FX Barrier Options

Applied Quantitative Finance series

Applied Quantitative Finance is a new series developed to bring readers the very latest market tested tools, techniques and developments in quantitative finance. Written for practitioners who need to understand how things work 'on the floor', the series will deliver the most cutting-edge applications in areas such as asset pricing, risk management and financial derivatives. Although written with practitioners in mind, this series will also appeal to researchers and students who want to see how quantitative finance is applied in practice.

Also available

Oliver Brockhaus
EQUITY DERIVATIVES AND HYBRIDS
Markets, Models and Methods

Enrico Edoli, Stefano Fiorenzani and Tiziano Vargiolu
OPTIMIZATION METHODS FOR GAS AND POWER MARKETS
Theory and Cases

Roland Lichters, Roland Stamm and Donal Gallagher
MODERN DERIVATIVES PRICING AND CREDIT EXPOSURE ANALYSIS
Theory and Practice of CSA and XVA Pricing, Exposure Simulation and Backtesting

Daniel Mahoney
MODELING AND VALUATION OF ENERGY STRUCTURES
Analytics, Econometrics, and Numerics

Ignacio Ruiz
XVA DESKS: A NEW ERA FOR RISK MANAGEMENT
Understanding, Building and Managing Counterparty and Funding Risk

Christian Crispoldi, Peter Larkin & Gérald Wigger
SABR AND SABR LIBOR MARKET MODEL IN PRACTICE
With Examples Implemented in Python

Adil Reghai
QUANTITATIVE FINANCE
Back to Basic Principles

Chris Kenyon, Roland Stamm
DISCOUNTING, LIBOR, CVA AND FUNDING
Interest Rate and Credit Pricing

Marc Henrard
INTEREST RATE MODELLING IN THE MULTI-CURVE FRAMEWORK
Foundations, Evolution and Implementation

FX Barrier Options

A Comprehensive Guide for Industry Quants

Zareer Dadachanji
Director, Model Quant Solutions, Bremen, Germany

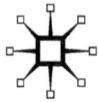

© Zareer Dadachanji 2015 Foreword © Adrian Campbell-Smith 2015

All rights reserved. No reproduction, copy or transmission of this publication may be made without written permission.

No portion of this publication may be reproduced, copied or transmitted save with written permission or in accordance with the provisions of the Copyright, Designs and Patents Act 1988, or under the terms of any licence permitting limited copying issued by the Copyright Licensing Agency, Saffron House, 6–10 Kirby Street, London EC1N 8TS.

Any person who does any unauthorized act in relation to this publication may be liable to criminal prosecution and civil claims for damages.

The author has asserted his right to be identified as the author of this work in accordance with the Copyright, Designs and Patents Act 1988.

First published 2015 by
PALGRAVE MACMILLAN

Palgrave Macmillan in the UK is an imprint of Macmillan Publishers Limited, registered in England, company number 785998, of Houndmills, Basingstoke, Hampshire RG21 6XS.

Palgrave Macmillan in the US is a division of St Martin's Press LLC,
175 Fifth Avenue, New York, NY 10010.

Palgrave Macmillan is the global academic imprint of the above companies and has companies and representatives throughout the world.

Palgrave® and Macmillan® are registered trademarks in the United States, the United Kingdom, Europe and other countries

ISBN: 978–1–137–46274–9

This book is printed on paper suitable for recycling and made from fully managed and sustained forest sources. Logging, pulping and manufacturing processes are expected to conform to the environmental regulations of the country of origin.

A catalogue record for this book is available from the British Library.

A catalog record for this book is available from the Library of Congress.

To Ulrike, Wolfgang and Helena.

Contents

List of Figures xii
List of Tables xix
Preface xx
Acknowledgements xxiv
Foreword xxv
Glossary of Mathematical Notation xxvii
Contract Types xxviii

1 Meet the Products 1
   1.1 Spot 1
       1.1.1 Dollars per euro or euros per dollar? 3
       1.1.2 Big figures and small figures 4
       1.1.3 The value of Foreign 4
       1.1.4 Converting between Domestic and Foreign 6
   1.2 Forwards 6
       1.2.1 The FX forward market 7
       1.2.2 A formula for the forward rate 8
       1.2.3 Payoff of a forward contract 10
       1.2.4 Valuation of a forward contract 12
   1.3 Vanilla options 12
       1.3.1 Put–call parity 15
   1.4 European digitals 16
   1.5 Barrier-contingent vanilla options 16
   1.6 Barrier-contingent payments 23
   1.7 Rebates 25
   1.8 Knock-in-knock-out (KIKO) options 25
   1.9 Types of barriers 26
   1.10 Structured products 27
   1.11 Specifying the contract 28
   1.12 Quantitative truisms 29
       1.12.1 Foreign exchange symmetry and inversion 29
       1.12.2 Knock-out plus knock-in equals no-barrier contract 29
       1.12.3 Put–call parity 30
   1.13 Jargon-buster 30

vii

2 Living in a Black–Scholes World 33
- 2.1 The Black–Scholes model equation for spot price 33
- 2.2 The process for ln S 35
- 2.3 The Black–Scholes equation for option pricing 38
  - 2.3.1 The lagless approach 38
  - 2.3.2 Derivation of the Black–Scholes PDE 39
  - 2.3.3 Black–Scholes model: hedging assumptions 42
  - 2.3.4 Interpretation of the Black–Scholes PDE 43
    - 2.3.4.1 Term 1: theta term 43
    - 2.3.4.2 Term 2: carry term 43
    - 2.3.4.3 Term 3: gamma term 44
    - 2.3.4.4 Term 4: cash account term 45
- 2.4 Solving the Black–Scholes PDE 45
- 2.5 Payments 45
- 2.6 Forwards 47
- 2.7 Vanilla options 47
  - 2.7.1 Transformation of the Black–Scholes PDE 48
    - 2.7.1.1 Transformation 1: Time direction 48
    - 2.7.1.2 Transformation 2: Discounting 49
    - 2.7.1.3 Transformation 3: From spot to forward 49
    - 2.7.1.4 Transformation 4: Log-space 51
  - 2.7.2 Solution of the diffusion equation for vanilla options 52
  - 2.7.3 The vanilla option pricing formulae 57
    - 2.7.3.1 Respecting the spot lags 57
    - 2.7.3.2 Expression in terms of forward and discount factors . 57
    - 2.7.3.3 Intrinsic value 58
    - 2.7.3.4 Moneyness 58
  - 2.7.4 Price quotation styles 59
  - 2.7.5 Valuation behaviour of vanilla options 60
- 2.8 Black–Scholes pricing of barrier-contingent vanilla options 64
  - 2.8.1 Knock-outs 65
  - 2.8.2 Knock-ins 69
  - 2.8.3 Quotation methods 70
  - 2.8.4 Valuation behaviour of barrier-contingent vanilla options . . . 70
- 2.9 Black–Scholes pricing of barrier-contingent payments 73
  - 2.9.1 Payment in Domestic 74
  - 2.9.2 Payment in Foreign 76
  - 2.9.3 Quotation methods 76
  - 2.9.4 Valuation behaviour of barrier-contingent payments 77
- 2.10 Discrete barrier options 80

		2.11	Window barrier options	80
		2.12	Black–Scholes numerical valuation methods	81
3	**Black–Scholes Risk Management**			82
	3.1	Spot risk		83
		3.1.1	Local spot risk analysis	83
		3.1.2	Delta	84
			3.1.2.1 Premium-adjusted Delta	84
			3.1.2.2 Delta quotation styles	85
		3.1.3	Gamma	85
		3.1.4	Results for spot Greeks	86
		3.1.5	Non-local spot risk analysis	97
	3.2	Volatility risk		97
		3.2.1	Local volatility risk analysis	98
			3.2.1.1 Results for vega and volgamma	100
			3.2.1.2 Vanna	110
		3.2.2	Non-local volatility risk	112
	3.3	Interest rate risk		113
	3.4	Theta		115
	3.5	Barrier over-hedging		117
	3.6	Co-Greeks		120
4	**Smile Pricing**			121
	4.1	The shortcomings of the Black–Scholes model		121
	4.2	Black–Scholes with term structure (BSTS)		123
	4.3	The implied volatility surface		125
	4.4	The FX vanilla option market		126
		4.4.1	At-the-money volatility	129
		4.4.2	Risk reversal	131
		4.4.3	Butterfly	132
		4.4.4	The role of the Black–Scholes model in the FX vanilla options market	133
	4.5	Theoretical Value (TV)		133
		4.5.1	Conventions for extracting market data for TV calculations	134
		4.5.2	Example broker quote request	135
	4.6	Modelling market implied volatilities		136
	4.7	The probability density function		137
	4.8	Three things we want from a model		141
	4.9	The local volatility (LV) model		141
		4.9.1	It's the smile dynamics, stupid	155
	4.10	Five things we want from a model		156
	4.11	Stochastic volatility (SV) models		157
		4.11.1	SABR model	157

Contents

- 4.11.2 Heston model 158
  - 4.11.2.1 Mean-reversion vs volatility 159
  - 4.11.2.2 Calibrating the Heston model 160
- 4.12 Mixed local/stochastic volatility (LSV) models 162
  - 4.12.1 Term structure of volatility of volatility 170
- 4.13 Other models and methods 171
  - 4.13.1 Uncertain volatility (UV) models 171
  - 4.13.2 Jump–diffusion models 172
  - 4.13.3 Vanna–volga methods 173

5 Smile Risk Management 175
- 5.1 Black–Scholes with term structure 175
- 5.2 Local volatility model 179
- 5.3 Spot risk under smile models 180
- 5.4 Theta risk under smile models 182
- 5.5 Mixed local/stochastic volatility models 182
- 5.6 Static hedging 183
- 5.7 Managing risk across businesses 184

6 Numerical Methods 186
- 6.1 Finite-difference (FD) methods 186
  - 6.1.1 Grid geometry 187
  - 6.1.2 Finite-difference schemes 189
- 6.2 Monte Carlo (MC) methods 193
  - 6.2.1 Monte Carlo schedules 194
  - 6.2.2 Monte Carlo algorithms 195
  - 6.2.3 Variance reduction 197
    - 6.2.3.1 Antithetic variables 197
    - 6.2.3.2 Control variates 198
  - 6.2.4 The Brownian Bridge 199
  - 6.2.5 Early termination 200
- 6.3 Calculating Greeks 200
  - 6.3.1 Bumped Greeks 200
    - 6.3.1.1 Bumping spot near a barrier 201
    - 6.3.1.2 Arbitrage in bucketed vega reports 201
  - 6.3.2 Greeks from finite-difference calculations 202
  - 6.3.3 Greeks from Monte Carlo 203

7 Further Topics 205
- 7.1 Managed currencies 205
- 7.2 Stochastic interest rates (SIR) 206
- 7.3 Real-world pricing 210
  - 7.3.1 Bid–offer spreads 210
  - 7.3.2 Rules-based pricing methods 212

| 7.4 | Regulation and market abuse | 213 |

Appendix A: Derivation of the Black–Scholes Pricing Equations for Vanilla Options 215

Appendix B: Normal and Lognormal Probability Distributions 220
- B.1 Normal distribution 220
- B.2 Lognormal distribution 220

Appendix C: Derivation of the Local Volatility Function 221
- C.1 Derivation in terms of call prices 221
- C.2 Local volatility from implied volatility 225
- C.3 Working in moneyness space 227
- C.4 Working in log space 228
- C.5 Specialization to BSTS 229

Appendix D: Calibration of Mixed Local/Stochastic Volatility (LSV) Models 230

Appendix E: Derivation of Fokker–Planck Equation for the Local Volatility Model 232

Bibliography 234

Index 237

List of Figures

1.1	EURUSD forward curve as of end of September 2014	8
1.2	Payoff profile of a EURUSD forward contract in EUR 100,000 struck at 1.2647	11
1.3	Payoff profile of a EUR call/USD put option in EUR 100,000 struck at 1.2647	13
1.4	Payoff profile of a EUR put/USD call option in EUR 100,000 struck at 1.2647	15
1.5	Payoff profile of a EURUSD call spread in EUR 100,000 per leg; strikes at 1.2647/1.35	17
1.6	Payoff profile of a EURUSD put spread in EUR 100,000 per leg; strikes at 1.2647/1.20	17
1.7	Setting the call option payoff to zero when the spot rate is above 1.35	18
1.8	Payoff profile diagram of a 1.2647-strike EUR call/USD put option with an up-side knock-out at 1.35	20
1.9	Payoff profile diagram of a 1.2647-strike EUR call/USD put option with a down-side knock-out at 1.25	20
1.10	Payoff profile diagram of a 1.2647-strike EUR put/USD call option with a down-side knock-out at 1.25	21
1.11	Payoff profile diagram of a 1.2647-strike EUR call/USD put option with an up-side knock-in at 1.35	22
1.12	Payoff profile of a six-month EURUSD 1.30 one-touch in EUR 100,000	24
2.1	Conceptual inputs and output of the Black–Scholes model	38
2.2	Variation with spot of the value of a EURUSD 1.28-strike vanilla call option at three maturities. The strike is marked with a triangle	61
2.3	Variation with maturity of the value of a 1.28-strike EUR call/USD put vanilla option	62
2.4	Variation with spot of a EURUSD 1.28-strike vanilla put option at three maturities. The strike is marked with a triangle	63
2.5	Variation with maturity of the value of a 1.28-strike EUR put/USD call vanilla option	63
2.6	Variation with volatility of the value of a 6-month EUR call/USD put vanilla option at three different strikes	64
2.7	Illustration of the method of images, showing the payoffs of the option and its image for a 1.25-strike EUR put/USD call option with an up-side knockout at 1.28	68

2.8	Variation with spot of the value of a 6-month 1.28-strike EUR call/USD put option with a down-and-out barrier at 1.25 (contract code CON).	70
2.9	Variation with spot of the value of a 6-month 1.25-strike EUR put/USD call option with an up-and-out barrier at 1.28 (contract code PNO).	71
2.10	Variation with spot of the value of a 6-month 1.25-strike EUR call/USD put option with an up-and-out barrier at 1.35 (contract code CNO).	72
2.11	Variation with spot of the value of a 6-month 1.28-strike EUR put/USD call option with a down-and-out barrier at 1.15 (contract code PON).	72
2.12	Variation with spot of the value of a 6-month 1.28-strike EUR put/USD call option with knock-out barriers at 1.20 and 1.38 (contract code COO).	73
2.13	Variation with spot of the value of a 6-month 1.28-strike EUR put/USD call option with knock-in barriers at 1.20 and 1.38 (contract code CII).	74
2.14	Value against spot of a six-month USDTRY 3.00 up-side one-touch, paying in USD at maturity (contract code FNI)	77
2.15	Value against spot of a three-month USDTRY double no-touch with barriers at 2.20 and 2.90, paying in USD (contract code FOO)	78
2.16	Variation with maturity of USDTRY pay-at-maturity one-touches with an up-side barrier at 2.70, paying in TRY (full line) and USD (dotted line)	79
2.17	Variation with maturity of USDTRY pay-at-maturity one-touches with a down-side barrier at 2.10, paying in TRY (full line) and USD (dotted line)	79
3.1	Variation with spot of delta (full line, primary y-axis) for a six-month 1.28-strike EUR call/USD put vanilla option. The value is shown alongside (dotted line, secondary y-axis). The strike level is marked with a triangle	87
3.2	Variation with spot of gamma (full line, primary y-axis) for a six-month 1.28-strike EUR call/USD put vanilla option. The delta is shown alongside (dotted line, secondary y-axis). The strike level is marked with a triangle	88
3.3	Variation with spot of delta (full line, primary y-axis) for a six-month 1.28-strike EUR put/USD call vanilla option. The value is shown alongside (dotted line, secondary y-axis. The strike level is marked with a triangle	89

List of Figures

3.4 Variation with spot of gamma (full line, primary y-axis) for a six-month 1.28-strike EUR put/USD call vanilla option. The delta is shown alongside (dotted line, secondary y-axis. The strike level is marked with a triangle 89

3.5 Variation with spot of delta (full line, primary y-axis) for a six-month EURUSD 1.28-strike EUR call/USD put option with down-side knock-out at 1.20. 91

3.6 Variation with spot of gamma (full line, primary y-axis) for a six-month EURUSD 1.28-strike EUR call/USD put option with down-side knock-out at 1.20. 92

3.7 Variation with spot of delta (full line, primary y-axis) for a six-month EURUSD 1.28-strike EUR call/USD put option with up-side knock-out at 1.38. 93

3.8 Variation with spot of gamma (full line, primary y-axis) for a six-month EURUSD 1.28-strike EUR call/USD put option with up-side knock-out at 1.38. 93

3.9 Variation with spot of value and delta for a one-minute EURUSD 1.28-strike EUR call/USD put option with up-side knock-out at 1.38. . . 94

3.10 Variation with spot of delta (full line, primary y-axis) for a six-month EURUSD 1.38 high-side no-touch, paying in EUR. The value is shown alongside (dotted line, secondary y-axis). The barrier level is marked with a cross 95

3.11 Variation with spot of gamma (full line, primary y-axis) for a six-month EURUSD 1.38 high-side no-touch, paying in EUR. The delta is shown alongside (dotted line, secondary y-axis). The barrier level is marked with a cross 95

3.12 Variation with spot of delta (full line, primary y-axis) for a six-month USDTRY double no-touch with barriers at 2.25 and 2.70, paying in USD. The value is shown alongside (dotted line, secondary y-axis). The barrier levels are marked with crosses 96

3.13 Variation with spot of gamma (full line, primary y-axis) for a six-month USDTRY double no-touch with barriers at 2.25 and 2.70, paying in USD. The delta is shown alongside (dotted line, secondary y-axis). The barrier levels are marked with crosses 96

3.14 Spot ladder for a six-month 1.28 strike EUR call/USD put with an upside knock-out at 1.38 98

3.15 Variation with spot of the vega (full line, primary y-axis) of a six-month 1.28-strike EUR call/USD put vanilla option. The value is plotted alongside (dotted line, secondary y-axis). The strike level is marked with a triangle 100

3.16 Variation with spot of the volgamma (full line, primary y-axis) of a six-month 1.28-strike EUR call/USD put vanilla option. The vega is plotted alongside (dotted line, secondary y-axis). The strike level is marked with a triangle 102

3.17 Variation with spot of the vega (full line, primary y-axis) of a six-month 1.28-strike EUR call/USD put option with a down-side knock-out at 1.20. The value is plotted alongside (dotted line, secondary y-axis). The strike level is marked with a triangle, the barrier level with a cross 103

3.18 Variation with spot of the volgamma (full line, primary y-axis) of a six-month 1.28-strike EUR call/USD put option with a down-side knock-out at 1.20. The vega is plotted alongside (dotted line, secondary y-axis). The strike level is marked with a triangle, the barrier level with a cross 103

3.19 Variation with spot of the vega (full line, primary y-axis) of a six-month 1.28-strike EUR call/USD put option with a down-side knock-out at 1.20. **The USD interest rate is artificially set to 15%.** The value is plotted alongside (dotted line, secondary y-axis). The strike level is marked with a triangle, the barrier with a cross 105

3.20 Variation with spot of the volgamma (full line, primary y-axis) of a six-month 1.28-strike EUR call/USD put option with a down-side knock-out at 1.20. **The USD interest rate is artificially set to 15%.** The vega is plotted alongside (dotted line, secondary y-axis). The strike level is marked with a triangle, the barrier with a cross 105

3.21 Variation with spot of the vega (full line, primary y-axis) of a six-month 1.28-strike EUR call/USD put option with an up-side knock-out at 1.38. The value is plotted alongside (dotted line, secondary y-axis). The strike level is marked with a triangle, the barrier with a cross 106

3.22 Variation with spot of the vega (full line, primary y-axis) of a six-month 1.28-strike EUR put/USD call option with a down-side knock-out at 1.20. The value is plotted alongside (dotted line, secondary y-axis). The strike level is marked with a triangle, the barrier with a cross 106

3.23 Variation with spot of the volgamma (full line, primary y-axis) of a six-month 1.28-strike EUR call/USD put option with an up-side knock-out at 1.38. The vega is plotted alongside (dotted line, secondary y-axis). The strike level is marked with a triangle, the barrier with a cross 107

3.24 Variation with spot of the volgamma (full line, primary y-axis) of a six-month 1.28-strike EUR put/USD call option with a down-side knock-out at 1.20. The vega is plotted alongside (dotted line, secondary y-axis). The strike level is marked with a triangle, the barrier with a cross 107

3.25 Variation with spot of the vega (full line, primary y-axis) of a six-month EURUSD 1.38 high-side no-touch paying in EUR. The value is plotted alongside (dotted line, secondary y-axis). The barrier level is marked with a cross 108

3.26 Variation with spot of the volgamma (full line, primary y-axis) of a six-month EURUSD 1.38 high-side no-touch paying in EUR. The vega is plotted alongside (dotted line, secondary y-axis). The barrier level is marked with a cross 109

3.27 Variation with spot of the vega (full line, primary y-axis) of a six-month EURUSD 1.22/1.30 (10% price) double no-touch paying in EUR. The value is plotted alongside (dotted line, secondary y-axis). The barrier levels are marked with crosses 109

3.28 Variation with spot of the vega (full line, primary y-axis) of a six-month EURUSD 1.15/1.45 double no-touch paying in EUR. The value is plotted alongside (dotted line, secondary y-axis). The barrier levels are marked with crosses 110

3.29 Variation with spot of the volgamma (full line, primary y-axis) of a six-month EURUSD 1.22/1.30 (10% price) double no-touch paying in EUR. The vega is plotted alongside (dotted line, secondary y-axis). The barrier levels are marked with crosses 111

3.30 Variation with spot of the volgamma (full line, primary y-axis) of a six-month EURUSD 1.15/1.45 double no-touch paying in EUR. The vega is plotted alongside (dotted line, secondary y-axis). The barrier levels are marked with crosses 111

3.31 Variation with spot of the vanna (full line, primary y-axis) of a six-month 1.28-strike EUR call/USD put option with an up-side knock-out at 1.38. The vega is plotted alongside (dotted line, secondary y-axis). The strike level is marked with a triangle, the barrier with a cross 113

3.32 Variation with spot of the Domestic and Foreign rhos (full lines) of a six-month 1.28-strike EUR call/USD put option with an up-side knock-out at 1.38. The vega is plotted alongside (dotted line). The strike level is marked with a triangle, the barrier with a cross 114

3.33 Variation with spot of the Black–Scholes practitioner theta of a six-month 1.28-strike EUR call/USD put vanilla option. The strike level is marked with a triangle 117

3.34 Variation with spot of the Black–Scholes practitioner theta (full line, primary y-axis) of a six-month 1.28-strike EUR call/USD put option with an up-side knock-out at 1.38. The vega is plotted alongside (dotted line, secondary y-axis). The strike level is marked with a triangle, the barrier with a cross 118

3.35 Variation with days-to-expiry of the delta gap of a 1.28-strike EUR call/USD put option with an up-side knock-out at 1.38 120

4.1 EURUSD implied volatility smiles for three-month (bold line) and six-month (dashed line) expiries. Circles mark the at-the-money points 127

4.2 USDTRY implied volatility smiles for three-month (bold line) and six-month (dashed line) expiries. Circles mark the at-the-money points 127

4.3 AUDJPY implied volatility smiles for three-month (bold line) and six-month (dashed line) expiries. Circles mark the at-the-money points 128

4.4 Three-month EURUSD risk-neutral smile PDF (full line) and TV PDF (dotted line) 139

4.5 EURUSD PDF skews for expiries of three months (full line) and six months (dotted line) 139

4.6 USDTRY PDF skews for expiries of three months (full line) and six months (dotted line) 140

4.7 AUDJPY PDF skews for expiries of three months (full line) and six months (dotted line) 140

4.8 Variation with barrier level of the LV model value (full line) of a 3-month EURUSD down-side one-touch paying in USD. The TV has been plotted alongside (dotted line) 145

4.9 Variation with barrier level of the LV model skew-to-TV of a three-month EURUSD down-side one-touch paying in USD 146

4.10 Variation with barrier level of the LV model skew-to-TV of a three-month USDTRY down-side one-touch paying in TRY 147

4.11 Variation with barrier level of the LV model skew-to-TV of a three-month AUDJPY down-side one-touch paying in JPY 148

4.12 Variation with TV of the LV model skews to TV of three-month down-side one-touches on EURUSD, USDTRY and AUDJPY, all paying in Domestic 149

4.13 Variation with TV of the LV model skews to TV of three-month up-side one-touches on EURUSD, USDTRY and AUDJPY, all paying in Domestic 149

4.14 Variation with TV of the LV model skews to TV of three-month EURUSD one-touches, paying in USD. The down-side touches are plotted in the left-hand half, the up-side touches in the right-hand half 150
4.15 Variation with TV of the LV model skews to TV of three-month double no-touches on EURUSD, USDTRY and AUDJPY, all paying in Domestic 151
4.16 Variation with TV of the skew to TV of three-month 1.26-strike (at-the-money) EURUSD up-and-out call options under the LV model 152
4.17 Variation with TV of the skew to TV of three-month 1.23-strike (in-the-money) EURUSD up-and-out call options under the LV model 152
4.18 Variation with TV of the skew to TV of three-month 1.30-strike (out-of-the-money) EURUSD up-and-out call options under the LV model 153
4.19 Variation with strike of the skew to TV of three-month EUR call/USD put vanilla options 153
4.20 Variation with TV of the skew to TV of three-month 1.26-strike (at-the-money) EURUSD double knock-out call options under the LV model 155
4.21 Variation with spot of the three-month EURUSD local volatility factor Λ for various different volatilities of volatility. The Dupire local volatility σ_{LV} is plotted alongside 166
4.22 Variation with TV of the LSV model skews to TV of three-month EURUSD down-side one-touches paying in USD. Results are shown for 2 different values of LSV model parameter α, and the LV result is plotted alongside 169
4.23 Variation with TV of the LSV model skews to TV of three-month EURUSD double-no-touches paying in USD. Results are shown for two different values of LSV model parameter α, and the LV result is plotted alongside 169
4.24 Variation with volatility-of-volatility of the LSV model skew to TV of a three-month EURUSD 10%-TV double-no-touch paying in USD 170
4.25 An example implied volatility smile for six-month EURUSD generated using an uncertain volatility model based on purely Black–Scholes calculations 172
5.1 Smile re-location of three-month EURUSD under various dynamics. The original spot level is marked with a plus sign, the re-located spot level with a diamond 181
7.1 Variation of the calibrated volatility of USDTRY spot with maturity of calibration forward contract, for various levels of correlation between spot and TRY interest rate. The FX forward volatility is 11% .. 210

List of Tables

2.1 Price quotation methods for vanilla options and barrier-contingent vanilla options 60
2.2 Market data values used for demonstration of Black–Scholes model results 61
4.1 Standardized expiry tenors for the three benchmark currency pairs. "D"=day; "W"=week; "M"=month; "Y"=year 129

Preface

'Can you really write a *whole book* on barrier options?' I was asked by a friend. 'Actually it's just *Foreign Exchange* barrier options,' I explained, 'and oh yes.'

Oh yes indeed. Whilst the non-practitioner may well infer a narrow scope from the title, aficionados will be all too aware that the devil is in the detail, and that the detail runs deep.

Barrier options are a class of exotic options which present particular challenges to practitioners in all areas of the financial industry, and across all asset classes. The Foreign Exchange options industry has always shown great innovation in this class of products and has committed enormous resources to studying them. This has resulted in a highly sophisticated understanding of these products and their risks, accompanied by a vast body of knowledge, in the form of concepts, models, theories, techniques, practices and numerical methods, all of which need to be mastered by the modern quantitative practitioner.

In the two decades straddling the start of the 21st century, this knowledge was in enormous flux. Out of the intense development and collision of ideas from that period has emerged a certain stability and structure. The aim of this book is to explain and record this stabilized body of knowledge, serving both as a learning experience and as a reference.

A learning experience must build on itself, with each new stage being supported by the one below, and one of the challenges that I faced when writing this book was to decide at what level I should begin. I have erred on the side of beginning quite low down, for example by discussing the FX spot market, forward contracts and vanilla options in some detail before tackling barrier options. I hope that many of you will find that to be a useful approach. To those of you who find that I start too low down: please do skip paragraphs or sections and pick up the narrative where it gets interesting for you.

The primary perspectives from which this book is written are those of the quantitative analyst, but it is not only quants (whether in front office or control functions) who will benefit from reading this book. All quantitatively minded traders, structurers, risk managers, marketers, IT developers and product controllers will benefit from a greater depth of understanding of the topics covered. So, it is a book for not only "professional quants" but also "quantitative professionals".

I have aimed to set the mathematical framework in this book at a level of abstraction close to the problem at hand. I have mostly preferred to concentrate on specific cases, on the basis that every step higher in abstraction risks blurring the resolution on the detailed understanding. For example, I focus on specific examples of mixed local/stochastic volatility models, rather than on generalized forms, because I believe that seeing a partial differentiation coefficient in terms of specific, "physical", model parameters is more meaningful and revealing than seeing it as a generalized function. Similarly, I introduce Itô's lemma in the context of the derivation of a specific financial result, with the intention that its significance and effect are more readily seen.

A more mathematically oriented approach to the state of FX barrier option modelling as it stood in 2001 is provided by Lipton's classic treatise on FX markets and products [1], which covers a wide variety of mathematical methods.

The trading of any financial product constitutes a legal agreement, and as such products will always contain features that are bound to the details of the specific market in which they are traded. This book introduces all the aspects of financial markets that are relevant for understanding FX barrier options, so readers do not need to be already familiar with the basics of the financial markets. Of course, readers who do have such familiarity, or who are familiar with derivatives in other asset classes, such as interest rates or equities, will naturally find it easier to take on the concepts presented.

Readers looking for a greater breadth of understanding about the financial markets are well served by a number of texts. The multi-edition classic by Hull [2] gives an excellent introduction to a wide variety of topics in financial markets. Wilmott's three-volume work [3] explains an enormous variety of topics relevant to quantitative analysts, and explains them brilliantly. A less technical but extremely well informed coverage of the financial markets is to be found in Pilbeam [4].

Structure of the book

A deep understanding of financial products in general, and FX barrier options in particular, is best achieved in stages. We first need to understand why there might be a need or desire for a particular product in the first place. Only after that does it make sense to consider exactly how the product is conventionally specified, and it then becomes much clearer why products are specified the way they are. Having learnt the mechanisms of a particular product, the next stage is to acquire a principled understanding of what will happen under different market scenarios – and not only the ones which motivated the product. Chapter 1 (Meet the Products) addresses all of the above stages for FX barrier options. Prerequisite to an understanding of barrier options is an understanding of simpler products and trades: vanilla options, forwards and spot. These too are covered in Chapter 1, which ends with a "Jargon-buster" section that summarizes the substantial product terminology that has been introduced.

Once we know how the barrier products work in principle, the next important stage of learning is to understand how to value them. Chapter 2 (Living in a Black–Scholes World) explains the Black–Scholes model and how it is applied to barrier products. I have restricted the treatment in this chapter to the version of the model with no time-dependence of volatility or interest rates – what some people call "pure" Black–Scholes.

Following closely on the heels of valuation is the topic of risk management: how does the value of an option *vary* as the world about it changes? The topic of risk management under the Black–Scholes model is covered in Chapter 3 (Black–Scholes Risk Management). Many of the concepts described here are applicable to more sophisticated models.

Such sophistication arrives in Chapter 4 (Smile Pricing), which explores the world of valuation beyond Black–Scholes. Indeed, the chapter title "Beyond Black–Scholes" would have been more technically correct than "Smile Pricing", since this chapter includes the version of the Black–Scholes model with term structure, which, strictly speaking, is not a smile model. However, this chapter deserves an appropriately assertive title, covering as it does some of the most central and important concepts in FX barrier options, indeed in derivatives modelling generally. And the Black–Scholes model with term structure belongs in this chapter, as it is best seen, and understood, as a stepping stone between the pure Black–Scholes model and smile models.

The extra valuation complexity of smile models needs to be accompanied by corresponding risk management techniques, and these are the subject of Chapter 5 (Smile Risk Management).

Chapter 6 (Numerical Methods) homes in on the practical side of financial engineering: the numerical methods that are used to actually compute the values and risks of derivatives.

Finally, Chapter 7 (Further Topics) presents brief discussions of a number of subjects: managed currencies, stochastic interest rates, real-world pricing practices, regulation and market abuse.

When explaining quantitative concepts, I distinguish the mathematics that is integral to the concept from that which supports it and is secondary to it. This applies even if – as is very often the case – the supporting mathematics is extremely interesting and illuminating in its own right. The mathematics that is integral to the key concepts in this book is always to be found in the main text; the supporting mathematics has mostly made its way to the appendices. My hope is that this will have the twin benefits of making the discussions in the main text less cluttered, and distilling into the appendices a rich source of interesting mathematical material that is of great value to the industry quant.

I, and all those involved in the production of this book, have made best efforts to ensure the accuracy of all the material presented, but errors can still slip through, and we do not assume any responsibility or liability for the information in this book or its use.

The introduction of a new concept often requires the introduction of new terminology, and there are a lot of both in this book. Key words and phrases are marked in **bold type** when they are first mentioned or defined.

Acknowledgements

I would especially like to thank my friend and FX options guru Adrian Campbell-Smith, who read the manuscript for this book with enthusiasm and made many valuable and illuminating comments. And a lot of entertaining ones too. Any errors that remain are purely mine. I am further grateful to Adrian for the great many valuable discussions we have enjoyed over the years.

I am also indebted to the many people who have taught me over the years. Prime amongst them is my friend and former manager Mark Jones, from whose immense talent I greatly benefited in the early days of my career as a quant. I am also very grateful to him for the many extremely useful comments he made on the manuscript for this book. Others who have been invaluable in helping me to understand the FX options world include Philippe Lintern, Mark Jex, Jeremy Gelber, Brian Hunton, Ian Robson, Ian White, David Shelton and Alex Sturt.

I believe that an understanding of any one asset class is greatly enhanced by an understanding of others, and I would like to add a special thank you to Karim Lari for his exemplary stewardship of the GMAG front-office quant team at Credit Suisse and for fostering its truly cross-asset nature and its highly collaborative spirit.

I am very grateful to my former employer, The Royal Bank of Scotland, for providing me with market data and allowing me to demonstrate model behaviour based on it.

The very idea of writing a book on FX Barrier Options was one that required much discussion and refinement, and I would like to express my gratitude to my commissioning editor at Palgrave Macmillan, Pete Baker, for the significant part he played in the birth of this book.

Lastly, I would like to thank my wife Ulrike for her tremendous support and encouragement as I was writing this book. Her daily comedy question 'So how many chapters have you written now?' became a source of entertainment for us both. I am pleased that she now has an unequivocal answer.

Foreword

Upon receiving the request, 'Can you write a foreword', a currencies trader is likely to reply, 'What currency pair?' Aside from an indication of a slightly strange and pedantic sense of humour, the reply is a signal for two features of the currencies markets which are relevant to the construction of this book: first, that participants have adopted a slightly opaque set of terminology and jargon to communicate about markets and products; and second, that as a fully over-the-counter (OTC) market, the concept of restrictions on products is fairly alien, and the market as a whole takes an accommodating can-do attitude to the provision of transactions and services. In combination these features can be an obstacle to professionals attempting to navigate the complicated zoo of products and models in use.

Currencies markets contain a rich set of products with a very sound structure. By far the most liquid product is simple 'spot' foreign exchange – exchanging one currency for another as travellers might do before a holiday – with trillions of US dollars (or equivalent) traded each day. For the options trader this is the 'underlying asset', with natural buyers and sellers of virtually all currencies creating depth and liquidity, and virtually unparalleled transparency and continuity; the market is closed only at weekends, and millisecond-scale pricing and transaction data are available for analysis. In short, it is a market that is relatively free of artificial deviations from the simplest assumptions of mathematical models, and hence a very solid foundation on which to begin modelling derivative products such as options. Simple ('vanilla') currency options – plain calls and puts – are also incredibly liquid, with hundreds of billions of US dollars (equivalent) traded each day[1] in a continuous and transparent way, again with natural buyers and sellers, and hence a relatively clear concept of 'fair value' to model. This is already an enviable starting point from which to consider modelling path-dependent and other exotic derivatives, but the currency options market has yet another ace up its sleeve, in the form of an active interdealer market in a large family of path-dependent transactions, namely barrier options: the one-touches, ranges and single and double-barrier options which are the subject of this book. These products occupy a very special and enviable niche in the financial markets: they are complex enough to be challenging and interesting from a mathematical modelling perspective, yet have tight, transparent market prices with sufficient liquidity to permit a careful critique, analysis and calibration of any modelling approach. Indeed the

---

[1] www.bis.org/publ/rpfx13fx.pdf

pricing is sufficiently tight that subtle nuances such as intraday variations in liquidity, term-structure and smile-surface shapes and dynamics, and events such as economic data releases or political statements, are all resolvable in the pricing of FX vanilla and barrier options. The barrier options market in turn provides a laboratory for testing models which can be extended to valuation of yet more complex derivatives such as window barriers, discrete barriers, target redemption forwards, and so on , knowing the valuations they provide are consistent with the prices of barrier and vanilla options that will likely form a part of any realistic hedging strategy.

The terminology used by traders to describe currencies, and currency options markets in particular, can be highly efficient, communicating large amounts of information quickly, succinctly and avoiding potentially disastrous ambiguity. Paradoxically, even though clarity is the aim, the jargon used can be quite difficult to learn, even for seasoned professionals in non-trading functions such as quant teams and risk functions. In this book Dr Dadachanji helps the reader begin to bridge this gap, as he carefully explains mathematical and technical concepts alongside intuitive explanations and realistic examples in a way that helps lift the veil on some of the jargon used by trading professionals.

Dr Dadachanji's book is an essential companion to those wishing to understand the tools and language of the FX barrier option laboratory: quants in both industry and academia, market risk managers, financial controllers, auditors and traders. His extensive experience in the financial industry has left him ideally placed to give his readers a valuable guide; requiring very little pre-requisite knowledge and building carefully from basic building blocks to very advanced concepts, it will equip his readers with the intuition, techniques and practical guidance they need to understand this fascinating and important area of the financial markets.

Adrian Campbell-Smith
Global Head of FX Exotic Options Trading at Royal Bank of Scotland Markets

Glossary of Mathematical Notation

Symbol	Meaning	Units
A_d	principal amount	Domestic
A_f	principal amount	Foreign
$B(T_1, T_2)$	discount factor between T_1 and T_2	dimensionless
F	forward rate	$\frac{\text{Domestic}}{\text{Foreign}}$
f	forward points	$\frac{\text{Domestic}}{\text{Foreign}}$
$F_X(\cdot)$	CDF of variable X	dimensionless
$f_X(\cdot)$	PDF of variable X	X^{-1}
H	barrier level (lower or upper)	$\frac{\text{Domestic}}{\text{Foreign}}$
K	option strike	$\frac{\text{Domestic}}{\text{Foreign}}$
L	lower barrier level	$\frac{\text{Domestic}}{\text{Foreign}}$
$N(\cdot)$	CDF of standard normal distribution	dimensionless
$n(\cdot)$	PDF of standard normal distribution	dimensionless
P	option payoff in Domestic currency	Domestic
$p(S,t)$	time-dependent PDF of spot	$\frac{\text{Foreign}}{\text{Domestic}}$
r_d	domestic interest rate	years^{-1}
r_f	foreign interest rate	years^{-1}
S	FX spot rate	$\frac{\text{Domestic}}{\text{Foreign}}$
T_e	option expiry time	Datetime
T_s	option settlement date	Date
T'_x	spot date of time T_x	Date
$\tilde{T}_x$	inverse spot date of date T_x	Date
t	time	Datetime
t'_x	spot date of time t_x	Date
$\tilde{t}_x$	inverse spot date of date t_x	Date
U	upper barrier level	$\frac{\text{Domestic}}{\text{Foreign}}$
V	option value in Domestic currency	Domestic
V_{ABC}	option value in currency ABC	ABC
Σ	implied volatility	$\text{years}^{-\frac{1}{2}}$
ϕ	option trait (+1 for call; -1 for put)	dimensionless
σ	process volatility	$\text{years}^{-\frac{1}{2}}$
τ	time to expiry	years
τ_H	first passage time to H	years

Contract Types

The table below lists the contract types that are frequently discussed in the main text. An option code and a long name are given for each contract type. The first letter of the code is used to denote the payoff type: [C]all, [P]ut, [D]omestic payment, [F]oreign payment, or for[W]ard. The second letter is used to denote the type of lower barrier: knock[O]ut, knock[I]n or [N]one. The third letter is used to denote the type of upper barrier: knock[O]ut, knock[I]n or [N]one. For one-touches, a suffix "_H" denotes that the option pays at hit. The absence of this suffix denotes that the option pays at maturity.

Code	Long Name
WNN	forward
WON	down and out forward
WNO	up and out forward
WOO	double knock-out forward
WIN	down and in forward
WNI	up and in forward
WII	double knock-in forward
CNN	vanilla call
PNN	vanilla put
CON	down and out call
CNO	up and out call
COO	double knock-out call
PON	down and out put
PNO	up and out put
POO	double knock-out put
CIN	down and in call
CNI	up and in call
CII	double knock-in call
PIN	down and in put
PNI	up and in put
PII	double knock-in put
DNN	payment in Domestic
FNN	payment in Foreign

Code	Long Name
DON	down-side no-touch payment in Domestic
DNO	up-side no-touch payment in Domestic
DOO	double no-touch payment in Domestic
FON	down-side no-touch payment in Foreign
FNO	up-side no-touch payment in Foreign
FOO	double no-touch payment in Foreign
DIN	down-side one-touch pay-at-maturity in Domestic
DIN_H	down-side one-touch pay-at-hit in Domestic
DNI	up-side one-touch pay-at-maturity in Domestic
DNI_H	up-side one-touch pay-at-hit in Domestic
DII	double one-touch pay-at-maturity in Domestic
DII_H	double one-touch pay-at-hit in Domestic
FIN	down-side one-touch pay-at-maturity in Foreign
FIN_H	down-side one-touch pay-at-hit in Foreign
FNI	up-side one-touch pay-at-maturity in Foreign
FNI_H	up-side one-touch pay-at-hit in Foreign
FII	double one-touch pay-at-maturity in Foreign
FII_H	double one-touch pay-at-hit in Foreign

1 Meet the Products

If barrier options did not exist, it would be necessary to invent them.

Were the financial products that we use today designed? Or did they evolve by natural selection? In today's complex world of financial products, it's very much a mixture of both. Structured products, such as FX accumulators, are the way they are very much by design: product developers have sat down together to discuss how to synthesize a product which matches their needs (which usually corresponds to the needs of their clients). In contrast, stand-alone barrier options are better seen as having evolved. This chapter traces that evolution process, via the simpler products of spot, forwards and vanilla options.

There is an inextricable link between a financial product and the market or markets in which that product is traded. The markets for vanilla and barrier options are of a highly esoteric nature, and we will describe them in Chapter 4, after we have covered a number of key prerequisite concepts. In contrast, the cases of spot and forwards are fairly straightforward, and this chapter additionally describes the nature of the markets in which they trade and the way in which we value them.

1.1 Spot

Consider a European company which has received revenues in US dollars and needs to pay bills in euros in the next few days. What should it do? It could enter a contract with a wholesale bank under which it must pay an agreed amount of dollars to the bank, and the bank must pay an agreed amount of euros to the company. The amounts paid are called the **principal amounts**, and the date on which the two cash payments must be made is called the **settlement date**.

The term **notional** is sometimes used in place of "principal", and one can talk of notional amounts and notional currencies. I prefer to use the term "notional" only when the amount really is notional and is not actually exchanged. For example, an FX volatility swap pays out according to a formula based on a notional amount that is not actually exchanged. Where cash flows really are exchanged (as they are for the vast majority of the products covered in this book), I will stick to the term "principal".

This kind of trade is exceedingly common and has been completely standardized in the wholesale markets. In its standard form it is called a **Foreign Exchange** (FX) **spot trade**. The on-market exchange rate at which the trade takes place (the number of dollars per euro in this case) is called the **spot rate** or **spot price**. In this book we will denote the spot rate by S. If we need to explicitly specify that we are referring to the spot rate at a specific time t, we will write $S(t)$. The date and time at which the trade is agreed are called the **trade date** and **trade time**.

The standardized settlement date is called the **spot date**, and is typically a few days after the trade date. The interval between the trade date and the spot date is referred to as the **spot lag** or **settlement lag**. The exact way in which the spot date is calculated for a given trade date depends on the currency pair, and is governed by a system of rules, known as **settlement rules**, which has evolved over time and which is now used by all market participants. Some details and examples are to be found in Clark [5]. Whilst the settlement rules themselves are somewhat involved, the underlying principle is plain: the time lag allows for a specified number of clear business days between the trade date and the settlement date. Typically, one clear business day is specified, with the result that the settlement date lies two business days after the trade date. This type of settlement rule is often referred to as a "$T+2$" rule.

The nature of the settlement rules ensures that for any given trade date, the spot date is determined unambiguously. Most often, the opposite is also true: for any given spot date, there is only one corresponding trade date. Occasionally, though, and usually due to holidays between the trade date and the spot date, there may be more than one trade date corresponding to a given spot date.

Historically, before the electronic age, the settlement lag would have been needed for operational reasons. These days, it may be perfectly possible to settle without any time lag, but the spot lag remains by convention.

Note that the spot contract does not specify the *time* at which the payments must be made, so they can be made at any time during business hours in the location in which the contract has been agreed.

A note on the language of foreign exchange: it is common to describe an FX spot trade as "converting dollars into euros", but this is very loose terminology. "Conversion" implies that dollars are destroyed and euros are created, but that is not the case – an FX spot trade certainly conserves both currencies. It is far better to speak of "exchanging cash flows". In the case above, our example company – let us suppose it is a German company called Davonda GmbH – is exchanging dollars for euros. If we want to be explicit about which way around the exchange is made, we say that Davonda is *buying euros and selling dollars*. There are of course times when we are merely changing the *quotation* of an asset value from one currency to another, as described in Section 1.1.4. In such cases, there is no exchange of cash flows, and the term "conversion" is appropriate.

1.1.1 Dollars per euro or euros per dollar?

For a given pair of currencies, C1 and C2, we may quote the exchange rate either as the number of C1 per C2 or the number of C2 per C1. The standardization of the FX spot market extends to the specification of the **quote order convention** – which way around the rate is quoted. For example, in the case of US dollars and euros, the convention is to quote the number of dollars per euro. For example, the spot rate in this book's benchmark market data (reflecting the real market as at the end of September 2014) is 1.2629. Typically, the quote order convention is chosen so that the spot rate is greater than 1, but that is not always the case: for example, the exchange rate between pounds sterling and euros is quoted as the number of pounds per euro, which has never been greater than 1 – though it has got tantalizingly close!

Saying "dollars per euro" is a bit too much of a mouthful when you need to say it a hundred times every day, and in the industry parlance we say "euro-dollar"[1] to refer to the currency pair and its exchange rate. Similarly, "pounds per euro" is spoken as "euro-sterling". When referring to the currency pair in written form, we use the currencies' three-letter ISO codes in place of their names, for brevity, so for our two examples above we would write "EURUSD' and "EURGBP" respectively. Going forward in this book, I will mainly use such six-letter symbols to specify the currency pair of interest.

An alternative notation is also sometimes to be seen in which a forward slash is written between the two currencies, like so: "EUR/USD". Confusingly, although this notation suggests EUR per USD, it actually means exactly the same as EURUSD.

For the most part in this book, we will be discussing the following three currency pairs:

1. **EURUSD**: US dollars per euro, spoken "euro-dollar".
2. **USDTRY**: Turkish lira per US dollar, spoken "dollar-Turkey".
3. **AUDJPY**: Japanese yen per Australian dollar, spoken "Aussie-yen".

With a given quotation order convention in place, industry parlance often regards the currency pair rather like an asset, and we talk of buying it, selling it or going long/short the currency pair. So "buying EURUSD" and "going long EURUSD" both mean the exchange of cash flows that involves buying EUR and selling USD. To describe the exchange of cash flows that involves selling EUR and buying USD, we would say "selling EURUSD" or "going short EURUSD".

We very often wish to discuss Foreign Exchange issues without having to specify a particular currency pair, and for that we require terminology that allows us to describe a general currency pair. A commonly used terminology, and the one that I shall use in this book, is to say that the spot rate describes the number of units of **Domestic** currency per unit **Foreign** currency. So, in our EURUSD example above, EUR is referred to as the Foreign currency and USD is referred

---

[1] This is not to be confused with "eurodollars" in the sense of US dollars deposited in Europe.

to as the Domestic currency. This is a global financial convention and has nothing to do with whether a currency is regarded as domestic or foreign by an individual participant. Indeed, our example German company Davonda would regard EUR as its domestic currency and USD as a foreign currency, but that is unrelated to the market convention.

As we shall see in greater depth later on, when discussing risk-neutral valuation, the Domestic currency is the natural currency in which we measure FX derivative values. Unless otherwise stated, "value" will refer to the value in Domestic currency.

If we abbreviate the word Foreign to the three-letter code "FOR", and the word Domestic to "DOM", the currency pair can be written as "FORDOM". The following equation then serves as a reminder of our conventions:

$$S_{FORDOM} = \text{number of units of DOM per unit of FOR} \tag{1.1}$$

1.1.2 Big figures and small figures

The precision with which exchange rates are quoted in the spot market is subject to market conventions, which, like so many FX conventions, vary with currency pair. EURUSD is quoted to four decimal places, with an optional fifth place which is usually (but not always) 0 or 5. For example, the benchmark market data used in this book has a EURUSD spot which would be quoted as 1.26290. The first and second decimal places are referred to as the **big figures**, so that, for instance, a "big-figure move" means a move equal to 0.01. The third and fourth decimal places are referred to as the **small figures**, so that, for instance, a move of ten small figures means a move equal to 0.001. The smaller of the two small figures (that is, the fourth decimal place) is often referred to as a **pip**. The term pip is normally used to describe the least significant digit of any quoted price, but when precision increases, the historical definition is preserved, and quotation in fractional pips becomes possible. On no account should a pip be confused with a **bip**, which is short for **basis point**, which means 1% of 1%, or 0.0001!

AUDJPY (benchmark spot 95.95) on the other hand is quoted to two decimal places, these being the small figures. The big figures are the two digits to the left of the decimal point.

1.1.3 The value of Foreign

What is the Domestic value V at time t of A_f units of Foreign currency? If we did not keep FX spot lags in mind, we might be tempted to write simply: $V(t) = A_f S(t)$. But this is not correct: $S(t)$, the spot price at time t, is the market exchange rate applicable for delivery on the *spot date* of t. We can therefore easily write down the Domestic value of having A_f units of Foreign currency on the spot date:

$$V(t') = A_f S(t) \tag{1.2}$$

where we have denoted the spot date of time t by t'.

Now, to get the value at time t of anything whose value at time t' is known, we simply multiply by a (dimensionless) **discount factor** between t and t' – this is the definition of a discount factor. In our current case, we require a Domestic currency discount factor between t and t', which we denote $B_d(t,t')$:

$$V(t) = B_d(t,t') A_f S(t) \qquad (1.3)$$

I was careful to write "a" discount factor, rather than "the" discount factor, in the last paragraph, because discounting is not a straightforward matter and there is a choice to be made about what discount factor to use in any given context. Specifically, there is the question of whether to include funding valuation adjustment (FVA) as part of the valuation calculation. The answer to this question is essentially: "it depends". And what it depends on is the purpose of the valuation. The subject of FVA does not have any specific bearing on FX barrier options and we will not discuss it in this book.

With the exception of the section on stochastic interest rates, Section 7.2, we will be assuming in this book that interest rates are deterministic. The discount factor B between two times T_1 and T_2 can be obtained by the expression:

$$B(T_1, T_2) = \exp\left(-\int_{T_1}^{T_2} r(t)\,dt\right) \qquad (1.4)$$

where the (deterministic) quantity $r(t)$ is known as the **instantaneous short rate curve** for the currency in question. Its dimension is one over time, so that the argument of the exponential function is dimensionless. Now, in the world of financial engineering, the standard unit for measuring time is a 365-day year (unlike the world of physical sciences, which respects the International System of Units and uses the second). Thus the unit of interest rate r is year^{-1}.

When the interest rate takes a constant value r, Equation 1.4 simplifies to:

$$B(T_1, T_2) = e^{-r(T_2 - T_1)} \qquad (1.5)$$

Note that Equation 1.3 implicitly involves a mixture of time systems. t can represent any time of any day, and as such is a "datetime", whereas t' can specify time only up to the resolution of a date. In practice, analytical and numerical methods used in financial engineering usually treat all time-like quantities as datetimes, and then adopt a convention for the representation of a date as a datetime, for example the start of the day or midday. This is not a problem as long as it is done consistently. For example, the value of T_2 used in our calculation of the discount factor, Equation 1.4, must be consistent with our calculation of spot date.

1.1.4 Converting between Domestic and Foreign

The spot price at time t effectively gives us the factor for converting between the Foreign and Domestic values of any asset at time t', the spot date of t. Therefore, to convert from an asset's Foreign value V_f to Domestic value V_d at a general valuation time t_{value}, we must apply the following procedure:

1. Apply a Foreign discount/accrual factor to $V_f(t_{\text{value}})$ to get the Foreign value of the asset at time t'.
2. Multiply by the spot rate at time t to get the Domestic value of the asset at time t'.
3. Apply a Domestic discount/accrual factor to get the Domestic value of the asset at time t_{value}.

In equations, these three steps are:

$$V_f(t') = B_f(t', t_{\text{value}}) V_f(t_{\text{value}})$$
$$V_d(t') = S(t) V_f(t')$$
$$V_d(t_{\text{value}}) = B_d(t_{\text{value}}, t') V_d(t')$$

which can be combined to give:

$$V_d(t_{\text{value}}) = V_f(t_{\text{value}}) S(t) B_d(t_{\text{value}}, t') B_f(t', t_{\text{value}}) \tag{1.6}$$

Note that t_{value} may be before or after t'.

1.2 Forwards

So Davonda can happily pay its imminent euro bills. Suppose instead that the company expects to receive revenues in dollars *in six months' time* and needs to pay bills in euros also in six months' time. Now what should it do? One option would be for it to wait six months and then enter a spot trade. But this approach would run a very large risk: if the EURUSD spot rate increased substantially, the same dollar revenues would result in substantially fewer euros. Instead, Davonda could enter a contract with a wholesale bank under which Davonda must pay a pre-agreed amount of dollars to the bank in six months' time, and the bank must pay a pre-agreed amount of euros to Davonda in six months' time. Davonda now knows exactly how much it will pay and receive, and is insensitive to the spot rate in six months' time. This kind of contract is called a **forward contract**, often called simply a **forward**, and the time until settlement (six months in this example) is called the **maturity** of the forward.

The number of dollars to be settled divided by the number of euros to be settled gives an effective exchange rate for the contract. When this effective exchange contract is such that the contract can be dealt at zero cost (that is, without either side paying to enter the contract), the effective exchange rate is called the **fair forward rate** or simply the **forward rate** (or even just the "forward"). During the life of the forward contract, as time moves forward and spot moves around, the fair forward rate will move around and will not generally be equal to the exchange rate fixed in the contract. The exchange rate fixed in any given forward contract is called the **strike rate** or simply **strike** of the forward contract. We will denote the strike rate by K. Two forward contracts which settle on the same date but which were traded on different dates will in general have different strikes.

Since Davonda is *buying* the Foreign currency, we say it is *long* the forward contract. If it instead entered a contract to sell the Foreign currency (euros) and buy the Domestic currency (dollars), we would say it was going *short* the forward contract. This is not an arbitrary choice of terminology but rather an illustration of the general meaning of "long" versus "short" in finance parlance: a counterparty is *long* any instrument if it benefits from the market price of that instrument going *up*; conversely, a counterparty is *short* an instrument if it benefits from the market price of that instrument going *down*. In our case here, the "market price" is the fair forward rate.

At any given trade time, the forward rate is a function of contract maturity, and this function is known as the **forward curve**. In this book we will denote the forward rate by $F(T)$, where T is the settlement date. As with spot, if we need to explicitly specify that we are referring to the forward rate as seen at a specific trade time t, we will write $F(t, T)$. Figure 1.1 shows the forward curve for EURUSD as at the end of September 2014. The six-month forward rate is 1.2647. As the maturity approaches the spot date, the forward rate approaches the spot rate (1.2629), since a spot contract is really just a special case of the forward contract where the settlement date is the spot date.

1.2.1 The FX forward market

Just as with FX spot, there is an extremely active market in FX forwards. Prices in this market are not quoted in terms of the fair forward rate, however. The reason for that is that forward rates are generally very close to the corresponding spot rate, as illustrated in the previous section. This is especially so for short-maturity (or "short-dated") trades. Therefore, as the spot rate moves around, the entire curve of forward rates moves around with it, meaning that the signal (variations in the difference between forward and spot) can be swamped by noise (variations in the spot rate). To reduce the spot-based noise in the forward rates, the forward market uses a quotation convention whereby what is quoted is not the forward rate itself, but the *difference* between the forward rate and the spot rate (forward rate minus

8 | FX Barrier Options

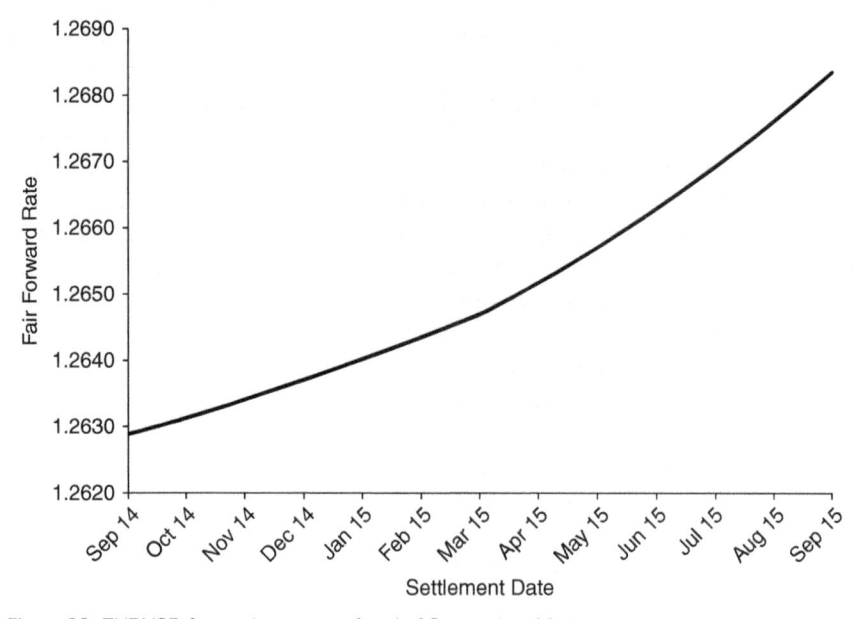

Figure 1.1 EURUSD forward curve as of end of September 2014

spot rate). This difference is called the **forward points** or **swap points**. Because forward points are often much less than 1, they are quoted after being multiplied by a scaling factor, which varies by currency pair. For example, the forward points scaling factor for EURUSD is 10,000. In this book we will denote the forward points by $f(T)$:

$$f(T) = F(T) - S \qquad (1.7)$$

The forward $F(T)$ is sometimes referred to as the **outright forward rate** in order to distinguish it from the forward points $f(T)$.

1.2.2 A formula for the forward rate

Once Davonda has entered the forward contract, it knows exactly how many dollars it will need to deliver and exactly how many euros it will receive, irrespective of what happens to the EURUSD market exchange rate. We say that it has **hedged its market risk**.

But suppose we are the bank on the other side. What should we do to ensure we have the agreed amount of euros to deliver? And how should we determine the fair forward rate? Let's address the first question first. We could simply buy the required number of euros now in the spot market (to be delivered on the spot date), hold them for six months and deliver them to Davonda on the settlement date. However, we would earn six months of interest on the euros, so that would yield too many euros. Instead, we should buy the discounted number of euros. To buy these euros in the spot market, we borrow dollars, paying six months of interest on the loan. Then at settlement, we deliver the euros to Davonda, receive the dollars from the company and pay off the dollar loan. If the number of dollars that we receive from the forward contract is exactly enough to pay off the dollar loan, then we have made neither a profit nor a loss on the trade, and the forward contract is worth zero. This is by definition what is meant by the *fair* forward rate, which then answers the second question.

The strategy described in the previous paragraph is known as **forward replication**. Let us now apply the replication strategy mathematically, step by step, to derive a formula for the fair forward rate.

- At time t:

    - We place an order in the EURUSD spot market, at spot rate $S(t)$, to buy $A_{\text{EUR}} B_{\text{EUR}}(t', T_s)$ euros, where A_{EUR} is the euro principal of the forward contract, and B_{EUR} is the euro discount factor between t' (the spot date of time t) and T_s (the settlement date of the forward contract).

- On date t' (the spot date corresponding to time t):

    - We borrow $A_{\text{EUR}} S(t) B_{\text{EUR}}(t', T_s)$ US dollars and pay it out to settle the spot trade.
    - We receive $A_{\text{EUR}} B_{\text{EUR}}(t', T_s)$ euros from the spot trade and deposit it.

- On date T_s:

    - We deliver A_{EUR} euros out of our deposit account to settle the forward contract.
    - We receive $A_{\text{EUR}} K$ US dollars from settlement of the forward contract, where K is the strike rate of the forward contract.
    - We repay the dollar loan, which has grown to $A_{\text{EUR}} S(t) B_{\text{USD}}^{-1}(t', T_s) B_{\text{EUR}}(t', T_s)$ US dollars.

Setting K equal to $F(t, T_s)$ and equating the two dollar amounts, we have:

$$A_{\text{EUR}} F(t, T_s) = A_{\text{EUR}} S(t) B_{\text{USD}}^{-1}(t', T_s) B_{\text{EUR}}(t', T_s)$$
$$\Rightarrow F(t, T_s) = S(t) B_{\text{USD}}^{-1}(t', T_s) B_{\text{EUR}}(t', T_s) \qquad (1.8)$$

Using Equation 1.4, we can alternatively write the expression for the fair forward rate in terms of instantaneous short interest rates:

$$F(t, T_s) = S(t) \exp\left(\int_{t'}^{T_s} (r_{\text{USD}}(u) - r_{\text{EUR}}(u)) \, du\right) \quad (1.9)$$

It is now easy to see that the forward rate is generally close to the spot rate, and furthermore, we see that the forward rate grows exponentially with maturity at a rate equal to the differential between the interest rates. For a general currency pair FORDOM:

$$F_{\text{FORDOM}}(t, T_s) = S_{\text{FORDOM}}(t) \exp\left(\int_{t'}^{T_s} (r_d(u) - r_f(u)) \, du\right) \quad (1.10)$$

where r_d and r_f are respectively the domestic and foreign interest rates. This is the formula for the **fair forward rate in terms of spot and instantaneous short interest rates**.

So – in a world where we unambiguously know the instantaneous short interest rate curves, we could calculate the fair forward rate from spot and interest rates. The practice, however, is a little more complicated. Taking the example of EURUSD, there is a highly active market in short-dated EURUSD forwards, and in practice we *derive* short-term EUR interest rates from the forward points in concert with a known USD interest rate curve. Indeed, the desk in a bank which typically makes markets in short-dated forwards is the short-term interest rate trading desk. A similar situation applies to any currency pair which contains USD. For currency pairs which do not contain USD, various other procedures are used by FX desks for deriving short-term interest rates.

Given this nature of the market, we should view Equation 1.10 as a formula that *relates* the forward rate to spot and interest rates, rather than as a formula for "how to get" the forward rate.

1.2.3 Payoff of a forward contract

Even when a hedger such as Davonda has entered a forward contract in order to offset some other risk, and has thereby reduced its uncertainty, it is natural for it to ask whether it would have been better off to gamble on the spot market. Davonda could have simply converted its dollars into euros in the spot market in six months time at the prevailing spot rate instead of at the agreed forward rate of 1.2647. The "prevailing spot rate" here means the spot rate at any time on a day whose spot date equals the settlement date of the forward contract. We denote this time by $\tilde{T}_s$

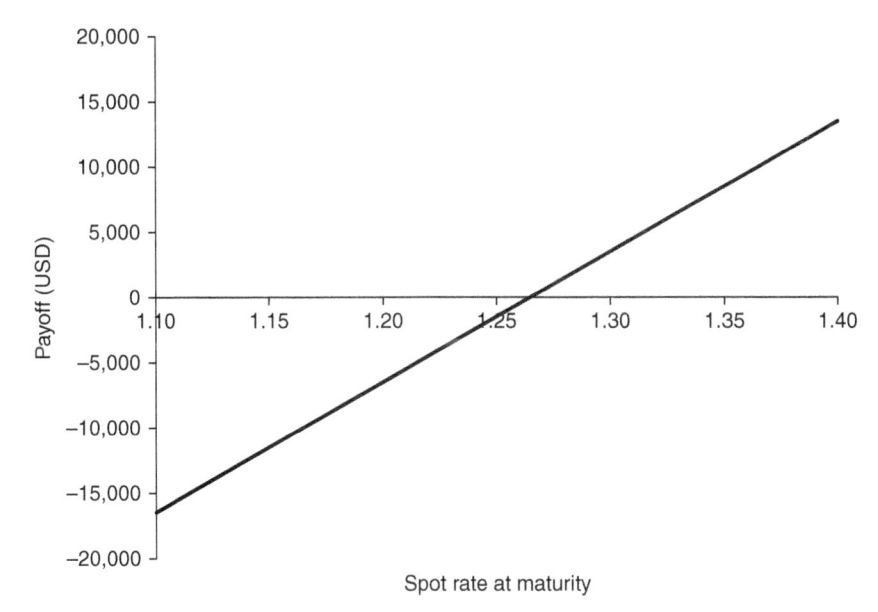

Figure 1.2 Payoff profile of a EURUSD forward contract in EUR 100,000 struck at 1.2647

and the corresponding spot rate by $S(\tilde{T}_s)$.[2] Let us suppose that the contract has a EUR principal of 100,000, and therefore a USD principal of 126,470. Adopting our natural measure currency of USD, the value on date T_s of the dollars paid is simply USD 126,470, whilst the value of the euros received is USD $100,000 \times S(\tilde{T}_s)$. The net USD value of the forward contract on date T_s is therefore given by:

$$P(T_s) = 100,000 \Big(S(\tilde{T}_s) - 1.2647 \Big) \tag{1.11}$$

This is called the **payoff** of the forward contract. Figure 1.2 shows a plot of its simple linear form, which we call the **payoff profile**.

A forward contract is an example of a **derivative**: a financial instrument whose payoff depends on the (generally future) market price of another financial instrument. The instrument on which a derivative depends (FX spot, in this case) is called the **underlying** instrument.

For a general currency pair and a forward contract with Foreign principal A_f and strike K, the payoff is given by:

$$P(T_s) = A_f \Big(S(\tilde{T}_s) - K \Big) \tag{1.12}$$

---

[2] It is tempting to call $\tilde{T}_s$ the "expiry date", in parallel with options, but I will reserve that term for contract types which actually have an expiry date.

1.2.4 Valuation of a forward contract

We have now established that the value of a forward contract before maturity is zero when it is struck at the fair forward rate, and we have derived an expression for the value of a forward contract *at* maturity for any strike (the result is given by the payoff). But how much is a forward contract worth when we are *before* maturity and when its strike is *not* equal to the fair forward rate? Inspection of the last two steps of the EURUSD replication strategy described in Section 1.2.2 shows that for a general strike K, the bank expects to end up with $A_{EUR}[K - F(t, T_s)]$ dollars on the settlement date. This is then the bank's expectation of the value in dollars of the contract on the settlement date. Davonda's valuation is simply the negative of this: $A_{EUR}[F(t, T_s) - K]$. The present value to Davonda is then obtained by discounting back to today:

$$V(t) = A_{EUR} B_{USD}(t, T_s) [F(t, T_s) - K] \tag{1.13}$$

Generalizing the currency pair, a long position in a forward contract with Foreign principal A_f has present Domestic value given by:

$$V(t) = A_f B_d(t, T_s) [F(t, T_s) - K] \tag{1.14}$$

This is the expression for the **present value of a forward contract** in terms of discount factor B and fair forward rate F.

Alternative expressions can be written in terms of spot and interest rates. Using constant interest rates for the sake of conciseness, two useful forms are:

$$V(t) = A_f e^{-r_d(T_s - t)} \left[S(t) e^{(r_d - r_f)(T_s - t')} - K \right] \tag{1.15}$$

$$V(t) = A_f e^{-r_d(t' - t)} \left[e^{-r_f(T_s - t')} S(t) - e^{-r_d(T_s - t')} K \right] \tag{1.16}$$

In the first expression, the square brackets contain the value of the (unit-Foreign-principal) forward contract on the settlement date T_s, the first term of which is precisely the fair forward rate. The square brackets of the second expression contain the value of the unit forward contract on the spot date t'.

1.3 Vanilla options

Wouldn't it be nice if the payoff profile in Figure 1.2 had no downside? As it stands, if the spot rate at maturity is below the strike of 1.2647, Davonda will be monetarily worse off than if it had not hedged its market risk with the forward contract. If the spot rate at maturity is above the strike, Davonda will be monetarily better

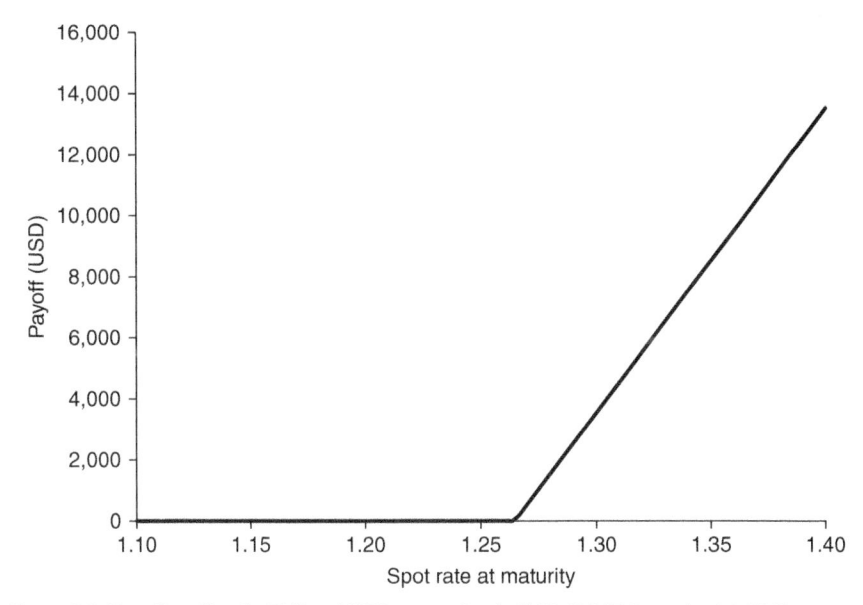

Figure 1.3 Payoff profile of a EUR call/USD put option in EUR 100,000 struck at 1.2647

off. I emphasize "monetarily" because the removal of risk achieved through the forward contract will always bring the company great benefit in terms of reduced uncertainty, regardless of the level of spot at maturity. Nevertheless, the presence of a potential downside remains psychologically unattractive to many hedgers. To have its cake and eat it, Davonda would like to floor the payoff at zero: it needs the payoff profile shown in Figure 1.3. This is the payoff of a **vanilla option**. Specifically, the vanilla option is a "EUR call/USD put option in EUR 100,000 struck at 1.2647". It is another example of a **derivative**.

Needless to say, the have-it-and-eat-it cake costs more money. It cost Davonda nothing to enter a forward contract struck at the fair forward rate with the bank, because the upside and downside effectively balanced each other out. In contrast, the vanilla option only has upside, so no choice of strike allows the upside and downside to balance out. Davonda must therefore *buy* the vanilla option from the bank. The amount it must pay is called the **option premium**. Davonda then becomes the **option holder**, and the bank is referred to as the **option writer**.

The vanilla option allows for the same exchange of cash flows as a forward, but the difference is that the option gives the option holder the *right but not the obligation* to exchange cash flows with the bank. If exchange of cash flows would result in a negative payoff for the option holder, the holder will clearly not exercise its right to exchange cash flows. As we saw when discussing the payoff profile of a forward contract, in Section 1.2.3, the payoff is dependent on $S(\tilde{T}_s)$, the spot rate at some time during a day whose spot date equals the settlement date. The exercise decision therefore needs to be taken on such a date, and in fact a vanilla option contract will specify not only the date but also the precise time when the exercise decision must be made by the option holder. These are called the **expiry date** and **expiry time** of the option. The optionality held by the option holder expires after this time.

Expiry times are standardized, and the different standards are referred to as **expiry cuts**. For instance, the "New York cut" is at 10am New York time. The expiry cut used for a given option depends on the currency pair and sometimes additionally on the time of day at which the request or quote was made.

The premium may be paid in either currency of the pair (either EUR or USD in this case). The premium currency, premium amount and premium payment date will all be agreed as part of the option contract.

A vanilla option thus has several dates and times associated with it:

1. The trade date – the date the contract is agreed between the option writer and holder.
2. The premium payment date – the date on which the premium must be paid by the holder.
3. The expiry date and time – the time at which the option holder must decide whether to exercise the option to exchange cash flows.
4. The settlement date – the time at which the cash flows settle, if the option has been exercised.

An option to perform the opposite exchange of cash flows (selling EUR and buying USD) is referred to as a "EUR put/USD call" option. The payoff profile for this option (with the same strike as before) is shown in Figure 1.4.

In the same way that we can say "buy EURUSD spot" to mean buy EUR and sell USD, it is common to use the abbreviated form "EURUSD call option" in place of the full form "EUR call/USD put option", and similarly to use the abbreviated form "EURUSD put option" in place of the full form "EUR put/USD call option". I will adopt the convention of using the abbreviated forms when it is getting too long-winded to write the full form. Other conventions exist, however: for example, in the inter-dealer FX options market (used when *both* counterparties are market-making banks), the unqualified term "call" means a call on the side that is not USD, if USD is one of the currencies in the pair, or otherwise the Foreign currency.

Irrespective of whether the option is a Foreign call/Domestic put or a Foreign put/Domestic call, the holder of an option is said to be "long" the option, whilst the writer is said to be "short" the option.

Vanilla call and put options are both examples of **European derivatives**, defined as a derivative whose payoff depends purely on the level of spot at maturity (also known as the "**terminal spot rate**"). A European derivative has no sensitivity to the spot path at times before the expiry time.

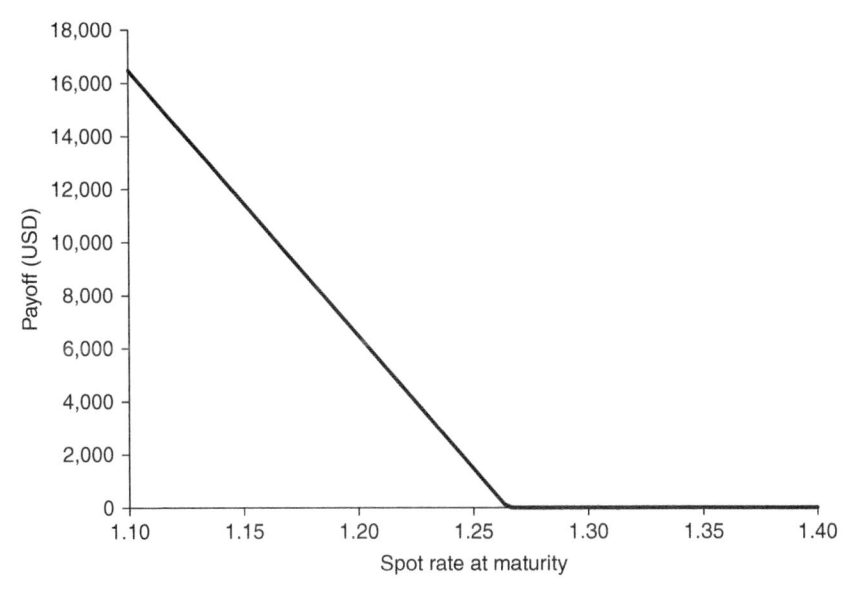

Figure 1.4 Payoff profile of a EUR put/USD call option in EUR 100,000 struck at 1.2647

1.3.1 Put–call parity

If we look at the payoff profiles of our EURUSD forward, call option and put option (Figures 1.2–1.4) it is visually obvious that a long position in the call combined with a short position in the put will give the same payoff profile as the forward. Two contracts which have exactly the same payoff profile at maturity must have the same value at any earlier time t, otherwise it would be possible to make a guaranteed riskless profit, known as **arbitrage**. Hence we can further conclude that the value of a call option minus the value of a put option equals the value of a forward contract. This general and important relationship is called **put–call parity**, and it applies as long as we keep all the other contract details the same: strike, settlement date and principals. Moreover, the expiry times of the call and put options must be equal (remember that the forward contract does not have an expiry time and it is sometimes possible for multiple trade dates to have the same spot date).

We will discuss the valuation of vanilla options in later chapters, but for the moment we can write the following schematic equation to describe put–call parity:

$$V_{\text{call}}(t, K, T_e, T_s) - V_{\text{put}}(t, K, T_e, T_s) = V_{\text{forward}}(t, K, T_s) \qquad (1.17)$$

The absence of principals in this equation simply means that all three contracts must have the same Foreign principal amount. As usual, the values are in the natural currency of Domestic.

1.4 European digitals

Another type of European derivative is the **European digital**, which pays out a fixed amount of cash (in either Domestic or Foreign) if the terminal spot rate is above/below an agreed level. For example, a "six-month EURUSD 1.30 digital call in EUR 100,000" pays out 100,000 euros if the spot rate in six months' time is at 1.30 or above, and pays out nothing otherwise. Strictly speaking, the European digital is not an option, because there is no optionality in the contract, but it is common to see it referred to as a "European digital option".

1.5 Barrier-contingent vanilla options

In flooring the payoff of a long forward position to get a call option, we removed all possible downside but did not touch the upside, which remains completely unlimited. The premium charged for a call option will of course reflect this unlimited upside. For our example case of a six-month EUR call/USD put option in EUR 100,000 struck at 1.2647, the fair USD premium is about 2,600. As a fraction of the the USD principal of 126,470, this USD premium is about 2.1%.

Whilst the payoff of the EUR put/USD call option is technically limited, it still has the potential to become very large, and again the premium charged reflects this potential. The premium for the put option is also about 2.1%. (This is not coincidence; we shall show later, in Section 2.7.3, that when the strike equals the forward, the option pricing formulae for call and put options have the same values.)

It is very common for hedgers to take their own views on future spot moves, and it is often the case that they do not wish to pay the full vanilla premium to participate in the unlimited potential upside. It then makes sense to somehow modify the contract so that it no longer has an unlimited upside, in order to make it cheaper without removing the desired hedging protection that was its purpose. One simple way to remove the unlimited upside is to *cap* the payoff, so that it does not continue to rise after some threshold high level of spot. For example, one could choose a threshold level of 1.35 and replace the payoff shown in Figure 1.3 with the one shown in Figure 1.5. This capped payoff can easily be constructed using a structure of two EUR call/USD put options: the original one (EUR call/USD put struck at 1.2647) plus a *short* position in another EUR call/USD put option with a strike at 1.35 and all the other parameters the same. This structure is called a EURUSD **call spread**. (With two options, it gets rather cumbersome using the "EUR call/USD put" terminology, so we will stick to the briefer "EURUSD call" terminology.) Similarly, the original EURUSD put option struck at 1.2647 can be combined with a short position in a 1.20-strike put to give the **put spread** whose payoff profile is shown in Figure 1.6.

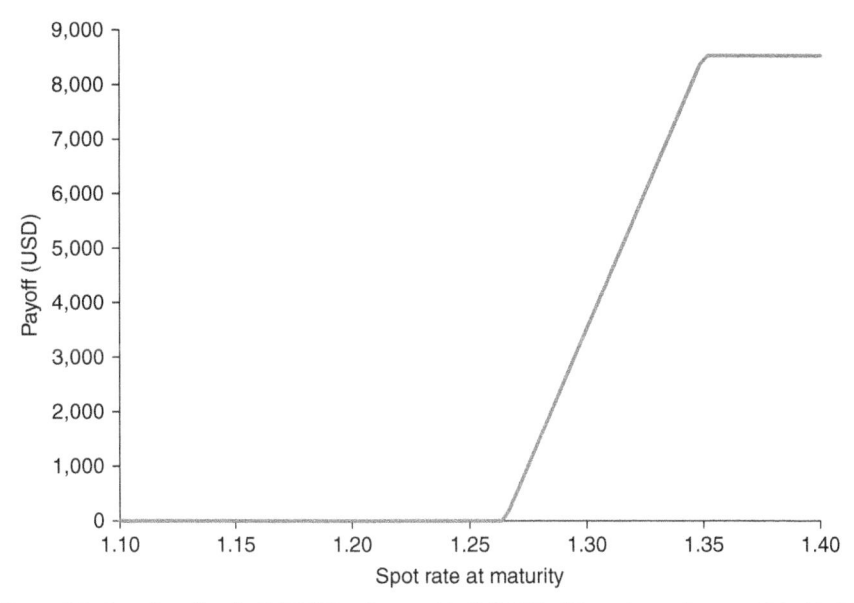

Figure 1.5 Payoff profile of a EURUSD call spread in EUR 100,000 per leg; strikes at 1.2647/1.35

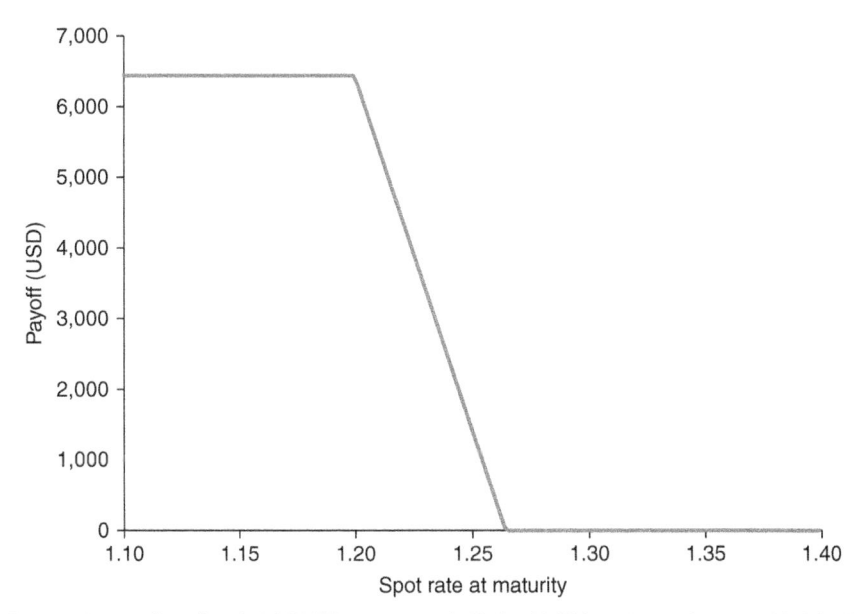

Figure 1.6 Payoff profile of a EURUSD put spread in EUR 100,000 per leg; strikes at 1.2647/1.20

18 | FX Barrier Options

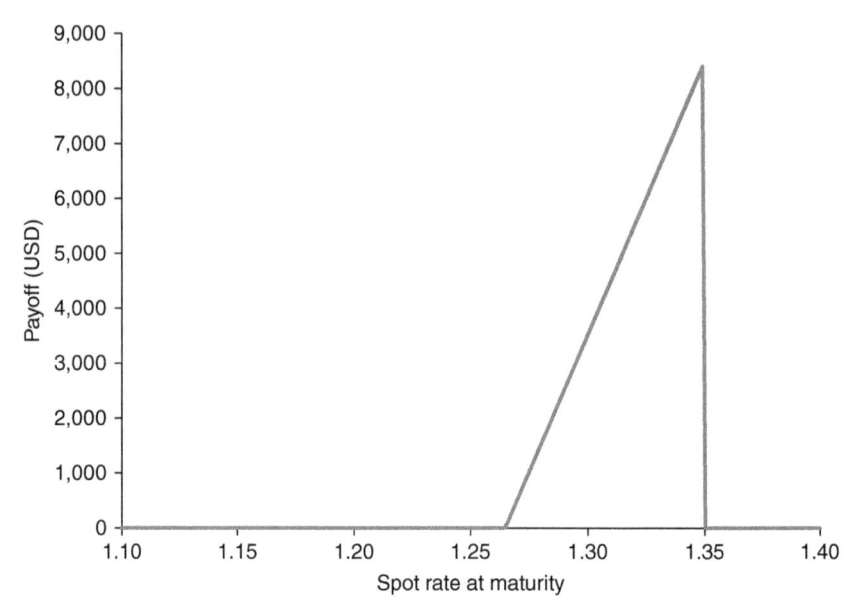

Figure 1.7 Setting the call option payoff to zero when the spot rate is above 1.35

Capping the payoff in this way only reduces the option premium a little bit: our call spread example has a premium of about 1.8% of principal, whilst our put spread example has a premium of about 1.7% of principal.

A slightly more draconian way of reducing the premium is to set the payoff to zero above the threshold level, as shown in Figure 1.7. This structure has a premium of around 1.1%.

However, there is a much better way of reducing the premium than simply playing with the payoff at maturity: we can make the entire payoff contingent on the condition that the spot rate stays below the threshold level *for the entire lifetime of the option*. The probability that spot goes above 1.35 *at some time* is much higher than the probability that it ends up above 1.35, because there are many possible spot paths which go above 1.35 and then come down again. But this is perfectly acceptable to a hedger whose view is based on whether spot will go above the threshold level during the lifetime of the option. For the same threshold spot level, this feature lowers the premium[3] more drastically, to 0.69%.

The construct above is an example of a **barrier option**. The term refers to a wide class of options where the payoff depends on whether spot has traded at a particular level at a particular set of time points. A barrier option is in turn an example of a

---

[3] The premium for a barrier option is model-dependent, and in this chapter we will quote premia based on the so-called Theoretical Value or TV. What this means is described in detail in Chapter 4.

path-dependent option: one whose payoff depends on the path spot takes and not just on the value of spot at maturity. There are many path-dependent options which are not barrier options; for example, an Asian option is based on the *average* level of spot over some set of time points.

While we are on the subject of terminology, it is worth mentioning the terms **exotic option** and **exotic contract**. Opinion is slightly divided regarding the meaning of "exotic" here: some use the term to mean exactly the same as a path-dependent option, whilst others mean "any option that is not a vanilla". The question boils down to whether non-vanilla European derivatives (such as European digitals) are exotics. I will adopt the approach that a derivative which is neither a forward nor a vanilla option is an exotic contract. Hence European digitals *are* exotic contracts.

Back to our example barrier option above. It is more specifically called a **knock-out barrier option**. The threshold spot level of 1.35 is called the **barrier level**, and we say that the call option *knocks out* if spot ever trades at the barrier level during the option's lifetime. In this context, the option's lifetime means the time interval starting at the trade time and ending at the expiry time, which is when the option holder must choose whether to exercise the option. Because the barrier level is higher than spot, this barrier option is described as an **up-and-out call option**. And because the barrier can be triggered at any time during the option's life, we say that it is a **continuously monitored barrier** or simply a **continuous barrier**.

In payoff profile diagrams, I will indicate the presence of the knock-out barrier by means of a cross (×) on the spot axis at the barrier level, as shown in Figure 1.8.

If we increase the barrier level (keeping all other parameters fixed), we allow a larger potential payoff, and the option must correspondingly have a greater premium. In the limit of very high barrier level, the option behaves like a vanilla. Conversely, if we decrease the barrier level, the potential payoff and the option premium become smaller. In the limit of a barrier level at spot, the option has no value. Hence for a fixed option strike level, the barrier level can be adjusted to give the desired balance of potential payoff and premium.

There is no reason why the barrier level has to be above spot. We can equally well consider a barrier level of say 1.25 and construct a barrier option whose payoff is contingent on the condition that spot stays *above* the barrier level. This **down-and-out call option** has a premium of 0.87%, and would suit a hedger who takes the view that spot is unlikely to go down to 1.25 during the option's lifetime. Its payoff profile diagram is shown in Figure 1.9.

There is an important qualitative difference between the two barrier option examples above. In the case of the up-and-out call, the barrier is placed at a level where the payoff would otherwise be non-zero, and hence a small change in spot which breaches the barrier will change the payoff from around USD 8,000 to zero. We say that there is a **spike** in the payoff. In contrast, in the case of the down-and-out call, the barrier is placed at a level where the payoff would anyway

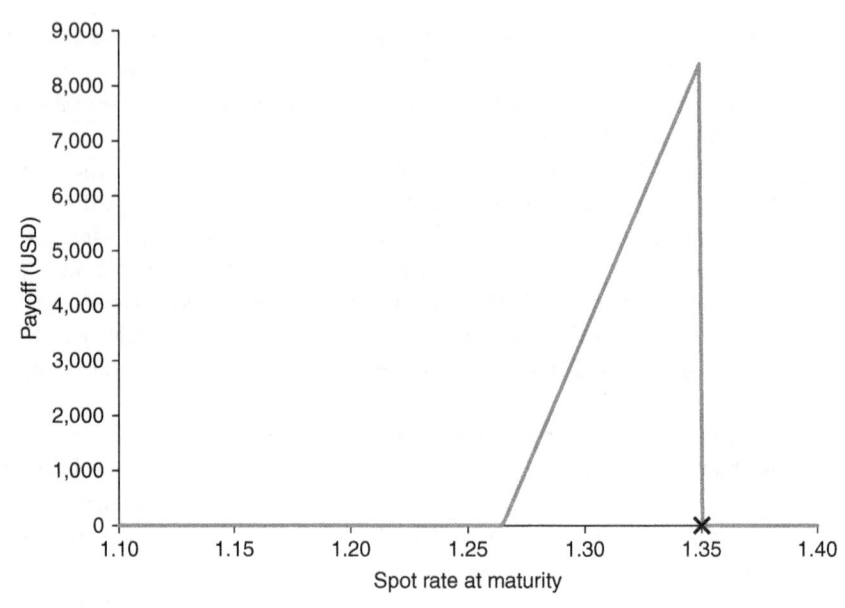

Figure 1.8 Payoff profile diagram of a 1.2647-strike EUR call/USD put option with an up-side knock-out at 1.35

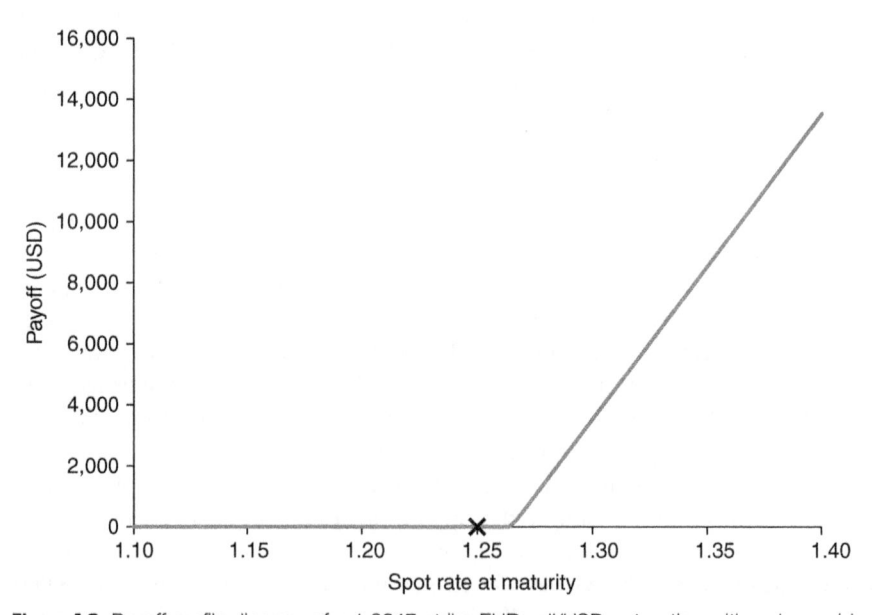

Figure 1.9 Payoff profile diagram of a 1.2647-strike EUR call/USD put option with a down-side knock-out at 1.25

be zero, and the breaching of the barrier causes no payoff spike. The qualitative difference in the forms of risk to be managed in these two situations motivates the use of some specialist terminology to distinguish them: a knock-out barrier at zero payoff is called a **normal knock-out**, whilst a knock-out barrier at non-zero payoff is called a **reverse knock-out**. In some contexts, the epithet "normal" is dropped. For example, a drop-down list in a software application may offer the choice of either "barrier option" or "reverse barrier option".

A **double knock-out call option** has two barrier levels, one above spot and one below, and the payoff is contingent on the condition that *neither* of the barriers is breached. This naturally reduces the option premium very effectively, whilst remaining suitable for a hedger whose view is that spot will remain in a given range around its current level. Typically (but not necessarily), the strike level will be between the barrier levels, with the result that one of the barriers will be a normal knock-out and the other will be a reverse knock-out.

I have described the barrier-related features above in the context of the payoff of a *call* option (EUR call/USD put), but all the features can be applied equally to a put option (EUR put/USD call). For example, we could construct a **down-and-out put option** where the payoff of a six-month 1.2647-strike EUR put/USD call option is contingent on spot never falling to 1.20. Its payoff profile diagram is shown in Figure 1.10. This reduces the premium from 2.1% to 0.39%. The barrier being placed at a level where the payoff would otherwise be non-zero, this is an example of a reverse knock-out.

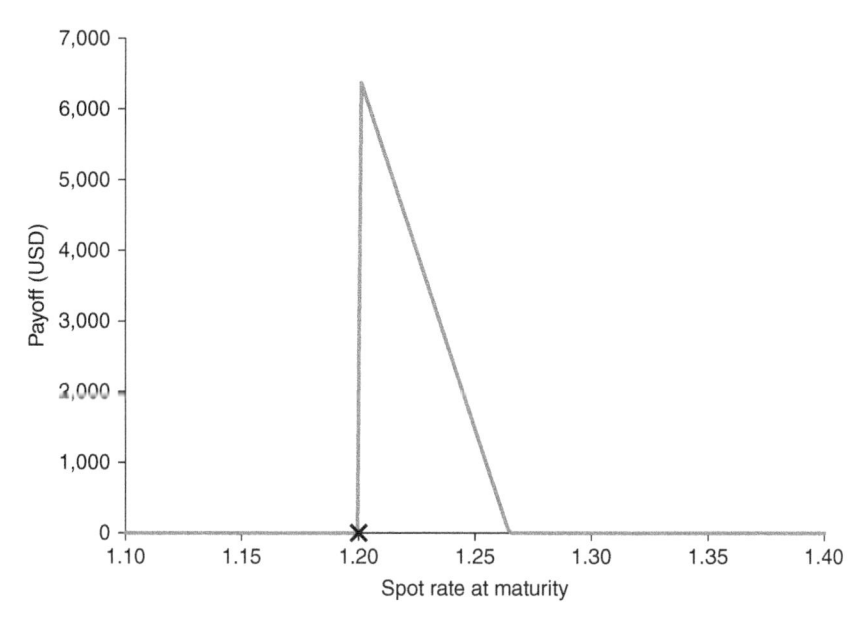

Figure 1.10 Payoff profile diagram of a 1.2647-strike EUR put/USD call option with a down-side knock-out at 1.25

Just as a hedger may take a view that a certain spot level *won't* be breached in a given time period, it is perfectly reasonable to hold a view that a certain spot level *will* be breached. There's an option for that: a **knock-in option**. For example, we could construct an **up-and-in call option** where the payoff of a six-month 1.2647-strike EUR call/USD put option is contingent on the condition that spot *does* trade at the barrier level of 1.35 at some point during the option's lifetime. In payoff profile diagrams, we indicate a knock-in barrier with an open circle (o), as illustrated in Figure 1.11. A **double knock-in option** has two barrier levels, and the payoff is contingent on the condition that *either* (one or both) of the barriers is breached.

Suppose we hold both a knock-out option and its "sibling" knock-in option (the knock-in option having all the other option properties the same as the knock-out option). If the barrier is triggered, the knock-out option expires worthless and the knock-in option knocks in to a vanilla option, so we end up with a vanilla option. If the barrier is not triggered, the knock-out option yields a vanilla option and the knock-in option expires worthless, so again we end up with a vanilla option. Thus the sum of the value of a knock-out option and the value of its sibling knock-in option must equal the value of the underlying vanilla option. This very useful relationship is independent of the choice of valuation model, and is presented again in Section 1.12 along with some other useful relationships.

It can easily be seen that we can construct a lot of different types of barrier option. We can start with a call payoff or a put payoff. We can add a barrier on

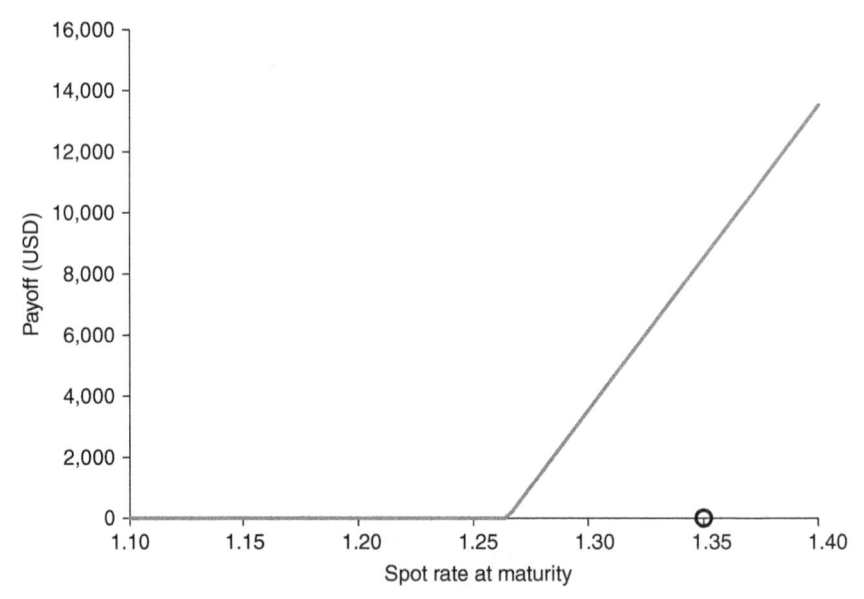

Figure 1.11 Payoff profile diagram of a 1.2647-strike EUR call/USD put option with an up-side knock-in at 1.35

the up-side only, the down-side only, or a double barrier. And the barriers can be knock-out or knock-in. What they all have in common is that a vanilla option payoff is contingent on whether a barrier has been triggered, and so I will use the term **barrier-contingent vanilla option** to describe this family of barrier option types. The table Contract Types at the front of the book lists the main contract types that we will be covering in this book, and includes numerous barrier-contingent vanilla option types. For each contract type, I have given a short code, which I will use for brevity in later sections of the book.

1.6 Barrier-contingent payments

When you're holding a hammer, everything starts to look like a nail. The technique of making payoffs contingent on barriers being triggered need not be restricted to vanilla option payoffs. Another very popular family of barrier-based contract types is **barrier-contingent payments**. Under such contracts, a future payment (in either Domestic or Foreign) is contingent on whether a barrier or barriers has/have been breached. For example, a "six-month EURUSD 1.30 **one-touch** in EUR 100,000" pays out 100,000 euros if (and only if) spot trades at or above a level of 1.30 at some point during the lifetime of the contract. Conversely, a "six-month EURUSD 1.30 **no-touch** in EUR 100,000" pays out 100,000 euros as long as spot *never* trades at or above a level of 1.30 at any point during the lifetime of the contract.

Strictly speaking, barrier-contingent payments such as a one-touch should not be described as *options*, because there is no optionality involved anywhere. They may however be described as "exotic", "path-dependent" and "derivatives". Having said that, the broad term "barrier options" is very often used colloquially to include barrier-contingent payments. It is unusual, for example, to hear the phrase "FX Barrier Derivatives", and the title of this book reflects the more colloquial, if less accurate, form.

Barrier-contingent payments go by various other names. They are commonly called **American binaries** or **American bets**. The "American" part of the name refers to the fact that the barrier can trigger at any time, by analogy with American options, which can be exercised at any time. The "binary" or "bet" terminology emphasizes that the option has just two discrete outcomes.

With two barriers in play, we get a **double one-touch** or a **double no-touch**. The double no-touch is particularly popular, and sometimes goes by the name of a **range**, paying out as it does only in the event that spot trades within a range during the contract's lifetime. The barrier levels for double one-touches and double no-touches are very often specified to be *symmetric about spot* at the time of trade.

Payments do not have an expiry time, only a settlement date, so when we introduce a barrier feature, we must also add an expiry time, which defines exactly when the barrier ceases to be active.

If a one-touch or double one-touch contract is triggered, we know immediately how much payment needs to be made, so the following question arises: should the payment be made immediately or on the contract's settlement date? In fact, two variants of every one-touch contract type exist, one which pays "immediately" (actually on the spot date of the date on which the barrier was triggered) and one which pays on the settlement date. The first variant is known as a **pay-at-hit** contract; the second variant is known as a **pay-at-maturity** contract.

Just as we discussed for the barrier-contingent vanilla options that a knock-out option plus a knock-in option gives us the barrier-free option (a vanilla option), so it is with touch contracts: if we hold both a no-touch and its sibling one-touch (which means the pay-at-maturity variant), we are assured of a payment at maturity. Hence the sum of the value of the no-touch and the value of the sibling one-touch equals the value of the underlying payment.

Payoff profile diagrams for barrier-contingent payments are less interesting and useful than for barrier-contingent vanilla options, but if we do draw them we must keep in mind the currency in which the payment will be made. If a payment is fixed in Foreign, its Domestic payoff will depend on the spot rate at maturity, so for example the payoff profile diagram for the euro-paying one-touch above will take the form of a sloped straight line that increases with spot, as shown in Figure 1.12. In the absence of a contract strike, it is often useful, for orientation, to plot the spot level, which I will do with a plus sign (+).

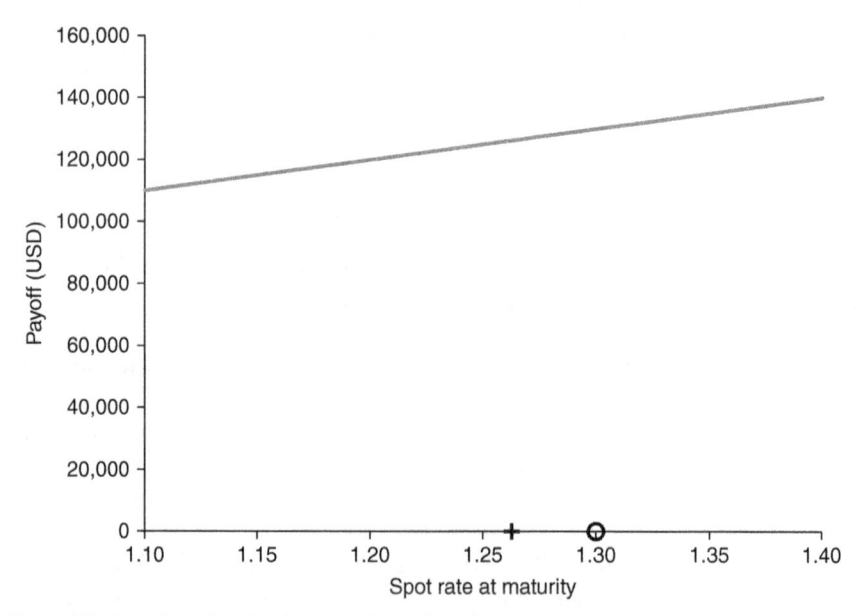

Figure 1.12 Payoff profile of a six-month EURUSD 1.30 one-touch in EUR 100,000

The list of contract types in the table Contract Types at the front of the book includes numerous barrier-contingent payment types, together with their short codes.

1.7 Rebates

When a knock-out option knocks out, all hopes of participating in the upside of the vanilla option payoff are dashed. To soften the blow, contracts are sometimes modified to include a feature whereby a fixed payment is made if the option knocks out. This fixed payment is called a **rebate**. It is not difficult to see that a barrier option with a rebate can be structured simply out of a rebate-less barrier option and a touch contract (barrier-contingent payment). For certain purposes, it is advisable to treat the rebate together with the barrier option: for structuring and product development, for counterparty credit risk analysis, and for real-world pricing (covered in Section 7.3). However, for the valuation and risk management purposes which are the primary focus of this book, it makes most sense to treat the two components separately. For the remainder of this book, we will assume that barrier options are rebate-free, unless otherwise stated.

1.8 Knock-in-knock-out (KIKO) options

The double barrier options and double touches described above had either both barriers being knock-out or both barriers being knock-in. A twist on this is provided by **KIKO** contracts, which combine one knock-in barrier and one knock-out barrier. There is plenty of scope for ambiguity as to how the contract works, and in fact there are two variants.

The first (and more popular) variant pays out only in the event that the knock-in barrier has been triggered *and* the knock-out barrier has not been triggered. All other combinations of trigger states result in the contract expiring worthless. For example, if both barriers are triggered, the contract expires worthless. (The order in which the barriers are triggered is immaterial.)

This variant of KIKO can be structured straightforwardly out of a double knock-out and a single knock-out. This is most easily seen using an example: let us take the case of a KIKO contract which has a knock-in on the downside and a knock-out on the upside. If we added to this contract a double knock-out contract (with the same barrier levels and other contract details), the combination would be guaranteed to have the same payoff as the corresponding contract with a knock-out barrier on the upside. If the lower barrier were triggered, the KIKO would turn into an up-side knock-out, whilst the double knock-out contract would be worthless.

And if the lower were not triggered, the KIKO would be worthless, whilst the double knock-out contract would be effectively an up-side knock-out.

The second variant is effectively a "first-to-trigger" option: if the knock-in barrier is triggered first, the option becomes active and can no longer be extinguished by the knock-out barrier. If the knock-out barrier is triggered first, the option becomes worthless and can no longer be activated by the knock-in barrier. This variant of KIKO cannot be structured out of basic contract types.

The terms **sequential KIKO** and **non-sequential KIKO** are sometimes used to distinguish the two variants. However, I am not convinced that all practitioners use the terms the same way around! Given the potential confusion, I prefer to refer to the first (and more popular) variant as the **structurable KIKO** and the second variant as the **non-structurable KIKO**.

1.9 Types of barriers

The barrier option types described so far are the most commonly traded. They are often referred to as **first-generation exotic options**, and thanks to their large trading volumes are also categorized as **flow products**.

Their barriers all have the following four properties:

1. They are active for the entire lifetime of the option.
2. They are at a constant level for the entire lifetime of the option.
3. They are continuously monitored – they can be triggered at any time of any day whilst the barrier is active.
4. They are triggered by first breach. That is to say, a barrier is breached as soon as spot trades at or beyond its level. It makes no difference whether spot continues to trade beyond the barrier level for one minute or for one month.

Each of these four properties can be varied, to construct a variety of other barrier types. For example, we may vary the first property by defining a barrier to be active for only part of the option's life. This is known as a **window barrier** or **partial barrier**. It is sensitive to the spot path only during a subset of the option's lifetime, which may suit certain views on the market. An additional attraction is that the option holder need not worry about the possibility of barrier trigger before the barrier's start time or after its end time.

We may vary the second property by allowing the barrier level to change during the life of the option. It may change in a pre-agreed manner – for example, a six-month up-and-out barrier option may have its barrier level set to 1.28 for the first three months and 1.30 for the last three months. This is referred to as a **time-dependent barrier**. Or, the barrier level may vary according to where spot trades in the future. For example, a contract may reset an upper barrier after three months at a level two big figures above the prevailing spot level at that time. This is known as a **resetting barrier**.

Varying the third property, we may define a barrier which is monitored only at discrete time points, say at 4pm London time[4] each business day. This is called a **discretely monitored barrier** or simply **discrete barrier**. Why is this a good idea? Well, one of the problems with continuously monitored barriers is that they really must be monitored continuously! The FX market operates around the clock, every day except on weekends and public holidays, and a barrier may be breached at a time which is in the middle of the night for one or both of the counterparties. Large global counterparties, such as multi-national investment banks, have the operational ability to monitor barriers around the clock, but not all hedgers who buy barrier options have such an ability. For them, the chief attraction of discrete barrier options is that they allow the monitoring times to be restricted to a manageable number of convenient time points. Typically, the barrier will be monitored once each business day during business hours for the hedger.

The fourth and last property may be varied by using **Parisian barriers**, which require spot to be "well and truly" over the barrier level. The exact specification used to determine whether the Parisian barrier has triggered varies, but a typical example would be to track the *average* spot rate in a moving window covering say the last 24 hours. If spot pokes briefly through the barrier level and then quickly retreats from it, the Parisian barrier will not be triggered, but if spot breaches the barrier for some time or pushes far beyond it, it will be triggered. Options based on Parisian barriers are generally known simply as **Parisian options**.

1.10 Structured products

A variety of FX structured products are based on barrier options. Where these can be broken down and expressed as a sum of individual barrier options, they can be priced and risk-managed to a large extent via the component options. Wystup [6] describes a variety of structured products based on barrier options.

A very common example of an FX barrier-based structured product is the **accumulator payment**, a simple version of which works as follows. The date and currency of a payment are fixed, but the payment amount is calculated in a manner depending on the spot path during the option's life. A sequence of time points, called the **schedule**, is defined, and at each time point in the schedule the payment amount *accrues* (grows), either by a fixed amount or at a rate depending on the level of spot. Additionally, a barrier level (possibly time-dependent) is defined, and if the spot rate ever triggers the barrier, the payment amount accrues no further for the remainder of the option's lifetime.

In this simple version, it is possible to break the structure down into individual barrier-contingent payments. If the payment amount accrues at a fixed rate, a

---

[4] This is not a random example: the main WM/Reuters benchmark FX fix is taken in a narrow time window surrounding 4pm London time. It is the nearest thing to a "closing" rate in FX.

single barrier-contingent payment is required at each schedule date, but if the payment amount is spot-dependent, this must in turn be structured out of multiple barrier-contingent payments at each schedule date.

Sometimes the structure is defined with an initial payment amount and a negative "accrual". The payment amount then *diminishes* at every time point in the schedule, again either by a fixed amount or at a rate depending on the level of spot. Triggering of the barrier causes the diminution of the payment to cease.

The final payoff need not be a payment – the essential part of the accumulator structure calculates a notional amount, and this same notional amount can instead be used to define the principal of a forward or an option, giving an **accumulator forward** or **accumulator option** respectively. Accumulators should thus be regarded as a *family* of structures.

Even when a structured product *can* be decomposed into multiple basic barrier options, it is often still worth developing a specialized valuation model for it, in the interests of optimized computational performance.

1.11 Specifying the contract

Every derivative trade constitutes a legal contract between two counterparties, and behind the headline option parameters that we have been discussing (strike, barrier level, expiry time and so on) there lies a detailed description of the terms of that contract, intended to ensure absolute legal clarity regarding the counterparties' rights and obligations. (Who decides, for example, if spot really did breach the barrier? What happens if the counterparties dispute whether the barrier was triggered?) The entirety of the documentation for an FX barrier option typically runs to a dozen or so pages, but apart from the headline option parameters, the details are the same for all contracts of a given type. For this reason, the option parameters themselves are generally recorded in a single short section of their own, referred to as the "term sheet" (and indeed often comprising just one sheet). I can illustrate this using the format of a "pseudo-term sheet". For example, the first barrier option that we discussed above would be specified using the following pseudo-term sheet:

Contract type:	Up and Out single barrier
Currency pair:	EURUSD
Maturity:	6 months
Call/Put:	EUR call; USD put
Strike K:	1.2647
Lower Barrier L:	N/A
Upper Barrier U:	1.35
EUR Principal A_f:	100,000
USD Principal A_d:	126,470

With larger principals, the abbreviation "mio" is often used to mean million.

Whilst term sheets are essential for legal contracts and other official documentation, it is also useful to be able to specify an option's parameters in a single short phrase that can be quickly spoken or written down for communication with colleagues. It's a bit like ordering a coffee in certain coffee shops, but instead of a "double tall dry skinny cappuccino", it's a "six-month 1.2647-strike euro call/dollar put in 100,000 euros, knock-out at 1.35". For the purposes of this book, I will mostly use the "coffee shop" phrase to specify contracts.

1.12 Quantitative truisms

In the course of meeting the products, we have discussed a number of important quantitative relationships. These can sometimes vastly simplify our work, and so I will give a brief summary of them here.

1.12.1 Foreign exchange symmetry and inversion

The clue is in the name: *exchange*. When we exchange cash flows in two currencies, we are simultaneously buying one and selling the other, and the overall trade can be viewed either as a buy trade or a sell trade. For example, a spot trade which involves buying euros and selling dollars may be regarded either as a buy trade in which we are buying euros denominated in dollars or as a sell trade in which we are selling dollars denominated in euros. Contrast this with say a share transaction, where if we pay out 100 shares and receive cash for them, there is unequivocal recognition that this transaction should be described as us selling 100 shares.

Foreign exchange symmetry allows us to represent the same option in two equivalent ways: either as the contractual option, specified in terms of the conventional quote-order currency pair (for example, EURUSD, USDTRY or AUDJPY), or as the **inverse option**, specified in terms of the **inverse currency pair** (USDEUR, TRYUSD or JPYAUD). For example, a three-month USDTRY 2.50 high-side one-touch in 200,000 USD can alternatively be represented as a three-month TRYUSD 0.40 low-side one-touch in 200,000 USD. In the contractual specification, the payment currency is the Foreign currency, whereas in the inverse option, the payment currency is the Domestic currency. The equivalence of the representations means we can choose to calculate the option's value based on whichever of the two representations is easier.

1.12.2 Knock-out plus knock-in equals no-barrier contract

We have already discussed this relationship in the context of barrier-contingent vanilla options, barrier-contingent payments and KIKOs. In general, we can write down:

$$\text{Contract X with knock-out} + \text{Contract X with knock-in} = \text{Contract X} \quad (1.18)$$

When we come to value knock-outs and knock-ins numerically, a prudent strategy is to value one of them directly and the other one using this relationship. This ensures that a portfolio containing the combination of the two barrier options and a short position in the no-barrier contract will always value correctly to zero, regardless of numerical error. When we deal with barrier-contingent vanilla options, we usually value the knock-out numerically and the knock-in as a vanilla minus the knock-out. The reason for doing it this way around is that in a finite-difference method, the boundary condition for a knock-out is trivial to impose (the value at the boundary is simply zero), whereas the boundary condition for a knock-in requires us to calculate the vanilla option value at the barrier level at the time of hit.

1.12.3 Put–call parity

A basic and standard result in the world of vanilla options of any asset class, put–call parity asserts that a call option minus a put option (on the same currency pair and with the same strike, expiry time, settlement date and principal amounts) is equal to a forward with the same properties. There sometimes arise situations in which the forward is known exactly, and the call and put need to be calculated using some difficult, slow or inaccurate numerical method. In such a situation, it is advisable to calculate either the call only or the put only using the numerical method, and then use put–call parity to calculate the other.

1.13 Jargon-buster

We have introduced a great deal of terminology in this chapter. This section gives a brief summary of the terms we have introduced.

Accumulator A type of structured product whereby the notional amount used in the calculation of the payoff depends on the spot path. At certain levels, the spot path accrues notional, but if spot goes beyond the barrier level, no more notional is accrued. The payoff may be a payment, forward or option.

Barrier-contingent payment A derivative which makes a future payment in an agreed currency contingent on whether the FX spot price of that currency against some other currency breaches a specified barrier level during the option's lifetime.

Barrier-contingent vanilla option A derivative under which a vanilla option is settled contingent on whether the FX spot price of the two principal currencies breaches a specified barrier level during the option's lifetime.

Big figure A more significant digit of an exchange rate, the exact definition depending on the currency pair. Compare: small figure.

Call spread A vanilla option structure comprising two call options: a long call position at strike K_1 and a short call position at strike K_2, with $K_1 < K_2$.

Discrete barrier A barrier which can only be triggered at certain discrete time points. Also called discretely monitored barrier.

Domestic/Foreign An exchange rate between two currencies is expressed as the number of units of the Domestic currency per unit of the Foreign currency.

European derivative A derivative whose payoff depends on the spot rate at maturity only, and not on the spot path leading up to maturity.

European digital A derivative which makes a payment in an agreed currency at maturity, contingent on whether the FX spot price of that currency against some other currency is higher or lower than a specified strike level at maturity.

Exotic derivative A derivative which is either path-dependent or a non-vanilla European.

Expiry date/time For an option, the time at which the optionality ceases. For a barrier contract without optionality, it is the last time at which the barrier is monitored. Some derivatives, such as forwards, do not have an expiry date/time.

Fair forward rate The strike of a forward contract which results in it having zero value.

Forward contract An agreement under which two counterparties agree to exchange fixed-size cash flows at a pre-agreed time in the future, the two cash flows being in different currencies.

Forward curve The function describing the variation of fair forward rates with maturity.

Forward points/Swap points The fair forward rate minus the spot rate.

Forward replication The strategy which allows the payoff of a forward contract to be reproduced using the FX spot and interest rate markets.

Inversion The procedure of transposing the quote order of a currency pair and correspondingly changing the representation of an FX option.

Maturity The end of a derivative's lifetime. Sometimes we need to be more specific, and distinguish between expiry time and settlement date.

Mio Abbreviation for million, for example "EUR 1.5 mio" means "1.5 million euros".

Normal knock-out A knock-out barrier-contingent vanilla option in which the barrier is at a spot level where the vanilla payoff would anyway be zero. Compare: reverse knock-out.

Option holder The counterparty in an option contract who holds the right but not the obligation to exercise the option.

Option writer The counterparty in an option contract who has no optionality but is obliged to settle the option if the option holder chooses to exercise it.

Outright forward Another term for the fair forward rate, used to explicitly distinguish it from the forward points.

Parisian barrier A barrier which monitors the recent average spot level to determine whether the barrier has been "substantially" triggered. The exact definition varies with contract.

Parisian option An option based on a Parisian barrier.

Payoff profile The function describing the variation of the Domestic value of an option's payoff with the terminal spot rate.

Pip The smaller of the two small figures in a spot rate quotation. If a third small figure is introduced, for higher precision, the pip remains as the second small figure.

Principal amount The size of a cash flow exchanged in an FX spot, forward or option transaction.

Put–call parity A key relationship between call options, put options and forward contracts. For a given strike, maturity and principal amounts, the value of a call option minus the value of the put option equals the value of the forward contract.

Put spread A vanilla option structure comprising two put options: a long put position at strike K_1 and a short put position at strike K_2, with $K_1 > K_2$.

Quote order convention The convention which determines which way around an exchange rate between two currencies is quoted: the number of units of currency1 per unit of currency2, or vice versa.

Range Another name for a double no-touch, a kind of barrier-contingent payment.

Rebate A fixed payment that may be made in the event that a knock-out option knocks out.

Resetting barrier A barrier which resets according to where spot lies in the future.

Reverse knock-out A knock-out barrier-contingent vanilla option in which the barrier is at a spot level where the vanilla payoff would otherwise be non-zero. Compare: normal knock-out.

Settlement date The date on which the exchange of cash flows takes place for an FX spot, forward or option transaction.

Settlement rules Rules describing how a spot date should be calculated from a trade date.

Small figure A less significant digit of an exchange rate, the exact definition depending on the currency pair. Compare: big figure.

Spot date For a given trade date, the spot date is the standardized settlement date for spot trades.

Spot lag The interval between the trade date and the corresponding spot date.

Spot rate The market exchange rate for a standard spot trade.

Spot trade The standardized Foreign Exchange trade in which cash flows in two currencies are exchanged on the spot date.

Strike The exchange rate between two cash flows that will be exchanged under a derivative contract.

Terminal spot rate The spot rate at the expiry time of an option.

Time-dependent barrier A barrier whose level changes in a pre-set manner during the life of an option.

Trade date/time The date/time at which a trade is agreed.

Vanilla option The option to exchange cash flows with a counterparty in pre-specified currencies and amounts on a pre-specified settlement date.

2 Living in a Black–Scholes World

Necessity is the mother of invention.

How many people in the world have heard of "the Black–Scholes model"? And how many people in the world *really understand* how it works? Whilst these questions are not well defined, they nonetheless illustrate a point: there is enormous variation in the depth of familiarity people have with this model. The aim of this chapter is to explore the model in sufficient depth to understand its mathematical and behavioural subtleties. Such an understanding is not only very valuable in its own right, but it also paves the way for a clearer understanding of the more advanced models which we will be covering later in the book.

2.1 The Black–Scholes model equation for spot price

If we ask ourselves what constitutes "large" or "small" moves in an FX spot price over a given time interval, we may think about moves either in terms of outright changes in spot price ("EURUSD is up a big figure") or in terms of relative changes in spot ("EURUSD is up 1 per cent"). Which of these is more useful depends partly on the context. When focusing on a single currency pair in a single market paradigm, it is common to consider certain spot levels as special, in which case outright changes are of greater significance. However, when we wish to compare moves in the spot rates of two currency pairs, for example EURUSD and AUDJPY, it is usually more helpful to consider relative changes in spot, especially when the two spot prices have very different magnitudes.

So, should our model be based on outright or relative moves? Well, when it comes to modelling FX spot prices, we are almost always attempting to come up with a single model that describes numerous currency pairs in a given market paradigm, such as free-floating spot rates between G10 currencies. In this situation, we are not modelling anything that depends on the importance of specific spot levels and it makes most sense to develop our model in terms of relative moves.

I wrote "almost always" in the previous paragraph, because sometimes we wish to model the idiosyncrasies of a specific currency pair, often one involving a currency which is in some way "managed," for example using a peg. Pegged currencies, and other forms of managed currency, are discussed in Section 7.1.

The relative change in spot price is also known as the **return**, and that is the term that we shall use going forward.

At the heart of the Black–Scholes model for FX spot prices lies the assumption that *the return follows a Brownian Motion*. Named after Robert Brown [7], a botanist who in 1827 observed the random motion of pollen-produced particles when suspended in water, the term Brownian Motion is used to describe both the physical phenomenon and the mathematical equation which models it. We can describe the physical phenomenon in words by saying that the quantity in question (the position of a pollen-produced particle, or the return) wiggles about randomly, by varying amounts, and that this wiggling is possibly accompanied by an overall non-random drift at a particular speed.

Formally, we consider a time interval $(t, t + \delta t)$ and define the return as equal to the change in spot price δS over this time interval, divided by the initial spot price S:

$$\text{return} \doteq \frac{\delta S}{S} \qquad (2.1)$$

Note that the return is a dimensionless quantity, since δS and S necessarily have the same dimensions (namely $\frac{\text{Domestic}}{\text{Foreign}}$).

The assumption that the FX spot price return follows a Brownian Motion can be written as follows:

$$\frac{\delta S}{S} = \mu \, \delta t + \sigma \, \delta W_t. \qquad (2.2)$$

We can alternatively say that the FX spot price S follows a **geometric Brownian Motion**. Let us now describe Equation 2.2.

The first term on the right-hand side is deterministic, with μ a constant number, and the term represents the non-random drift part of the Brownian Motion. It is the expectation of the return over the time interval $(t, t + \delta t)$. The quantity μ is correspondingly called either the **drift rate** or the **expected rate of return**. The term $\mu \, \delta t$ needs to be dimensionless (to ensure dimensional homogeneity of Equation 2.2), and so the drift rate has the dimension of one over time, and it is measured in units of years^{-1}.

In the second term on the right-hand side, the quantity W_t is called the **Wiener process**, and it is the standard mathematical representation of a (driftless) Brownian Motion. In words, we can say that the Wiener process represents the 'wiggly' part of the Brownian Motion, without any drift, and that it has its own standardized amount of wiggliness. Mathematically, the Wiener process has the dimensions of the square root of time, and possesses the property that its change δW over any time interval $[t, t+\delta t]$ is a Gaussian random variable with zero mean and variance equal to δt. Changes at different time points are independent, with the result that the variances over successive time steps simply add, and the value $W(t)$ of the Wiener process at time t is a random variable with zero mean and variance equal to t. (We define $W(0) = 0$.)

The quantity σ (Greek letter sigma) is called the **volatility**, and it scales the variance of the Wiener process up or down. The term $\sigma \delta W_t$ needs to be dimensionless (again to ensure dimensional homogeneity of Equation 2.2), and so volatility has the dimension of one over the *square root* of time, and it is measured in units of year$^{-\frac{1}{2}}$. In the context of the Black–Scholes model, the volatility takes a constant value.

So we now have an expression consisting of two parts, one that is purely non-random and one that is random with no drift:

$$\frac{\delta S}{S} = \underbrace{\mu \, \delta t}_{\text{non-random drift}} + \underbrace{\sigma \, \delta W_t}_{\text{random with no drift}} \qquad (2.3)$$

Taking the limit of infinitesimally small time steps and multiplying through by S, we get the following equation:

$$dS = \mu \, S \, dt + \sigma \, S \, dW_t \qquad (2.4)$$

This is the **Black–Scholes model equation for FX spot price.** It is named after Fischer Black and Myron Scholes, who in 1974 published a landmark paper [8] for option pricing which uses this model equation as its starting point for the dynamics of spot. The original paper examines the case of options on equity stocks, but the same approach can be applied to Foreign Exchange, and we will describe exactly that approach in Section 2.3.

Equation 2.4 is an example of a **stochastic process** – a stochastic differential equation which describes how a random quantity changes through time. Later in the book we shall encounter other stochastic processes, for example in Section 4.11 when we look at stochastic volatility models.

2.2 The process for ln S

The process for the natural logarithm of spot (or "log-spot") has a particularly interesting and significant form, and we discuss that now. Starting with the

Black–Scholes process of Equation 2.4, it can be shown that the process for the natural logarithm of spot is given by the following equation:

$$d(\ln S) = \left(\mu - \frac{1}{2}\sigma^2\right)dt + \sigma\, dW_t \qquad (2.5)$$

The derivation of this equation depends on a central and celebrated result in stochastic calculus developed by Kiyosi Itô[1] [9] and called **Itô's lemma**, or the Itô formula. A summary of the result is that if a stochastic variable X follows the process

$$dX = a(X, t)\, dt + b(X, t)\, dW \qquad (2.6)$$

then a function Y of X and t follows the process

$$dY = \left(\frac{\partial Y}{\partial t} + a\frac{\partial Y}{\partial X} + \frac{1}{2}b^2\frac{\partial^2 Y}{\partial X^2}\right)dt + b\frac{\partial Y}{\partial X}\, dW \qquad (2.7)$$

To say that Equation 2.7 is a remarkable result is something of an understatement, as there are several remarkable aspects to it. One remarkable aspect is that the process for Y takes the *same form* as that for X: a dt term whose coefficient is a function of X and t, and a dW term whose coefficient is also a function of X and t. Any stochastic process that takes this form is called an **Itô process**.

Another remarkable aspect of the Itô result is that the Wiener process in the Itô process for Y is the *same Wiener process* as in the Itô process for X. As we shall see, this allows us to build models in which the risk from one financial instrument is offset by that from another. A great deal of modern financial engineering in derivatives is built upon this single crucial fact, hyperbolic as that may sound.

Equation 2.7 can alternatively be written as follows:

$$dY = \frac{\partial Y}{\partial t}dt + \frac{\partial Y}{\partial X}dX + \frac{1}{2}b^2\frac{\partial^2 Y}{\partial X^2}dt \qquad (2.8)$$

which highlights the difference between stochastic and non-stochastic calculus in differentiation: the first two terms of Equation 2.8 are exactly as for non-stochastic calculus. The third term is the one to remember. For our Black–Scholes log-spot example, b equals σS and $\frac{\partial^2 \ln S}{\partial S^2}$ equals $-S^{-2}$, giving the result in Equation 2.5.

Itô's lemma is very widely described and discussed in financial engineering literature. Shreve [10] presents the result very nicely, referring to it as the Itô–Doeblin

---

[1] Alternatively written as Itō or Ito.

formula in recognition of the relatively recent discovery that Wolfgang Döblin [11] had constructed a similar result some years earlier. Hull [2], Wilmott [3] and Austing [12] each also give the result a very clear treatment.

So, what is so interesting and significant about Equation 2.5? The answer is that it has no mention of S on the right-hand side, and we can trivially integrate the process over large time steps, something that is not generally the case for stochastic processes. We perform the integral as follows:

$$\int_{t_1}^{t_2} d(\ln S(t)) = \left(\mu - \frac{1}{2}\sigma^2\right)\int_{t_1}^{t_2} dt + \sigma\int_{t_1}^{t_2} dW(t)$$

$$\Rightarrow \ln S(t_2) - \ln S(t_1) = \left(\mu - \frac{1}{2}\sigma^2\right)(t_2 - t_1) + \sigma(W(t_2) - W(t_1)) \quad (2.9)$$

The time points t_1 and t_2 may take any (non-historic) values. Setting t_1 to t, representing the current time, and t_2 to be some future time T yields the following:

$$\ln S(T) = \ln S(t) + \left(\mu - \frac{1}{2}\sigma^2\right)(T - t) + \sigma(W(T) - W(t)) \quad (2.10)$$

This is a particularly useful result – knowing the properties of W, we can deduce that *the logarithm of spot at some future time T is distributed normally*, with mean and variance given by:

$$\text{mean} = \ln S(t) + \left(\mu - \frac{1}{2}\sigma^2\right)(T - t)$$

$$\text{variance} = \sigma^2(T - t)$$

The mean equals the logarithm of current spot plus a drift correction at an **adjusted drift rate** $(\mu - \frac{1}{2}\sigma^2)$.

So why is the adjusted drift rate *less* than the drift rate? We can get an intuitive understanding for this by remembering that geometric Brownian Motion effectively means that equal *proportional* moves are equally likely. If a spot rate starts at 100, moves 1% up, and then 1% down, it ends up at ...99.99.

Using the help of Appendix B, we can write down an explicit expression for the probability density function $f_{S(T)}$ of future spot price $S(T)$:

$$f_{S(T)}(s) = \frac{1}{\sqrt{2\pi\sigma^2(T-t)}} \frac{1}{s} \exp\left(-\frac{(\ln S(t) + \mu(T-t) - \ln s)^2}{2\sigma^2(T-t)}\right) \quad (2.11)$$

2.3 The Black–Scholes equation for option pricing

Conceptually, it is constructive to think about the Black–Scholes option pricing model as a theory with three fundamental ideas as inputs, and one equation as output. This is illustrated in Figure 2.1. The three inputs are as follows:

1. An assumed process model for spot. (This is the one given by Equation 2.4.)
2. A strategy for hedging the risk of any derivative by spot trading. (We will expound this strategy in Section 2.3.2).
3. A set of assumptions about how we can hedge. (We will examine these assumptions more closely in Section 2.3.3.)

The output of the model is the Black–Scholes partial differential equation (PDE) for option pricing. This equation is written out at the end of Section 2.3.2 in Equation 2.21.

2.3.1 The lagless approach

Before we embark on the derivation of the Black–Scholes PDE, we will describe an approach that simplifies the treatment of spot lags. Recall from Section 1.1.3 that the spot rate at time t, $S(t)$, tells us the Domestic value of a unit of Foreign currency not at time t, but at t', the spot date of t. We therefore need to distinguish these time dependencies in our option value function V:

$$\text{option value} = V(S(t), t') \tag{2.12}$$

Maintaining the distinction between t and t' throughout all of our forthcoming mathematical derivations would not only be tedious and distracting, but also unnecessary: with a little bit of thought, we can see where each of the time points is applicable. For example, given that the spot rate is quoted at time t, we know

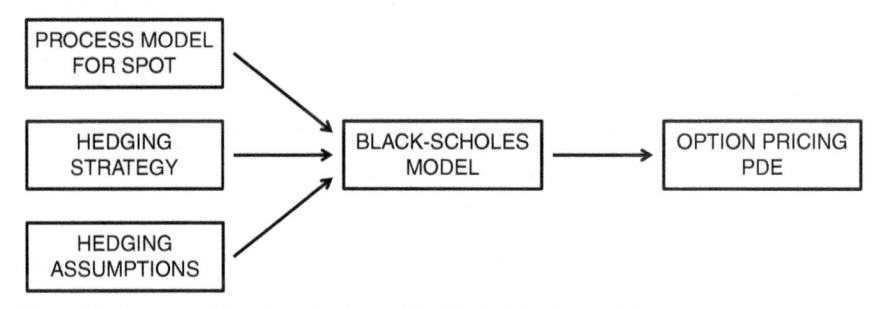

Figure 2.1 Conceptual inputs and output of the Black–Scholes model

that its changes must be affected by the volatility at time t, not t'. Similarly, the discounting and accrual of values must be based on the time t' because that is when the cash flows occur (and in models other than Black–Scholes, where interest rates are not constant, we must accordingly use the interest rates at that time). In addition to these observations, we know that the settlement time T_s of a vanilla option is the spot date of the expiry time T_e, as explained in Section 1.3. Putting this all together, we can happily ignore the spot lag for the purposes of mathematical derivation, and then add its effects back in at the end.

In detail, this approach requires the following procedure:

- Set the spot date t' equal to the trading time t.
- Set the expiry time T_e and settlement time T_s both equal to a time T, which we will call the **maturity**.
- Work through the mathematics and derive valuation formulae in terms of t, T and $S(t)$.
- For volatilities, dependencies on t remain unchanged, and dependencies on T must be switched to T_e.
- For interest rates, dependencies on t must be switched to t', and dependencies on T switched to T_s.
- The time dependency of spot remains $S(t)$.
- The valuation formulae give the value at t'.

I will call this approach the **lagless approach**.

2.3.2 Derivation of the Black–Scholes PDE

We will now go through the derivation of the partial differential equation step by step. We consider any option on a single currency pair FORDOM, and denote the Domestic value of the option by a function V that depends on both of the two independent variables in our problem, spot and time. Under the lagless approach described in Section 2.3.1, the option value is denoted by $V(S, t)$, where the stochastic differential equation (SDE) for spot S is given by the Black–Scholes model equation (Equation 2.4):

$$dS = \mu S\,dt + \sigma S\,dW_t$$

When spot moves, so will the Domestic value of our option (in general). The same is true of a Foreign cash position: the Domestic value of an amount A_f of Foreign cash is SA_f. The Black–Scholes hedging strategy is to *cancel out spot-related moves in the option value by holding a position in Foreign cash*. The Foreign cash position is adjusted continuously to ensure that it balances out the option value move at all times. This is known as **dynamic hedging**.

We now introduce the concept of **delta**, and define the **Spot-Delta-in-Foreign** as the rate of change of Domestic value V with respect to spot:

$$\text{Spot-Delta-in-Foreign} = \frac{\partial V}{\partial S} \quad (2.13)$$

Delta is an example of an **option Greek** and is denoted by the corresponding Greek upper-case letter: Δ. In general, an option Greek is a risk measure that is equal to or proportional to a partial derivative of option value with respect to some risk factor. We will revisit the subject of Greeks, and examine them much more closely, in Chapter 3, when we discuss Black–Scholes Risk Management. As we will see then, there are several other flavours of delta, but for now this particular flavour of delta, Spot-Delta-in-Foreign, will suffice.

The Spot-Delta-in-Foreign of a Foreign cash position is simply A_f. We don't (yet) know what the Spot-Delta-in-Foreign of our option is, but we know how to denote it mathematically:

$$\Delta_{\text{option}} = \frac{\partial V(S,t)}{\partial S} \quad (2.14)$$

Hence we deduce that the number of units x of Foreign cash that will exactly cancel out the delta risk of the option is given by:

$$x = -\frac{\partial V(S,t)}{\partial S} \quad (2.15)$$

Note that this quantity may be positive or negative.

This position in Foreign cash is our **delta hedge**. We can now construct a portfolio consisting of our option plus the delta hedge. We denote the Domestic value of the portfolio by function Π and we can write it down as follows:

$$\text{portfolio value} \quad \Pi(S,t) = V(S,t) + xS \quad (2.16)$$

This portfolio is hedged at the current time, t. After an infinitesimal time step dt, the Domestic portfolio value will (in general) have changed, through four dependencies:

1. The option value depends explicitly on time.
2. The option value depends on spot, which changes stochastically with time.
3. The Domestic value of the delta hedge depends on spot.
4. The Foreign cash position earns interest, at rate r_f.

The change in option value, arising from the first and second dependencies, is computed using Itô's Lemma (dropping the (S, t) arguments of V for brevity):

$$dV = \frac{\partial V}{\partial t}dt + \frac{\partial V}{\partial S}dS + \frac{1}{2}\frac{\partial^2 V}{\partial S^2}(\sigma^2 S^2 dt) \qquad (2.17)$$

The change in value of the delta hedge xS due to the third dependency is given by xdS, since the hedge is fixed during the infinitesimal time step.

The interest earned on the Foreign cash position (the fourth dependency) is given by $xr_f dt$, and its Domestic value is $Sxr_f dt$.

Collecting together the various component changes, the total change in the Domestic value of the portfolio, $d\Pi$, is given by:

$$d\Pi = \left\{\frac{\partial V}{\partial t} + \frac{1}{2}\sigma^2 S^2 \frac{\partial^2 V}{\partial S^2} + Sxr_f\right\}dt$$
$$+ \left\{\frac{\partial V}{\partial S} + x\right\}dS \qquad (2.18)$$

Our choice of x, given by Equation 2.15, means that the whole of the dS term cancels out, leaving:

$$d\Pi = \left\{\frac{\partial V}{\partial t} + \frac{1}{2}\sigma^2 S^2 \frac{\partial^2 V}{\partial S^2} - S\frac{\partial V}{\partial S}r_f\right\}dt \qquad (2.19)$$

All terms in dW_t have vanished. What does that mean? It means that – in the context of our model – the portfolio we have constructed is *free of risk*.

This is of course a mathematical modelling mirage – in the real world, there are no portfolios or financial instruments which are truly free of risk. However, within the context of our mathematical modelling world, we can easily conceive of instruments which have no risk (in terms of their Domestic value). We can then assert that all these instruments must have the same rate of return r_d, because if they didn't, an unrealistic opportunity would arise: we could sell one risk-free instrument with a low rate of return, and invest the proceeds in a risk-free instrument with a higher rate of return, and thereby make a guaranteed risk-free profit with zero net capital outlay. The principle that such a too-good-to-be-true opportunity should never arise is known as the **principle of no-arbitrage**. And by the same no-arbitrage argument, our portfolio too must yield the same rate of return r_d, which gives us another expression for dΠ:

$$\begin{aligned}d\Pi &= \Pi r_d \, dt \\ &= \left\{ V - S\frac{\partial V}{\partial S} \right\} r_d \, dt \end{aligned} \qquad (2.20)$$

We now combine the two expressions for dΠ given by Equations 2.19 and 2.20, and deduce the following relationship:

$$\frac{\partial V}{\partial t} + (r_d - r_f) S \frac{\partial V}{\partial S} + \frac{1}{2}\sigma^2 S^2 \frac{\partial^2 V}{\partial S^2} = r_d V \qquad (2.21)$$

This equation is the **Black–Scholes Partial Differential Equation (PDE) for FX Option Pricing.**

The Black–Scholes PDE is an example of a **risk-neutral valuation method**. Its derivation proceeded via a portfolio which was free of risk, and as a result we are able to describe the behaviour of an option's value without any knowledge or assumptions regarding future market moves. This is the essence of risk-neutrality.

When the value of a financial instrument is derived via a risk-neutral approach (such as by deriving and solving a **risk-neutral PDE**), it is known as the **risk-neutral value** or the **fair value** of the instrument.

2.3.3 Black–Scholes model: hedging assumptions

It is in the nature of assumptions that, even without examining them, you can get quite far. Sometimes further than if you do examine them. It is now time to discuss the third conceptual input to the Black–Scholes model: the hedging assumptions. Scanning through our derivation in Section 2.3.2 and analysing the statements we made there reveals a number of assumptions. Each model assumption has a practical implication, and in the following list of assumptions, each item states first the model assumption and then, in square brackets [], the practical implication:

1. There is no distinction between the price at which we buy and the price at which we sell. [The bid–offer spread in the spot market is zero.]
2. There are no transaction costs of any kind. [We can access the FX spot market for free.]
3. We can perform spot trades at any time. [The FX spot market is fully active throughout the day, every day, including at weekends and on public holidays.]
4. We are able to perform spot trades continuously throughout the life of the option. [There is no limit to the frequency with which we can order (and settle) FX spot trades.]
5. We can perform spot trades in any size. [The FX market is infinitely liquid.]

Living in a Black–Scholes World | 43

6. There is no connection between the size of spot trade and the spot price. [The FX spot market is infinitely deep.]
7. We know exactly what interest rate the Foreign cash position earns at every time point between now and option expiry, and what interest rate the conceptual Domestic-risk-free instrument earns. [Future interest rates are deterministically known to us.]
8. When we lend cash, we are sure to get it back. [Interest-paying counterparties have zero credit risk.]

The assumptions in the above list, whilst significant, are present in many models that are more sophisticated, including those models which on the whole yield prices close to the market. We should in no way lose confidence in the Black–Scholes model due to the assumptions above. However, the most serious assumption of the Black–Scholes model is one that lies not in the list above, but rather in the assumed model process itself: the assumption that spot moves in a geometric Brownian Motion with constant volatility σ. We will discuss the ramifications of this assumption in Chapter 4, just before we embark on the modelling adventure that is Smile Pricing. For the moment, however, we will accept the Black–Scholes model for what it is, and continue to deepen our analysis and understanding of it.

2.3.4 Interpretation of the Black–Scholes PDE

It is instructive to examine each of the terms in the Black–Scholes PDE (Equation 2.21) and interpret it intuitively. We split the equation up as follows:

$$\underbrace{\frac{\partial V}{\partial t}}_{\text{Term 1}} + \underbrace{(r_d - r_f)S\frac{\partial V}{\partial S}}_{\text{Term 2}} + \underbrace{\frac{1}{2}\sigma^2 S^2 \frac{\partial^2 V}{\partial S^2}}_{\text{Term 3}} = \underbrace{r_d V}_{\text{Term 4}} \qquad (2.22)$$

2.3.4.1 Term 1: theta term

Term 1 is relatively straightforward to interpret: the partial derivative $\frac{\partial V}{\partial t}$, being taken at constant spot, measures the rate at which the option value changes due to the passage of time alone. Even if spot does not move, the option changes in value. In general, the rate of change in option value with respect to time is termed **option theta**, and denoted by the Greek upper-case letter Θ, as discussed in Section 3.4. We may therefore call Term 1 the **theta term**.

2.3.4.2 Term 2: carry term

Term 2 readily admits interpretation if we recall that the delta hedge specified by the model consists of a position in Foreign cash of amount $-\frac{\partial V}{\partial S}$. Given a Foreign interest rate of r_f, we expect to earn Foreign interest on this cash position at the rate $-r_f \frac{\partial V}{\partial S}$, which when converted to Domestic gives $-r_f S\frac{\partial V}{\partial S}$. In order to buy a Foreign cash position of $-\frac{\partial V}{\partial S}$, we must have had to borrow an amount of Domestic cash equal to $-S\frac{\partial V}{\partial S}$, which will be costing us interest at the rate $-r_d S\frac{\partial V}{\partial S}$, or equivalently earning us interest at the rate $r_d S\frac{\partial V}{\partial S}$. The difference between the rates at which we earn Domestic interest and pay Foreign interest is what gives us Term 2.

The term **carry trade** is often used to describe a trade whose economics depend to a large extent on the difference between two currencies' interest rates. Hence, we may call Term 2 the **carry term**.

2.3.4.3 Term 3: gamma term

To interpret Term 3, let us ask ourselves: what are the dynamics of an option portfolio which we are keeping continuously delta-hedged? A Taylor expansion of the change δV in portfolio value due to a change δS in spot gives us:

$$\delta V \doteq V(S+\delta S) - V(S)$$
$$= \frac{1}{2}\frac{\partial^2 V}{\partial S^2}(\delta S)^2 + \cdots \qquad (2.23)$$

where we have dropped the delta term to reflect the fact that the option portfolio is delta-hedged.

This is not Term 3, but it is already a very interesting result. The change in spot appears squared, meaning that regardless of whether spot moves up or down, the factor is always positive (or zero in the rare case where spot does not change). The sign of the term then is governed by the sign of the second derivative $\frac{\partial^2 V}{\partial S^2}$. This is clearly an important quantity, and indeed it has its own name: **gamma**. It is another example of an option "Greek", and is denoted by the Greek upper-case letter Γ. We shall discuss gamma, and how it looks for different option types, at greater length in Chapter 3, but we can already make a fundamental observation: a positive (negative) gamma contributes to a *systematically* positive (negative) change in the value of the option over every time step. Owning gamma (that is, having a long gamma position) therefore has value, and it is worth paying to hold an option that has a positive gamma. The Black–Scholes PDE automatically includes this effect via Term 3, which we will call the **gamma term**.

Now let us go back to Equation 2.23 and take a closer look at the effect of δS. It is a random number, but we know its stochastic properties: given that spot in our model follows a geometric Brownian Motion, the standard deviation of $\frac{\delta S}{S}$ is equal to $\sigma\sqrt{\delta t}$, and therefore the standard deviation of δS is $\sigma S\sqrt{\delta t}$. Substituting the δS in Equation 2.23 by its standard deviation, we obtain:

$$\delta V = \frac{1}{2}\frac{\partial^2 V}{\partial S^2}\sigma^2 S^2 \delta t \qquad (2.24)$$

We can easily see that Term 3 is the same expression but without the δt, and hence it is the rate of change in value of the delta-hedged portfolio that arises when the spot change occurs at a rate equal to its standard deviation.

2.3.4.4 Term 4: cash account term

Interpretation of Term 4 is achieved by remembering that we needn't have bought an option at all. Given that V is the fair Domestic value of the option, if we were to invest this amount of Domestic cash in a risk-free cash account, it would earn interest at the Domestic risk-free rate r_d. The portfolio would thus grow at a rate $r_d V$. We call Term 4 the **cash account term**.

The equality sign between the left and right-hand sides of Equation 2.22 is then asserting that there is no arbitrage between option valuation and the cash market. Good thing too.

2.4 Solving the Black–Scholes PDE

The Black–Scholes option pricing PDE holds for options of all types. More than that: it holds for all types of tradable financial instruments based on a single currency pair. For the PDE to be useful, we must solve it, and to solve it we must additionally know the *boundary conditions* of the problem. These boundary conditions come from the payoff description of the specific instrument whose value V we wish to calculate. The various different types of barrier options involve various different boundary conditions, and we will discuss them in detail shortly, in Sections 2.8 and 2.9. But before that, we are going to build up the complexity gradually, by working through the solution of the Black–Scholes PDE for a series of three successively richer instruments: payments, forwards and vanilla options.

2.5 Payments

Let's start with the simplest of the simplest: a payment in Domestic currency (contract type code DNN). Suppose the payment contract has principal A_d and settlement date T_s. Taking the lagless approach described in Section 2.3.1, we replace the settlement date by maturity T, and then, by definition, we can write down the value of the payment at maturity:

$$V_{\text{DNN}}(S, T) = A_d \qquad (2.25)$$

Equation 2.25 is our boundary condition. Since the payment is completely independent of FX spot, we can expect the value to depend only on time, and can therefore set to zero the partial derivatives with respect to S in the Black–Scholes PDE of Equation 2.21. The PDE then becomes:

$$\frac{dV_{\text{DNN}}}{dt} = r_d V_{\text{DNN}}$$

which can be solved straightforwardly to give:

$$V_{\text{DNN}}(t) = A_d e^{-r_d(T-t)} \tag{2.26}$$

The lagless approach then tells us that, to recover the spot lags, we must replace the T by T_s, and the t by t', which yields the – unsurprisingly but somehow satisfyingly – correct result:

$$V_{\text{DNN}}(t') = A_d e^{-r_d(T_s-t')} \tag{2.27}$$

How about a payment in Foreign (contract type code FNN)? This time our (Domestic) payment value V *is* spot-dependent, as is its boundary condition:

$$V_{\text{FNN}}(S, T) = A_f S(T) \tag{2.28}$$

Since the boundary condition is linear in spot, let us try a solution of the same form:

$$V(S, t) = S(t) V_1(t)$$

Just as for the Domestic payment, the PDE simplifies:

$$\frac{dV_1}{dt} = r_f V_1$$

giving the following solution for $V(S, t)$:

$$V_{\text{FNN}}(S, t) = A_f S(t) e^{-r_f(T-t)}$$

Again following the lagless approach, we replace the T by T_s, and the t in the discount factor (but not in the spot rate) by t', to get the Domestic value at time t':

$$V_{\text{FNN}}(S, t') = A_f S(t) e^{-r_f(T_s-t')} \tag{2.29}$$

2.6 Forwards

As described in Section 1.2, settlement of a forward (contract type code WNN) involves the (guaranteed) exchange of Domestic and Foreign cash flows on the forward's settlement date T_s. A long position in a forward corresponds to a long position A_f in the Foreign payment and a short position $A_f K$ in the Domestic payment, where K is the strike of the forward. The Black–Scholes solution for the forward contract can then simply be written down based on the solutions for the two payments:

$$V_{\text{WNN}}(S, t') = A_f S(t) e^{-r_f (T_s - t')} - A_f K e^{-r_d (T_s - t')}$$

If we discount this value from time t' back to time t (by multiplying by the discount factor $e^{-r_d(t'-t)}$) and rearrange, we can obtain either of the forms that we presented in Equations 1.15 and 1.16, before we encountered the Black–Scholes model.

Note that when interest rates are constant, as they are in the Black–Scholes model, the expression for the fair forward rate given by Equation 1.10 simplifies to:

$$F_{\text{FORDOM}}(t, T_s) = S_{\text{FORDOM}}(t) e^{(r_d - r_f)(T_s - t')} \qquad (2.30)$$

2.7 Vanilla options

Our solutions of the Black–Scholes PDE have hitherto been illustrative in nature: we merely showed that we could reproduce expressions that we had already derived. We are now going to start using the Black–Scholes model in anger: to derive formulae that we have not already seen. In this section, we are going to show how to derive formulae for the prices of vanilla options, given as our starting point the Black–Scholes option pricing PDE. This exercise will give us the opportunity to discuss a number of important new ideas that are relevant to barrier options but not specific to them. The benefit of this approach is that when we embark on the barrier problems, we will be better equipped to recognize the ideas that *are* specific to barriers. The non-barrier-specific topics we will cover include:

- transformation of the Black–Scholes PDE to the diffusion equation;
- solution of the diffusion equation;
- recognition of the similarity between vanilla options and all other European options;
- the concept of **risk-neutral expectation**.

If you are familiar with the above topics, you may skip the corresponding sections and go straight to Section 2.8.

2.7.1 Transformation of the Black–Scholes PDE

Our first mission is to transform the Black–Scholes PDE of Equation 2.21 into a simpler form that lends itself more easily to mathematical solution. We will carry out the overall transformation by successively performing a number of transformation steps.

2.7.1.1 Transformation 1: Time direction

Our first transformation is motivated by the recognition that the option's maturity time T is special: it is the point in time at which the option's value is known with certainty, irrespective of the valuation model. As we move back in time from maturity, the uncertainty increases. Furthermore, we have no interest in modelling what happens *after* maturity. Therefore, the natural time-like quantity in our problem is the *time remaining to maturity*, which we denote by τ:

$$\tau \doteq T - t \tag{2.31}$$

We transform function V to function $\tilde{V}$, given by:

$$\tilde{V}(S, \tau) \doteq V(S, t) \tag{2.32}$$

The transformed partial derivatives are very straightforward to compute:

$$\frac{\partial V}{\partial t} = \frac{\partial \tilde{V}}{\partial \tau} \frac{\partial \tau}{\partial t} \tag{2.33}$$

$$= -\frac{\partial \tilde{V}}{\partial \tau} \tag{2.34}$$

$$\frac{\partial V}{\partial S} = \frac{\partial \tilde{V}}{\partial S} \tag{2.35}$$

$$\frac{\partial^2 V}{\partial S^2} = \frac{\partial^2 \tilde{V}}{\partial S^2} \tag{2.36}$$

The transformed PDE is then:

$$-\frac{\partial \tilde{V}}{\partial \tau} + (r_d - r_f) S \frac{\partial \tilde{V}}{\partial S} + \frac{1}{2}\sigma^2 S^2 \frac{\partial^2 \tilde{V}}{\partial S^2} = r_d \tilde{V} \tag{2.37}$$

Since τ runs in the opposite direction to time (it decreases as time goes forward), transformation from t to τ has the sole effect of a change of sign in the time derivative.

2.7.1.2 Transformation 2: Discounting

We may think of the present option value $\tilde{V}$ as a value that has been discounted from option maturity T back to t. We then define the undiscounted value U as follows:

$$U(S,\tau) \doteq \tilde{V}(S,\tau)e^{r_d\tau} \qquad (2.38)$$

and transform the PDE by using U in place of $\tilde{V}$. Transformation of the S-derivatives follows trivially:

$$\frac{\partial \tilde{V}}{\partial S} = \frac{\partial U}{\partial S}e^{-r_d\tau} \qquad (2.39)$$

$$\frac{\partial^2 \tilde{V}}{\partial S^2} = \frac{\partial^2 U}{\partial S^2}e^{-r_d\tau} \qquad (2.40)$$

Transformation of the τ-derivative is slightly more interesting:

$$\frac{\partial \tilde{V}}{\partial \tau} = \frac{\partial U}{\partial \tau}e^{-r_d\tau} - r_d U e^{-r_d\tau} \qquad (2.41)$$

The second term of Equation 2.41 causes cancellation of Term 4 in the PDE, which then becomes:

$$-\frac{\partial U}{\partial \tau} + (r_d - r_f)S\frac{\partial U}{\partial S} + \frac{1}{2}\sigma^2 S^2 \frac{\partial^2 U}{\partial S^2} = 0 \qquad (2.42)$$

Recall that in Section 2.3.4 we interpreted the $r_d V$ term as the growth rate of a deposit of Domestic cash in an amount equal to the present value of the option. The effect of this growth rate is to discount the present value V relative to the value at expiry time, so it makes sense that when we switch to the undiscounted value U, the term disappears.

2.7.1.3 Transformation 3: From spot to forward

The third transformation step also involves the option maturity: we transform from spot to the forward. Specifically, we transform from current spot, $S(t)$, to the current forward rate to maturity, $F(t, t+\tau)$. The expression for the forward in terms of spot is:

$$F(t, t+\tau) = S(t)e^{(r_d - r_f)\tau} \qquad (2.43)$$

We transform the value variable from U to $\tilde{U}$:

$$\tilde{U}(F,\tau) \doteq U(S,\tau) \qquad (2.44)$$

Since the forward itself depends on τ, we need to take care when transforming the partial derivatives, and be clear about what is being held constant. In particular, the partial derivative $\frac{\partial U}{\partial \tau}$ in Equation 2.42 is at constant S, which we can emphasize by writing $\frac{\partial U}{\partial \tau}\big|_S$. We cannot simply equate this to $\frac{\partial \tilde{U}}{\partial \tau}\big|_F$, the partial derivative of $\tilde{U}$ at constant F, because when τ changes at constant S, F will clearly change too. A nice way of avoiding confusion in this situation is to equate the "total" derivatives with respect to τ of U and $\tilde{U}$:

$$\frac{dU}{d\tau} = \frac{d\tilde{U}}{d\tau}$$

$$\Rightarrow \frac{\partial U}{\partial \tau}\bigg|_S + \frac{\partial U}{\partial S}\bigg|_\tau \frac{dS}{d\tau} = \frac{\partial \tilde{U}}{\partial \tau}\bigg|_F + \frac{\partial \tilde{U}}{\partial F}\bigg|_\tau \frac{dF}{d\tau}$$

$$\Rightarrow \frac{\partial U}{\partial \tau}\bigg|_S = \frac{\partial \tilde{U}}{\partial \tau}\bigg|_F + \frac{\partial \tilde{U}}{\partial F}\bigg|_\tau \frac{dF}{d\tau}$$

$$= \frac{\partial \tilde{U}}{\partial \tau}\bigg|_F + (r_d - r_f)F \frac{\partial \tilde{U}}{\partial F}\bigg|_\tau \quad (2.45)$$

where we have used the fact that S does not depend on τ.

The S partial derivatives (at constant τ) are transformed as follows:

$$\frac{\partial U}{\partial S} = \frac{\partial \tilde{U}}{\partial F} \frac{dF}{dS}$$

$$= e^{(r_d - r_f)\tau} \frac{\partial \tilde{U}}{\partial F} \quad (2.46)$$

$$\frac{\partial^2 U}{\partial S^2} = \frac{\partial}{\partial F}\left(e^{(r_d - r_f)\tau} \frac{\partial \tilde{U}}{\partial F}\right) \frac{dF}{dS}$$

$$= e^{2(r_d - r_f)\tau} \frac{\partial^2 \tilde{U}}{\partial F^2} \quad (2.47)$$

This transformation results in the following PDE:

$$\frac{\partial \tilde{U}}{\partial \tau}\bigg|_F = \frac{1}{2}\sigma^2 F^2 \frac{\partial^2 \tilde{U}}{\partial F^2} \quad (2.48)$$

Here the F subscript on the τ-derivative serves to emphasize that it is F, not S, that we must hold constant when evaluating the partial derivative.

2.7.1.4 Transformation 4: Log-space

For our final transformation, we recall that the Black–Scholes model equation for spot is a geometric Brownian Motion (GBM), and that the distribution of future spot values is lognormal. More specifically, $\ln S(T)$, the logarithm of spot at some future time T, is distributed normally with the mean equal to $\ln F(T) - \frac{1}{2}\sigma^2 T$. This motivates us to transform to a new variable equal to this expression for the mean. Given the antipathy many physical scientists feel towards taking the logarithm of a dimensioned quantity, such as F, let us introduce an arbitrary fixed constant F_0 of the same dimensionality, and define a new variable X as:

$$X \doteq \ln\left(\frac{F}{F_0}\right) - \frac{1}{2}\sigma^2 \tau \tag{2.49}$$

We denote the corresponding new value variable by v:

$$v(X, \tau) \doteq \tilde{U}(F, \tau) \tag{2.50}$$

Using the "total derivative" approach described for Transformation 3, we transform the τ partial derivative of Equation 2.48 as follows:

$$\begin{aligned}\left.\frac{\partial \tilde{U}}{\partial \tau}\right|_F &= \left.\frac{\partial v}{\partial \tau}\right|_X + \left.\frac{\partial v}{\partial X}\right|_\tau \frac{dX}{d\tau} \\ &= \left.\frac{\partial v}{\partial \tau}\right|_X - \frac{1}{2}\sigma^2 \left.\frac{\partial v}{\partial X}\right|_\tau \end{aligned} \tag{2.51}$$

The F partial derivative in Equation 2.48 is transformed as follows:

$$\begin{aligned}\frac{\partial^2 \tilde{U}}{\partial F^2} &= \frac{\partial}{\partial F}\left(\frac{\partial \tilde{U}}{\partial F}\right) \\ &= \frac{\partial}{\partial X}\left(\frac{\partial v}{\partial X}\frac{dX}{dF}\right)\frac{dX}{dF} \\ &= \frac{\partial}{\partial X}\left(\frac{\partial v}{\partial X}F_0^{-1}e^{-X-\frac{1}{2}\sigma^2\tau}\right)F_0^{-1}e^{-X-\frac{1}{2}\sigma^2\tau} \\ &= \left(\frac{\partial^2 v}{\partial X^2} - \frac{\partial v}{\partial X}\right)F_0^{-2}e^{-2X-\sigma^2\tau} \\ &= \left(\frac{\partial^2 v}{\partial X^2} - \frac{\partial v}{\partial X}\right)F^{-2}\end{aligned} \tag{2.52}$$

The PDE thereupon becomes:

$$\frac{\partial v}{\partial \tau} = \frac{1}{2}\sigma^2 \frac{\partial^2 v}{\partial X^2} \tag{2.53}$$

This completes the transformation of the Black–Scholes PDE.

It is immediately clear that the new form, Equation 2.53, is significantly simpler than the original form, Equation 2.21. Moreover, it takes the form of an equation which has been studied for centuries (literally): the **diffusion equation**.

Have we lost any generality in the course of transforming the equation? No, not at all. The transformed equation is every bit as general as the original equation. Our choice of option maturity T does *not* restrict the equation to options with that maturity. T is simply a quantity that appears in the mathematical transformations. Similarly, the quantity F_0 that we introduced is completely arbitrary. Having said that, it is nevertheless the case that the *simplifications* we achieved are more simplifying for some contract types than for others. In particular, we shall see that the use of the variable F (forward to maturity) is vastly more helpful when dealing with vanilla options (and other European options) than it is when dealing with barrier options.

Our next mission is to solve the diffusion equation in Equation 2.53 for vanilla options.

2.7.2 Solution of the diffusion equation for vanilla options

Our approach here starts with the boundary conditions. First we will determine the boundary conditions for vanilla options in the original financial variables, and then we will transform them to the variables of our diffusion equation.

So, what are the appropriate boundary conditions for a vanilla option? Well, one thing we certainly know about a vanilla option is its payoff profile, through which we in fact introduced vanilla options in Chapter 1. The payoff profiles of call and put options are displayed respectively in Figures 1.3 and 1.4. The mathematical representations of these payoff profiles are given by:

$$P_{\text{call}}(S(T)) = A_{\text{f}} \max(0, S(T) - K) \tag{2.54}$$

$$P_{\text{put}}(S(T)) = A_{\text{f}} \max(0, K - S(T)) \tag{2.55}$$

where A_{f} is the Foreign currency principal, $S(T)$ is the spot rate at maturity (the "terminal spot rate") and K is the strike.

The payoff formulae for the call and put options are very similar to each other, and can be merged into a single expression $P_{\text{vanilla}}(S(T))$:

$$P_{\text{vanilla}}(S(T)) = A_{\text{f}} \max(0, \phi(S(T) - K)) \tag{2.56}$$

where the quantity ϕ distinguishes between call and put:

$$\phi = \begin{cases} +1 & \text{(call)} \\ -1 & \text{(put)} \end{cases} \tag{2.57}$$

I will call this quantity ϕ the **trait** of the vanilla option.

By definition, the value of a European option (such as a vanilla option) at maturity is equal to the option payoff. Writing the option payoff as $P(S(T))$, we can express this as follows:

$$V(S(T), T) = P(S(T)) \tag{2.58}$$

Equation 2.58 gives us the boundary condition under which we must solve the Black–Scholes PDE in order to calculate the price of a vanilla option.

Since we have transformed the Black–Scholes PDE to the diffusion equation, we must apply the same transformations to the boundary conditions. At maturity, we have $t = T$, and the transformations 1, 2 and 4 are straightforward:

$$U(S, 0) = V(S, T) \tag{2.59}$$

$$F(T, T) = S(T) \tag{2.60}$$

$$\tau = 0 \tag{2.61}$$

For the remaining transformation, we define:

$$\bar{P}(X) \doteq P(e^X) \tag{2.62}$$

which gives:

$$v(X, 0) = \bar{P}(X) \tag{2.63}$$

This is the boundary condition for our vanilla option in the transformed coordinates.

Equations 2.53 and 2.63 together define the problem that we need to solve in order to compute vanilla option prices. Mathematically speaking, it is a classic example of an **initial-value problem** of the one-dimensional diffusion equation.

Unlike the 19th-century mathematicians [13] who first examined the diffusion equation, we do not need to start from first principles in order to solve this problem. For the current discussion, I will simply state that the solution can be written in the following form:

$$v(X, \tau) = \int_{-\infty}^{\infty} \frac{1}{\sqrt{2\pi\sigma^2\tau}} e^{-\frac{(X'-X)^2}{2\sigma^2\tau}} \bar{P}(X') \, dX' \tag{2.64}$$

54 | FX Barrier Options

and invite interested readers to perform the exercise in differentiation needed to confirm that it satisfies the PDE and boundary condition.

The form of the solution in Equation 2.64 is strongly suggestive of an *expectation* under a probability distribution. Indeed it is so, and we will very shortly spell out exactly how that is the case, and show that such an interpretation is of fundamental importance. But first – let us transform back to our original financial variables.

Successively undoing each of our transformations, we arrive at the following expression for the present option value V:

$$V(S,t) = e^{-r_d(T-t)} \int_0^\infty \frac{1}{\sqrt{2\pi\sigma^2(T-t)}} \frac{1}{S'} \exp\left(-\frac{(\ln S' - \ln F)^2}{2\sigma^2(T-t)}\right) P(S') \, dS' \tag{2.65}$$

The form of the integral in this expression is also strongly suggestive of an expectation under a probability distribution. This time the expectation is multiplied by the Domestic discount factor between today and option maturity. Let us now spell out the nature of the expectations in Equations 2.64 and 2.65.

First let us recall that if a continuous random variable Z has a probability density function f_Z, then the expectation of $g(Z)$, a general function of Z, is given by:

$$\mathbb{E}[g(Z)] = \int_{-\infty}^{\infty} f_Z(z) g(z) \, dz \tag{2.66}$$

Comparing Equations 2.64 and 2.66, we can interpret $\bar{P}$ (the transformed option payoff function) as the function whose expectation we are taking. The other factor in the integrand is then the probability density function. We can immediately see that this has the form of a *normal distribution*, and we can read off the mean and variance of the distribution as follows:

$$\text{normal mean} = X \tag{2.67}$$

$$\text{normal variance} = \sigma^2 \tau \tag{2.68}$$

Now comparing Equations 2.65 and 2.66, we can interpret P (the option payoff function) as the function whose expectation we are taking. This time the density function has the form of a *lognormal distribution*. There are multiple convenient ways of parameterizing a lognormal distribution, and we follow the notation used in Appendix B, which describes properties of the normal and lognormal distributions. Under that notation, we can read off from Equation 2.65 the parameters of the lognormal distribution as: $\mu_Z = F$ and $\sigma_Z = \sigma\sqrt{\tau}$.

Now, what is the random variable S' underlying this lognormal distribution? Interestingly, we have not actually had to identify it explicitly in order to make our interpretations so far. However, given that function P has a very specific physical meaning – it is the option payoff as a function of spot price at maturity – the only obvious physical interpretation is that the random variable S' is the spot price at maturity, $S(T)$.

We therefore make a crucial conclusion: the fair present value of the option is equal to the discounted expectation of the payoff under a lognormal distribution for the spot price at maturity, with distribution parameters F and $\sigma\sqrt{\tau}$.

Denoting the density function for this distribution by $f_{S(T)}$, we have:

$$f_{S(T)}(s) = \frac{1}{\sqrt{2\pi\sigma^2(T-t)}} \frac{1}{s} \exp\left(-\frac{(\ln F - \ln s)^2}{2\sigma^2(T-t)}\right) \qquad (2.69)$$

With F expanded in terms of spot and interest rates, we obtain:

$$f_{S(T)}(s) = \frac{1}{\sqrt{2\pi\sigma^2(T-t)}} \frac{1}{s} \exp\left(-\frac{(\ln S + (r_d - r_f)(T-t) - \ln s)^2}{2\sigma^2(T-t)}\right) \qquad (2.70)$$

Let us have a think about what we have just concluded. Did we not deduce in Section 2.2 that the logarithm of spot followed a normal distribution? Comparing Equations 2.11 and 2.70, we see that they are the same expression *except* that where we previously had μ, we now have $r_d - r_f$. It is as if we had simply set μ in Equation 2.4 equal to $(r_d - r_f)$, rewritten our stochastic process as follows:

$$dS = (r_d - r_f) S \, dt + \sigma S \, dW \qquad (2.71)$$

and then blithely used the resulting lognormal probability distribution to compute the expectation of the payoff.

Because the distribution specified by Equation 2.69 was derived on the basis of our risk-neutral PDE (the Black–Scholes option pricing PDE), it is known as the **risk-neutral distribution** of future spot. We can then say that **the fair value of an option is equal to the discounted expectation of the payoff under the risk-neutral distribution.**

As noted above, the mean of this distribution is F, which means that **the forward is the risk-neutral expectation of future spot**. Similarly, the SDE given by Equation 2.71 is known as the **risk-neutral process** for spot under the Black–Scholes model, and the drift rate $(r_d - r_f)$ is called the **risk-neutral drift rate**. All in all, we say that we are modelling under the **risk-neutral measure**. Shreve [10] gives a thorough mathematical description of risk-neutral valuation.

The μ-based quantities are often referred to as "real-world" equivalents: Equation 2.4 is a **real-world stochastic process**, Equation 2.11 is a **real-world distribution**, and so on. I prefer to write "a" real-world quantity, rather than "the", because there is no single value of μ that everybody agrees on. (Not in the real world, anyway.) The most important point to appreciate is that the risk-neutral drift rate does not necessarily match what *anyone* might estimate for μ in the real world. It is simply what comes out of the risk-neutral valuation approach.

Let us emphasize at this point that the result we have derived is not specific to vanilla options. We have left the payoff P in its general form, so this result is applicable to all options (and other derivatives) whose payoff can be written in the form of a function of a single spot price. As discussed in Chapter 1, derivatives in this class are known as European derivatives.

A similar result applies to *any* option, including path-dependent exotics. In general, we can write the option value as the risk-neutral expectation of the discounted payoff of the option, noting that the payoff may not be expressed simply as a function of terminal spot. The discount factor goes inside the expectation because it may itself be random, either because the time at which the payoff is made is random (such as for a pay-at-hit one-touch) or (going beyond Black–Scholes) in the context of a model with stochastic interest rates.

To calculate the value for a specific given form of payoff, we simply need to insert the specific payoff function into Equation 2.65 and perform the integral. Alternatively, we can go via the transformed-solution route: we make the minimal transformation $P \to \bar{P}$, perform the integral in Equation 2.64 to get v, and then transform to V. Whether the integrals can be performed analytically depends on the form of P. In the specific case of vanilla options, the integrals *can* be performed analytically. The procedure is described in Appendix A, and the result is:

$$V_{\text{vanilla}}(S,t) = A_f \phi \left[S e^{-r_f(T-t)} N(\phi d_1) - K e^{-r_d(T-t)} N(\phi d_2) \right] \quad (2.72)$$

where:

$$d_1 = \frac{\ln\left(\frac{S}{K}\right) + (r_d - r_f + \frac{1}{2}\sigma^2)(T-t)}{\sigma\sqrt{T-t}} \quad (2.73)$$

$$d_2 = \frac{\ln\left(\frac{S}{K}\right) + (r_d - r_f - \frac{1}{2}\sigma^2)(T-t)}{\sigma\sqrt{T-t}} \quad (2.74)$$

Note that these formulae are still using the lagless approach of Section 2.3.1. To respect the spot lags, we need to apply the guidelines described there, and we will do this explicitly in Section 2.7.3.

Equations 2.72, 2.73 and 2.74 together comprise the **pricing formulae for vanilla options under the Black–Scholes model.**

2.7.3 The vanilla option pricing formulae

A comprehensive discussion of the Black–Scholes vanilla option pricing formulae given by Equations 2.72, 2.73 and 2.74 could fill a book of its own. This book being about barrier options, we will discuss just the most important and relevant aspects of the vanilla formulae.

2.7.3.1 Respecting the spot lags

For the sake of simplicity, we derived, transformed and solved the Black–Scholes equation using the "lagless approach" described in Section 2.3.1. Following the guidelines explained in that section, we can now add the effects of the spot lag back in, to give the following results:

$$V_{\text{vanilla}}(S(t), t') = A_f \phi \left[S(t) e^{-r_f(T_s - t')} N(\phi d_1) - K e^{-r_d(T_s - t')} N(\phi d_2) \right] \quad (2.75)$$

where

$$d_{\genfrac{}{}{0pt}{}{1}{2}} = \frac{\ln\left(\frac{S(t)}{K}\right) + (r_d - r_f)(T_s - t') \pm \frac{1}{2}\sigma^2(T_e - t)}{\sigma\sqrt{T_e - t}} \quad (2.76)$$

Recall that the lagless approach also tells us that the formula in Equation 2.75 gives the value on the *spot date*, not today.

2.7.3.2 *Expression in terms of forward and discount factors*

Using the expression for the forward rate given by Equation 2.30 and the expression for the discount factor given by Equation 1.5, we can rewrite the vanilla pricing formulae in the following, simpler, form:

$$V_{\text{vanilla}} = A_f \phi B_d [FN(\phi d_1) - KN(\phi d_2)] \quad (2.77)$$

where:

$$d_{\genfrac{}{}{0pt}{}{1}{2}} = \frac{\ln\left(\frac{F}{K}\right) \pm \frac{1}{2}\sigma^2(T_e - t)}{\sigma\sqrt{T_e - t}} \quad (2.78)$$

For ease of reading, I have dropped the date dependencies of the forward and discount factor, which are as follows:

$$F = F(t, T_s)$$
$$B_d = B_d(t', T_s)$$

2.7.3.3 Intrinsic value

We define the **intrinsic value** $V_{\text{intrinsic}}$ of an option as the value that the option would have in the absence of volatility:

$$V_{\text{intrinsic}} = \lim_{\sigma \to 0} V(S,t) \qquad (2.79)$$

Taking the limit of the vanilla option formulae as volatility tends to zero, we get the following result:

$$\lim_{\sigma \to 0} V_{\text{vanilla}} = A_f B_d \max[0, \phi(F - K)] \qquad (2.80)$$

This result is easily derived by considering separately the cases of $\phi = +1$ and $\phi = -1$, and within each ϕ case, the sub-cases of $F < K$ and $F > K$.

The vanilla option intrinsic value given by Equation 2.80 is similar to the payoff function, but the two are not the same thing. The intrinsic value is computed at times *before* the expiry time, and it is effectively the *discounted* payoff function computed at the *forward rate*.

2.7.3.4 Moneyness

Inspection of Equation 2.78 shows that the strike only ever appears in its ratio with the forward. A minor rearrangement of Equation 2.77 shows that the same is true of it, and therefore of the whole vanilla option value:

$$V_{\text{vanilla}} = A_f \phi B_d F \left[N(\phi d_1) - \frac{K}{F} N(\phi d_2) \right] \qquad (2.81)$$

This leads us naturally to focus on the ratio $\frac{K}{F}$ as a useful quantity, which we call the **moneyness**. Unlike strike, moneyness is dimensionless and allows easy comparison across maturities and different currency pairs. Moneyness is therefore a more natural coordinate than strike in many situations, and we often work in moneyness space in both mathematical formalism and in numerical analysis.

Formally, for a given strike K and settlement date T_s, we define the moneyness $k(T_s)$ by:

$$\text{moneyness} \quad k(T_s) \doteq \frac{K}{F(t, T_s)} \qquad (2.82)$$

The expression for the intrinsic value given by Equation 2.80 motivates some further terminology relating to moneyness: a strike level is said to be **in the money** if it leads to a non-zero intrinsic value. For a call option ($\phi = +1$), a strike is in the money if it is less than the forward; for a put option ($\phi = -1$), a strike is in the money if it is greater than the forward. Conversely, a strike level is said to be **out of the money** if for a call option it is greater than the forward, or for a put option it is less than the forward. If the strike level is exactly equal to the forward, it is said to be **at the money**. (Alternative definitions of at-the-money will arise when we look at smile pricing, in Chapter 4.)

The vanilla option pricing formulae for at-the-money options have a particularly simple form. Setting $K = F$ in Equation 2.78 gives:

$$d_1 = -d_2 = \frac{1}{2}\sigma\sqrt{T_e - t} \qquad (2.83)$$

whereupon the pricing formula Equation 2.77 becomes:

$$\begin{aligned}V_{\text{vanilla}} &= A_f \phi B_d F \left[N\left(\phi \frac{1}{2}\sigma\sqrt{T_e - t}\right) - N\left(-\phi \frac{1}{2}\sigma\sqrt{T_e - t}\right) \right] \\ &= A_f B_d F \left(2N\left(\frac{1}{2}\sigma\sqrt{T_e - t}\right) - 1 \right) \end{aligned} \qquad (2.84)$$

Not only has the formula simplified, but ϕ has disappeared, showing that *at-the-money call and put options have the same value.*

2.7.4 Price quotation styles

The quantity V_{vanilla} in Equation 2.72 gives us the value of the vanilla option in the Domestic currency. It scales linearly with the Foreign principal A_f of the option. For many purposes, this is exactly the quantity that we are interested in quoting as a price, but sometimes other forms of price quotation are more useful. For a start, we may be more interested in quoting the option price in the Foreign currency. To calculate the Foreign value of the option, we simply divide V by the spot rate.

Alternatively, we may be interested in quoting the Domestic price *per unit Foreign principal*. For example, this might be useful if we are not sure what size of Foreign principal our contract is going to have. This is calculated simply by dividing the Domestic price by the Foreign principal, and is referred to as the "Domestic per Foreign" price. For a specific currency pair, say AUDJPY, we would denote it as the "JPY/AUD" (spoken "yen per Aussie") price.

At other times, we wish to obtain a dimensionless number that can nicely be expressed in percentage form. We can do this in one of two ways: we can convert the Domestic price to a Foreign price (by dividing by the spot rate), and then divide the Foreign price by the Foreign principal to get the "Foreign per Foreign" price, also called the "percent Foreign" price. Or, we can convert the Foreign principal to the Domestic principal (by multiplying by the option's strike rate), and then divide the Domestic price by the Domestic principal to get the "Domestic per Domestic" price, also called the "percent Domestic" price.

Table 2.1 Price quotation methods for vanilla options and barrier-contingent vanilla options

Quotation name for general currency pair	Quotation name for AUDJPY	Formula to calculate quote
Domestic	JPY	V
Foreign	AUD	$\frac{V}{S}$
Domestic per Foreign	JPY per AUD	$\frac{V}{A_f}$
Foreign per Domestic	AUD per JPY	$\frac{V}{A_f KS}$
%Foreign	%AUD	$\frac{V}{A_f S}$
%Domestic	%JPY	$\frac{V}{A_f K}$

All of the above quotation styles are commonly used for vanilla option prices, and indeed exactly the same quotation methods are also used for barrier-contingent vanilla options.

When we are dealing with multiple options, for example if we are making a price for a call spread structure, the options may have different principals (in one or both currencies). In such cases, we must take care to limit the use of the "per-unit-principal" quotation styles to cases where the principals are equal.

Note that we are describing quotation styles for *price-making* purposes here. For *valuation* purposes (for example when we are aggregating the values of options in a portfolio), we would simply express our values in either Domestic or Foreign.

Table 2.1 gives a summary of the different methods of price quotation.

2.7.5 Valuation behaviour of vanilla options

Mathematical analysis gives us one perspective on a model, but to really understand any model, we must become familiar with its *behaviour*. We will now examine the behaviour of values calculated using the Black–Scholes vanilla option pricing formulae.

Before we can evaluate the pricing formulae for a given option contract, we must choose the values of the market data parameters. Table 2.2 lists three sets of Black–Scholes market data parameters, which represent respectively the EURUSD, USDTRY and AUDJPY markets.

Figure 2.2 shows the variation with current spot rate of the values of three EURUSD 1.28-strike vanilla call options at three different maturities: one month, six months and one year. The strike is marked with a triangle, and the payoff is plotted with a dotted line.

There are a number of important observations we can make:

1. The curves all look like smoothed out versions of the call option payoff (see Figure 1.3, but note the strike is different). This is a classic sign of diffusion, linked to the fact that the dynamics of option valuation are closely related to the

Table 2.2 Market data values used for demonstration of Black–Scholes model results

	EURUSD	USDTRY	AUDJPY
Spot	1.26	2.28	96
Volatility	7%	11%	9%
Foreign Interest Rate	−0.02%	0.2%	3%
Domestic Interest Rate	0.2%	9%	−0.2%

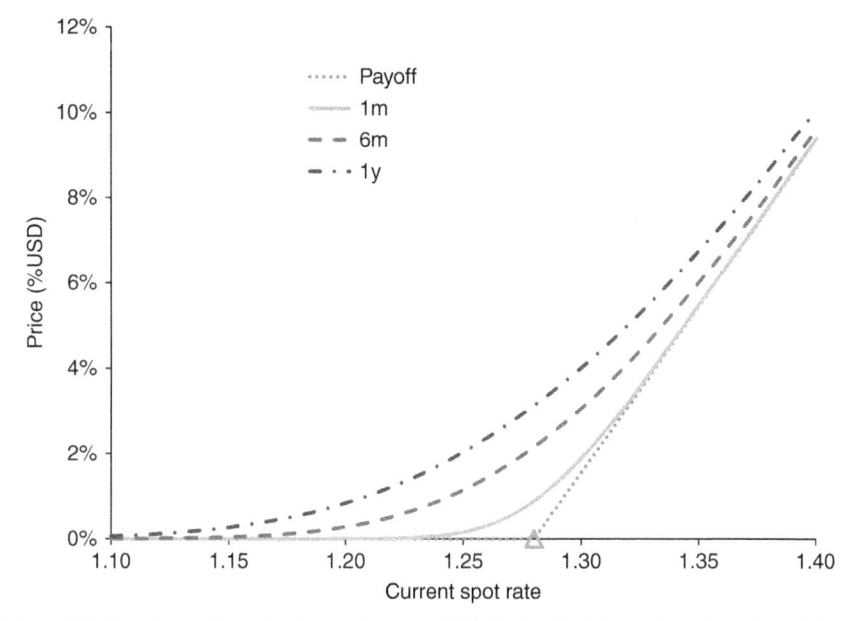

Figure 2.2 Variation with spot of the value of a EURUSD 1.28-strike vanilla call option at three maturities. The strike is marked with a triangle

diffusion equation: the option value at times before expiry is a diffused version of the final payoff.
2. The option value increases significantly with maturity at all spot levels.
3. At low spot levels, the value tends to zero for all maturities, with the shorter maturities approaching the limit faster than the longer maturities.
4. At high spot level, the value tends to the payoff, again with the shorter maturities approaching the limit faster.
5. At all spot levels, and for all maturities, the option value is greater than the payoff profile.
6. The greatest difference between option value and payoff level occurs in the region of the strike.

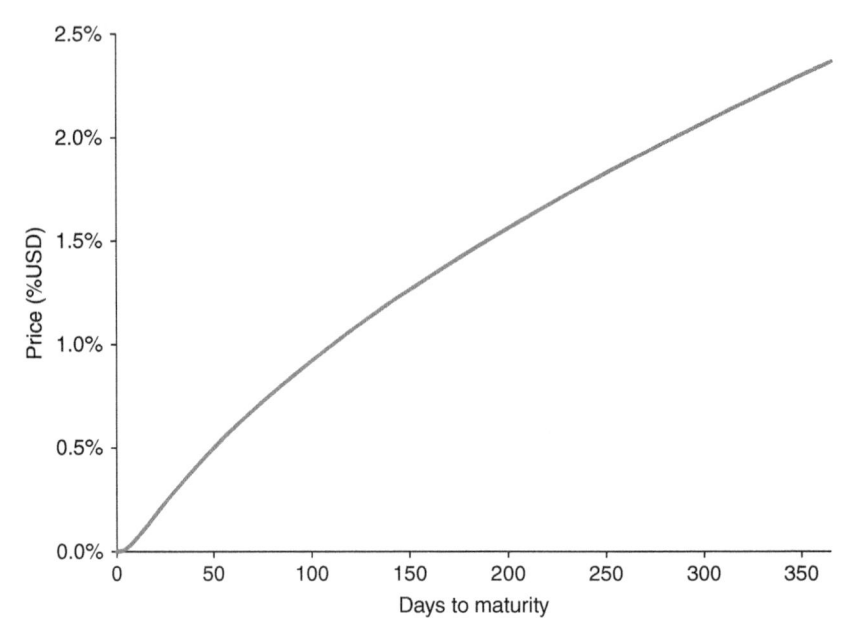

Figure 2.3 Variation with maturity of the value of a 1.28-strike EUR call/USD put vanilla option

We can formalize some of these observations using the concept of **time value**. We define the time value V_{time} of an option as the part of the option value that does not come from the intrinsic value:

$$V_{\text{time}} = V(S,t) - V_{\text{intrinsic}} \qquad (2.85)$$

(The concept of intrinsic value was introduced in Section 2.7.3.)

Figure 2.3 examines the behaviour of time value more closely, by showing how an option value changes with maturity. As expected, the value is monotonically increasing with maturity. At short maturities, of a few days, the value is very small but increases very steeply. At longer maturities, of around a year, the value is much greater, but increases less steeply.

Vanilla put options show similar behaviour in many ways. Figures 2.4 and 2.5 show the values against spot and maturity for a put option. Note that at very short maturities, the value of the call option is nearly zero whereas the value of the put option is non-zero. This is to do with intrinsic value: the same strike of 1.28 is out of the money for a call but in the money for a put. An in-the-money option has non-zero intrinsic value, whereas an out-of-the-money option has zero intrinsic value.

Why are option values so sensitive to the time to maturity? We can understand this intuitively, in the following way: the more time there is to maturity, the wider

Living in a Black–Scholes World | 63

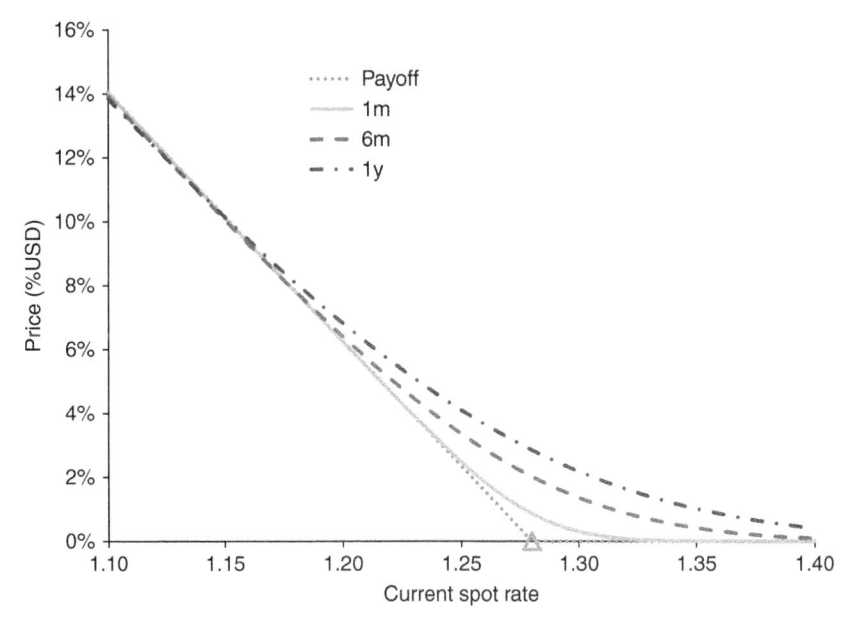

Figure 2.4 Variation with spot of a EURUSD 1.28-strike vanilla put option at three maturities. The strike is marked with a triangle

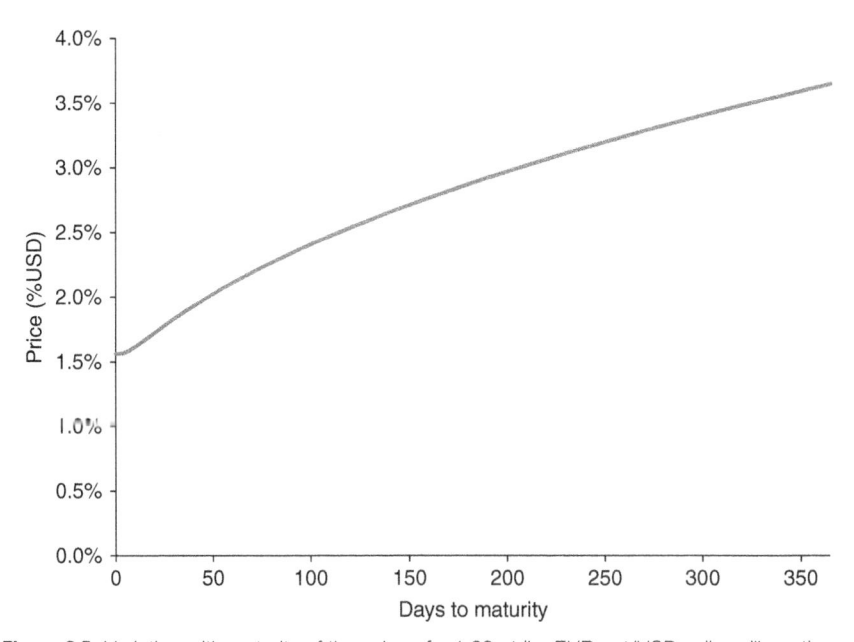

Figure 2.5 Variation with maturity of the value of a 1.28-strike EUR put/USD call vanilla option

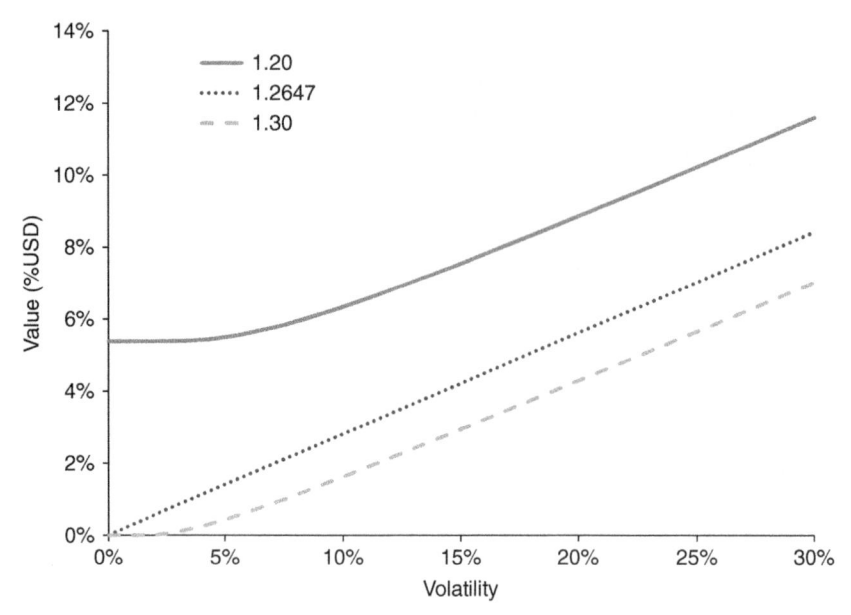

Figure 2.6 Variation with volatility of the value of a 6-month EUR call/USD put vanilla option at three different strikes

is the probability distribution of the terminal spot rate. Now, a wider distribution means more likelihood of both large moves up and large moves down. But, the vanilla payoff is *asymmetric*: for a call option, large upward moves always increase the payoff, whilst large downward moves below the strike make no difference because of the zero floor. Conversely, for a put option, large downward moves always increase the payoff, whilst large upward moves above the strike make no difference. This asymmetry results in a net *increase* in value with greater maturity.

There is another way that the probability distribution can become wider: an increase in *volatility*. We should therefore expect that the value of a vanilla option increases with volatility. Figure 2.6 demonstrates just that.

Vanillas are arguably the simplest product which have a monotonic and highly sensitive dependence on volatility, albeit combined with a high sensitivity to spot, and this goes a long way to explaining their popularity.

2.8 Black–Scholes pricing of barrier-contingent vanilla options

Having seen how we can use the Black–Scholes option pricing PDE (Equation 2.21) to compute prices for vanilla options, we are now primed to turn our attention to barrier options. Our starting point is the determination of the boundary conditions. For vanilla options, it was relatively easy to state the boundary conditions – the payoff function was all we needed. With a barrier-contingent vanilla, we have a

"2-state" contract: the contract may be 'untriggered' or 'triggered', and the payoff depends on the state. The contract starts in the untriggered state, and remains in that state for as long as spot does not trade at the barrier level. If spot reaches the barrier level at any time before the option's expiry time, the contract becomes triggered and remains in that state for the remainder of the option's lifetime.

Let us divide our barrier-contingent vanilla options into two sets: knock-outs and knock-ins. Let us first examine knock-out options – that is, single- and double-barrier knock-out calls and puts.

2.8.1 Knock-outs

At expiry time, if the knock-out contract is in an untriggered state, the payoff is as for the underlying vanilla option. If the contract is in the triggered state, the payoff is zero. Once a contract enters the triggered state, it has a value which is unequivocally zero at all times, and we clearly do not need a model for it. Thus, when we talk about the valuation of a knock-out option, we are implicitly interested only in valuation of the contract in its *untriggered* state. By definition, this further means we are interested only in valuation of the contract at *spot levels* which do not trigger the barrier, and at times before the barrier has been triggered.

What then are the boundary conditions of an untriggered knock-out call/put option? At maturity, an untriggered knock-out option has no further chance of being triggered, so the boundary condition at $t = T$ is just as for the underlying vanilla option:

$$V(S, T) = P_{\text{vanilla}}(S(T)) \tag{2.86}$$

We call this the **payoff boundary condition**.

Now, what about a boundary condition at the barrier(s)? We know that if spot touches a barrier, the value of the contract will become zero. That is precisely the boundary condition we need to impose:

$$V(H, t) = 0 \quad \forall t \leq T$$

where H is the barrier level[2], and we explicitly state that this condition must hold for all times up to and including expiry time. We call this the **barrier boundary condition**.

If an option has both a lower barrier at L and an upper barrier at U, we must impose two barrier boundary conditions:

$$V(L, t) = 0 \quad \forall t \leq T$$
$$V(U, t) = 0 \quad \forall t \leq T$$

---

[2] Opinions are divided as to why the quant community tends to use H to denote a barrier level. One theory is that it stands for the Hit level.

Let us start with the specific case given by the following pseudo-termsheet:

Contract type:	Up and Out single barrier
Currency pair:	EURUSD
Maturity:	6 months
Call/Put:	EUR put; USD call
Strike K:	1.25
Lower Barrier L:	N/A
Upper Barrier U:	1.28
EUR Principal A_f:	1,000,000
USD Principal A_d:	1,250,000

The payoff boundary condition is:

$$V(S, T_{6m}) = \max(0, 1.25 - S(T_{6m})) \qquad (2.87)$$

and the barrier boundary condition is:

$$V(1.28, t) = 0 \quad \forall t \leq T \qquad (2.88)$$

Equations 2.87 and 2.88, together with the Black–Scholes PDE, given in Equation 2.21, define the barrier-option problem, which we must solve in order to calculate the option price of the normal knock-out put option. As before, when we looked at solving the vanilla-option problem, we are dealing with a much-studied problem, with well known solutions [14, 15, 16]. However, before we present the solution, it will be instructive for us briefly to think intuitively about how the barrier-problem solution might relate to the vanilla-problem solution.

For a start, we know that we can find a solution which satisfies the PDE and payoff condition only, namely the solution for the 6-month 1.25-strike EUR put/USD call vanilla option. Let us call this partial solution the **payoff solution**. We also know that this payoff solution will give a value that is too large, since (as discussed in Section 1.12) the knock-out option must necessarily have a lower value than the corresponding vanilla option. Further, since we are only interested in valuation of the contract at spot levels *below* the barrier level of 1.28, we know that we can supplement our payoff solution with the solution for any vanilla option which has a zero payoff below this level, because such an option will satisfy the PDE and will not disturb the payoff in the region of interest. Put together, these observations mean that we can subtract the solution for any call option (of the same 6-month maturity) whose strike is greater than or equal to 1.28, and in any principal amount. We can then conceive of a **supplementary solution**, consisting of a short position in a call option (or a set of such positions), which exactly cancels out the value of the payoff solution (which is a long put position) at the barrier (at all times), thereby ensuring that the barrier boundary condition is met. Can we find such a supplementary solution? Yes, we can. But we'll see that there's a twist.

The supplementary solution is indeed a short position in a single 6-month call option. Its strike K' is related to the strike K and barrier U of the up-and-out put option like so:

$$K' = \frac{U^2}{K} \qquad (2.89)$$

This gives a strike of $K' = 1.3107$ in the present example.

The Foreign principal A'_f of the supplementary solution is related not only to the contract data but also to the market data:

$$A'_f = \left(\frac{K}{U}\right)\left(\frac{U}{S}\right)^{\frac{r_d - r_f}{\frac{1}{2}\sigma^2}} A_f \qquad (2.90)$$

Taking from our benchmark market data for EURUSD a spot price of 1.2629, a EUR interest rate of -0.04%, a USD interest rate of 0.25% and a volatility of 7.45%, this expression evaluates to EUR 990,385.

Another way of writing the expression for the supplementary strike K' is:

$$\frac{K'}{U} = \frac{U}{K}$$

and this emphasizes that, in proportional terms, the strike of the supplementary solution is exactly as far above the barrier as the barrier option's strike is below it. For example, in the present case, because we have to multiply the strike of the barrier option by 1.024 to get the barrier level, we have to multiply the barrier level by 1.024 to get the strike of the supplementary solution. In such geometric terms, the barrier is exactly half way between the two strikes. If we think of the barrier level as a reflecting mirror, and we place the strike of the barrier option in front of it, then the strike of the supplementary option is the *image* of the barrier strike, as illustrated in Figure 2.7. There are many other barrier-option problems which can also be solved using a combination of payoff and 'image' options, and the general method of solving a PDE in this way is called **the method of images**.

So, it seems that everything is reflected: for a payoff which is a *long put* with a strike on one side of the barrier, our supplementary option comprises a *short call* with a strike on the other side of the barrier. And now for the twist: the supplementary solution is not simply the value of the supplementary option – it is *the value we would get if we interchanged the Domestic and Foreign interest rates*. It is the entire dynamics of the problem that are being reflected. For example, if our market has an upward-sloping forward curve, the value of the image option will be calculated under a downward-sloping forward curve.

68 | FX Barrier Options

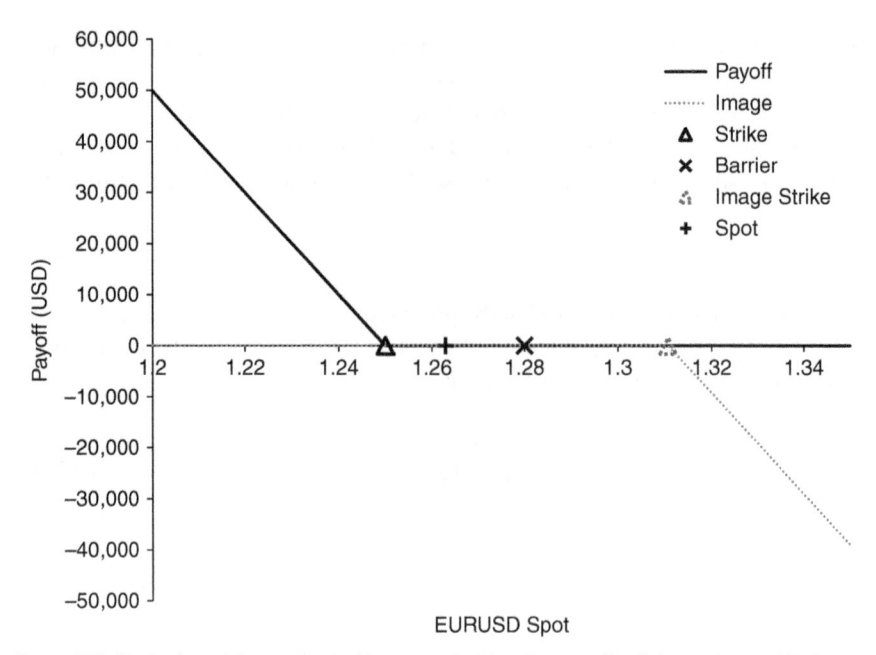

Figure 2.7 Illustration of the method of images, showing the payoffs of the option and its image for a 1.25-strike EUR put/USD call option with an up-side knockout at 1.28

Let us now write out the complete solution for our example up-and-out put option:

$$V_{\text{PNO}} = A_f \left[K e^{-r_d(T-t)} N(-d_2) - S e^{-r_f(T-t)} N(-d_1) \right]$$
$$- A'_f \left[S e^{-r_d(T-t)} N(\tilde{d}_1(K')) - K' e^{-r_f(T-t)} N(\tilde{d}_2(K')) \right] \quad (2.91)$$

where A'_f is given by Equation 2.90, K' is given by Equation 2.89, and the quantities $\tilde{d}_1$ and $\tilde{d}_2$ are like the normal versions defined in Equations 2.73 and 2.74, but with the Domestic and Foreign interest rates transposed:

$$\tilde{d}_{\substack{1 \\ 2}}(K) \doteq \frac{\ln\left(\frac{S}{K}\right) + (\overbrace{r_f - r_d}^{\text{transposed}} \pm \frac{1}{2}\sigma^2)(T-t)}{\sigma\sqrt{T-t}} \quad (2.92)$$

The method of images can be applied in a similar way to all the barrier-contingent vanilla options. In the case of double-barrier options, the method leads to an infinite series of image options, which in practice must be evaluated to as many terms as are necessary for the precision required.

Although we have spent some effort on a heuristic discussion of the solution in terms of the method of images, it is rare in practice that we need to go through such a procedure in order to calculate Black–Scholes prices, since formulae are well documented for all FX barrier products for which formulae exist. Notably, Haug [15] includes many different cases of barrier-contingent vanilla options in his immensely valuable and well-established book of option pricing formulae.

It is well worth clarifying how Haug's terminology and notation correspond to those used in this book, as the differences are a potentially serious pitfall. Crucially, his K refers not to the strike but to the option rebate, which we assume without loss of generality to be zero (Section 1.7 explains why). His strike is denoted instead by X. His quantity b equals $r_d - r_f$ from this book. In terms of contract type names, he refers to barrier-contingent vanilla options with single and double barriers as "Standard Barrier Options" and "Double-Barrier Options" respectively. Lastly, Haug's formulae ignore spot lags; for example, they do not distinguish between expiry time T_e and settlement date T_s. As a reminder, the "lagless approach" that we discussed in Section 2.3.1 prescribes a straightforward procedure for applying the spot lag.

The method of images is essentially a PDE-based method, and originates from PDE-based techniques in the physical sciences. However, it is not the only way in which the values of barrier-contingent vanilla options can be derived. The **reflection principle** is an alternative approach which starts from the symmetry properties of the SDE. Shreve discusses the reflection principle for discrete [17] and continuous [10] stochastic processes. Austing [12] derives barrier option values using a method which includes the use of the reflection principle.

2.8.2 Knock-ins

As explained in Chapter 1 and summarized in Section 1.12.2, a contract with a knock-in feature can be valued in terms of its "sibling" knock-out contract and the equivalent no-barrier contract. Employment of this technique should not be seen as a wily trick, but rather a matter of good practice, as it ensures consistency between the related contract types. Furthermore, when we are valuing contracts using numerical methods, use of this technique allows greater efficiency in terms of software development, and it is commonly the case that this technique is the only one used, that is, no numerical functionality is developed to calculate the knock-in value directly. With analytic formulae, however, it is usually easier to to implement the knock-in valuation formulae directly than to go via the knock-out and no-barrier contracts.

70 | FX Barrier Options

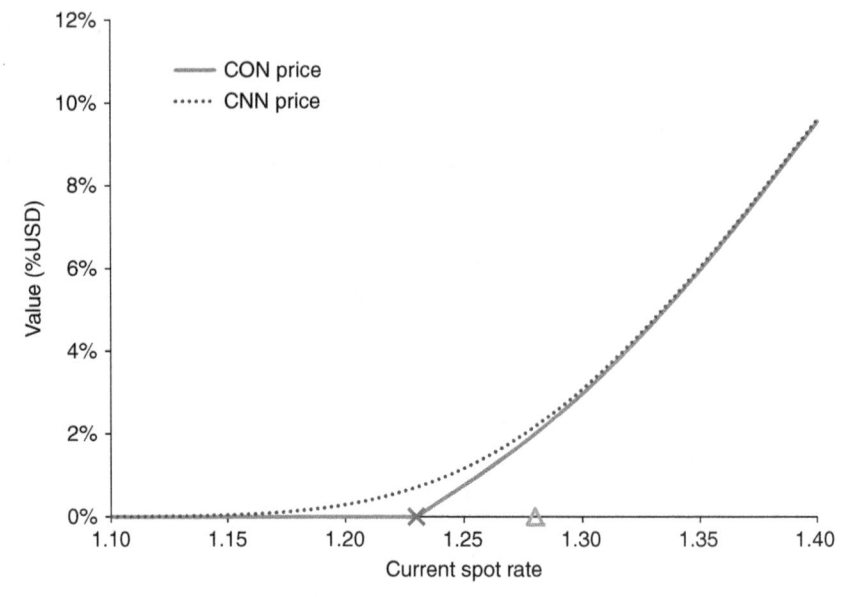

Figure 2.8 Variation with spot of the value of a 6-month 1.28-strike EUR call/USD put option with a down-and-out barrier at 1.25 (contract code con). The corresponding vanilla option (cnn) is shown alongside. The strike is marked with a triangle, the barrier with a cross

2.8.3 Quotation methods

The quotation methods used for barrier-contingent vanilla options are the same as for vanilla options, as summarized in Table 2.1. This facilitates comparison between the values of options which differ only in the presence of a barrier or barriers.

2.8.4 Valuation behaviour of barrier-contingent vanilla options

Figure 2.8 shows the variation with current spot rate of the value of a 6-month 1.28-strike EUR call/USD put option with a down-and-out barrier at 1.23. The barrier is marked with a cross, the strike is marked with a triangle, and the corresponding vanilla value is plotted alongside.

It is clear to see that for high spot values, far away from the barrier, the barrier option has a value very close to that of the vanilla option. This tells us that there is only a negligible probability that the option will knock out. As spot comes down towards 1.30, it becomes clear that the barrier option value is lower than the vanilla option value. There is now some non-negligible probability of knocking out. As spot goes further lower, the effect of the barrier becomes increasingly strong, with the difference between the barrier option and vanilla option values increasing, until at the barrier level the value of the barrier option is zero.

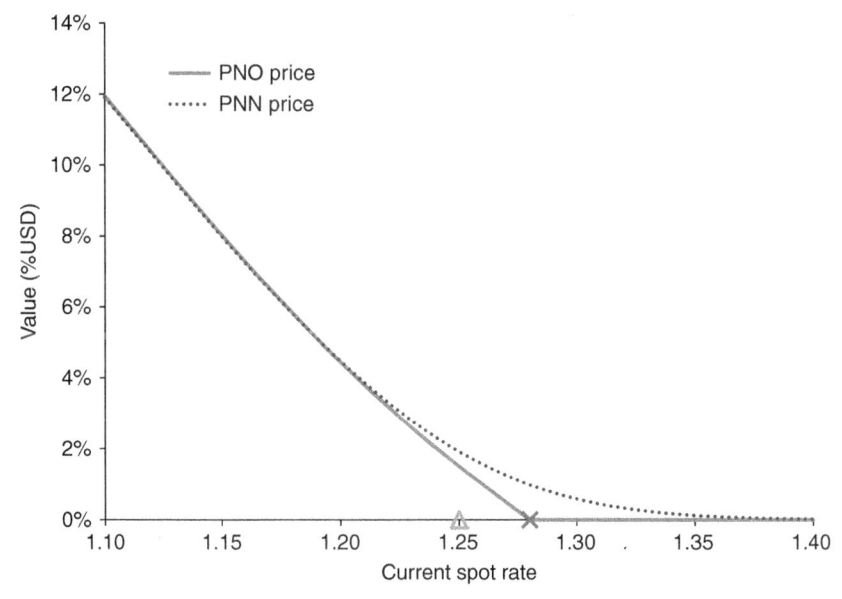

Figure 2.9 Variation with spot of the value of a 6-month 1.25-strike EUR put/USD call option with an up-and-out barrier at 1.28 (contract code PNO). The corresponding vanilla option (PNN) is shown alongside. The strike is marked with a triangle, the barrier with a cross

The pattern of behaviour just described is typical for down-and-out call options. A very similar pattern is seen for *up*-and-out *put* options, except that the value profile is reflected about the barrier, as shown in Figure 2.9. It is this close qualitative similarity that motivates us to describe both cases as examples of a "normal" knock-out barrier, as introduced in Section 1.5.

Reverse knock-outs exhibit qualitatively different behaviour, as demonstrated by Figures 2.10 and 2.11, which show the value against spot of a reverse knock-out call option and a reverse knock-out put option respectively. This time the barrier option value is near the vanilla option value in the out-of-the-money region, where the values are near zero. As spot moves towards the strike (upwards for the call; downwards for the put), two effects are in play: a greater chance of ending up in the money contributes value to the option value, whereas a greater chance of knocking out removes value from the option. The balance between these two effects means that the option value first increases and then decreases down to zero, with a maximum somewhere in the middle.

Double knock-out call and put options (typically) have one normal knock-out and one reverse knock-out, and correspondingly display a combination of the effects seen in normal and reverse knock-outs. For example, Figure 2.12 shows the value against spot of a double knock-out call option.

As we discussed in Section 1.12.2, the value of any *knock-in* option equals the difference between the values of the no-barrier option and the sibling knock-out

72 | FX Barrier Options

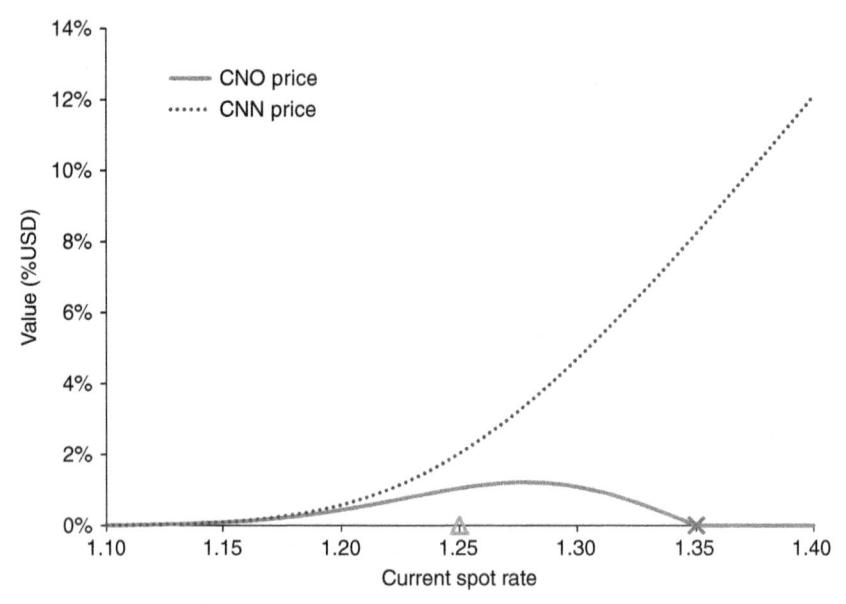

Figure 2.10 Variation with spot of the value of a 6-month 1.25-strike EUR call/USD put option with an up-and-out barrier at 1.35 (contract code CNO). The corresponding vanilla option (CNN) is shown alongside. The strike is marked with a triangle, the barrier with a cross

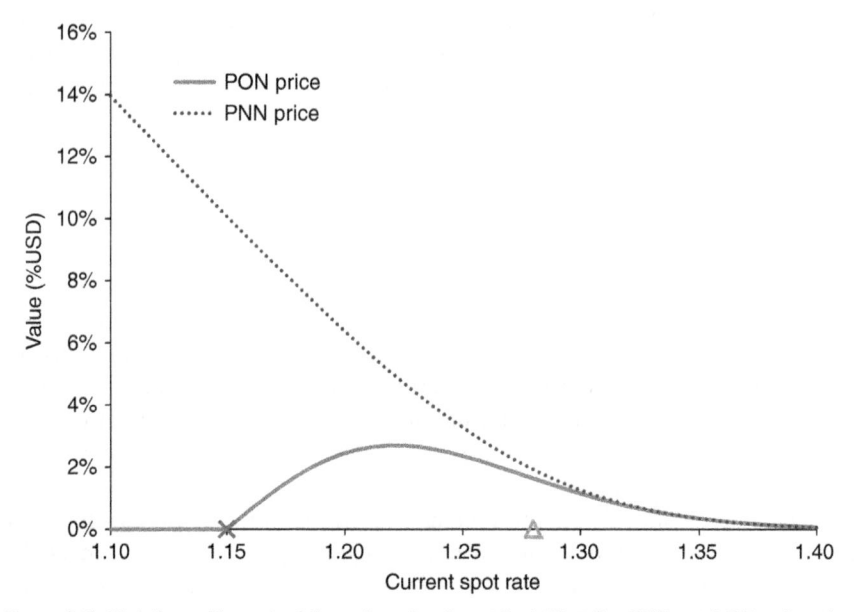

Figure 2.11 Variation with spot of the value of a 6-month 1.28-strike EUR put/USD call option with a down-and-out barrier at 1.15 (contract code PON). The corresponding vanilla option (PNN) is shown alongside. The strike is marked with a triangle, the barrier with a cross

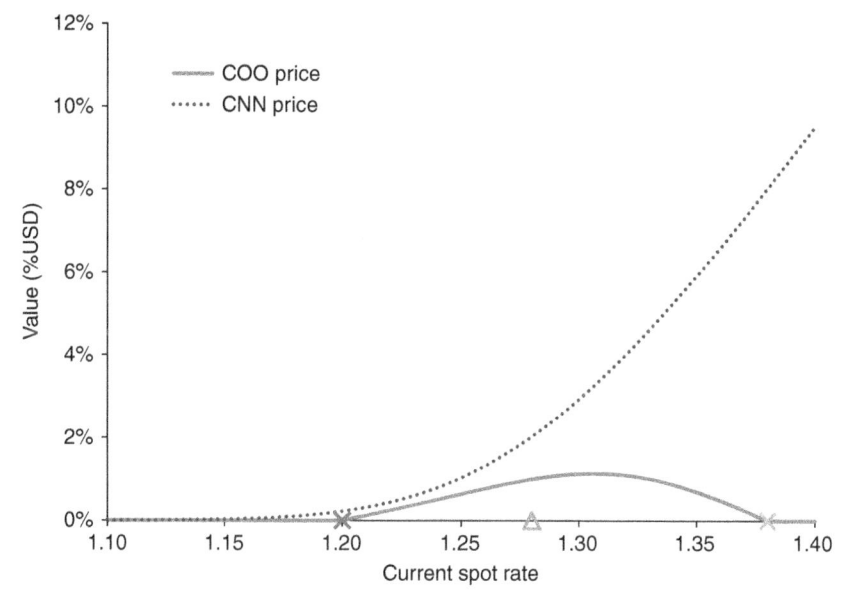

Figure 2.12 Variation with spot of the value of a 6-month 1.28-strike EUR put/USD call option with knock-out barriers at 1.20 and 1.38 (contract code COO). The corresponding vanilla option (CNN) is shown alongside. The strike is marked with a triangle, the barriers with crosses

option. I find it very helpful, when considering the value profile of a knock-in option, to keep in mind the value profiles of both the vanilla option and the sibling knock-out option. For example, Figure 2.13 builds on Figure 2.12 by adding the value profile of the sibling double knock-in option.

2.9 Black–Scholes pricing of barrier-contingent payments

At first sight it may appear that barrier-contingent payments cannot be handled using the method of images described for barrier-contingent vanilla options in Section 2.8. The analogue of the vanilla payoff solution is the payment, and a payment, after all, has either no dependence at all on spot (in the case of Domestic payments) or a simple linear dependence on spot (in the case of Foreign payments). No combination of such simple solutions is going to exhibit the effects of a barrier. In fact we could use the method of images if we re-interpreted a barrier-contingent payment as a barrier-contingent *European digital* in which the barrier level and the digital strike level are equal. However, instead of going down that route, we are now going to take the opportunity to approach the barrier problem from an alternative angle.

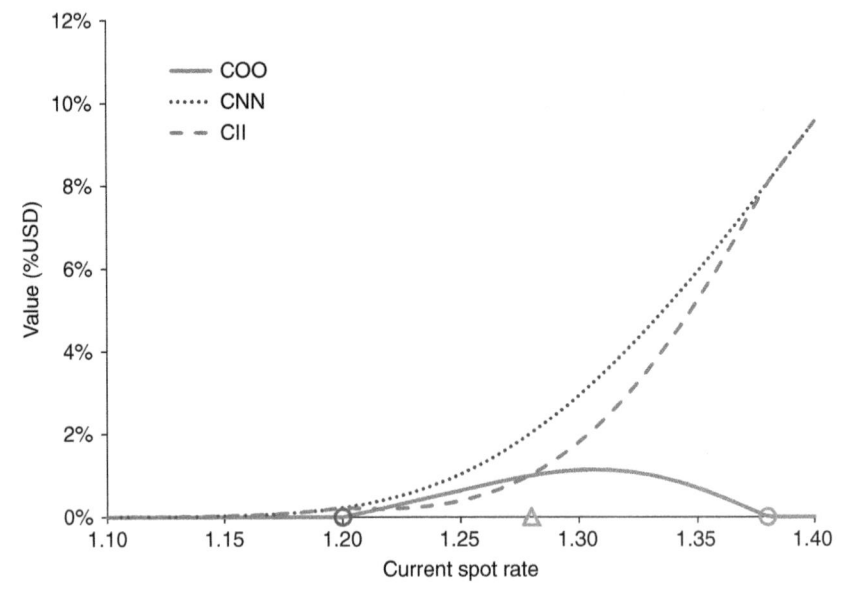

Figure 2.13 Variation with spot of the value of a 6-month 1.28-strike EUR put/USD call option with knock-in barriers at 1.20 and 1.38 (contract code cii). The corresponding vanilla option (cnn) and knock-out option (coo) are shown alongside. The strike is marked with a triangle, the barriers with circles

2.9.1 Payment in Domestic

Let us for a moment drop all references to contract types, and just consider the future path of the spot rate. Suppose EURUSD spot is currently trading at 1.26, and we are interested in when and whether it will trade at a level of 1.28. We can then ask ourselves various questions, such as:

1. What is the probability that spot will trade at 1.28 at some time in the next three months?
2. What is the probability that spot will not trade at 1.28 at any time in the next three months?
3. How long will it be before spot next trades at 1.28?

These specific questions motivate some specific terminology. The first question is answered by a quantity called the **barrier trigger probability**. It is specified for a given barrier level H and time interval (T_1, T_2). (In this example, T_1 equals the current time, and T_2 equals the three-month time point.) Question 2. is answered by the **barrier survival probability**. For a given barrier level H and time interval (T_1, T_2), the sum of the trigger probability and the survival probability is 1.

The answer to Question 3. is of course a stochastic quantity, and is known as the **first passage time** (or **first exit time**) to 1.28. Being a time interval, the first passage time is measured in years and can take any non-negative value. For example, a value of 0.5 corresponds to a scenario in which spot first trades at 1.28 in half a year.

Shreve [10] has shown how, under a geometric Brownian Motion, the probability distribution of the first passage time can be expressed in closed form. Wystup [18] has used Shreve's result to derive an expression for the risk-neutral probability distribution of the first passage time under the Black–Scholes model. Wilmott [3] discusses first passage times and the equations that govern their distributions and expectations. Denoting the first passage time to upper barrier level U by τ_U, the probability density function f_{τ_U} is given by:

$$f_{\tau_U}(t) = \frac{\ln(\frac{U}{S})}{\sqrt{2\pi\sigma^2 t^3}} \exp\left(-\frac{\left(\ln(\frac{U}{S}) - (r_d - r_f)t + \frac{1}{2}\sigma^2 t\right)^2}{2\sigma^2 t}\right) \qquad (2.93)$$

First passage time distributions can similarly be found for a lower barrier level and for double barriers.

Whatever barriers we have, integration of the probability density function of the first passage time between two time intervals τ_1 and τ_2 gives us the probability that barrier trigger occurred at a time point in that time interval:

$$\Pr(\tau_1 \leq \tau \leq \tau_2) = \int_{\tau_1}^{\tau_2} f_\tau(\tau) \, d\tau \qquad (2.94)$$

For example, using results from Chapter 4 in Haug [15], we can write the following expressions for the probability that an upper barrier U is triggered between now (time t) and some future time T:

$$p_{\text{trigger}} = N\left(\frac{\ln(\frac{S}{U}) + (r_d - r_f)(T - t) - \frac{1}{2}\sigma^2(T - t)}{\sigma\sqrt{T - t}}\right)$$
$$+ \left(\frac{U}{S}\right)^{\frac{r_d - r_f}{\frac{1}{2}\sigma^2} - 1} N\left(\frac{\ln(\frac{S}{U}) + (r_f - r_d)(T - t) + \frac{1}{2}\sigma^2(T - t)}{\sigma\sqrt{T - t}}\right) \qquad (2.95)$$

Now let us go back to the contracts. By definition, the fair value of a Domestic no-touch (DON, DNO or DOO contract) equals the discounted risk-neutral expectation of its payoff. This is simply equal to the value of the underlying Domestic payment multiplied by the risk-neutral *survival probability* for the relevant barrier(s). Similarly, the value of a Domestic one-touch pay-at-maturity (DIN, DNI or DII contract) equals the value of the underlying Domestic payment multiplied by the *trigger probability*. This means that the problem of calculating the values of these touch contracts is essentially the same as the problem of calculating the barrier survival or trigger probabilities.

For one-touch contracts which pay in Domestic *at hit* (DIN_H, DNI_H or DII_H contract), the value of the underlying Domestic payment is itself dependent on the first passage time, since the discount factor depends on the time of hit. Now, the discount factor must be taken inside the integral over the first passage time. For example, for an up-side one-touch pay-at-hit contract with Domestic principal A_d:

$$V_{\text{DNI\_H}} = A_d \int_0^{T-t} e^{-r_d \tau} f_{\mathcal{T}}(\tau) \, d\tau \qquad (2.96)$$

2.9.2 Payment in Foreign

The risk-neutral value of a touch contract which pays in Foreign requires us to compute the expectation of future spot *conditional* on the barrier having (or not having) been triggered. To compute this expectation explicitly, we would need the risk-neutral joint probability density function of future spot and first passage time. However, there is a simpler approach: as discussed in Section 1.12, we can use the method of *currency-pair inversion*. As an example, consider a EURUSD 1.28 up-side no-touch paying in EUR (contract type FNO). We invert our underlying currency pair from EURUSD to USDEUR, so that our EURUSD FNO contract with an upper barrier at 1.28 turns into a USDEUR DON contract with a lower barrier at 1/1.28. And that is something we can handle as described in Section 2.9.1, yielding a value in EUR (the Domestic currency of the inverted pair), which can be converted to USD using the current spot rate.

As with barrier-contingent vanilla options, the formulae that result from the above approach are well documented. Again, Haug [15] includes many different cases of barrier-contingent payments in his compendium of option pricing formulae. As before, it is worth clarifying the terminology differences. Haug refers to barrier-contingent payments with single and double barriers as "Binary Barrier Options" and "Double-Barrier Binary Options" respectively, with the respective formulae being credited to Reiner and Rubinstein [19] and Hui [20]. And he refers to payments in Domestic and Foreign as payments in "cash" and "asset" respectively.

2.9.3 Quotation methods

Not all of the quotation methods used for vanilla options and barrier-contingent vanilla options (as summarized in Table 2.1) are valid for a given barrier-contingent payment. A payment has only one principal, which is in *either* Domestic *or* Foreign, and it does not make any sense to quote a value as, say, Domestic per unit Foreign principal when the principal is in Domestic. If the payment is in Domestic, we can

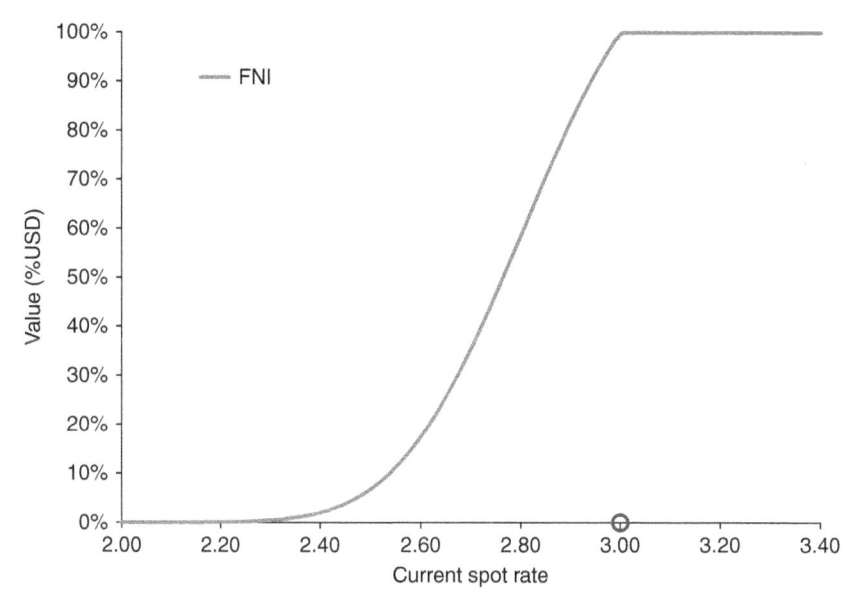

Figure 2.14 Value against spot of a 6-month USDTRY 3.00 up-side one-touch, paying in USD at maturity (contract code FNI)

quote the %Domestic value (Domestic value per unit Domestic principal) and we can quote the Foreign/Domestic value (Foreign value per unit Domestic principal). Conversely, if the payment is in Foreign, we can quote the %Foreign value (Foreign value per unit Foreign principal) and we can quote the Domestic/Foreign value (Domestic value per unit Foreign principal). Of course, we can always quote values in Domestic or Foreign.

2.9.4 Valuation behaviour of barrier-contingent payments

Let us now take a look at some value profiles for barrier-contingent payments. We will take USDTRY as our example currency pair, and use the market data values given in Table 2.2. Most commonly, USDTRY barrier-contingent payments pay out in USD, and their prices are also quoted in USD, so the most practically important price quotation method is %USD. Figure 2.14 shows the value against spot of a 6-month USDTRY 3.00 up-side one-touch, paying (in USD) at maturity (contract type code FNI).

As expected, the option value at low spot levels is close to zero, because is there is negligible chance that the barrier will be triggered and the payment will occur. And at high spot levels, the value is very close to 100% (actually it is equal to the discount factor because the payoff will occur in the future), reflecting the certainty that the

78 | FX Barrier Options

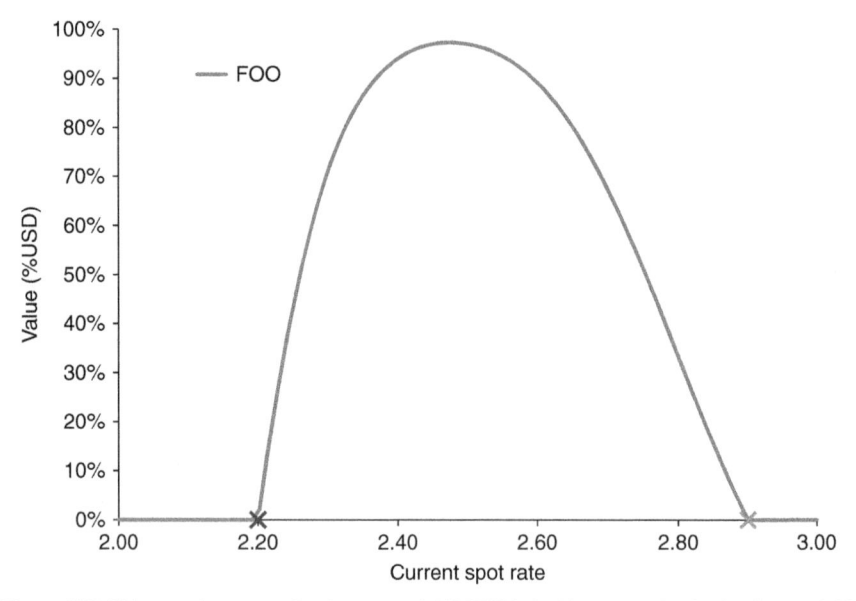

Figure 2.15 Value against spot of a three-month USDTRY double no-touch with barriers at 2.20 and 2.90, paying in USD (contract code FOO)

payment will be made. In between, the option value rises smoothly, though with a kink at the barrier level: the gradient of the value function has a discontinuity.

Next let us look at a double no-touch (or "range") option. Figure 2.15 shows the value against spot of a three-month USDTRY double no-touch with barriers at 2.20 and 2.90, paying in USD. As expected, the option value is zero at the barrier levels and outside them, and rises to a peak in between.

Lastly, let us look at the effect of maturity. Figure 2.16 shows how the values of Domestic and Foreign pay-at-maturity USDTRY one-touches vary with maturity with a fixed up-side barrier of 2.70. The values plotted use the %Domestic (TRY) and %Foreign (USD) quotation conventions respectively. At short maturities, the barrier is very unlikely to be triggered, and the values are correspondingly low. As the maturity increases, the barrier is ever more likely to be triggered, and the values increase. The fact that the USD-paying contract is more valuable than the TRY-paying contract is the result of two effects: first, the high TRY interest rates mean that its discount factor is much lower than the USD discount factor. And second, the Domestic value of a Foreign payment is proportional to spot, which is positively correlated with barrier trigger, since the barrier is on the up-side. For down-side one-touches, the discount factor effect applies in the same way, but the correlation effect is reversed: spot is *negatively* correlated with barrier trigger. The two effects therefore compete, with the discount factor effect dominating for longer maturities, as illustrated in Figure 2.17.

Living in a Black–Scholes World | 79

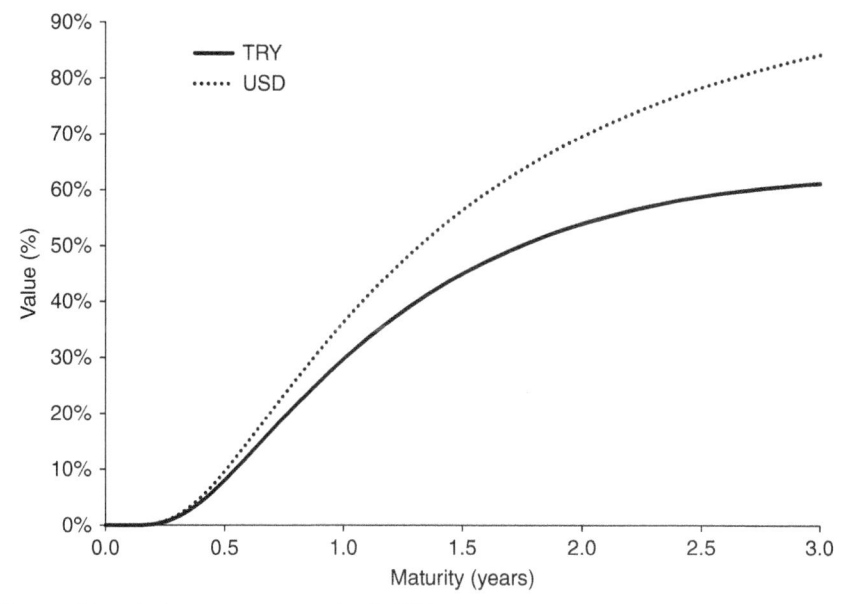

Figure 2.16 Variation with maturity of USDTRY pay-at-maturity one-touches with an up-side barrier at 2.70, paying in TRY (full line) and USD (dotted line)

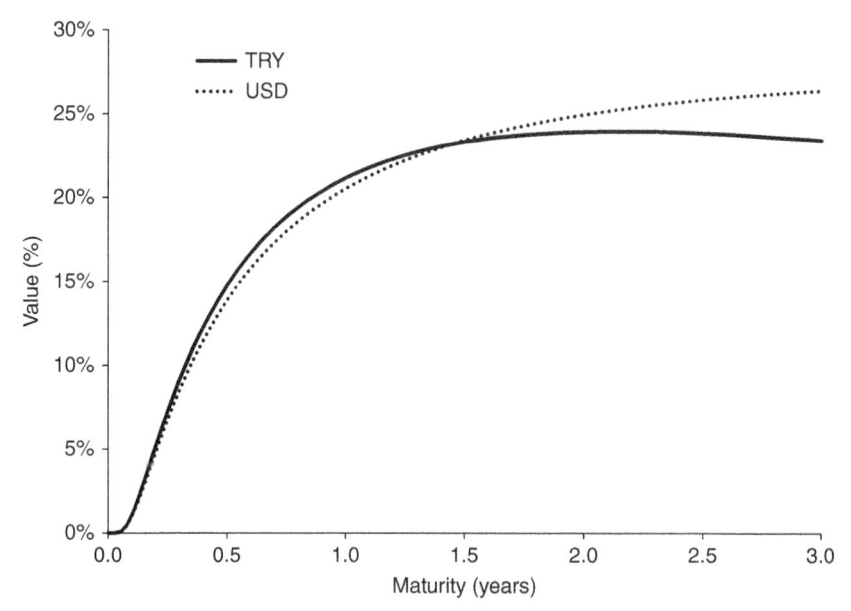

Figure 2.17 Variation with maturity of USDTRY pay-at-maturity one-touches with a down-side barrier at 2.10, paying in TRY (full line) and USD (dotted line)

2.10 Discrete barrier options

The probability of triggering a discrete barrier is always less than the probability of triggering the equivalent continuous barrier, since there will always exist spot paths which trigger the continuous version but not the discrete version. Conversely, we can say that for a given discrete barrier level, the continuous barrier that has the same trigger probability must be further away from the current spot rate. Analytical solutions are not in general available for the valuation of discrete barrier options, so in order to solve the Black–Scholes option pricing PDE subject to the boundary conditions of a discrete barrier option, numerical methods must be used, as described in Chapter 6. However, a highly effective analytical technique exists for calculating an *approximation* to the value of any given discrete barrier option in terms of its continuous-barrier equivalent. Broadie, Glasserman and Kou [21] have derived a result which shows that discrete barrier options can be accurately valued using the formulae for continuous barrier options by *adjustment* of the barrier level. The adjustment shifts the barrier away from spot by a factor $\tilde{h}$ given by:

$$\tilde{h} = e^{\beta \sigma \sqrt{\Delta t}} \tag{2.97}$$

where $\beta \sim 0.5826$, σ is the volatility and Δt is the discrete barrier monitoring interval. As an example, suppose we wish to value a USDTRY normal knock-out call option where the low-side barrier level of 2.10 is monitored daily. The adjusted barrier level $\tilde{H}$ is then calculated as follows:

$$\tilde{H} = \frac{2.10}{\exp\left(0.5826 \times 11\% \times \sqrt{\frac{1}{365}}\right)}$$
$$= 2.092968 \tag{2.98}$$

Broadie et al. call this adjustment a **barrier continuity correction for discrete barrier options**, but it is important to appreciate that the technique can also be extremely valuable when applied the other way around: to adjust the barrier level of a *continuous* barrier option and value it as a *discrete* barrier option. This is useful in the context of Monte Carlo simulation, which inherently performs only discrete barrier monitoring. Use of the technique in this way is discussed in Section 6.2.1.

2.11 Window barrier options

Analytical formulae for the valuation of window barrier options under the Black–Scholes model are available in Haug [15], where he credits Heynen and Kat [22] for the derivation.

2.12 Black–Scholes numerical valuation methods

As we have seen, it is possible to calculate the value of many types of option under the Black–Scholes model using **analytical methods**: that is, a closed-form formula, possibly in combination with one of the quantitative relationships described in Section 1.12. Sometimes, however, we are unable to derive a closed-form pricing formula, and we need to use **numerical methods**.

There are two classes of numerical methods that are by far the most useful for option valuation: **finite-difference methods** and **Monte Carlo simulation**. We describe these numerical methods, and a number of accompanying techniques, in Chapter 6.

3 | Black–Scholes Risk Management

A good decision is based on knowledge and not on numbers.

Plato

Risk management takes many forms, but common to all of them is the following set of aims:

- identify risk;
- measure risk;
- reduce risk;
- report risk.

The goal of this chapter is to discuss the market risk management of FX barrier options in a Black–Scholes world, and with that definition of scope we have largely achieved the first of the aims: we can identify all the market variables that appear in the Black–Scholes model as sources of risk. The first part of this chapter (Sections 3.1 to 3.4) discusses these sources of risk, and also how we measure and report the risks. (The reduction of risks is best done after taking into account the effects of Smile Pricing, so we will defer that aspect of risk management to Chapter 4.) The sections are structured by market variable: we first look at spot risk, then at volatility risk, and so on.

But there are sources of risk other than the market variables. As we described in Chapter 2, the Black–Scholes model is built upon a set of assumptions about how we can hedge. These assumptions are not wholly realistic (as emphasized and detailed in Section 2.3.3), and in the second part of this chapter we will discuss the risks that arise from the assumptions not being met.

We are implicitly describing the practical risk situation from the point of view of an option market-maker (such as a bank), rather than an option hedger. The hedger has entered the option contract precisely in order to reduce or eliminate its risk, and in doing so has passed the risk on to the market-maker, who must then manage it. A market-maker might have tens of thousands of live options on its book at any given time, so it manages its risk at the level of an option portfolio or "trading book".

The risk management methods presented in this chapter cover both the micro-level (individual options) and the macro-level (trading book).

3.1 Spot risk

Management of spot risk requires us to understand how the value of an option or the value of a portfolio of options changes with spot. In broad terms, we can do this in two ways: local risk analysis and non-local risk analysis.

3.1.1 Local spot risk analysis

Local spot risk analysis involves looking at the change δV in an option's value in response to a *small* change δS in spot. If we didn't know anything about where our option pricing formulae came from, we might take a standard approach by writing down the Taylor series expansion in spot of δV:

$$\delta V = V(S+\delta S) - V(S)$$
$$= \frac{\partial V}{\partial S} \delta S + \frac{1}{2} \frac{\partial^2 V}{\partial S^2} \delta S^2 + \frac{1}{6} \frac{\partial^3 V}{\partial S^3} \delta S^3 + \ldots \quad (3.1)$$

and then computing a few terms. Whilst correct, that approach would miss the point. We know exactly where our option pricing formulae come from, and we recognize the first partial derivative, $\frac{\partial V}{\partial S}$, as the quantity **delta** from our discussion of the Black–Scholes model in Chapter 2. There, we not only met the concept of delta, but we moreover discussed it in its most important context: *delta-hedging* as a strategy that is crucial to the very meaning of a risk-neutral option value. Our option only has its risk-neutral value if we keep it continuously delta-hedged, so it is clearly very important that we know our option's delta at all times.

Our hedging strategy requires us to continuously eliminate the (instantaneous) delta risk of an option by hedging with Foreign currency. As spot moves, we will need to re-delta-hedge (by performing a spot trade), so it is also very important that we know how our option's delta *changes* with spot. This is given by the second partial derivative $\frac{\partial^2 V}{\partial S^2}$, which is again a quantity we have met: it is **gamma**. As we mentioned in Section 2.3.2, in the context of deriving the Black–Scholes PDE, delta and gamma are examples of **option Greeks**. In general, an option Greek measures the local sensitivity of a derivative value to one or more market risk factors. Greeks are also sometimes called **risk ratios** or **hedge ratios**. We will now take a closer look at delta and gamma.

3.1.2 Delta

I wrote in Chapter 2 without much explanation that the flavour of delta given by the first partial derivative of value with respect to spot, $\frac{\partial V}{\partial S}$, is called the **Spot-Delta-in-Foreign**. The "in-Foreign" part of that term refers to the units of the delta. The value V is as ever in the natural units of Domestic currency, so when divided by spot, which has units of Domestic per Foreign, we get a result whose units are Foreign. This Foreign number has a fundamental meaning: we delta-hedge our option by taking a spot position whose Foreign principal is the opposite. To take the specific example of EURUSD, if the option delta is +EUR 50,000, we delta-hedge the option by selling EURUSD in 50,000 euros. If the option delta is −EUR 50,000, we delta-hedge by buying EURUSD in 50,000 euros.

So Spot-Delta-in-Foreign tells us the Foreign principal of the spot position we need to take in order to delta-hedge our option. Now what is the Domestic principal of the spot position? Quite simply, it is the Foreign principal multiplied by spot: $S\frac{\partial V}{\partial S}$. This quantity is called the **Spot-Delta-in-Domestic**.

The "Spot-Delta" part of the term refers to the fact that it tells us the principals (in either Foreign or Domestic) of the spot trade that would delta-hedge our option. But spot trades are not the only possible hedge. We could alternatively use a *forward contract* to hedge our delta. We would need to choose a particular maturity, but that would not be an obstacle, and in the case of a European option, there would be a natural choice: the option settlement date. This approach yields two more flavours of delta: the **Forward-Delta-in-Foreign** and the **Forward-Delta-in-Domestic**. To calculate the Forward-Delta-in-Foreign of the option, we calculate the Spot-Delta of the option and divide by the Spot-Delta of a forward contract having unit Foreign principal. Similarly, to calculate the Forward-Delta-in-Domestic of the option, we calculate the Spot-Delta of the option and divide by the Spot-Delta of a forward contract having unit Domestic principal. (The Spot-Deltas used for the calculation can be either in Foreign or in Domestic, as long as they are consistent.) An expression for the value of the forward is given by Equation 1.15.

3.1.2.1 Premium-adjusted Delta

To any of the four flavours of delta defined above can be applied a variation called **premium adjustment**. To see how it works, let us imagine that the premium for the option was paid as an amount of Foreign currency cash. This Foreign premium has its own delta, and we can therefore compute an *aggregate* delta which is long the option-only delta and short the delta of the premium. (Whichever counterparty is long the option is short the premium.) This aggregate delta is the **premium-adjusted delta**. Note that whilst the short delta of the premium is always negative, the option-only delta may be positive or negative, with the result that the premium adjustment may either increase or decrease the absolute size of the delta.

Premium adjustment of delta is often a source of confusion, possibly because many of the quantities involved are mathematically similar but conceptually different. Let us therefore now briefly run through the quantities involved.

Let us suppose that the Foreign premium amount equals p_f. The subtle but crucial point to note is that once the premium has been agreed, p_f does not depend on spot. The Domestic (natural-currency) value of the premium is p_d, given by:

$$p_d = S p_f$$

The Spot-Delta-in-Foreign of p_d therefore equals p_f, and the Spot-Delta-in-Domestic of p_d equals $S p_f$. We can now substitute in the value of p_f: it equals the Domestic option value V divided by spot: $p_f = \frac{V}{S}$. Then we can calculate for example the premium-adjusted Spot-Delta-in-Foreign as the premium-unadjusted Spot-Delta-in-Foreign minus $\frac{V}{S}$. The premium-adjusted Spot-Delta-in-Domestic equals the premium-unadjusted Spot-Delta-in-Domestic minus V. Premium adjustment of the forward deltas proceeds by first calculating the premium-adjusted Spot-Delta and then calculating the Forward-Delta.

The practical usefulness of premium-adjusted delta actually has precious little to do with the currency in which option premia are paid, despite the terminology. Rather, it is to do with the currency with respect to which we wish to manage our risk. In all our mathematical formalism in this book, such as the derivation and discussion of the Black–Scholes model, we have consistently sought to hedge the *Domestic* value of portfolios. The appropriate deltas in this situation are the premium-unadjusted ones, and a real-life risk manager who wished to preserve the Domestic value of an option portfolio would be interested in looking at premium-unadjusted delta. On the other hand, a risk manager who wished to preserve the *Foreign* value of an option portfolio would be interested in looking at premium-adjusted delta. A very common example is a trader who needs to preserve the USD value of a USDJPY option portfolio.

3.1.2.2 Delta quotation styles

Just as prices and values can be quoted in the various forms given in Table 2.1, so too can the deltas. For example, Spot-Delta-in-Foreign may be divided by the Foreign principal of the option to yield a %Foreign quote.

3.1.3 Gamma

The purpose of gamma is to help us risk-manage the change in delta that occurs as a result of spot changing. The derivative $\frac{\partial^2 V}{\partial S^2}$ gives us a number which measures the rate of change of delta with respect to spot. We will refer to this gamma as the **mathematical gamma**. It is not a very useful measure, for two reasons. First, it has units of $\frac{\text{Foreign} \times \text{Foreign}}{\text{Domestic}}$, which is not very intuitive! Secondly, its magnitude is effectively based on a spot change of 1, whatever the spot rate. The likelihood of

EURUSD spot moving up by 1 (from around 1.26) is clearly completely different from the likelihood of AUDJPY spot moving up by 1 (from around 96.).

A far better measure is the change in delta for a *1%* move in spot. Even with widely varying volatilities amongst currency pairs, this measures gives us a much more realistic idea of the likely change in delta when spot changes. This measure is given (to a good approximation) by the **practitioner gamma**, defined as:

$$\text{practitioner gamma} = \frac{S}{100} \frac{\partial^2 V}{\partial S^2} \qquad (3.2)$$

Specifically, this expression gives the **Spot-Gamma-in-Foreign**, where our terminology mirrors that used for Delta. Gamma can be calculated in various flavours as for delta, except that the premium adjustment is not applicable, since a Foreign cash premium has no gamma.

3.1.4 Results for spot Greeks

In a Black–Scholes world, the spot Greeks delta and gamma can be calculated in one of two ways for any given option. We can either differentiate the closed-form expression for the option value with respect to spot (to get so-called "**analytic Greeks**") or we can calculate the derivatives numerically (to get so-called "**bumped Greeks**"). In probably the majority of contexts, it is preferable to use analytic Greeks, because they are fast, accurate and not subject to all the problems associated with numerical differentiation. Furthermore, the analytic expressions lend themselves to a great deal of powerful analysis beyond merely the Greeks. For example, we can use them to accurately locate the zeros, maxima and minima of the value and Greeks. Nevertheless, there are sometimes good and legitimate reasons for using bumped Greeks. Section 6.3, in the chapter on numerical methods, explains these reasons, describes some of the numerical challenges associated with their calculation and describes methods to overcome them.

Irrespective of the calculation method, let us now try to get a feel for the behaviour of the spot Greeks. To start with, let us consider the following vanilla option:

Currency pair:	EURUSD
Contract type code:	CNN
Contract description:	EUR call/USD put
Maturity:	6 months
Strike K:	1.28
Lower Barrier L:	N/A
Upper Barrier U:	N/A
EUR Principal A_f:	10 mio
USD Principal A_d:	12.8 mio

Given that the fair forward rate is 1.2647, this option is out of the money. Using the %EUR quotation method, its value is 1.5%, its Spot-Delta-in-Foreign is 41% and its Spot-Gamma-in-Foreign is 7%. If we now change the strike to 1.24, the option (now in the money) has a value of 3%, a Spot-Delta-in-Foreign of 64% and a Spot-Gamma-in-Foreign of 7%. As this example illustrates, an in-the-money vanilla option has a much larger value and Spot-Delta-in-Foreign than an out-of-the-money option (all other option properties being equal). But it is clear that gamma does not vary in the same way.

A good way to visualize the variation of value, delta and gamma with moneyness is to plot these quantities against varying spot. (We could alternatively plot against varying strike, but when we come to barrier options, it will be far simpler to vary spot than to try to vary both strike and barriers, so for comparability we will plot against spot for vanilla options too.) Plotting value, delta and gamma all on the same graph can get a little busy, so I will restrict plots to two quantities at a time. For consistency, I will focus on the Spot-Delta-in-Foreign flavour of delta, and for conciseness, the unqualified term "delta" will mean this flavour, unless otherwise stated.

Figure 3.1 shows the variation of value and delta for a six-month 1.28-strike EUR call/USD put vanilla option, whilst Figure 3.2 shows the variation of delta and gamma for the same option. Several important observations can be made. First

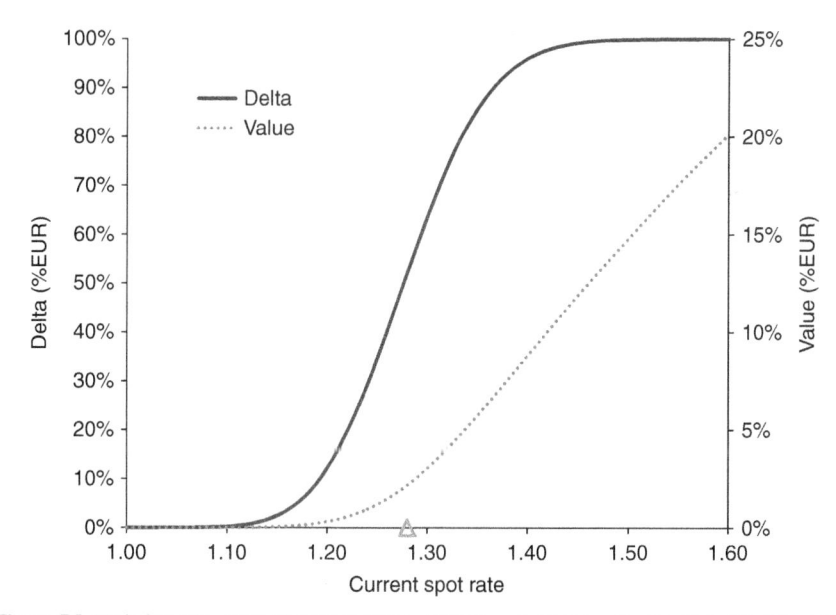

Figure 3.1 Variation with spot of delta (full line, primary y-axis) for a six-month 1.28-strike EUR call/USD put vanilla option. The value is shown alongside (dotted line, secondary y-axis). The strike level is marked with a triangle

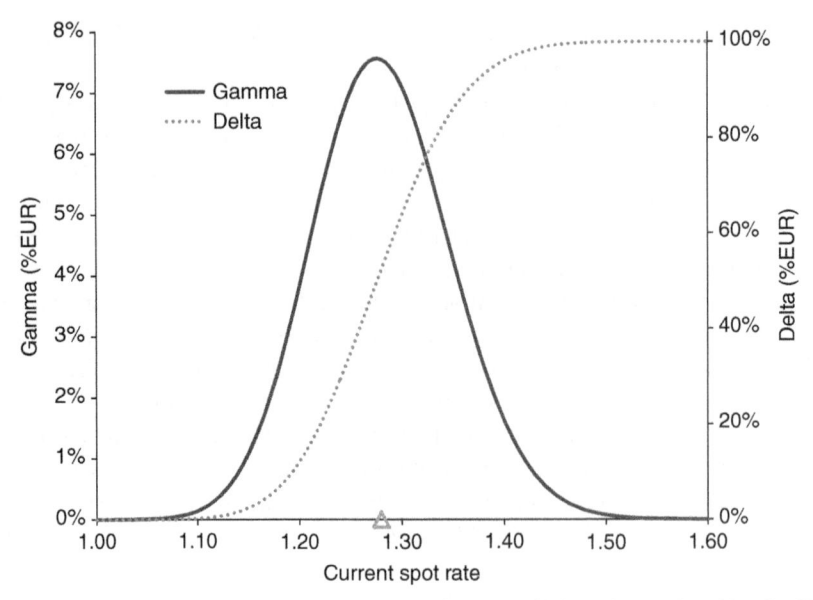

Figure 3.2 Variation with spot of gamma (full line, primary *y*-axis) for a six-month 1.28-strike EUR call/USD put vanilla option. The delta is shown alongside (dotted line, secondary *y*-axis). The strike level is marked with a triangle

of all, the graphs illustrate very clearly that the delta is the gradient of the value, and the gamma is the gradient of the delta. The limits of delta for small and large spot are of particular importance: at very low spot levels, the delta is nearly zero – meaning we hardly need any delta-hedge. This is because the option is hardly worth anything. At very high spot levels, the delta tends to a number close to 100% (actually the limit is the EUR discount factor), meaning that to delta-hedge the option, we need to hold an amount of euros equal to the euro principal of the option. This is because the option has effectively become a forward. It is almost certain that it will be exercised and that cash flows will be exchanged, so the delta hedge involves the reverse position. Gamma, meanwhile, is positive everywhere and has a bell shape which tends to zero for both low and high spot levels, and whose peak is near the strike.

The graphs for the corresponding put option are given in Figures 3.3 and 3.4. As these illustrate, the delta is always negative for a put option, and the gamma of a put option is exactly the same as the gamma of a call option (all other properties being equal).

Knowing that gamma is always positive for both call and put vanilla options, we can conclude that the value of any vanilla option is always a *convex function of spot*. This important property is inherent to vanilla options, but it does not extend to all options in general.

Black–Scholes Risk Management | 89

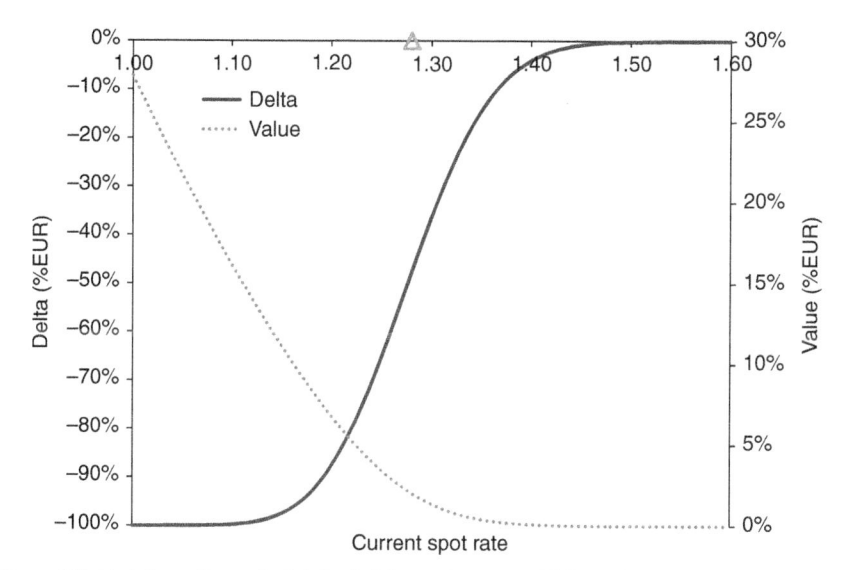

Figure 3.3 Variation with spot of delta (full line, primary y-axis) for a six-month 1.28-strike EUR put/USD call vanilla option. The value is shown alongside (dotted line, secondary y-axis. The strike level is marked with a triangle

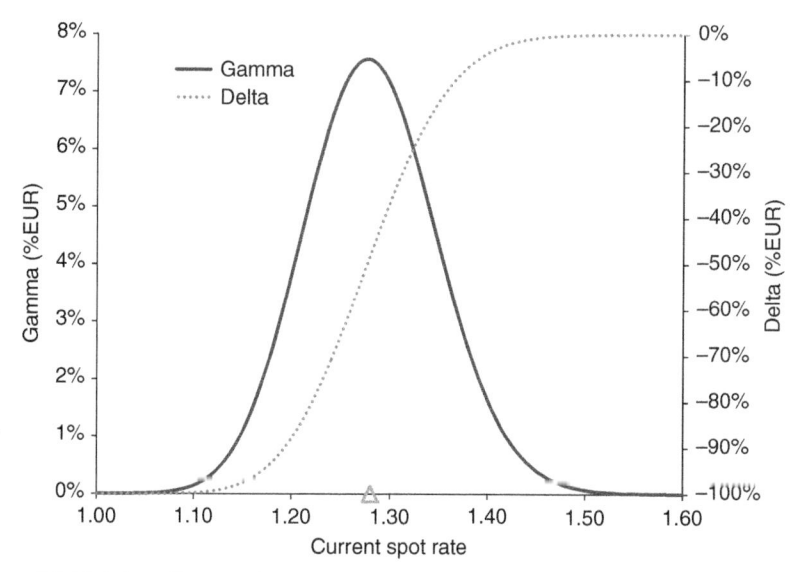

Figure 3.4 Variation with spot of gamma (full line, primary y-axis) for a six-month 1.28-strike EUR put/USD call vanilla option. The delta is shown alongside (dotted line, secondary y-axis. The strike level is marked with a triangle

The fact that Spot-Delta-in-Foreign varies monotonically between zero and (approximately) 100% of the Foreign principal makes it a very useful measure indeed. The simple limits allow us very easily to specify strike levels in a consistent way across all currency pairs, regardless of their spot and volatility levels and for any maturity. We simply need to think of a delta level between 0 and 1, such as 0.25, and convert it to strike – which we can do unambiguously because of the monotonic variation. My choice of delta value was far from arbitrary: the so-called **25-delta** level is ubiquitous in the FX options markets as a way to specify a strike that is "just nicely" out of the money. The 10% and 15% levels are also extremely commonly used to specify strike levels.

Given the FX market's tendency to quote strikes in terms of delta, the Black–Scholes formulae for the Spot-Delta-in-Foreign of vanilla options are extremely useful. Differentiating with respect to spot the value function given by Equations 2.72, 2.73 and 2.74, we get:

$$\frac{\partial V_{\text{vanilla}}}{\partial S} = \begin{cases} A_f e^{-r_f(T-t)} N(d_1) & \phi = +1 \\ -A_f e^{-r_f(T-t)} N(-d_1) & \phi = -1 \end{cases} \quad (3.3)$$

The simplicity of these results slightly belies the working required to obtain them, for which the following two relationships are extremely useful:

$$S e^{-r_f(T-t)} n(d_1) = K e^{-r_d(T-t)} n(d_2) \quad (3.4)$$

$$\frac{\partial}{\partial S}(d_1 - d_2) = 0 \quad (3.5)$$

The first of these relationships, Equation 3.4, can alternatively be written in the easily memorable form:

$$F n(d_1) = K n(d_2) \quad (3.6)$$

A common misconception is that delta represents the probability that an option will be exercised. Whilst for a vanilla option the delta and the probability of exercise are closely related, they are *not* the same quantity. And when it comes to barrier options, as we shall soon see, delta is not even bounded by zero and one, which completely debunks the idea that it corresponds to any kind of probability. In summary, I would advise against conflating the concepts of delta and exercise probability.

Let us now turn our attention to barrier options, and start by adding to our above-specified call option a lower knock-out barrier at 1.10. This barrier option has the delta profile shown in Figure 3.5. It is immediately clear that there is a large discontinuity in delta: across the barrier level of 1.20, the delta jumps

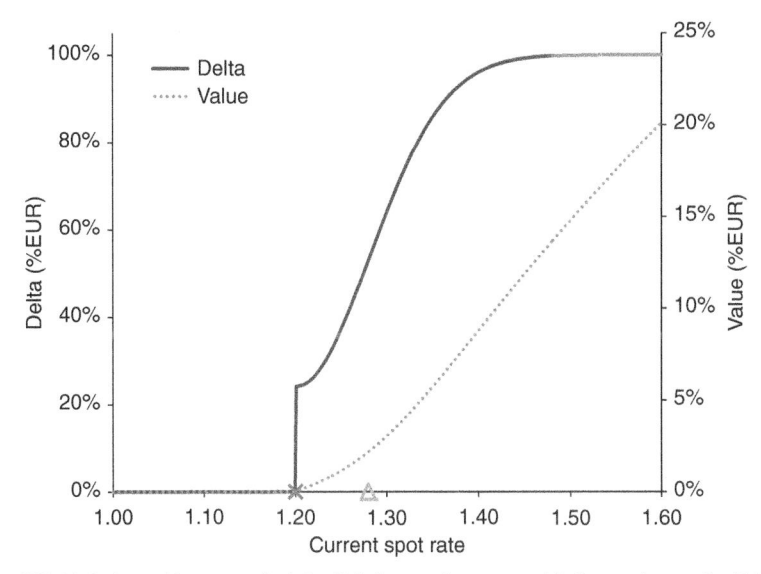

Figure 3.5 Variation with spot of delta (full line, primary y-axis) for a six-month EURUSD 1.28-strike EUR call/USD put option with down-side knock-out at 1.20. The value is shown alongside (dotted line, secondary y-axis). The strike level is marked with a triangle, the barrier level with a cross

discontinuously from zero to around 20%. Equivalently, we can state that the value function has a discontinuity in its gradient.

To understand the ramifications of this discontinuity, let us rehearse our delta-hedging strategy in the context of spot moving gradually downwards across the barrier level. To make the process more concrete, let us suppose that the option has a EUR principal of EUR 10 million. When the spot rate is 1.25, the delta is 30% in %EUR terms, so we need to hold a short position in EUR 3 million in order to delta-hedge the option. Now, as the spot rate gradually comes down from 1.25 to just over 1.20, where the option delta is around 20%, we need to gradually buy back EUR 1 million in order to bring our EUR position to short EUR 2 million. Then when spot crosses the barrier, we need to buy back all the remaining EUR 2 million – but this time it's not gradual! We must do the spot trade immediately, otherwise we are running a delta position through the EUR cash that we are short.

A discontinuity in delta such as we have just seen is known as a **delta gap**, and its presence presents a significant delta-hedging challenge. In practice, spot does not always move around slowly and smoothly (to put it mildly), so we cannot afford to assume that we will always be able to close out our delta hedge at a spot rate exactly equal to the barrier level. We must take the delta gap into account when calculating option values, and this is typically done using one of a set of techniques collectively known as **barrier over-hedging** methods, which we will discuss in Section 3.5.

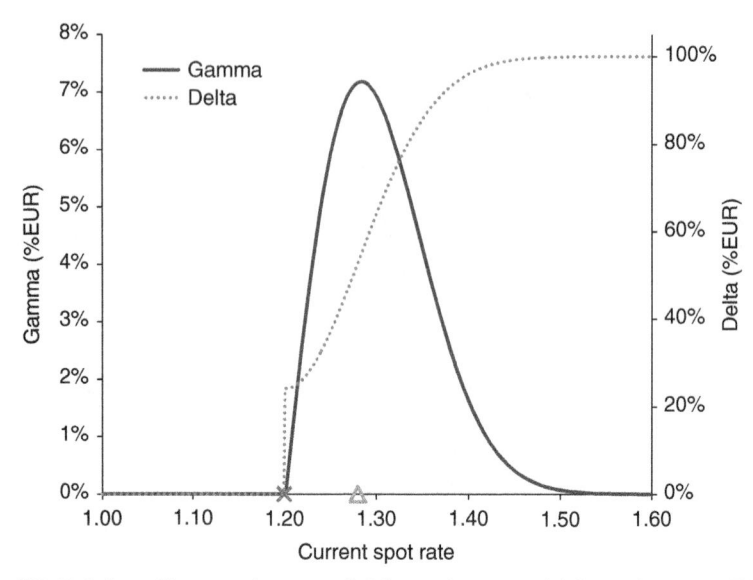

Figure 3.6 Variation with spot of gamma (full line, primary y-axis) for a six-month EURUSD 1.28-strike EUR call/USD put option with down-side knock-out at 1.20. The infinite gamma spike at the barrier level is not represented. The delta is shown alongside (dotted line, secondary y-axis). The strike level is marked with a triangle, the barrier level with a cross

The delta gap results in gamma being infinite when spot is at the barrier level. Figure 3.6 shows how the gamma varies with spot at all levels other than the barrier.

The delta and gamma profiles for a reverse knock-out call are shown Figures 3.7 and 3.8. Again, the delta profile shows a very large gap, but this time it is *negative*. The entire delta profile changes sign: at low spot levels far from the barrier, the delta is positive (as for a vanilla option), whilst at high spot levels near the barrier, the delta goes negative. Naturally, this means that there is a spot level at which the delta is zero.

I have often heard it remarked that it is counter-intuitive that a call option can ever have a negative delta, even in the presence of barriers. If we have sold such an option, the argument goes, our delta hedge when spot is near the barrier and will be a *short* position in the Foreign currency, even though settlement would only ever involve us having to deliver Foreign currency, for which we would need to be *long* the Foreign currency. But this is to fall into the trap of regarding delta as some kind of "preparation of funds for delivery" – it is not. It is a *through-the-life* hedging mechanism, and we do not need to prepare our funds for delivery until the option is just about to expire. And at that time, the delta profile looks rather different, as illustrated by Figure 3.9. The profile is essentially discretized now, and it tells us the following: if spot lies below the strike, delta is zero because we won't have to deliver any euros. If spot lies between the strike and the barrier, delta is 100% because

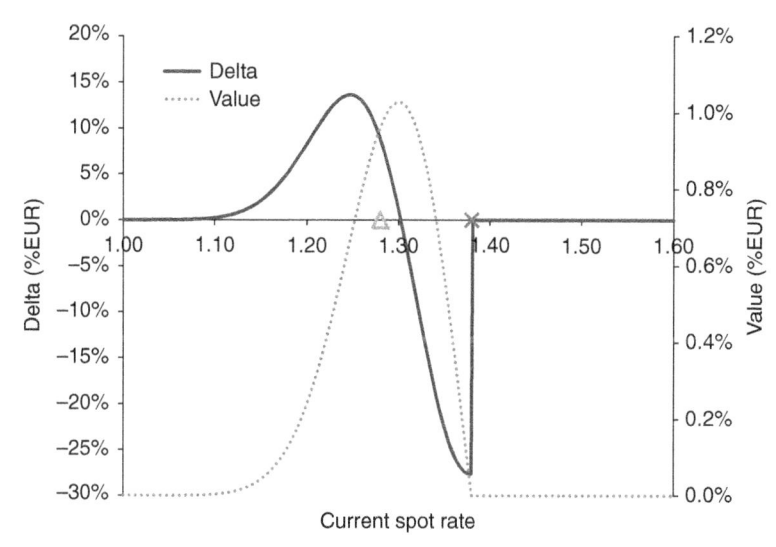

Figure 3.7 Variation with spot of delta (full line, primary y-axis) for a six-month EURUSD 1.28-strike EUR call/USD put option with up-side knock-out at 1.38. The value is shown alongside (dotted line, secondary y-axis). The strike level is marked with a triangle, the barrier level with a cross

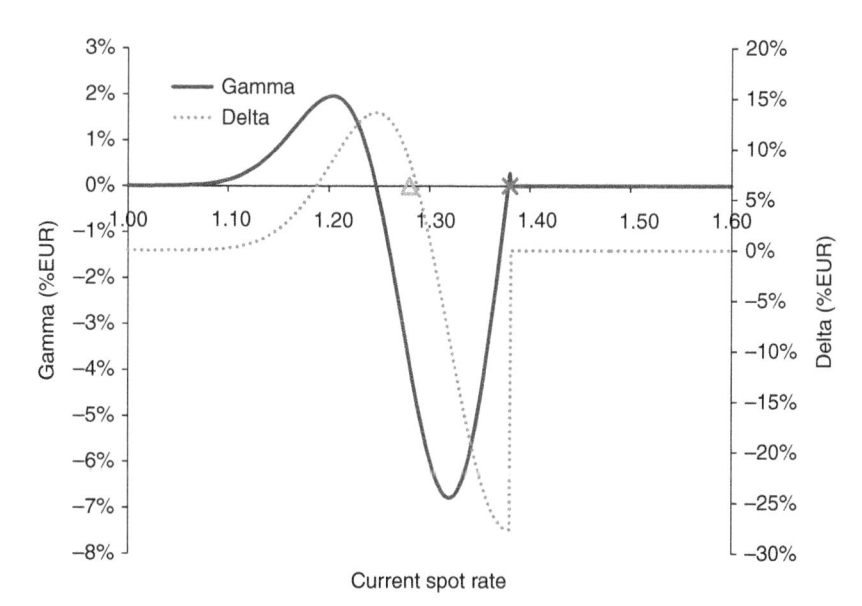

Figure 3.8 Variation with spot of gamma (full line, primary y-axis) for a six-month EURUSD 1.28-strike EUR call/USD put option with up-side knock-out at 1.38. The infinite gamma spike at the barrier level is not represented. The delta is shown alongside (dotted line, secondary y-axis). The strike level is marked with a triangle, the barrier level with a cross

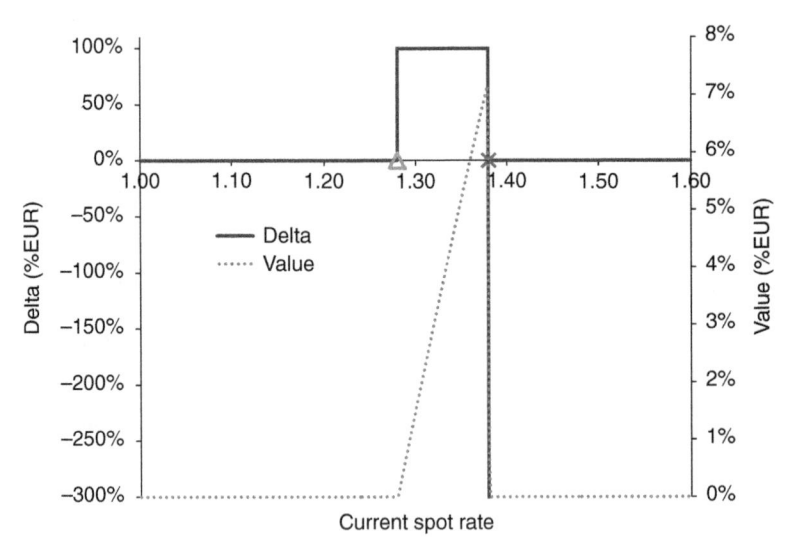

Figure 3.9 Variation with spot of value and delta for a one-minute EURUSD 1.28-strike EUR call/USD put option with up-side knock-out at 1.38

we will certainly have to deliver the EUR principal. If spot is above the barrier, delta is again zero, because again we won't have to deliver any euros. Only in the highly singular case of spot hovering *just* below the barrier level *just* before expiry do we still have a negative spike – and that is fine. It is fine theoretically speaking, because our option's value really is still changing with spot and must continued to be delta-hedged. And it is fine practically speaking, because when we really are 1 minute before expiry and offer-side spot is just a few ticks below the barrier, we have no practical way to continue delta-hedging. At that point, we are essentially presiding over a binary bet: either the barrier does not trigger, and we exchange cash flows whose net value is around 7% of EUR principal, or the barrier does trigger and no payments are made.

My reference to "binary bets" above is not accidental: the situation for reverse knock-outs is very similar to that for barrier-contingent payments, which, as we noted in Section 1.6, are also called American binaries or American bets. The barrier-contingent payment analogous to a reverse knock-out call option is an up-side no-touch, and Figures 3.10 and 3.11 show the delta and gamma profiles for a six-month EURUSD 1.38 high-side no-touch, paying in EUR. As we expected, in the region of the barrier level, the delta and gamma of the barrier-contingent payment are qualitatively similar to those for the reverse knock-out. Quantitatively, the barrier-contingent payment has a far larger %EUR value than the barrier-contingent vanilla, and consequently the spot Greeks are also far larger in magnitude for the barrier-contingent payment.

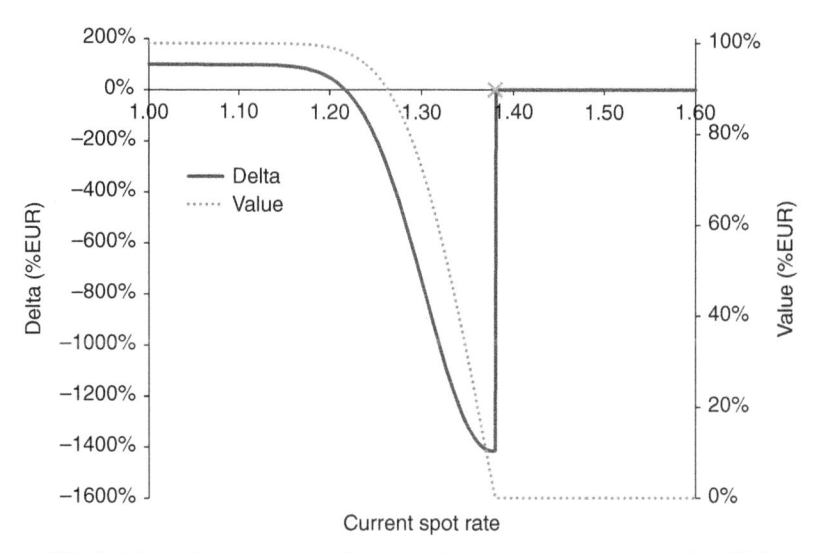

Figure 3.10 Variation with spot of delta (full line, primary y-axis) for a six-month EURUSD 1.38 high-side no-touch, paying in EUR. The value is shown alongside (dotted line, secondary y-axis). The barrier level is marked with a cross

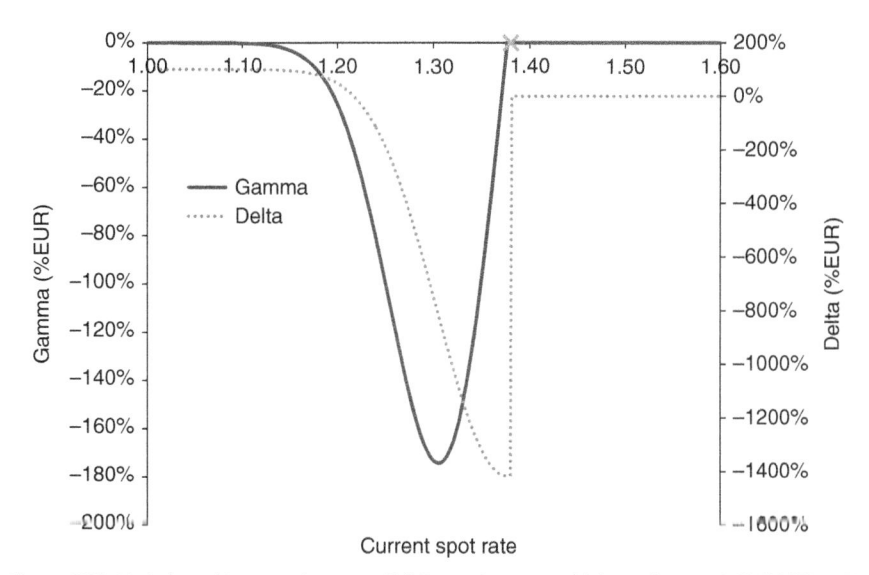

Figure 3.11 Variation with spot of gamma (full line, primary y-axis) for a six-month EURUSD 1.38 high-side no-touch, paying in EUR. The delta is shown alongside (dotted line, secondary y-axis). The barrier level is marked with a cross

Double no-touches have delta gaps at both barriers, as illustrated by Figures 3.12 and 3.13, which show the delta and gamma of a six-month USDTRY double no-touch.

96 | FX Barrier Options

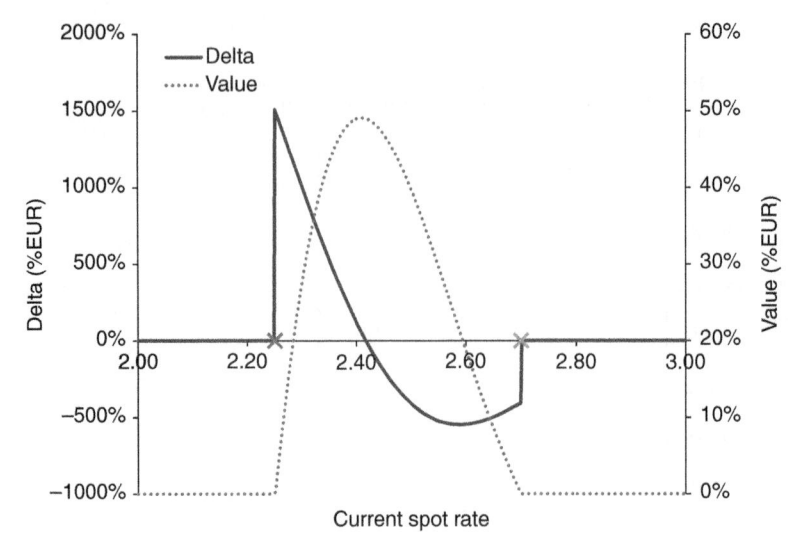

Figure 3.12 Variation with spot of delta (full line, primary y-axis) for a six-month USDTRY double no-touch with barriers at 2.25 and 2.70, paying in USD. The value is shown alongside (dotted line, secondary y-axis). The barrier levels are marked with crosses

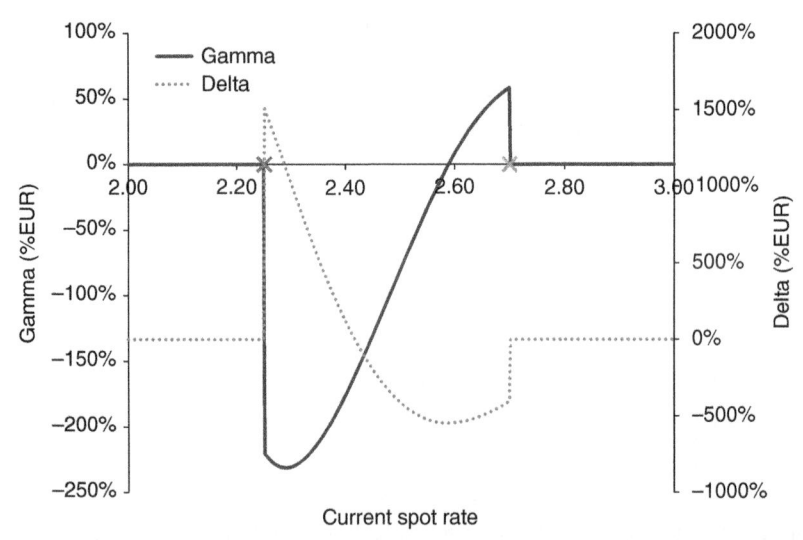

Figure 3.13 Variation with spot of gamma (full line, primary y-axis) for a six-month USDTRY double no-touch with barriers at 2.25 and 2.70, paying in USD. The delta is shown alongside (dotted line, secondary y-axis). The barrier levels are marked with crosses

3.1.5 Non-local spot risk analysis

Non-local spot risk analysis involves examination of the behaviour of an option as spot changes by *large* amounts. We have already effectively been performing such analysis: we have been plotting our numerous graphs of value profiles and Greek profiles against widely varying levels of spot. But whilst these plotted profiles are very good for heuristic purposes, they do not really help for *quantitative* risk analysis, especially at the portfolio level, where we need to add, subtract and compare numeric results for values and Greeks. For such purposes, a far better approach is to simply compute the values and Greeks at multiple regularly spaced spot levels and display the results in a table. The table is called a **spot risk report**, or colloquially a **spot ladder**.

Whilst this is a very simple method in principle, some care is needed to optimize the scope and the resolution of the spot ladder. In a typical risk management system, the bounds of the spot ladder (the minimum and maximum spot levels) and the number of spot levels (or **rungs**) in the ladder will be configurable, to allow the risk-manager to obtain a useful report. Spot ladders are most often run for an entire portfolio, not for individual contracts, but for the purposes of illustration, Figure 3.14 shows the spot ladder for a EURUSD reverse knock-out. Note how the effect of the reverse knock-out barrier at 1.38 is clear to see: the value goes gradually to zero, delta becomes negative and shows a large gap at the barrier, and gamma shows a huge spike at the barrier. Value-conditional formatting, such as red colouring for negative values, is often employed to improve the readability of a spot ladder.

3.2 Volatility risk

Black–Scholes volatility risk is a fundamentally different concept from spot risk, for the following reason: the Black–Scholes model assumes that spot moves around, so it is entirely natural and sensible to ask what happens to the value of an option when spot moves. However, the model inherently assumes that volatility is constant, so how can it then make sense to try and compute the change in option value due to a change in volatility? We can make partial sense of the situation by saying that we are effectively considering an infinite *family* of Black–Scholes models, each with its own volatility, and asking what happens if we switch from one model to another one (nearby for local risk, or distant for non-local risk). I say "partial sense", because this interpretation opens a can of worms: if volatility can move around, which volatility should we use to calculate the option price? We will explore the ramifications of this question thoroughly in Chapter 4, but for now, let us sweep the issue under the carpet by simply assuming that we know the volatility and are just wondering what life would be like under a different one.

98 | FX Barrier Options

Spot	Value(USD)	Delta(USD)	Gamma(USD)
1.10	19	1,352	892
1.11	35	2,438	1,520
1.12	65	4,234	2,486
1.13	114	7,084	3,903
1.14	194	11,429	5,882
1.15	320	17,787	8,504
1.16	510	26,714	11,787
1.17	789	38,726	15,639
1.18	1,181	54,193	19,815
1.19	1,716	73,193	23,889
1.20	2,419	95,364	27,242
1.21	3,310	119,763	29,091
1.22	4,399	144,772	28,567
1.23	5,678	168,091	24,827
1.24	7,118	186,834	17,215
1.25	8,669	197,763	5,423
1.26	10,253	197,635	−10,357
1.27	11,770	183,643	−29,341
1.28	13,105	153,880	−50,141
1.29	14,134	107,764	−70,854
1.30	14,739	46,336	−89,257
1.31	14,818	−27,633	−103,081
1.32	14,301	−109,762	−110,325
1.33	13,154	−194,420	−109,562
1.34	11,391	−275,281	−100,176
1.35	9,075	−345,998	−82,493
1.36	6,308	−400,913	−57,774
1.37	3,231	−435,680	−28,073
1.38	4	−223,865	447,729,490
1.39	0	0	0
1.40	0	0	0

Figure 3.14 Spot ladder for a six-month 1.28 strike EUR call/USD put with an upside knock-out at 1.38

3.2.1 Local volatility risk analysis

In practical terms, we compute Black–Scholes local volatility risk[1] very much as we do for spot risk. Where we can analytically derive a formula for the value of an

---

[1] The "local" refers to the risk, not the volatility, and this discussion has nothing to do with local volatility in the sense described in Chapter 4!

option, we can simply differentiate that formula with respect to volatility to get the **mathematical vega**:

$$\text{mathematical vega} \doteq \frac{\partial V}{\partial \sigma} \qquad (3.7)$$

Vega is another example of an option Greek – despite the fact that no such letter of the Greek alphabet exists!

Like mathematical gamma, mathematical vega is not a very useful risk measure, corresponding as it does to an unrealistic volatility move of 100%. The volatility risk ratio used in practice is one which scales the mathematical vega to correspond to a change in volatility of 1%. (For the avoidance of doubt, this means an absolute change of 1%, not a relative change of 1%. For example, a volatility of 7% would change to 8%, not 7.07%.) We will call this risk ratio the **practitioner vega**, and it is defined by:

$$\text{practitioner vega} \doteq \frac{1}{100} \frac{\partial V}{\partial \sigma} \qquad (3.8)$$

It is commonly stated loosely that the practitioner vega measures the change in value for a 1% move in volatility. Though roughly true, this is not quite accurate: we do not shift the volatility by 1% and recalculate the value – that would strictly be a non-local risk measure. (Indeed, in a low-volatility environment, a change in volatility of 1% might constitute a paradigm shift.) As described above, we calculate the local risk sensitivity and then *scale* it up.

An estimate of the difference between the local volatility risk (practitioner vega) and the non-local volatility risk (got by actually shifting volatility by 1% and re-calculating the value) can of course be obtained by looking at the second derivative of the option value with respect to volatility $\frac{\partial^2 V}{\partial \sigma^2}$. A Taylor expansion makes this explicit:

$$V(\sigma + 1\%) - V(\sigma) \simeq \frac{\partial V}{\partial \sigma} \times 1\% + \frac{1}{2} \frac{\partial^2 V}{\partial \sigma^2} \times 0.01\% \qquad (3.9)$$

Partly for this reason, the second derivative of value with respect to volatility is a quantity of great significance in option risk management, and by analogy with gamma, this option Greek is given the name: **volgamma**. Volgamma also goes by a remarkable variety of other names, such as "volga", "gamma of vol", "gamma of vega", "dVega", "vomma", "d-Vega-d-Vol" and "vol convexity", but "volgamma" is the term I shall use. The definition of practitioner volgamma is:

$$\text{practitioner volgamma} \doteq \frac{1}{10,000} \frac{\partial^2 V}{\partial \sigma^2} \qquad (3.10)$$

I wrote "partly for this reason" in the previous paragraph because there is another reason why we are very interested in volgamma, and it is in fact much more significant. Let us recall our discussion of the gamma term of the Black–Scholes option pricing PDE in Section 2.3.4. There, we saw that the option gamma (second order spot risk) is intimately connected with the value of an option. Specifically, a positive gamma contributes to a systematically positive change in the value of the delta-hedged portfolio. Option gamma is worth something, and we are willing to pay for it. If that is the case under a model in which spot is stochastic and volatility is constant, we can intuitively deduce that if we were to use a model in which volatility is also stochastic, we would expect the option value to be intimately connected with volgamma. We shall see in Chapter 4 that that is indeed the case.

3.2.1.1 Results for vega and volgamma

Figure 3.15 shows the variation with spot of the vega of a six-month 1.28-strike EUR call/USD put vanilla option. The prominent bell-shaped curve with a peak around the strike is a key feature of all vanilla options. Let us try to bring our intuition to bear on this result. The fact that vega is everywhere positive tells us that an increase in volatility *always* increases the value of a vanilla option. This is exactly consistent with our discussion in Section 2.7.5. There we noted that either an increase in time to maturity or an increase in volatility widens the risk-neutral probability distribution of terminal spot, and that, due to the asymmetric nature of the vanilla payoff, this always increases the value of the option. At spot levels far

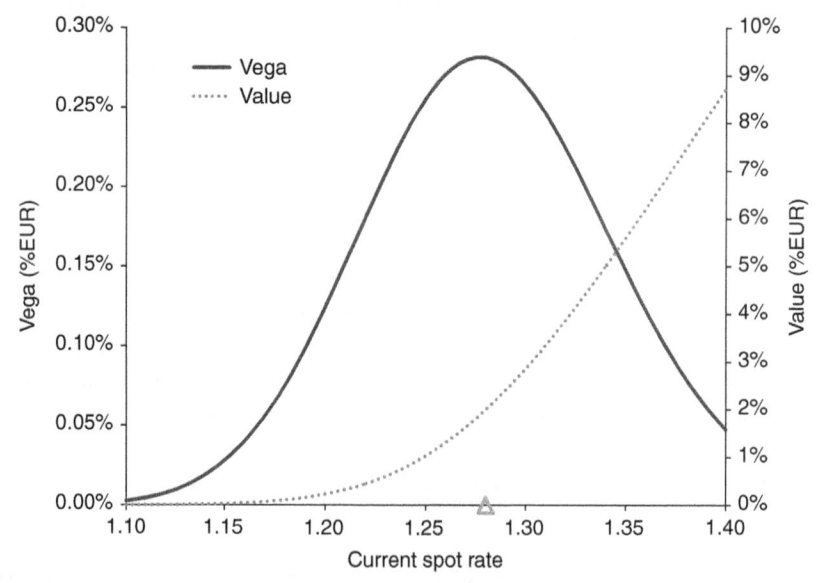

Figure 3.15 Variation with spot of the vega (full line, primary *y*-axis) of a six-month 1.28-strike EUR call/USD put vanilla option. The value is plotted alongside (dotted line, secondary *y*-axis). The strike level is marked with a triangle

below the strike, the option value is close to zero, and an increase in volatility can only increase the value a tiny amount, hence the low vega. At spot levels far above the strike, the option behaves increasingly like a forward, with a linear payoff that is unaffected by volatility, again leading to a low vega.

It is clear to see that the vega profile is very similar to the gamma profile. A degree of similarity exists for all option types, which is no coincidence – there is a fundamental mathematical relationship between the two Greeks. This relationship has been derived and discussed by Mercurio [23], and his result can be written in the following form:

$$\sigma \frac{\partial V}{\partial \sigma} = \sigma^2 (T-t) S^2 \frac{\partial^2 V}{\partial S^2} + 2(r_d - r_f)\left[(T-t)S\frac{\partial V}{\partial S} + \frac{\partial V}{\partial r_f}\right] \quad (3.11)$$

Mercurio also shows that for European options (such as vanilla options), the result simplifies to:

$$\sigma \frac{\partial V}{\partial \sigma} = \sigma^2 (T-t) S^2 \frac{\partial^2 V}{\partial S^2} \quad (3.12)$$

which demonstrates mathematically the close similarity between the vega and gamma profiles. From an intuitive point of view, we can say that gamma effectively quantifies how much money can be made as a result of random movements in spot in the immediate future, whilst vega effectively tells us how much money can be made from random movements in spot in the future (as-yet-unrealized gamma).

The vega of the corresponding put option is exactly the same as for the call. This can easily by seen by recalling the principle of put–call parity, as expressed by Equation 1.17. The value of a forward has no dependence on volatility, so the put and call *must* have exactly the same vega.

Figure 3.16 displays the variation with spot of the volgamma of the same option. The double bell shape is another hallmark of vanilla options. What does it tell us? Well, the very low volgamma around the strike tells us that the value of an at-the-money vanilla option varies linearly with volatility (up to second order). We have seen this fact already: in Figure 2.6, the option struck at 1.2647 is at the money, and sure enough, its value increases linearly with volatility. Meanwhile, the positive peaks on either side of the strike tell us that both in-the-money and out-of-the-money vanilla options have a positive convexity with respect to volatility, which is again illustrated nicely by Figure 2.6. The volgamma falls away again at very low and very high spot levels because the vega itself is getting very small.

It is often found harder to get an intuitive feel for volgamma than for say vega or the spot Greeks. I find the following method of analysis to be a good way of bringing intuition to bear on volgamma:

- Think of volatility moves as either *value-adding* or *value-subtracting*. When vega is positive, an increase in volatility is value-adding, and a decrease in volatility is

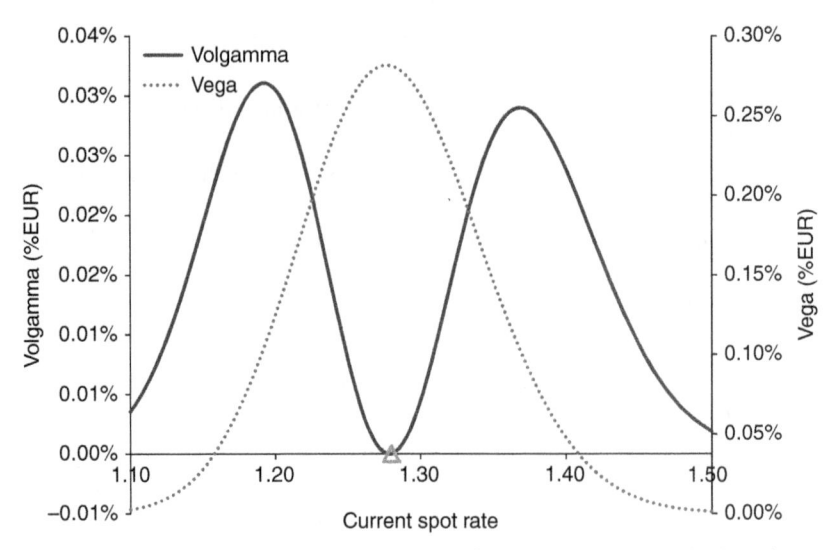

Figure 3.16 Variation with spot of the volgamma (full line, primary y-axis) of a six-month 1.28-strike EUR call/USD put vanilla option. The vega is plotted alongside (dotted line, secondary y-axis). The strike level is marked with a triangle

value-subtracting. Conversely, when vega is negative, an increase in volatility is value-subtracting, and a decrease in volatility is value-adding.
- A *positive* volgamma means that the valued added by a value-adding move in volatility is *greater* than the value subtracted by the (same-sized) value-subtracting move in volatility.
- A *negative* volgamma means that the valued added by a value-adding move in volatility is *less* than the value subtracted by the (same-sized) value-subtracting move in volatility.

Let's call this approach the **volgamma heuristic**. We will apply it to various different cases as we go along.

Adding a low-side barrier to obtain a normal knock-out call, we obtain the vega and volgamma profiles shown in Figures 3.17 and 3.18. At high spot levels, where the likelihood of triggering the barrier is low and the option is similar to a vanilla, the vega and volgamma profiles both have much the same form as for the corresponding vanilla, as expected. But as spot comes down towards the barrier, there are two competing effects in play: an increase in volatility on the one hand contributes value via the vanilla aspect of the payoff, but on the other hand makes knock-out more likely, which has a detractive effect on the value of the option. In the present case, this balance of effects causes the vega to fall steeply as spot approaches the barrier, hitting zero at the barrier level.

Black–Scholes Risk Management | 103

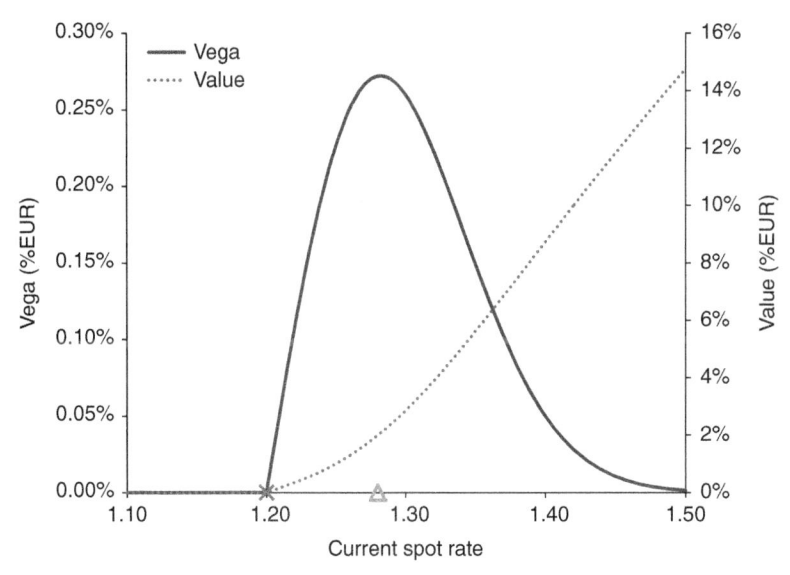

Figure 3.17 Variation with spot of the vega (full line, primary y-axis) of a six-month 1.28-strike EUR call/USD put option with a down-side knock-out at 1.20. The value is plotted alongside (dotted line, secondary y-axis). The strike level is marked with a triangle, the barrier level with a cross

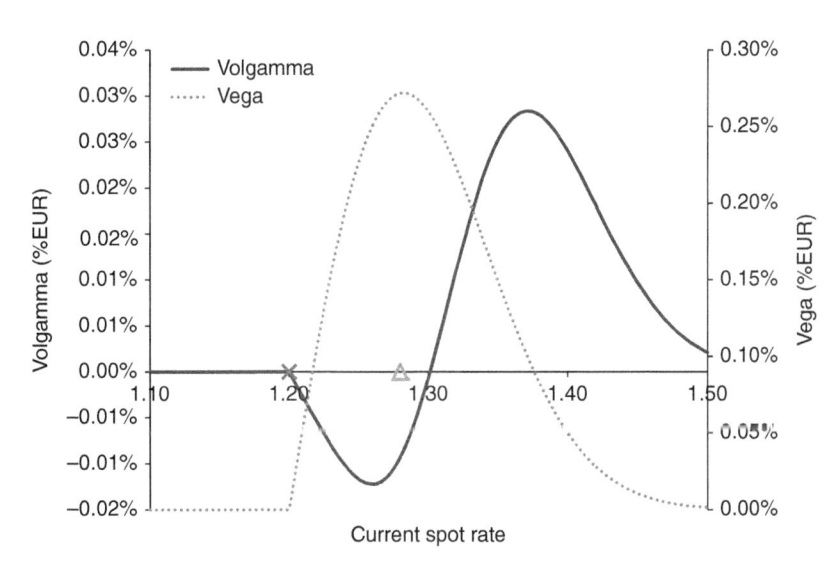

Figure 3.18 Variation with spot of the volgamma (full line, primary y-axis) of a six-month 1.28-strike EUR call/USD put option with a down-side knock-out at 1.20. The vega is plotted alongside (dotted line, secondary y-axis). The strike level is marked with a triangle, the barrier level with a cross

The volgamma profile meanwhile goes substantially negative in a region between the barrier and just above the strike. Applying the volgamma heuristic described above, and keeping in mind that the vega is positive, we can interpret this negative volgamma as follows: the value added by an increase in volatility is less than the value subtracted by the (same-size) decrease in volatility. In terms of the two competing effects at play, this can be understood as showing that the knock-out effect has a strong negative volgamma (since we know that the volgamma of the vanilla aspect is positive nearly everywhere).

Can the vega of a normal knock-out go negative? Yes, in certain circumstances, and the crucial relevant quantity is the *forward*. If spot is close to the barrier but the forward is in the money, the optimal scenario (that is, the one which results in the greatest option value) is one in which volatility is very small or even zero. (In the latter case, the option value would be equal to its intrinsic value.) In such a scenario, an increase in volatility above its optimal level will reduce the value of the option, leading to a negative vega. This is a good illustration of how option valuation is affected by both spot drift (represented by the forward) and spot randomness (represented by the volatility), two effects which are in this case competing.

Given the very low interest rates of EUR and USD, the six-month forward is very close to spot, so when spot is close to the barrier level of 1.20, the forward is around 1.201 – well out of the money for a 1.28 strike. But let us hypothesize for a moment that the USD interest rate rose to 15%. The forward rate (with spot at 1.20) would then be 1.29 – nicely in the money for a 1.28 strike. The vega and volgamma profiles for such a hypothetical market are shown in Figures 3.19 and 3.20, and the negative vega is clear to see. The value profile itself is noticeably different too, and in fact has a negative gamma in a small region above the barrier level.

When it comes to reverse knock-outs, negative vega arises as a matter of course, as shown by Figures 3.21 and 3.22 (the USD interest rate is back to normal now). This is straightforward to understand intuitively: when spot is near the barrier, the payoff is almost as high as it can ever be, so an increase in volatility has relatively little effect on the vanilla aspect of the payoff. However, an increase in volatility substantially increases the likelihood of triggering the barrier, which would eliminate the entire payoff, and it therefore has a substantial negative effect on the option value. The net effect is that the option value decreases substantially when volatility increases, hence the substantially negative vega.

As spot moves, the balance shifts back and forth between the positive volgamma due to the vanilla aspect and the negative volgamma due to the knock-out, giving rise to regions of positive and negative volgamma, as illustrated by Figures 3.23 and 3.24.

As we discussed in the context of the spot Greeks, there are similarities between the payoff spike of a reverse knock-out and that of a barrier-contingent payment, such as a no-touch. However, a no-touch has no optionality or strike, and there is only one effect in play – the barrier knock-out – which makes it a much easier

Black–Scholes Risk Management | 105

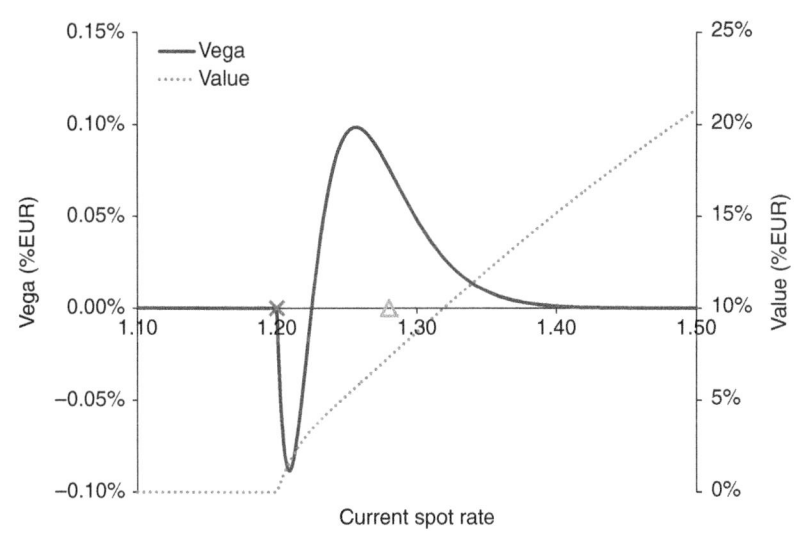

Figure 3.19 Variation with spot of the vega (full line, primary y-axis) of a six-month 1.28-strike EUR call/USD put option with a down-side knock-out at 1.20. **The USD interest rate is artificially set to 15%.** The value is plotted alongside (dotted line, secondary y-axis). The strike level is marked with a triangle, the barrier with a cross

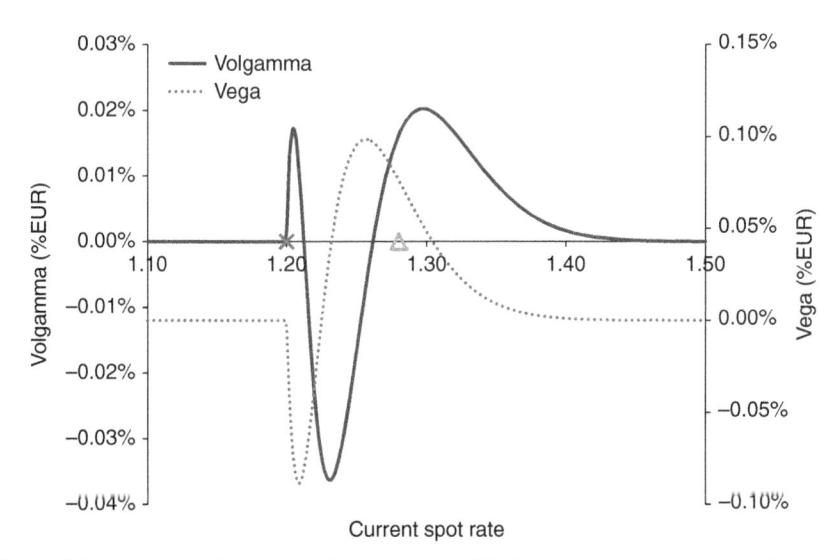

Figure 3.20 Variation with spot of the volgamma (full line, primary y-axis) of a six-month 1.28-strike EUR call/USD put option with a down-side knock-out at 1.20. **The USD interest rate is artificially set to 15%.** The vega is plotted alongside (dotted line, secondary y-axis). The strike level is marked with a triangle, the barrier with a cross

106 | FX Barrier Options

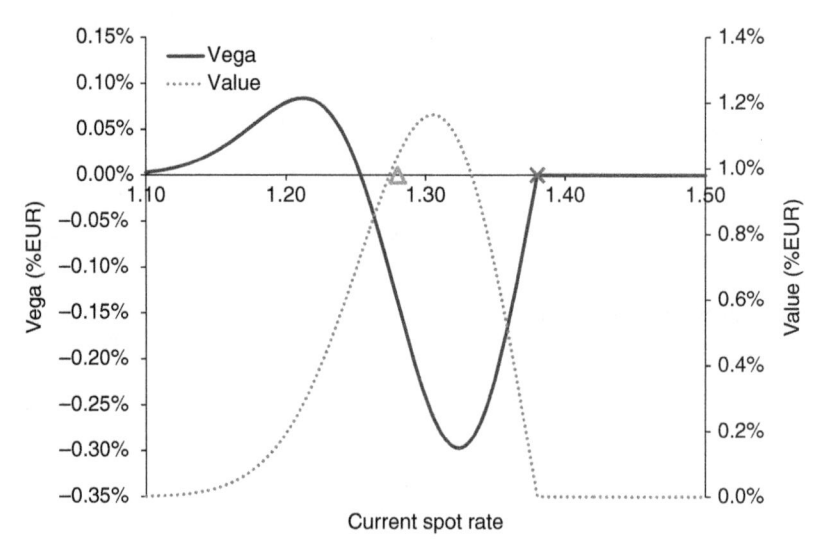

Figure 3.21 Variation with spot of the vega (full line, primary y-axis) of a six-month 1.28-strike EUR call/USD put option with an up-side knock-out at 1.38. The value is plotted alongside (dotted line, secondary y-axis). The strike level is marked with a triangle, the barrier with a cross

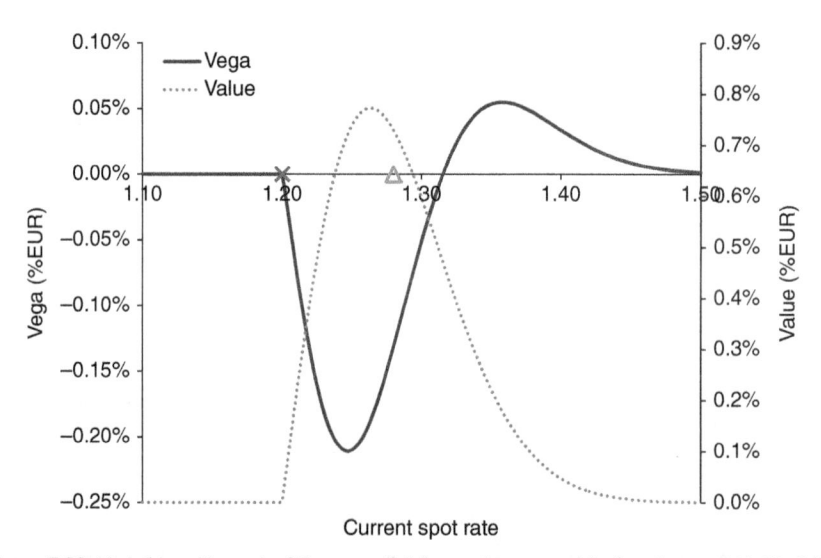

Figure 3.22 Variation with spot of the vega (full line, primary y-axis) of a six-month 1.28-strike EUR put/USD call option with a down-side knock-out at 1.20. The value is plotted alongside (dotted line, secondary y-axis). The strike level is marked with a triangle, the barrier with a cross

Black–Scholes Risk Management | 107

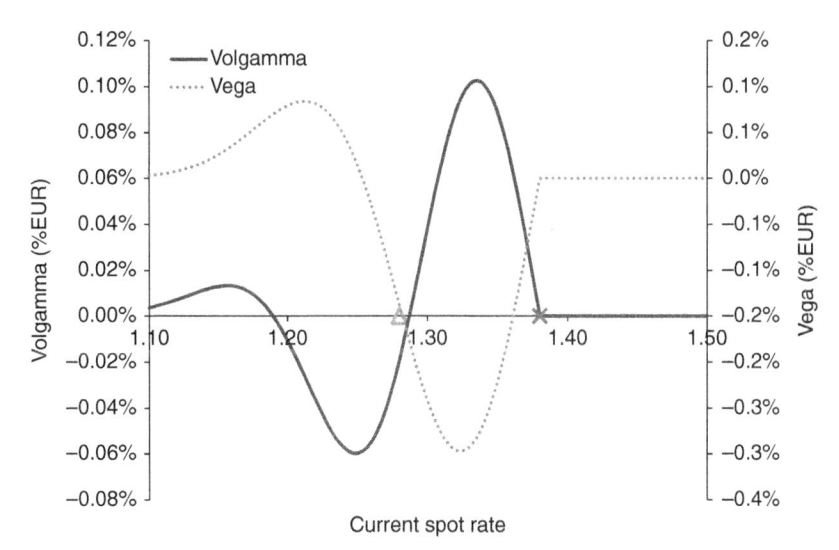

Figure 3.23 Variation with spot of the volgamma (full line, primary y-axis) of a six-month 1.28-strike EUR call/USD put option with an up-side knock-out at 1.38. The vega is plotted alongside (dotted line, secondary y-axis). The strike level is marked with a triangle, the barrier with a cross

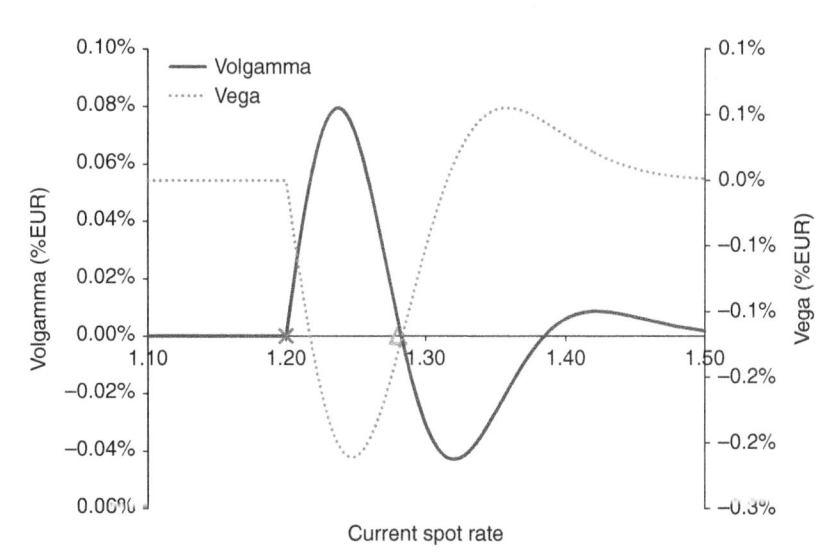

Figure 3.24 Variation with spot of the volgamma (full line, primary y-axis) of a six-month 1.28-strike EUR put/USD call option with a down-side knock-out at 1.20. The vega is plotted alongside (dotted line, secondary y-axis). The strike level is marked with a triangle, the barrier with a cross

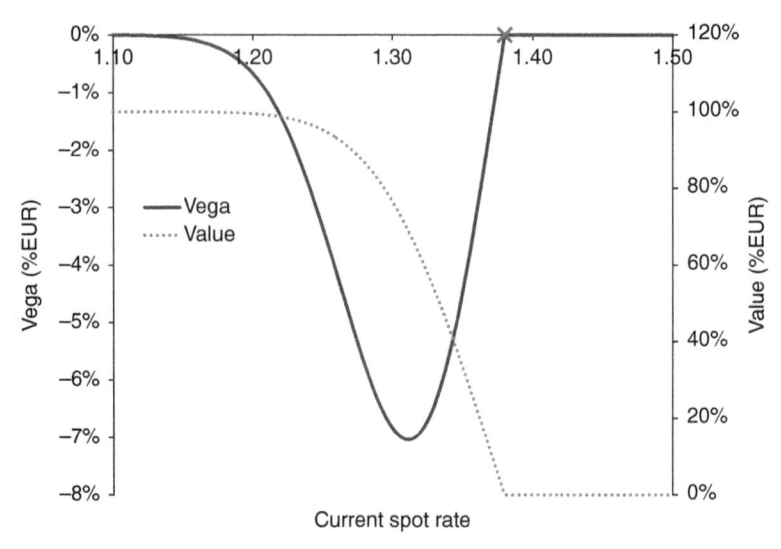

Figure 3.25 Variation with spot of the vega (full line, primary *y*-axis) of a six-month EURUSD 1.38 high-side no-touch paying in EUR. The value is plotted alongside (dotted line, secondary *y*-axis). The barrier level is marked with a cross

contract to analyse. Higher volatility is *never* beneficial for a no-touch, since its sole effect is to increase the likelihood of knock-out, and thus reduce the value of the option. We would therefore expect the vega to be negative everywhere. That is indeed the case, as demonstrated by Figure 3.25, which shows the vega for a six-month EURUSD 1.38 high-side no-touch, paying in EUR. What about the volgamma? Let us again try to analyse it using the volgamma heuristic. When spot is far from the barrier, the option value is close to its maximum, so there is very little scope for the value to increase, but plenty of scope for the value to decrease. A value-subtracting move in volatility is therefore bound to have a greater effect than a value-adding move, which means a negative volgamma. Conversely, when spot is close to the barrier, the option value is close to zero, so there is very little scope for the value to decrease, but plenty of scope for the value to increase. A value-adding move in volatility is therefore bound to have a greater effect than a value-subtracting move, which means a positive volgamma. This is all borne out by the volgamma profile shown in Figure 3.26. The final contract type for which we will examine vega and volgamma is the double no-touch. Once again, we expect the vega to be negative everywhere, since it can never be value-adding to increase the volatility. The exact shape of the vega profile varies somewhat depending on the distance between the barriers. If the barriers are not too far apart, as is the case for the highly liquid 10%-price contract, the vega will take the simple form of a trough, mirroring the peak-shaped form of the value profile. This is demonstrated by Figure 3.27. However, if the barriers are sufficiently far apart, there will be a

Black–Scholes Risk Management | 109

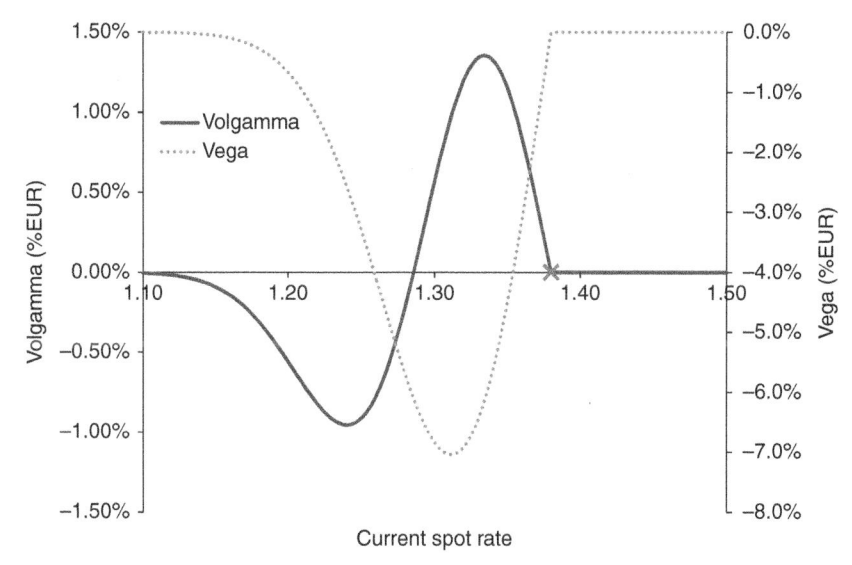

Figure 3.26 Variation with spot of the volgamma (full line, primary y-axis) of a six-month EURUSD 1.38 high-side no-touch paying in EUR. The vega is plotted alongside (dotted line, secondary y-axis). The barrier level is marked with a cross

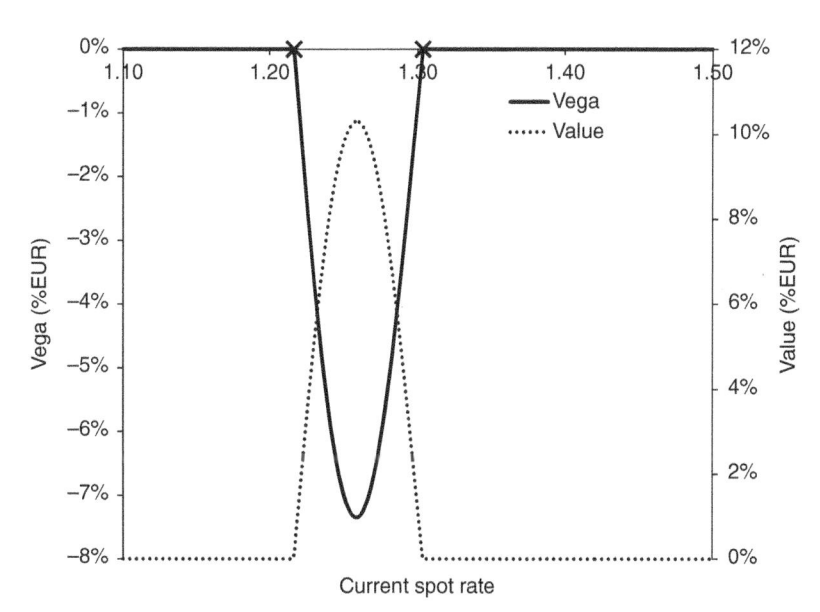

Figure 3.27 Variation with spot of the vega (full line, primary y-axis) of a six-month EURUSD 1.22/1.30 (10% price) double no-touch paying in EUR. The value is plotted alongside (dotted line, secondary y-axis). The barrier levels are marked with crosses

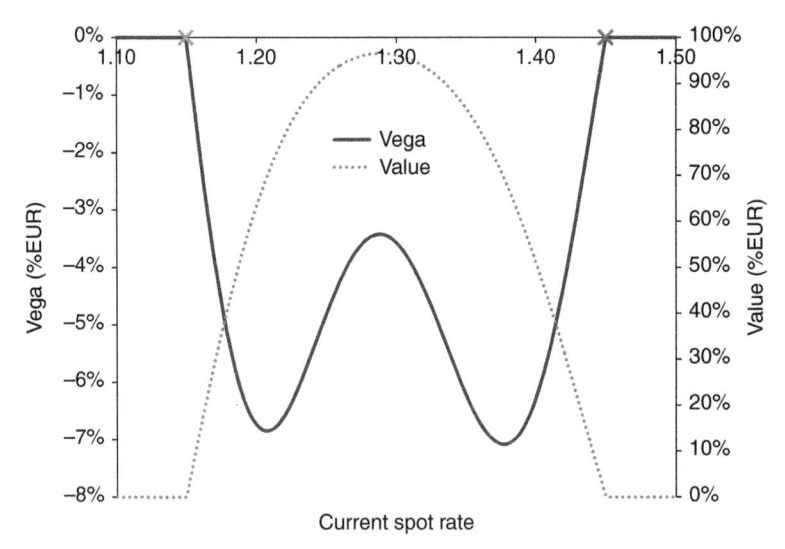

Figure 3.28 Variation with spot of the vega (full line, primary y-axis) of a six-month EURUSD 1.15/1.45 double no-touch paying in EUR. The value is plotted alongside (dotted line, secondary y-axis). The barrier levels are marked with crosses

region in the middle where knock-out is very unlikely, the value is close to 100%, a change in volatility has little effect, and the vega is small. This results in a "dimple" in the trough, as illustrated by Figure 3.28.

Unsurprisingly, the shape of the volgamma profile also varies according to barrier separation. Let us again use the volgamma heuristic to contemplate its form. When spot is in the vicinity of a barrier, and the value is low, there is much more scope for volatility to add value (by falling) than to remove it (by rising), so volgamma is positive. When spot is halfway between the barriers, and the value is neither very low nor near 100%, there is roughly equal scope for volatility to either add or remove value, so we can expect scenarios in which the volgamma is positive, negative or zero. Figures 3.29 and 3.30 show how all these scenarios arise.

Scanning through the various volgamma profiles above reveals stark differences in the *magnitude* of this Greek for different contracts. In particular, the volgamma of double no-touches is very large in magnitude: over 4% for the 10%-price contract. For comparison, the volgamma profile for the vanillas had a maximum absolute value of 0.03%, whilst for knock-outs the volgamma was never larger in size than 0.1%. As a general rule, *large volgamma is a feature of all double no-touches*.

3.2.1.2 Vanna

Just as our all-important delta varies with spot (at a rate measured by gamma), so delta also varies with volatility. Even if spot remains constant, we will need to re-delta-hedge our option if volatility moves. The rate at which delta changes with

Black–Scholes Risk Management | 111

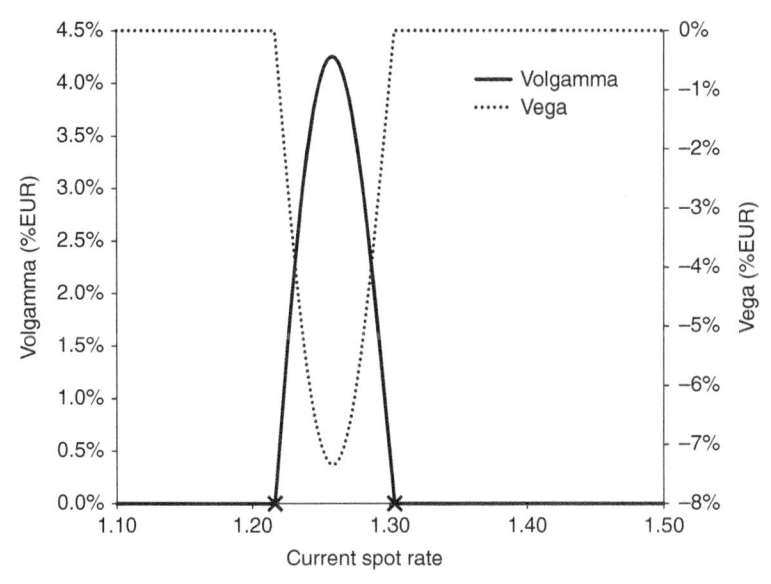

Figure 3.29 Variation with spot of the volgamma (full line, primary y-axis) of a six-month EURUSD 1.22/1.30 (10% price) double no-touch paying in EUR. The vega is plotted alongside (dotted line, secondary y-axis). The barrier levels are marked with crosses

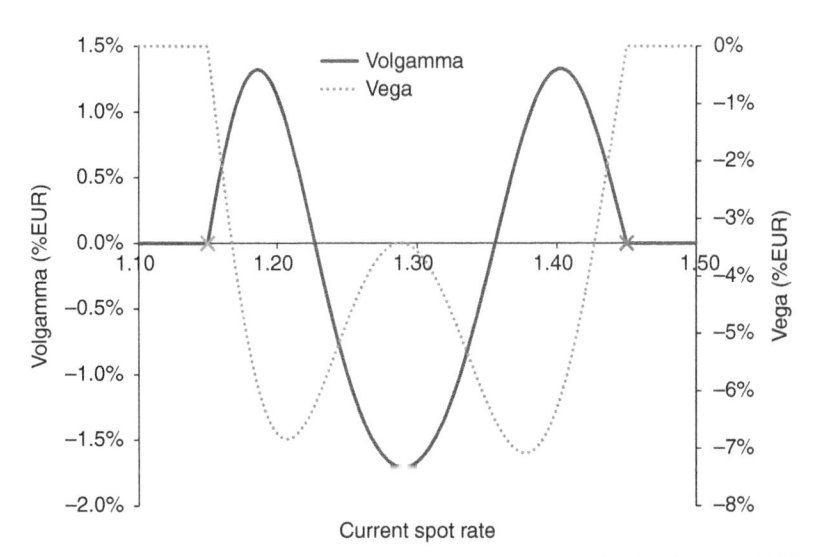

Figure 3.30 Variation with spot of the volgamma (full line, primary y-axis) of a six-month EURUSD 1.15/1.45 double no-touch paying in EUR. The vega is plotted alongside (dotted line, secondary y-axis). The barrier levels are marked with crosses

respect to volatility is measured by a Greek called **vanna**. (As with vega, no such letter actually exists in the Greek alphabet.) Vanna is defined along the same lines as practitioner vega, computing the local sensitivity of delta to volatility and scaling to represent the effect of a 1% move:

$$\text{vanna} \doteq \frac{1}{100} \frac{\partial \Delta}{\partial \sigma} \qquad (3.13)$$

I have written the delta symbol without specifying any particular type of delta, because in principle a vanna can be computed from any of the flavours of delta.

Although we have introduced vanna as the sensitivity of delta to volatility, it is essentially a second-order cross-derivative between spot and volatility, and we can think of it alternatively as the sensitivity of vega to spot. For example, choosing Spot-Delta-in-Foreign as our specific flavour of delta, we can write:

$$\begin{aligned}
\text{vanna} &= \frac{1}{100} \frac{\partial}{\partial \sigma} \left(\frac{\partial V}{\partial S} \right) \\
&= \frac{\partial}{\partial S} \left(\frac{1}{100} \frac{\partial V}{\partial \sigma} \right) \\
&= \frac{\partial \text{vega}}{\partial S}
\end{aligned}$$

How we choose to think about vanna will depend on the context. In the context of risk management, I find it more helpful to think about vanna as the change in delta that arises from a move in volatililty. But when intuitively gauging the sign and size of an option's vanna, I find it more helpful to picture an option's vega profile (against spot), and consider the gradient of vega with respect to spot.

As an illustration, the vanna profile of a reverse knock-out call option is shown in Figure 3.31, with the vega profile shown alongside. Note that since this option has a delta gap, it naturally also has a **vanna gap**.

3.2.2 Non-local volatility risk

In order to examine non-local volatility risk, we typically take the same approach as for non-local spot risk, and compute the quantities of interest (the value and selected Greeks of an option or portfolio) at multiple regularly spaced volatility levels, and display the results in a table. The table is called a **volatility risk report**, **volatility ladder** or **vega ladder**. As with spot ladders, it is important to choose the bounds and the number of rungs carefully in order to obtain a report which is both readable and has the necessary scope and resolution for risk management.

The non-local cross-risk between spot and volatility can be examined using a two-dimensional table which varies spot along one direction and volatility along

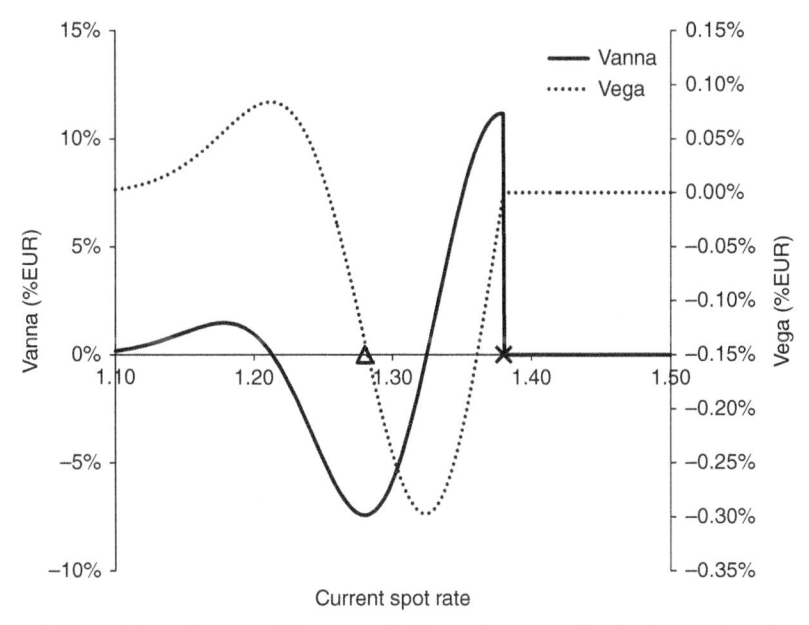

Figure 3.31 Variation with spot of the vanna (full line, primary y-axis) of a six-month 1.28-strike EUR call/USD put option with an up-side knock-out at 1.38. The vega is plotted alongside (dotted line, secondary y-axis). The strike level is marked with a triangle, the barrier with a cross

the other. Only one quantity can be displayed at a time in such a risk report, which is usually referred to as a **spot-vol matrix**.

3.3 Interest rate risk

On the one hand, interest rate risk is treated a lot like volatility risk. The Black–Scholes model assumes that, like volatility, the Domestic and Foreign interest rates are constant, and interest rate risk involves asking what would happen if we switched to a model with different interest rates. We define the option Greeks **Domestic rho** and **Foreign rho** (denoted by lower-case Greek letter ρ) to measure the local interest rate risks along the same lines as for vega. The practitioner versions of rho scale the risk measure for a 1% move in interest rate:

$$\text{practitioner } \rho_d \doteq \frac{1}{100}\frac{\partial V}{\partial r_d} \quad (3.14)$$

$$\text{practitioner } \rho_f \doteq \frac{1}{100}\frac{\partial V}{\partial r_f} \quad (3.15)$$

On the other hand, however, it is arguably the case that FX option risk managers devote *vastly* less attention to interest rate risk than to volatility risk. For example, it is uncommon to see an "interest rate ladder" for an option portfolio. And it is

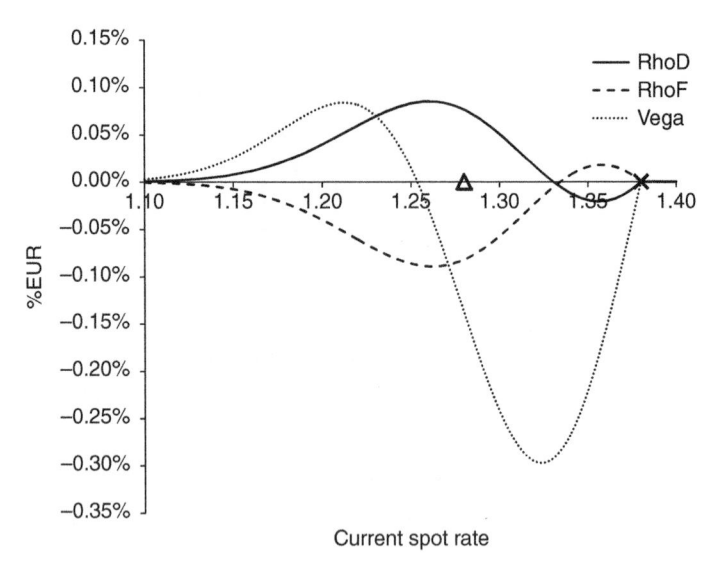

Figure 3.32 Variation with spot of the Domestic and Foreign rhos (full lines) of a six-month 1.28-strike EUR call/USD put option with an up-side knock-out at 1.38. The vega is plotted alongside (dotted line). The strike level is marked with a triangle, the barrier with a cross

extremely rare that risk managers engage with second-order interest rate risks ($\frac{\partial^2 V}{\partial r_d^2}$ and $\frac{\partial^2 V}{\partial r_f^2}$) or cross-risks with spot ($\frac{\partial^2 V}{\partial S \partial r_d}$ and $\frac{\partial^2 V}{\partial S \partial r_f}$).

Why is there less focus on interest rate risk than on volatility risk? It is certainly not the case that rho values are insignificant in size compared to vega values. As an example, Figure 3.32 shows the variation of Domestic and Foreign rhos for a reverse knock-out call, alongside its vega, and it is clear that the rho Greeks are by no means insignificant in comparison with vega. But of course to compare the size of interest rate risk with volatility risk, we need to look further than the Greeks: we must also look at the size of *likely moves* in the risk variable. For many currency pairs, likely moves in interest rates are indeed smaller than likely moves in FX volatility, but that is not true of all currency pairs, and in any case the interest rate risk is still worthy of the same attention as volatility risk. No, the real explanation requires us to look beyond Black–Scholes. As we shall recognize in Chapter 4, the biggest drawback by far of the Black–Scholes model is its simplistic treatment of volatility. Its simplistic treatment of interest rates presents far less of a problem. For that reason, more sophisticated models for option valuation and risk management begin by focusing on the uncertainty in volatility, rather than on the uncertainty in interest rates. The extra effort we make to examine volatility risk under the Black–Scholes model is really a precursor of these more sophisticated models, which we will discuss in Chapter 4.

Irrespective of the above discussion, it is nevertheless worth gaining an intuitive understanding of how interest rates affect option valuation. There are two effects via which option valuation depends on interest rates. The first effect is the **discounting effect**. Even a simple future payment has a rho risk, since its present value depends on the discount factor, which in turn depends on the interest rate. For example, for a Domestic payment (contract code DNN), we can derive the Domestic interest rate sensitivity as follows:

$$V_{\text{DNN}} = e^{-r_d(T-t)} A_d$$
$$\Rightarrow \frac{\partial V_{\text{DNN}}}{\partial r_d} = -(T-t) e^{-r_d(T-t)} A_d \quad (3.16)$$

Equation 3.16 illustrates that this rho effect has a sign opposite to that of the derivative value and is dominated by a factor that is linear in time to maturity. Assuming that our derivative value is calculated in the Domestic currency (the "natural" currency), the discounting effect will contribute this type of Domestic currency rho risk to every type of contract.

The second effect is the **forward effect**. The fair forward rate depends on the interest rate differential between the Domestic and Foreign currencies, as expressed by Equation 2.30. An increase in the forward rate may be brought about by an increase in the Domestic interest rate or a decrease in the Foreign interest rate. Conversely, a decrease in the forward rate may be brought about by a decrease in the Domestic interest rate or an increase in the Foreign interest rate. Then, if we recall that the fair forward rate is the risk-neutral expectation of future spot, it is straightforward to see how it affects option valuation. For example, an increase in the forward rate makes a call option *more* in the money and a put option *less* in the money. Similarly, it makes a high-side barrier *more* likely to be triggered, and a low-side barrier *less* likely to be triggered. A decrease in the forward rate has the opposite effects. In summary, the forward effect contributes both Domestic and Foreign currency rho risks to every type of contract which is sensitive to the forward rate.

3.4 Theta

Even if spot, volatility and interest rates all remain constant, the value of an option will change, due to the passage of time, and we refer to such changes in value as **theta risk** (despite the fact that it is comical to describe the passage of time as a risk!). As a first attempt to measure theta risk, we could simply calculate the partial derivative of option value with respect to current time, to get the **mathematical theta**, denoted Θ_{math}:

$$\Theta_{\text{math}} \doteq \frac{\partial V}{\partial t} \quad (3.17)$$

We have already met this form of theta: it is Term 1 of the Black–Scholes option pricing PDE, which we discussed in Section 2.3.4 and called the "theta term". Whilst this form of theta is of fundamental importance in the derivation, interpretation and solution of the Black–Scholes PDE, for practical risk management purposes I don't think it is going too far to say that mathematical theta is useless. One minor reason is that the measure relates to a change in time of one year, which is far too long a timescale given that other risks, such as delta, are managed on perhaps an hourly basis. A common practice is to divide the mathematical theta by 365, to obtain a risk measure that is scaled for a time change of one day, which I will call the **scaled mathematical theta**, denoted Θ_{scaled}:

$$\Theta_{\text{scaled}} \doteq \frac{1}{365} \frac{\partial V}{\partial t} \qquad (3.18)$$

Although this risk measure is more helpful, it still isn't what is needed in practice. To understand why, let us imagine that we are risk-managing a position on a Friday, and we would like to obtain some idea of how our position will look on the following Monday, even if spot, volatility and interest rates have not changed. No local risk measure will give us this information. What we need is a *non-local* theta which measures the change in option value between today and the *next business day*, denoted by t_{1b}. We will call this risk measure the **Black–Scholes practitioner theta**, denoted by Θ_{BS} and defined as:

$$\Theta_{\text{BS}} \doteq V(t_{1b}) - V(t) \qquad (3.19)$$

where all the market data parameters (spot, volatility and interest rates) are held constant.

I have named this risk measure specifically in terms of the Black–Scholes model, because when we move beyond the Black–Scholes model (as we will do in Chapters 4 and 5), we will see that there are all sorts of different ways in which we can calculate theta.

When the option maturity is a long way off, the difference between the mathematical and practitioner theta will be small. But as we approach expiry, the difference will become much larger.

For the specific case of vanilla options, the rate of change in option value with respect to time is always negative, and is termed *time decay*. This is illustrated by Figure 3.33. It is no coincidence that the theta profile looks like the negative of the vega and gamma profiles: just as vega and gamma are fundamentally related to each other, so too is theta intimately connected. We can understand this intuitively if we consider the option value as a function of variance $\sigma^2(T-t)$, so that an increase in volatility σ increases the variance, and a step forward in time t decreases the variance. In practice, the option value will also depend on the forward and the discount factor, which will bring the Domestic and Foreign interest rates into the

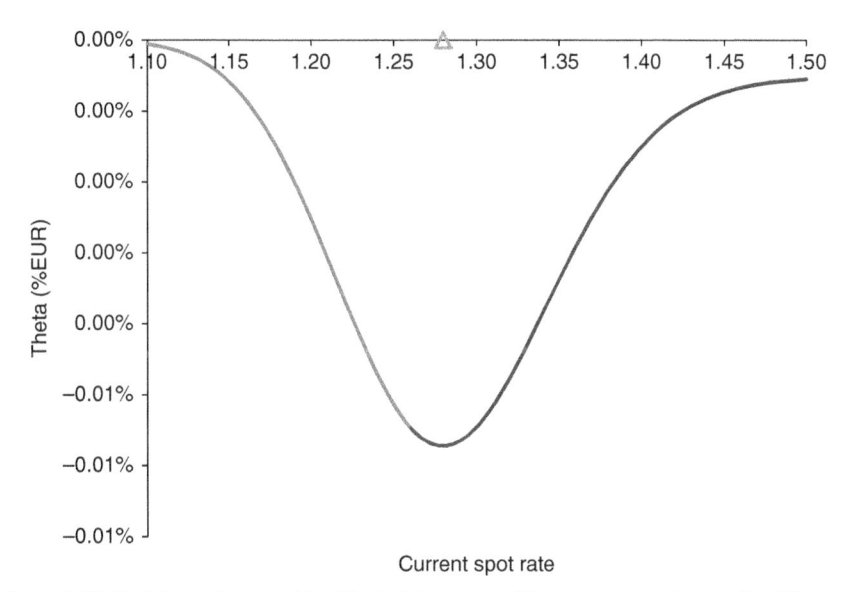

Figure 3.33 Variation with spot of the Black–Scholes practitioner theta of a six-month 1.28-strike EUR call/USD put vanilla option. The strike level is marked with a triangle

relationship. A relationship between theta, vega and the rhos has been derived by Reiss and Wystup [24], and can be written in the following form:

$$(T-t)\frac{\partial V}{\partial t} = -\frac{1}{2}\sigma\frac{\partial V}{\partial \sigma} - r_d\frac{\partial V}{\partial r_d} - r_f\frac{\partial V}{\partial r_f} \qquad (3.20)$$

As one further illustration, Figure 3.34 shows the theta profile for a reverse knock-out call option, with the vega profile plotted alongside. The close relationship between the two Greeks is clear to see.

3.5 Barrier over-hedging

The fair value that comes out of the Black–Scholes model – indeed the very assertion that there is a fair value – is valid only in the circumstances that the hedging strategy specified by the model is employed, and is therefore contingent on the hedging assumptions (detailed in Section 2.3.3) being met. Any departure from the assumptions entails a potential departure from the price that comes out of the model, and requires our attention. This is true for all option types, but for the specific case of barrier options, there is one critical risk feature that stands out as requiring special attention: the *delta gap*.

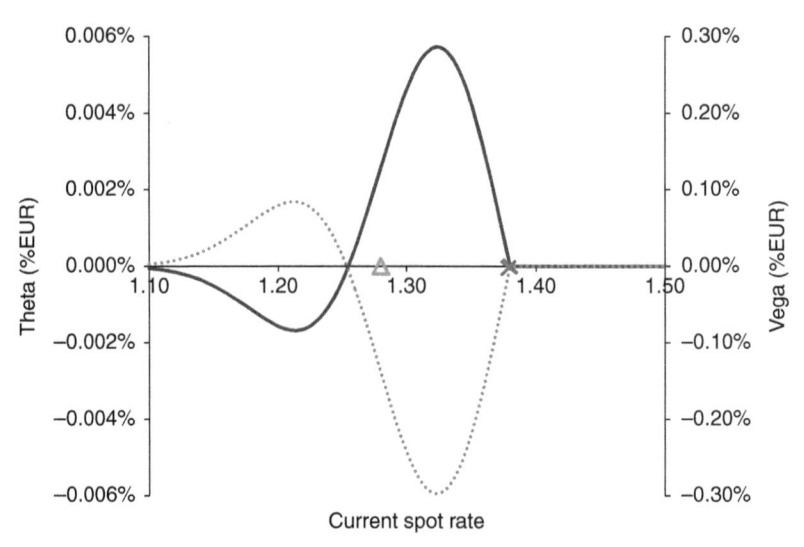

Figure 3.34 Variation with spot of the Black–Scholes practitioner theta (full line, primary y-axis) of a six-month 1.28-strike EUR call/USD put option with an up-side knock-out at 1.38. The vega is plotted alongside (dotted line, secondary y-axis). The strike level is marked with a triangle, the barrier with a cross

In Section 3.1, we showed how the delta profiles of barrier options can show discontinuities across the barrier level. In some cases, this discontinuity can be very large: Figure 3.7, for example, shows a reverse knock-out call with a delta gap of over 25% of principal. To close out the delta hedge on this option in 20 million euros would involve a spot trade in 5 million euros. The Black–Scholes model assumes that at the very moment that spot triggers the barrier level, we will be able to close out the delta position by performing this spot trade at a spot rate exactly equal to the barrier level. In practice, this is seldom possible, so let us work through the consequences of an unfavourable scenario.

Suppose that we have sold the reverse knock-out call to a hedging client. The long option position has a negative delta near the barrier, which means that our short position has a positive delta, which in turn means that we must delta-hedge the option with a short EURUSD spot position. When spot trades at the barrier level of 1.38, we must *buy* EURUSD in 5 million euros. If spot is undergoing a rally and pushes rapidly through the barrier level of 1.38, we might not be able to achieve a close-out spot rate of better than 1.3850, costing us 25,000 euros relative to the Black–Scholes assumption. This could be a very substantial proportion of the premium that was charged for the option. It is therefore clear that, when we are making the price, we must apply some method to account for such an unfavourable scenario. The various such methods for achieving this go under the name of **barrier over-hedging**.

Let us suppose that we need to make an offer price for the above reverse knock-out option: a six-month 1.28-strike EUR call/USD put option with an up-side knock-out at 1.38, in 20 million euros. As a first step towards over-hedging, a typical technique is to value the contract with an **adjusted barrier level**, chosen so that the contract is worth *more* to the counterparty than the contract with the true barrier level. For example, we might choose an adjusted barrier level of 1.3830. This would add about four basis points (0.04%) or around EUR 7,500 to the value of the option, and we would then base our price quotation on this adjusted-barrier calculation. This builds in some valuation cushion for the fact that the true cost of hedging is greater than the Black–Scholes-theoretical cost of hedging, hence the term "over"-hedging.

Once we have entered a trade that has been priced in this way, we do two things: risk-manage the adjusted-barrier option, and recalculate the valuation cushion. Operationally, this is typically achieved by having one trading book which contains the adjusted-barrier options, and another trading book which contains the true (client-confirmed) counterparts, back-to-back with internally booked reverse positions in the adjusted-barrier options. The former book is the main one that is risk-managed. The latter book is not risk-managed, but its value is monitored, consisting entirely as it does of all the valuation cushions.

There must of course be mechanisms in place that link each adjusted-barrier option with its true-barrier counterpart. In particular, there must be a mechanism that ensures that if the true barrier is triggered, the adjusted counterpart is cancelled. Practically speaking, this mechanism may live in the trade booking system software, in the valuation software or in some combination of the two. Industrial FX option risk management systems will usually also have a facility to highlight the options in the portfolio whose barriers are nearby. This is sometimes called a **barrier radar report**.

In the above simple over-hedging method, the barrier level adjustment is constant in time. Techniques used in practice are a bit more sophisticated, and account for the fact that the delta gap has different sizes at different points in time. Figure 3.35 shows how the delta gap of a reverse knock-out call option varies with time to expiry. It is clear that the delta gap that potentially needs to be closed out increases very steeply as we approach the expiry time of the option. A more sophisticated over-hedging technique might therefore adjust the barrier by a time-dependent amount, with very little or no adjustment early in the barrier option's life, and more adjustment later in its life. Any technique involving time-dependent barrier adjustment has the effect of converting a constant barrier to a "bent" barrier, and the technique is consequently known as **barrier bending**.

Options with general time-dependent barriers, such as those arising from barrier-bending over-hedging techniques, must be valued using numerical methods, as described in Chapter 6.

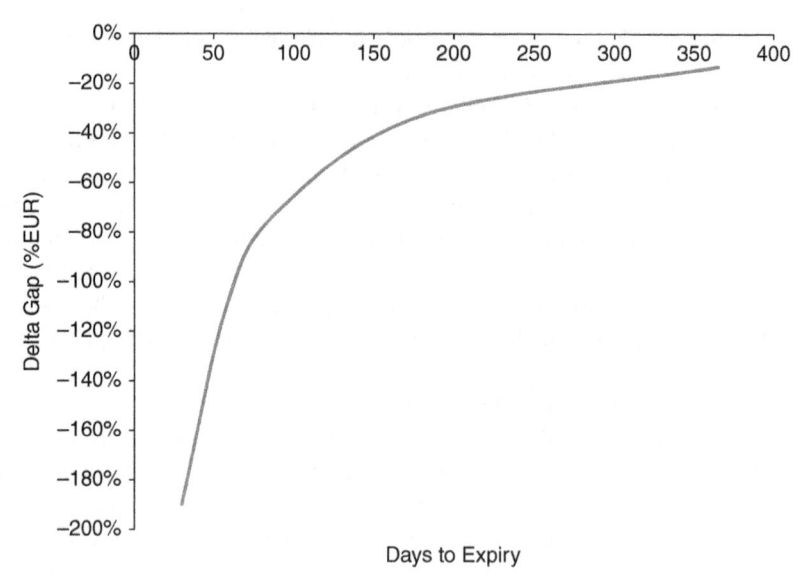

Figure 3.35 Variation with days-to-expiry of the delta gap of a 1.28-strike EUR call/USD put option with an up-side knock-out at 1.38

3.6 Co-Greeks

Just as we are interested in the sensitivity of an option value to market data parameters, such as spot or volatility, so too are we often interested in its sensitivity to the option parameters, such as strike and expiry time. Whilst these latter sensitivities are not themselves market risk measures, they are very closely related, and so I will allow myself to include them in this chapter.

Their close similarity to Greeks motivates their name of **co-Greeks**, also sometimes called **dual Greeks**. First- and second-order sensitivities with respect to strike are known as **co-Delta** and **co-Gamma** respectively, whilst the sensitivity with respect to expiry time is known as **co-Theta**:

$$\text{co-Delta} = \frac{\partial V}{\partial K} \qquad (3.21)$$

$$\text{co-Gamma} = \frac{\partial^2 V}{\partial K^2} \qquad (3.22)$$

$$\text{co-Theta} = \frac{\partial V}{\partial T_e} \qquad (3.23)$$

4 | Smile Pricing

> I do not agree with the price you make, but I'll defend to the death your right to make it.

4.1 The shortcomings of the Black–Scholes model

Let's cut to the chase: what value should the volatility σ in the Black–Scholes model take? To see why we should home in on this particular question, consider the pricing formula for a vanilla option, Equation 2.72. Its inputs are:

- spot;
- Domestic interest rate;
- Foreign interest rate;
- volatility;
- strike;
- maturity.

How do we determine these inputs? Well, the strike and maturity are simply read off the contract, whilst spot is taken from the FX spot market. The interest rates are, as we discussed, conceptual risk-free rates, rather than rates from any specific market or contract, but these too can be established satisfactorily in some fairly uncontentious way, for example from inter-bank lending rates. But the volatility is left dangling as the unknown input.

This is true for both vanilla and exotic options, since the pricing formulae differ only in the contract parameters, which are uncontentious. Now, if we apply all of the uncontentious inputs, the Black–Scholes pricing functions effectively become functions to convert from volatility to price. In the specific case of vanilla options, the price is a monotonic function of volatility, as we showed in our discussion of Vega, in Section 3.2. We can therefore invert the function and convert from price to volatility. A volatility calculated in this way is called an **implied volatility**, and if the vanilla option price input is a market price, we say that the volatility is a **market implied volatility**.

We are now ready to make the observation that is crucial to understanding the shortcomings of the Black–Scholes model as a valuation model. The observation is as follows: if we calculate market implied volatilities for options of different strikes and maturities (on the same currency pair), *we get completely different numbers*. For example, the market implied volatility for a three-month EURUSD vanilla option struck at 1.38 is around 5%. If we change the strike to 1.20, the market implied volatility is around 9%. And if we keep the strike at 1.38 and change the maturity to one year, the implied volatility is around 7%. These results make it very clear that the market is not using the Black–Scholes model to make prices.

Going forward, it will be imperative that we be clear about what kind of volatility we are discussing. We will adopt a notation whereby a small letter sigma (σ) denotes a process model volatility (such as the volatility in the Black–Scholes process model), and a capital letter sigma (Σ) denotes an implied volatility.

Being a process model volatility, σ may depend on market variables such as current time and spot, but it would not make sense for it to depend on strike, maturity or any other details of a contract, because the idea of a process model is that it applies to multiple contracts. We will distinguish the process model volatilities for different models by using a subscript suffix, for example σ_{BS} for the Black–Scholes model.

The implied volatility Σ may, by definition, depend on option strike K and expiry time T_e. For all models other than pure Black–Scholes, the implied volatility may also depend on the current time t and spot level S. Its full dependency is thus written as $\Sigma(S, t; K, T_e)$. Often, we are not explicitly discussing the variation with current time and spot, and it is then common to drop the current time and spot arguments, and write: $\Sigma(K, T_e)$.

Incidentally, there is a subtlety regarding the calculation and quotation of market implied volatilities that we need to be aware of, especially for short-dated options, and it is to do with the *time inputs*. The conversion between price and implied volatility always uses a *whole number of days* for the time to maturity ($T_e - t$) in Equations 2.72, 2.73 and 2.74. The reason for this market convention is its simplicity: it facilitates agreement between counterparties of option prices in markets which are quoted in terms of volatility. For a given option expiry time, this convention has the effect that whilst[1] the true current time varies through a given calendar day, the t that is used for the conversion calculation remains fixed. At some point late in the day, the market switches to using the t for the next day. This is known as the **market roll**, and we say that the market quotation calculation "rolls forward" to the next day.

---

[1] Wordsmiths may enjoy noting that the use of *whilst* here involves both its temporal and contrastive senses simultaneously.

To return to the question with which we started this chapter: there is *no* single value of volatility which we can reasonably use in the Black–Scholes model. We simply need a different model – one with more flexibility.

4.2 Black–Scholes with term structure (BSTS)

As a first way of increasing the flexibility of the Black–Scholes (BS) model, we make the volatility that appears in the Black–Scholes stochastic differential equation of Equation 2.4 a function of time:

$$dS = \mu(t) S\,dt + \sigma_{BSTS}(t) S\,dW_t \qquad (4.1)$$

The function $\sigma_{BSTS}(t)$ is called the **instantaneous volatility** curve, and Equation 4.1 is called the **Black–Scholes with term structure (BSTS) model** equation for FX spot price.

If we repeat the procedures of Chapter 2 with this process, we can derive the following partial differential equation for option pricing:

$$\frac{\partial V}{\partial t} + (r_d(t) - r_f(t))S\frac{\partial V}{\partial S} + \frac{1}{2}(\sigma_{BSTS}(t))^2 S^2 \frac{\partial^2 V}{\partial S^2} = r_d(t) V \qquad (4.2)$$

where we have also allowed the interest rates to become functions of time. Equation 4.2 is the **partial differential equation for FX option pricing under the Black–Scholes with term structure model**.

It can be shown (see Appendix C.5 in the Appendix) that the BSTS model's implied volatility Σ_{BSTS} – a function of expiry time T_e but not spot or strike – is given by the following expression:

$$\Sigma_{BSTS}(t; T_e) = \sqrt{\frac{1}{(T_e - t)} \int_t^{T_e} (\sigma_{BSTS}(u))^2 \, du} \qquad (4.3)$$

When implied volatility depends on expiry time but not strike, as does $\Sigma_{BSTS}(t; T_e)$, we refer to the function as the **implied volatility curve** or the **implied volatility term structure**.

The relationship between the instantaneous and implied volatilities of the BSTS model can easily be interpreted intuitively by writing Equation 4.3 in the following form:

$$(\Sigma_{BSTS}(t; T_e))^2 (T_e - t) = \int_t^{T_e} (\sigma_{BSTS}(u))^2 \, du \qquad (4.4)$$

We thereby recognize that we are adding up lots of little variances $(\sigma_{BSTS}(u))^2 \delta u$ over time intervals $(u, u + \delta u)$ to get a total variance $(\Sigma_{BSTS}(t; T_e))^2 (T_e - t)$ over time interval (t, T_e). The variances in question are those of moves in log-spot, which are independent and normally distributed.

An expression for the instantaneous volatility in terms of the implied volatility is easily obtained by differentiating both sides of Equation 4.4 with respect to T_e.

$$\sigma_{\text{BSTS}}(T_e) = \sqrt{\frac{\partial}{\partial T_e}\left[(\Sigma_{\text{BSTS}}(t; T_e))^2 (T_e - t)\right]} \quad (4.5)$$

This expression is derived in Appendix C.5, using the first-principles methods in Appendix C.

For Equation 4.5 to yield a real number for the instantaneous volatility, the following condition must hold:

$$\frac{\partial}{\partial T_e}\left[(\Sigma_{\text{BSTS}}(t; T_e))^2 (T_e - t)\right] \geq 0 \quad (4.6)$$

This condition makes perfect sense: the implied variance (which, as we recognized above, is the sum of lots of little variances over small time steps) must not decrease as the maturity increases. If it does decrease, we have a form of arbitrage called **falling variance arbitrage** or **calendar arbitrage**. Equation 4.6 is called the **no-arbitrage condition on the implied volatility curve of the BSTS model**.

Let us now try to understand the effect on pricing behaviour that arises when we extend our model from BS to BSTS. As a first step, we can recognize that the BS model corresponds to an instantaneous volatility curve which is constant in time (a "flat" volatility curve). Let us consider an example where this constant level is 6%. Now consider a second instantaneous volatility curve, where the volatility increases with time (is "upward sloping") and whose six-month implied volatility is exactly 6%. The upward-sloping curve will have values lower than 6% in the early expiries (say, one to three months) but values higher than 6% at later expiries (say, three to six months). Now suppose we need to price a window barrier option where the barrier is only active in the last three months. A spot process under the upward sloping volatility curve will be much more likely to trigger the barrier than a spot process under the flat-volatility curve, since the former will be much more volatile in the period when the barrier is active. This will result in a significantly lower price for a knock-out or no-touch option and a significantly higher price for a knock-in or one-touch option.

Conversely, we could consider an instantaneous volatility curve where the volatility *decreases* with time (is "downward sloping") and whose six-month implied volatility is exactly 6%. A spot process under this curve will be much less likely to trigger the barrier than either the flat or upward-sloping cases.

It is not just window barrier options which are sensitive to volatility term structure. I just chose that example because it is clear to see that the three-month–six-month period is the one of interest. But even standard (whole-life) barrier options can be very sensitive to the shape of the volatility curve, because the probability that the barrier is triggered varies greatly through its life. A common situation is that the forward curve is much closer to the barrier level at some points in time than at others (even when interest rates are constant). If the volatility curve has its highest values when the forward is close to the barrier level, the probability of barrier trigger will be significantly increased.

Similar arguments explain why the time-dependence of interest rates has an effect on option pricing. With its fixed interest rates, the BS model assumes that the forward curve is an exponential function of maturity, whereas the BSTS model will allow the forward curve to take a variety of different shapes, even for the same forward to option maturity as the BS model. Some shapes may make the barrier much more likely to trigger in the middle of the option's lifetime, whilst other shapes may make the barrier much less likely to trigger.

Closed-form solutions for option prices under the BSTS option pricing PDE, Equation 4.2, do not in general exist, and numerical methods must be employed. The most common approach is to use finite-difference methods to solve Equation 4.2 subject to the boundary conditions imposed by the contract. Another approach is to perform Monte Carlo simulation of the BSTS risk-neutral SDE, which by analogy with the Black–Scholes version, Equation 2.71, can be written down as:

$$dS = (r_d(t) - r_f(t))\,S\,dt + \sigma_{\text{BSTS}}(t)\,S\,dW \qquad (4.7)$$

These approaches, and a number of specific techniques applicable to each, are discussed in Chapter 6.

4.3 The implied volatility surface

Implied volatility Σ is a function of strike and maturity, and its formal definition is that it is the volatility which, when plugged into the Black–Scholes vanilla option pricing formula (denoted C_{BS} for call options), gives the desired price C_{desired} for the option with chosen strike K and maturity T. Mathematically:

$$C_{\text{BS}}(K, T, \Sigma(K, T)) = C_{\text{desired}}(K, T) \qquad (4.8)$$

The nature of the "desired" price depends on the context, but most often it is either a market price (yielding a "market implied volatility") or a model price (yielding a **model implied volatility**).

The principle of put–call parity, described in Section 1.12.3, means that (in the absence of arbitrage opportunities) the implied volatility for calls and puts is the same.

Depending as it does on two variables, the implied volatility function is very often called the **implied volatility surface**. Indeed, a "3-dimensional" surface plot against strike and maturity can often be a very good way of examining the properties of the implied volatility function.

In many contexts, we wish to fix the maturity parameter T and think only about how the implied volatility varies with strike. The function $\Sigma(K)$ that results from partial application of the maturity to the implied volatility surface function is called the **implied volatility smile**. For example, if we were analysing EURUSD six-month vanilla options, we would set the maturity equal to the six-month expiry time to obtain the EURUSD six-month smile.

Any model which recognizes that implied volatility is a function of strike is referred to as a "smile model", and valuation under such models is referred to as "smile pricing".

Different currency pairs unsurprisingly have different market implied volatility surfaces, and for a given currency pair, the market implied volatility surface also varies with trading time, with the most liquid pairs being re-marked several times per hour of every trading day. Substantial changes to the surface can take place within a few minutes if there is a major unexpected political or economic event, such as an unexpected referendum result or a surprise move in interest rates. In practice, the use of any model to calculate option values and risks necessarily entails the choice of an appropriate implied volatility surface to plug into the model. For example, a pricing tool used by an option trading desk would likely plug in the latest surface marked by traders, whereas an end-of-day risk report calculator used by a firm's risk management department would send in some form of "official end-of-day" volatility surface.

For the purposes of this book, we shall consider three currency pairs: **EURUSD**, **USDTRY** and **AUDJPY**. For each of these pairs, we will use an implied volatility surface based on the FX options markets at the end of September 2014. I will refer to these market implied volatility surfaces as our **benchmark volatility surfaces**. Figures 4.1, 4.2 and 4.3 show the three-month and six-month implied volatility smiles for our three benchmark currency pairs.

Also shown in each figure are the so-called at-the-money points: around 7% for EURUSD, 11% for USDTRY and 9% for AUDJPY. The precise meaning of "at-the-money" is discussed in detail in Section 4.4.1, but for now we just need to know that it is near or at the point where the strike equals the forward rate for the maturity of interest.

A common misconception is that the at-the-money volatility is at the minimum point of the smile, but as these figures show, that is not always the case.

4.4 The FX vanilla option market

It is commonly said – especially by those more familiar with exotic options and structured products than with vanilla options – that the implied volatility surface

Smile Pricing | 127

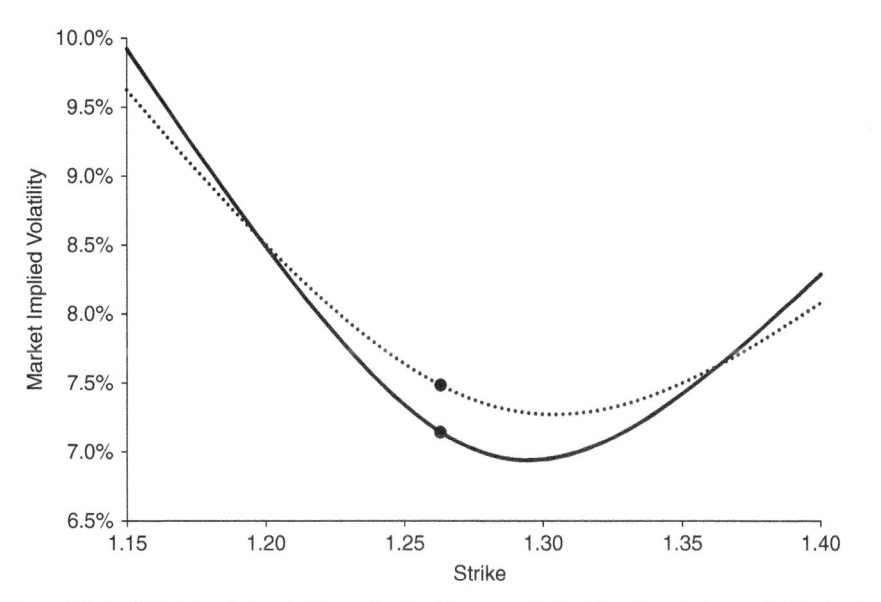

Figure 4.1 EURUSD implied volatility smiles for three-month (bold line) and six-month (dashed line) expiries. Circles mark the at-the-money points

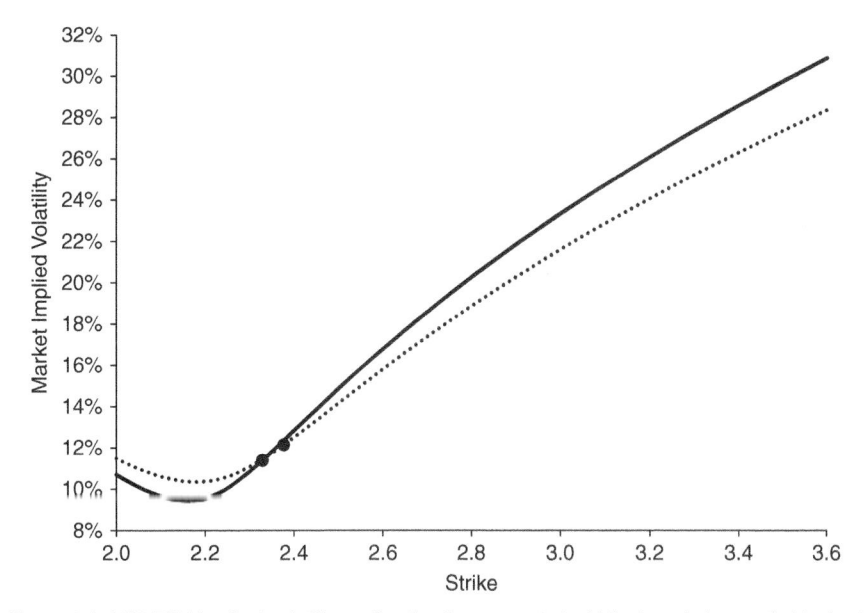

Figure 4.2 USDTRY implied volatility smiles for three-month (bold line) and six-month (dashed line) expiries. Circles mark the at-the-money points

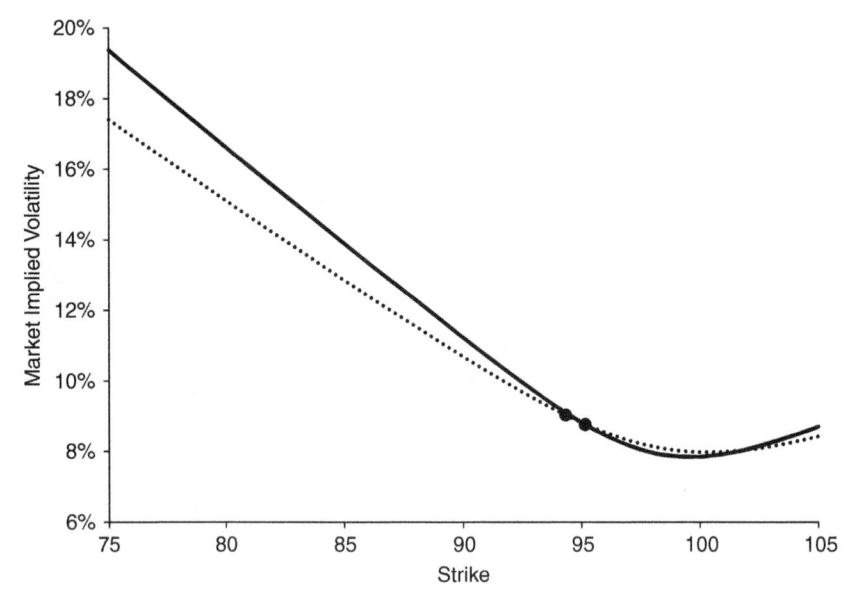

Figure 4.3 AUDJPY implied volatility smiles for three-month (bold line) and six-month (dashed line) expiries. Circles mark the at-the-money points

'comes from the vanilla market'. But what exactly does this mean? In this section, we will examine the nature of the wholesale FX vanilla options market in some detail, looking at what instruments are traded, how they are quoted, and what conventions are used in the process. And we will come to understand that the vanilla market alone is in fact not quite enough to give us the implied volatility surface.

A hedger or speculator seeking to buy or sell an FX vanilla option may naturally request from a market-maker a quote for *any* option or option structure. That is essentially what defines a market-maker: it is a market participant who can be relied upon to quote a price. However, irrespective of what specific price quotes have been requested, all FX vanilla option market-makers additionally maintain a set of "standardized market quotes" on each currency pair for which they make a market. This may involve publishing the quotes externally or merely marking them in internal systems. For example, a G10 FX vanilla options desk might publish the following five EURUSD market quotes:

1. At-the-money volatility;
2. 25-delta risk reversal;
3. 25-delta butterfly;
4. 10-delta risk reversal;
5. 10-delta butterfly.

Table 4.1 Standardized expiry tenors for the three benchmark currency pairs. "D"=day; "W"=week; "M"=month; "Y"=year

Currency pair	List of tenors
EURUSD	1D, 1W, 2W, 1M, 2M, 3M, 6M, 1Y, 2Y, 3Y, 4Y, 5Y ...
USDTRY	1D, 1W, 2W, 1M, 2M, 3M, 6M, 1Y, 2Y, 3Y, 4Y, 5Y ...
AUDJPY	1D, 1W, 2W, 1M, 2M, 3M, 6M, 9M, 1Y, 2Y, 3Y, 4Y, 5Y ...

Each of the above quotes is made for each of a number of **standardized expiry times** (also called the **straight dates**), resulting in a matrix of quotes. The straight dates are recalculated every day, based on a standardized set of **tenors**, such as one week, one month, two months, three months, six months and so on. The set of tenors varies slightly by currency pair, and Table 4.1 lists them for our three benchmark currency pairs. For many currency pairs, the one-month tenor is the most liquid for vanilla options, so let us now go through each of the quotes in the list above, referring to the one-month expiry for the sake of example.

4.4.1 At-the-money volatility

The one-month at-the-money volatility is by definition the implied volatility of a one-month option with an at-the-money strike. Simple? Far from it – for there are a number of different definitions of the at-the-money strike! One definition of at-the-money strike is that it is the forward to the settlement date that is the spot date of the option expiry time. This type of at-the-money strike is called **at-the-money forward** or ATMF for short. It has two significant advantages: it is easy to compute, and (unlike the other definitions) it does not depend on volatility, making it easier for counterparties to agree on. It is equivalent to the definition of at-the-money that we introduced in Section 2.7.3 in the context of the Black–Scholes model.

Another definition of at-the-money strike is that it is the strike at which a straddle has zero delta. Recall from Section 3.1.4 that a call option has a (non-premium-adjusted) delta that runs from near 1 (when the strike is zero) to zero (when the strike is infinite), whilst a put has a delta that runs from zero (when the strike is zero) to near −1 (when the strike is infinite). The delta of a straddle (call plus put at the same strike) therefore runs from 1 (when the strike is zero) to −1 (when the strike is infinite), and it is clear then that somewhere in the middle is a strike at which delta is zero. Such a straddle is called a **delta-neutral straddle** or DNS. Occasionally it is called a 'zero-delta straddle' or ZDS. The definition of the at-the-money strike as the delta-neutral straddle strike may seem very arcane, but it has a distinct advantage: it allows us to construct a vanilla structure which has zero delta but plenty of vega. I write 'plenty' because vega is actually near its peak value at this strike. A delta-neutral straddle is thus the ideal instrument for gaining exposure to implied volatility without taking on delta risk. It actually has a further interesting property, namely that volgamma is zero at the DNS strike, which means that to second order the value of the straddle is linear in volatility.

As explained in Section 3.1.2, there are at least eight different types of delta, so what do we use for the delta-neutral straddle? Several of the variations in delta type have no effect on the delta-neutral straddle strike. For example, the difference between spot and forward deltas is a discount factor, so a straddle that has zero spot delta also has zero forward delta. Similarly, a straddle that has zero delta measured in Foreign currency also has zero delta measured in Domestic currency. The only delta distinction of significance that we care about is whether the delta is premium-adjusted. If it is premium-adjusted, it corresponds to the premium being in Foreign, so we may call it delta-neutral straddle (Foreign), or DNSF. If it is not premium-adjusted, it corresponds to the premium being in Domestic, so we may call it delta-neutral straddle (Domestic), or DNSD. This results in two different definitions of delta-neutral straddle strike.

Whether the delta is premium-adjusted is a market convention, and is determined by the **default premium currency** for the currency pair. If the default premium currency is the Foreign currency in the pair, the delta is premium-adjusted; if it is the Domestic currency, the delta is not premium-adjusted. The default premium currency is determined as follows. If USD is present in the pair, it is the default premium currency. If USD is not present in the pair, the default premium currency is the Foreign currency, unless the Foreign currency is "non-deliverable", meaning that it cannot be transferred freely out of its native country. For example, the Brazilian real is non-deliverable, so in the currency pair Japanese yen per Brazilian real, BRLJPY, the default premium currency is JPY.

A further advantage of the delta-neutral straddle (DNS) strike definition is that, given the DNS volatility, we can obtain the corresponding DNS strike (with either delta convention) analytically. The formula that defines the strike is:

$$\Delta_c(K_{DNS}, \Sigma(K_{DNS})) + \Delta_p(K_{DNS}, \Sigma(K_{DNS})) = 0 \quad (4.9)$$

Taking first the example of non-premium adjusted delta, and inserting the formulae for delta that we showed in Equation 3.3, we can easily solve to obtain:

$$K_{DNSD} = F e^{\frac{1}{2} \Sigma(K_{DNSD})^2 (T-t)} \quad (4.10)$$

With premium-adjusted delta, the corresponding result is:

$$K_{DNSF} = F e^{-\frac{1}{2} \Sigma(K_{DNSF})^2 (T-t)} \quad (4.11)$$

We have now described three different definitions of at-the-money strike: ATMF, DNSF and DNSD. It is market conventions that dictate which definition should be used for a given at-the-money quote, depending on the currency pair and tenor. In the case of the EURUSD one-month at-the-money volatility market quote, market convention dictates that we use DNSD.

Whichever definition of at-the-money is used, the at-the-money volatility has the same intuitive interpretation in terms of its relationship with the smile: it represents the base level of volatility in the smile. If, for example, we were to shift the at-the-money volatility from 5% to 6% whilst keeping the risk reversal and butterfly unchanged, the entire volatility smile would move up by roughly 1%. Implied volatility being a forward-looking quantity, the at-the-money implied volatility for a given currency pair is a good guide to general levels of future volatility in the spot market, as expected in the options market.

4.4.2 Risk reversal

A **risk reversal option structure** is constructed from a spread (difference) of two positions: an out-of-the-money call ("high-strike call") and an out-of-the-money put ("low-strike put"). The two strikes in the structure have (in general) different implied volatilities, and what is quoted in the market is the *difference* between the implied volatilities. This difference is called the **risk reversal of the implied volatility smile** or simply the **smile risk reversal**.

Which way around the difference is taken (long call/short put or vice versa) is subject to a market convention of sorts: the convention is essentially to choose whichever way around results in a positive number – which only works when everyone already knows on which side (high or low strikes) volatilities are higher for the market in question! In case of doubt, a trader might indicate which side is higher by saying that the risk reversal is "bid for" that side or "favouring" that side. The side itself is often described via the option trait (call or put) of one of the currencies (the non-USD currency if USD is present) for an out-of-the-money option. For example, the USDTRY smile has the higher volatilities on the high-strike side, so it would be described as "bid for the high side" or "bid for TRY puts". The smile risk reversal would then be computed as long the high-strike volatility and short the low-strike volatility. Conversely, the EURUSD smile has the higher volatilities on the low-strike side, so it would be described as "bid for the low side" or "bid for EUR puts", and the smile risk reversal would then be computed as long the low-strike volatility and short the high-strike volatility. For our last benchmark currency pair, AUDJPY, the smile has the higher volatilities on the low-strike side, and so the smile risk reversal is computed as long the low-strike volatility and short the high-strike volatility.

The phrase "risk reversal" on its own may be used to refer to either the pair of options (the *risk reversal structure*) or the difference in volatilities (the *risk reversal of the implied volatility smile*). The context usually makes clear which one is meant.

To compute the risk reversal of an implied volatility smile, we first determine each of the two strikes in the risk reversal structure so as to yield the appropriate delta. For example, the EURUSD one-month 25-delta risk reversal structure comprises a long one-month EUR put/USD call at a strike that yields a delta of −0.25, and a short one-month EUR call/USD put at a strike that yields a delta of 0.25. As with the delta-neutral straddle, the choice of delta type matters, and again the choice is dictated by convention. This time though, the result *does* vary depending on whether we have spot delta or forward delta, and *does* vary with the currency in which it is measured. In the case of the EURUSD one-month risk reversals, we use premium-unadjusted spot delta measured in Foreign. So, for example, the strike of the put option in the risk reversal is such that the premium-unadjusted spot delta in Foreign is −0.25 times the Foreign currency principal of the option.

The risk reversal represents how asymmetric (or "skewed") the smile is. A smile whose volatilities for high strikes are much higher than those for low strikes will have a large positive risk reversal.

4.4.3 Butterfly

Lastly, let me try and explain the market quotes for butterflies. The term "butterfly", or "fly", is a general term used to describe a structure of three options, of which two are bought and one is sold. Here we use the term to describe a specific form based on an implied volatility smile. As with the risk reversals, we may talk in terms of option structures or of volatilities. A **butterfly option structure** comprises a long high-strike call, a long low-strike put, a short position in an at-the-money call, and a short position in an at-the-money put. It would be nice if the market quotation method for a butterfly followed the pattern of the risk reversal and simply combined the volatilities at the options' strikes. But alas, it's not as simple as that. Such a quotation method certainly exists, and is called the **smile butterfly**, often shortened to 'smile fly'. Explicitly, the smile butterfly equals the average of the volatilities at the strikes of the out-of-the-money options minus the at-the-money volatility.

Given that the information about the at-the-money volatilities is already provided by the market quote for the at-the-money volatility, it is very common to drop the at–the-money options and consider the out-of-the-money options (long call and put) alone. This is called a **strangle** option structure. Then the average of the call volatility and the put volatility is called the **smile strangle**.

The conventional market quotation method for butterflies is a bit more complicated than the smile butterfly. To explain it, I will describe it first in words, and then in equations. In words: let's pretend that we have an implied volatility smile under which the out-of-the-money strikes in the butterfly both have the same volatility, equal to the ATM volatility plus a volatility offset $\Delta\Sigma$. The strike of the out-of-the-money call is such that its delta under the pretend smile equals 0.25, and the strike of the out-of-the-money put is such that its delta under the pretend smile is −0.25. The total value of the butterfly structure under the pretend smile is the same as the total value of the butterfly structure under the true smile. Then, the market quote for the butterfly is the offset $\Delta\Sigma$.

In equations now:

$$\Delta_c(K_c, \Sigma_{ATM} + \Delta\Sigma) = 0.25 \quad (4.12)$$

$$\Delta_p(K_p, \Sigma_{ATM} + \Delta\Sigma) = -0.25 \quad (4.13)$$

$$V_c(K_c, \Sigma_{ATM} + \Delta\Sigma) + V_p(K_p, \Sigma_{ATM} + \Delta\Sigma) = V_c(K_c, \Sigma(K_c)) + V_p(K_p, \Sigma(K_p)) \quad (4.14)$$

We have three equations in three unknowns: K_c, K_p and $\Delta\Sigma$, and we solve for and quote the **market butterfly** $\Delta\Sigma$. The 'pretend' volatility $\Sigma_{ATM} + \Delta\Sigma$ used for pricing the out-of-the-money options is called the **market strangle**.

The butterfly (whether of the market or smile variety) represents, roughly speaking, how convex the smile is. If out-of-the-money volatilities for both high and low strikes are significantly higher than the at-the-money volatility, the shape of the smile will be very convex, and the smile and market butterflies will both be large.

Interestingly, market butterflies can sometimes be negative. This isn't caused by the smile turning upside down (into a "frown" ⌢), but rather because the at-the-money strike (invariably under a non-ATMF convention) ends up somewhere very far from the central region of the smile, at a point well outside the region enclosed by the out-of-the-money pair of options. In such a case, the butterfly isn't measuring the convexity of the smile in the normal sense.

4.4.4 The role of the Black–Scholes model in the FX vanilla options market

I stated towards the start of this chapter, in Section 4.1, that "the market is not using the Black–Scholes model to make prices". It should now be clear why I included the qualification "to make prices" – the way in which the FX vanilla options market is quoted is totally reliant on the use of implied volatility, which in turn is defined in terms of the Black–Scholes model. Thus the Black–Scholes model plays a very important role in the market, and is deeply embedded in it.

4.5 Theoretical Value (TV)

In Chapter 2, we showed how to calculate FX barrier option values using the Black–Scholes model, which involves a single constant volatility and a single constant interest rate for each currency. However, as we have been discussing in this chapter, the FX options market does not deal with volatility in the form of a single constant value. Rather, the vanilla options market deals with an entire two-dimensional surface of implied volatility, where volatility depends on the strike and expiry time of the option. In a similar way, the interest rate markets deal not with a single constant interest rate, but with term structures of rates. How then can the Black–Scholes model ever be relevant for FX barrier options? The answer is that a market convention has evolved which specifies how the volatility and interest rates should be extracted from the market. When these market data parameters are extracted according to the conventions and then used in a Black–Scholes model valuation calculation, the barrier option value which comes out is called the **Theoretical Value** (TV) of the option. The market data parameters are referred to as the 'TV volatility' and the 'TV interest rates'.

The TV is neither the value used to make tradable prices, nor is it the fair value used for revaluation of trading books. It is, however, the de facto standard reference price that is used to accompany requests for price quotations. An option price-maker (human or machine) benefits greatly from having the TV quoted alongside the trade details, for a number of reasons: first, it acts as a check that the trade details have been communicated and set up correctly and that the same uncontentious market data is seen by both sides of the request for price. Secondly, the rough value of the TV (1%? 10%? 90%?) immediately tells the price-maker what kind of moneyness level the trade involves, and this is often crucial to the way in which a smile price will be calculated. And third, many FX option market-makers think of TV as a "base price", and then regard any non-Black–Scholes model in terms of the adjustment to TV that the model brings about. The adjustment to TV is known as the "skew to TV", and we will discuss it in greater length later in the chapter.

Furthermore, the TV is often used to specify the parameters of a contract. A common example is that the barrier levels of a double no-touch are very often set (symmetrically about spot) in such a way that the TV of the contract is exactly 10%. The contract is then referred to as a "10%-TV symmetric double no-touch".

4.5.1 Conventions for extracting market data for TV calculations

The conventions for extracting TV volatility and interest rates are as follows:

- The TV volatility is the implied volatility for an expiry time equal to that of the barrier option and for a strike equal to the market-conventional at-the-money (ATM) strike at the expiry time. At-the-money conventions vary between currency pairs and to a limited extent with tenor. For our three benchmark currency pairs, Figures 4.1–4.3 display the at-the-money points on top of the

implied volatility smiles, and thereby give us a nice visual appreciation of how much difference there might be between TV prices and smile-based prices.
- For each currency, the TV interest rate R is the effective zero-coupon-bond (ZCB) rate for the *settlement date* T_s of the barrier option. It can be obtained from the instantaneous short interest rate curve $r(\cdot)$:

$$R(T_s) = \frac{1}{T_s - t_0} \int_{t_0}^{T_s} r(s) \, ds \qquad (4.15)$$

where t_0 is the current time, at which we are valuing the option.

4.5.2 Example broker quote request

Many FX barrier option trades are quoted and booked directly between two counterparties, for example between a bank and one of its corporate clients. One of the benefits of such a relationship is that trades can be customized to the individual needs of a client. In addition to such direct channels, there are highly active **broker markets**, in which trades between counterparties are brokered. FX options brokers are generally *introducing brokers*, that is, they sit between counterparties only for the purpose of price quoting, but the deals that are agreed are booked directly between counterparties without washing through the broker. The participant counterparties are typically market-making banks, and in fact the majority (though not all) of the inter-bank market is conducted via broker markets.

Note that both the direct channels and the broker markets are examples of so-called **over-the-counter** (OTC) markets, where no exchange house is involved.

A broker receiving a price quotation request from one participant bank will show the contract specification to all other participants and invite them to make 2-way prices. The name of the requesting participant is kept confidential until a deal is agreed.

The high level of sophistication on both sides allows requests for price quotes, and the contract specifications therein, to be written in an esoteric form that is highly concise, if cryptic. For example, a bank might see the following price quote request:

```
8m 28-30 Oct 15 Nyk / Eur-Usd One Touch / 0.9600 Trigger / Spot
1.1350 / Tv 2.0 vol 9.05 / Delta E700k / P.Out E1-2m ... fwd +43.0 ; $
depo 0.55 .... asked with VH ... Pls
```

We can decipher the sections of this price quote request as follows:

- "8m 28-30 Oct 15 Nyk" gives the expiry information: eight-month tenor, an expiry date of 28 October 2015 and a settlement date of 30 October 2015. The expiry cut is the New York cut.

- "`Eur-Usd One Touch`" gives the contract type information.
- "`0.9600 Trigger`" tells us the barrier level and, implicitly, that the barrier is on the down-side.
- "`Spot 1.1350`" is the spot reference. It is used both for calculating the TV and as the exchange rate for the "delta exchange" (described below).
- "`Tv 2.0`" tells us that the TV of the contract is 2%, in %EUR terms.
- "`vol 9.05`" tells us that volatility reference is 9.05%. This is used for calculating both the TV and the vega hedge.
- "`Delta E700k`" indicates that the option trade will be accompanied by a spot trade in 700,000 euros, at the spot reference. This is known as **delta exchange**. The delta is conventionally specified for a principal of 1 million euros.
- "`P.Out E1-2m`" means that the principal ("payout") will be between 1 and 2 million euros. That is to say, the trade is in normal size.
- "`fwd +43.0`" tells us that the forward points reference is 0.0043. (As explained in Section 1.2.1, the quoted number is a scaled version of the forward points, and the scaling factor for EURUSD is 10,000.) This is used for calculating both the TV and the vega hedge.
- "`$ depo 0.55`" means that the US dollar interest rate to use for the TV calculation is 0.55%.
- "`asked with VH`" indicates that the option trade will be accompanied by a vega hedge, which will be calculated using the reference market data.
- "`Pls`" stands for Please. How could one refuse?

The above quote request illustrates very nicely how TV is used as an essential means of communication in the FX barrier options markets.

4.6 Modelling market implied volatilities

Our discussion of the vanilla option market, in Section 4.4, described how to calculate market quotes once we have an implied volatility smile. But often our aim is the opposite: we wish to calculate the smile from market quotes. Being a continuous function of strike, the smile has more degrees of freedom than can be uniquely fitted to, say, five market quotes. To achieve our aim, we need an **implied volatility smile model** which we can *calibrate* to the five market quotes. As a simple illustration, consider a smile model which is a quartic polynomial in strike. A quartic polynomial has five parameters, so we should be able to calibrate such a model exactly to the five market quotes.

A common misconception about the FX vanilla options market is that the market quotes at a given expiry give us, say, five known points in (strike, volatility) space, and the role of the implied volatility model is merely to interpolate between them. As we have seen, that is not the case – the form of the market quotes is more complicated than that.

Once we have a calibrated implied volatility smile model, we can read off the implied volatility at any strike we choose. We can do this for any of the straight dates, but we must of course calibrate a separate smile model for each of these dates. But what about expiry times in between the straight dates? The simple answer is that we need another model, and this time its role is to interpolate between implied volatilities at the straight dates. It is often referred to as a **term structure interpolation model**. The implied volatility smile model and the term structure interpolation model are usually two separate models, but we very often refer to the combination of the two as the **implied volatility surface model** or simply "implied volatility model". The BSTS model can be thought of as a special case where we are effectively ignoring the smile, and it requires a term structure interpolation model only.

There is no single correct way of modelling implied volatility, and so the implied volatility models that are used in the industry are generally proprietorial, and the subject of ongoing research. Their status is therefore fundamentally different from that of the Black–Scholes model, which is a well-defined industry standard.

The absolute requirement to have an implied volatility surface model is the reason I wrote at the start of Section 4.4 that the vanilla market alone is not quite enough to give us the implied volatility surface.

4.7 The probability density function

For a given future time, we can compute the risk-neutral probability density function (PDF) of spot at that future time from two ingredients: the implied volatility smile for options expiring at that time, and the forward to the corresponding settlement date. This is a standard method in mathematical finance, but let us briefly outline it now. The key to the relationship is vanilla option prices: the undiscounted call option price C can be written in terms of the PDF of spot f_S as follows:

$$C(K) = \int_K^\infty f_S(s)(s-K)\,ds \quad (4.16)$$

Differentiating twice with respect to strike, we obtain the following elegant result:

$$f_S(K) = \frac{d^2 C}{dK^2} \quad (4.17)$$

Using the definition of implied volatility, Equation 4.8, we can express Equation 4.17 in terms of implied volatility:

$$f_S(K) = \frac{d^2}{dK^2} C_{BS}(K, \Sigma(K)) \quad (4.18)$$

where we have dropped the explicit dependence on maturity T as we are currently considering a fixed maturity.

The strike-derivative in Equation 4.18 may be evaluated numerically, allowing the PDF to be computed for any choice of implied volatility smile $\Sigma(K)$. Alternatively, we may use the chain rule to expand Equation 4.18, obtaining the following (inelegant) expression for the PDF in terms of call option Greeks (and co-Greeks) and the strike-derivatives of the implied volatility:

$$f_S(K) = \frac{\partial^2 C_{BS}}{\partial K^2} + 2\frac{\partial^2 C_{BS}}{\partial K \partial \Sigma}\frac{d\Sigma}{dK} + \frac{\partial^2 C_{BS}}{\partial \Sigma^2}\left(\frac{d\Sigma}{dK}\right)^2 + \frac{\partial C_{BS}}{\partial \Sigma}\frac{d^2 \Sigma}{dK^2} \qquad (4.19)$$

Analytic expressions for the call option Greeks and co-Greeks may be derived straightforwardly, and if we additionally have analytic expressions for the strike-derivatives of the implied volatility, Equation 4.19 allows us to calculate the PDF entirely in terms of analytic expressions. If we do not have access to analytic expressions for the strike-derivatives of the implied volatility, these would need to be computed numerically, and in this case it may be simpler just to numerically perform the derivative in Equation 4.18.

Figure 4.4 shows the risk-neutral PDF corresponding to the three-month EURUSD implied volatility smile (the "smile PDF"), and alongside it is the PDF corresponding to the constant volatility that would be used for the TV calculation of a three-month option (the "TV PDF").

We can see that moving from the TV PDF to the smile PDF has the following effects: the values at and around the peak become greater ("taller peak"), the values at very low and high strikes become greater ("fatter tails") and in between (around the points of inflexion), the PDF becomes lower ("thinner peak"). These three effects – taller peak, thinner peak and fatter tails – are found, to varying degrees, for all smile-shaped implied volatility smiles, and the pdfs are all examples of a "leptokurtic" distribution.

The effects described above can be magnified by plotting the **PDF skew**, which is defined as the smile PDF minus the TV (constant-volatility) PDF:

$$\text{PDF skew} \doteq \text{smile PDF} - \text{TV PDF} \qquad (4.20)$$

Figures 4.5, 4.6 and 4.7 show the PDF skews for the three-month and six-month smiles for, respectively, EURUSD, USDTRY and AUDJPY (our three benchmark pairs). We shall shortly see, in Section 4.9, that a knowledge of the shape of the PDF skew, and its variation with expiry time, can help us interpret and explain the effects of smile pricing.

Smile Pricing | 139

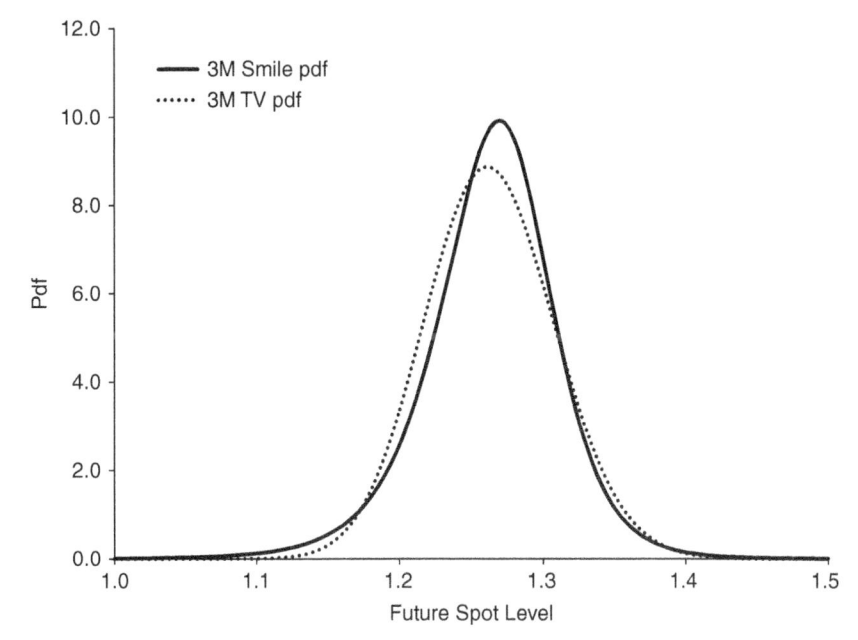

Figure 4.4 Three-month EURUSD risk-neutral smile PDF (full line) and TV PDF (dotted line)

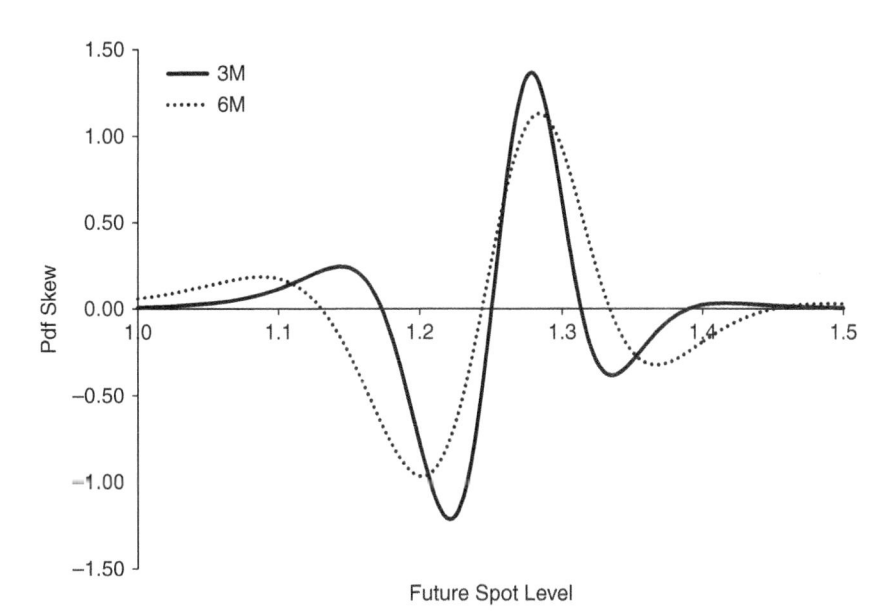

Figure 4.5 EURUSD PDF skews for expiries of three months (full line) and six months (dotted line)

140 | FX Barrier Options

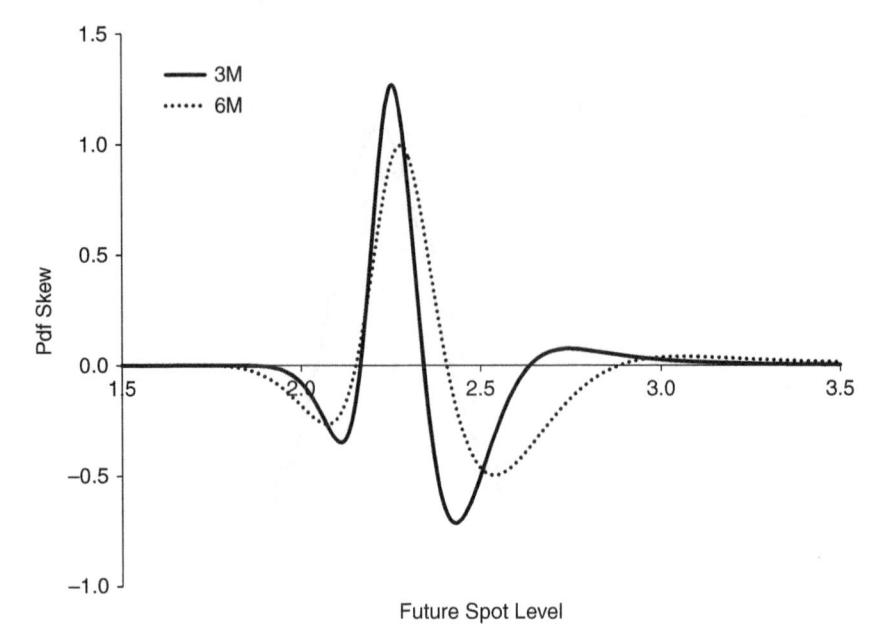

Figure 4.6 USDTRY PDF skews for expiries of three months (full line) and six months (dotted line)

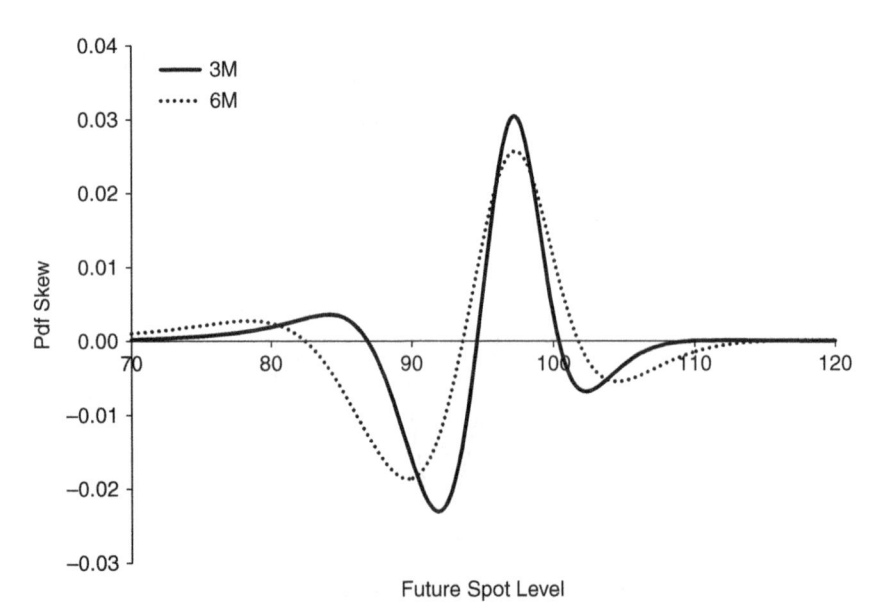

Figure 4.7 AUDJPY PDF skews for expiries of three months (full line) and six months (dotted line)

4.8 Three things we want from a model

Now is a good time to ask ourselves what exactly we want from an FX barrier option valuation model. Our discussions so far would suggest that we need the following properties:

- The model can be calibrated to exactly price vanilla options at all strikes and maturities in any FX market.
- Calibration is straightforward and fast.
- The model may be used to calculate prices for all our barrier options consistently with each other and with vanilla options.

This wish list brings us neatly to....

4.9 The local volatility (LV) model

In going from the Black–Scholes (BS) process model of Equation 2.4 to the Black–Scholes-with-term-structure (BSTS) process model of Equation 4.1, we took the step of extending the instantaneous volatility from being a constant value to being a function of time. This extra degree of freedom was just enough to allow us to calibrate our model to a term structure of implied volatilities, that is, to an implied volatility that is a function of option maturity. The **local volatility** (LV) **model** of Bruno Dupire [25] goes a giant leap further, and makes the instantaneous volatility additionally a function of spot. The risk-neutral process is then given by:

$$dS = (r_d - r_f) S \, dt + \sigma_{LV}(S, t) \, S \, dW_t \qquad (4.21)$$

The volatility function $\sigma_{LV}(S, t)$ is a *deterministic function*, but it takes *random values* due to its dependence on spot. The interest rates are implicitly time-dependent.

Dupire showed in 1994 that the extra spot-dependence introduced by the LV model allows us to calibrate the model to an *entire implied volatility surface*. More than that, he showed how the local volatility function can be calculated directly in terms of the implied volatility and the derivatives of the implied volatility with respect to maturity and strike. Once we have computed the local volatility function $\sigma_{LV}(S, t)$ in this way, we have at our disposal a single self-consistent model under which all the vanilla options in the market are repriced. Like the genie from the bottle, the local volatility model grants us the three wishes we made in Section 4.8.

Dupire's 1994 article describes the problem in terms of the equity index option market, but his derivation is applicable to foreign exchange, and in Appendix C we give an FX-specific derivation of the local volatility, expressing the result in a number of different forms. We now discuss two of those forms. The formula in terms of undiscounted call prices C is (from Equation C.18):

$$\sigma_{\text{LV}}(K, T) = \sqrt{\frac{\frac{\partial C}{\partial T} - (r_{\text{d}} - r_{\text{f}})(C - K\frac{\partial C}{\partial K})}{\frac{1}{2}K^2 \frac{\partial^2 C}{\partial K^2}}} \qquad (4.22)$$

The formula in terms of implied volatility Σ is (from Equation C.36):

$$\sigma_{\text{LV}}(K, T) = \sqrt{2\frac{\frac{\partial \Sigma}{\partial T}(T-t) + \frac{1}{2}\Sigma + (r_{\text{d}} - r_{\text{f}})(T-t)K\frac{\partial \Sigma}{\partial K}}{K^2 \frac{\partial^2 \Sigma}{\partial K^2}(T-t) + K\frac{\partial \Sigma}{\partial K}(T-t) + \Sigma^{-1}\left(1 + d_1 K\frac{\partial \Sigma}{\partial K}\sqrt{T-t}\right)\left(1 + d_2 K\frac{\partial \Sigma}{\partial K}\sqrt{T-t}\right)}}$$
$$(4.23)$$

There are a number of useful remarks we can make about these formulae. First, we can see by inspection of Equation 4.23 that this formula has the correct limiting behaviour for constant volatility (the BS model) and for strike-independent volatility (the BSTS model). For BS, if we set all the implied volatility derivatives to zero, we obtain the result: $\sigma_{\text{LV}} = \Sigma$, which formally shows that the process volatility (σ_{LV}) is the same as the implied volatility (Σ). For BSTS, we obtain a formula for calculating the (time-dependent) process volatility in terms of the term structure of implied volatility:

$$\sigma_{\text{LV}}(T) = \sqrt{2\Sigma \dot{\Sigma}(T-t) + \Sigma^2}$$

This equation can be re-written in the following form:

$$\sigma_{\text{LV}}^2(T) = \frac{\partial}{\partial T}\left[\Sigma^2(t, T)(T-t)\right] \qquad (4.24)$$

which tallies with the result presented in Equation 4.5.

The quantity in the square brackets of Equation 4.24 – the square of the implied volatility multiplied by the time to maturity – is known as **implied variance**. The term is not specific to the BSTS model, and is also used when the implied volatility depends on strike, so that in general the definition is:

$$\text{implied variance} \doteq \Sigma^2(S, t; K, T_{\text{e}})(T_{\text{e}} - t) \qquad (4.25)$$

Similarly, the square of the local volatility σ_{LV}^2 is often called the **local variance**, although I prefer to avoid this term as the quantity isn't really variance-like. So, in words, Equation 4.24 shows that, under the BSTS model, *the local volatility squared is the rate of change of implied variance with respect to maturity.*

The second useful remark we can make is that the local volatility is not guaranteed to be a real number! What is to stop the argument of the square root being negative? The question sounds rhetorical, but actually we can answer it literally: if the numerator and denominator of the fraction both remain non-negative, *that* will stop the argument of the square root being negative. The LV model thus requires the following two conditions on the call price function $C(K, T)$ to be satisfied:

$$\frac{\partial C}{\partial T} \geq (r_d - r_f)(C - K\frac{\partial C}{\partial K}) \qquad (4.26)$$

$$\frac{\partial^2 C}{\partial K^2} \geq 0 \qquad (4.27)$$

Conditions on the implied volatility can similarly be written down by inspection of Equation C.36, by requiring that both the numerator and the denominator of the fraction in the square root argument be non-negative. Equations 4.26 and 4.27 represent **no-arbitrage conditions** on the call price in the LV model.

Let us now look at Equations 4.26 and 4.27 in detail. Equation 4.26 asserts that undiscounted call prices must increase with maturity at a certain minimum rate. This minimum rate may be negative, in which case we may prefer to say that undiscounted call prices must "decrease less quickly" than a certain rate. The partial derivative with respect to T is taken at constant strike, since the function C is defined to depend on strike and maturity. If we instead look at the corresponding condition for the function $\tilde{C}$ which depends on *moneyness* and maturity (introduced and derived in Appendix C), we have:

$$\frac{\partial \tilde{C}}{\partial T} \geq (r_d - r_f)\tilde{C} \qquad (4.28)$$

This is easier to interpret: the rate of change in value of the call option with maturity must be at least as large as the drift rate of the spot process. This can be explained as follows: even in the limiting case where the variance is not increasing at all with maturity, the option value will still respond to the drift rate (note that $(r_d - r_f)$ can be either positive or negative). The reason that the strike derivative in Equation 4.26 is not present in Equation 4.28 is that, in the latter, we are moving through time along a line of constant moneyness. Violation of Equation 4.26 is called **calendar arbitrage**.

The second equation is most easily interpreted by referring back to Equation 4.17 and recalling that $\frac{\partial^2 C}{\partial K^2}$ is exactly equal to the risk-neutral probability density function. It makes perfect sense that the PDF must be non-negative to avoid arbitrage. Violation of Equation 4.27 is called **distributional arbitrage**.

Mathematical analysis of the kind performed above gives us a valuable perspective on the LV model, but as I have emphasized before, to really understand any model, we must become familiar with its *valuation behaviour*. Valuation of options under the LV option pricing PDE involves techniques very similar to those we discussed for valuation under the BSTS model. Repeating once more the procedures described in detail in Chapter 2, we can derive the following LV option pricing PDE:

$$\frac{\partial V}{\partial t} + (r_d(t) - r_f(t))S\frac{\partial V}{\partial S} + \frac{1}{2}(\sigma_{LV}(S,t))^2 S^2 \frac{\partial^2 V}{\partial S^2} = r_d(t)V \quad (4.29)$$

This PDE can solved by finite-difference methods, under the boundary conditions imposed by the contract being valued. Alternatively, and again similarly to the BSTS model, we can perform Monte Carlo simulation of the LV-model risk-neutral process, given by:

$$dS = (r_d(t) - r_f(t))S\,dt + \sigma_{LV}(S,t)S\,dW \quad (4.30)$$

Chapter 6 discusses these numerical methods and some associated techniques. For the current chapter, we can assume we have the necessary tools, and so it is now time to examine the valuation behaviour of various options under the LV model.

In Chapter 1, we discussed products in an order which corresponded to their evolutionary development, covering barrier-contingent vanilla options before barrier-contingent payments. In Chapter 2, we saw that in terms of valuation behaviour, the complexity is rather the other way around, since barrier-contingent vanilla options combine two effects, that of the barrier and that of the optionality. For that reason, we will in this chapter examine barrier-contingent payments before barrier-contingent vanilla options.

Another difference in the way we will examine valuation behaviour is the parameters that we will vary. In Chapter 2, we generally plotted the variation of values and Greeks against *spot*. However, with smile pricing, variation with spot is not uniquely defined. As we will discuss in Chapter 5, when spot moves, there are various different assumptions that can be made regarding what happens to the implied volatility surface. Until we explicitly wish to examine the effects of these assumptions, it makes more sense to hold spot constant and vary the contract strike and/or barrier levels.

Figure 4.8 shows the variation with barrier level of the LV model value of a three-month EURUSD down-side one-touch paying in USD. The corresponding TV results have been plotted alongside.

It is immediately clear that the LV and TV results are different, but not wildly different. An obvious way to highlight and magnify the differences is to plot the *differences* in value rather than the values themselves. The standard terminology for

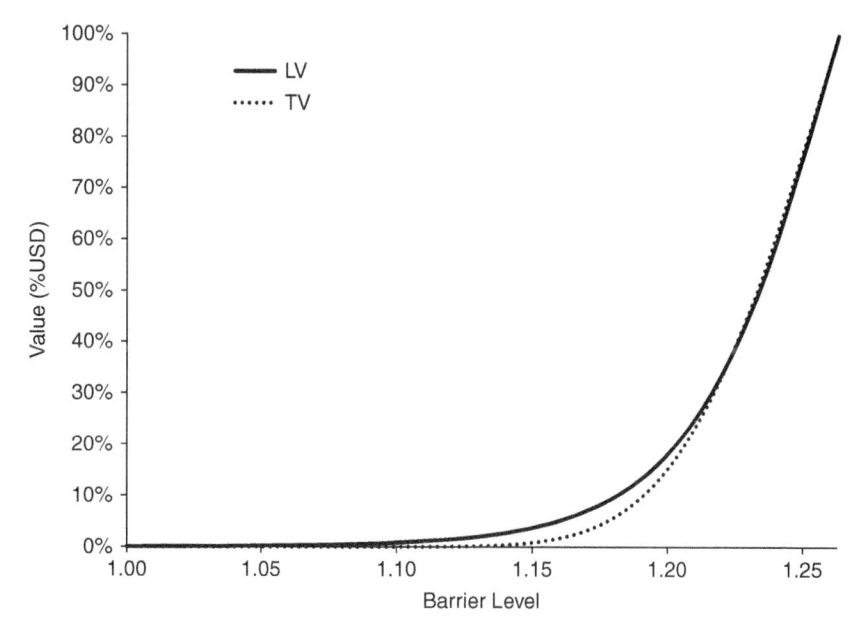

Figure 4.8 Variation with barrier level of the LV model value (full line) of a three-month EURUSD down-side one-touch paying in USD. The TV has been plotted alongside (dotted line)

this difference is the **skew-to-TV**, which I will denote by ΔV_{lv}, and which is defined as follows:

$$\Delta V_{lv} \doteq V_{lv} - V_{tv} \quad (4.31)$$

Plotting the skew-to-TV instead of the values, we obtain the results shown in Figure 4.9. The substantial size of the peak – over 4% – illustrates that the LV model can have a substantial valuation effect for certain trade parameters. And clearly, there are features that we cannot make out from the graphs of values.

Let us now try to interpret and explain the pattern of behaviour exhibited by Figure 4.9. To aid this process, let us recall the effect of the smile on the shape of the PDF, described in Section 4.7. The fatter low-strike tail of the EURUSD PDF means that, relative to TV, there is a higher probability that EURUSD spot will end up somewhere in the low-side tail. For down-side one-touches, this means a higher probability of touching barriers in this low-side tail, and hence a higher price. Sure enough, we can see that the EURUSD skew to TV is positive when the barrier is low (up to about 1.23). Now, for spot levels that are just a little bit lower than at-the-money, the PDF skew is negative, meaning a reduced probability of ending up in this region. This explains the slightly negative skew to TV for barriers above 1.23. As we might well expect, the skew to TV at extremely low barrier levels is zero, since the probability of touching such distant barriers vanishes for both TV and LV pricing. Similarly, when the barrier is extremely close to spot, the probability

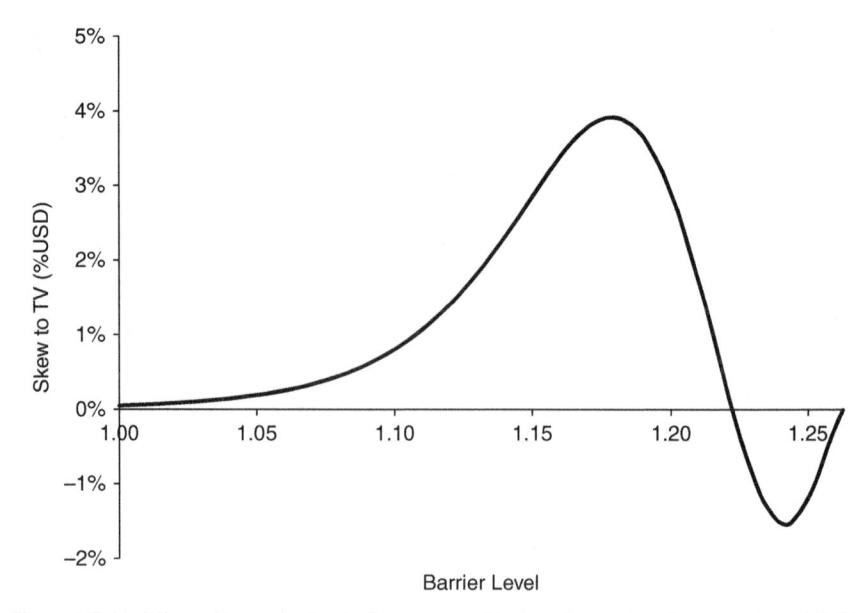

Figure 4.9 Variation with barrier level of the LV model skew-to-TV of a three-month EURUSD down-side one-touch paying in USD

of touching is so close to unity that there is little room for difference between the pricing methods and again the skew to TV tends to zero.

The analysis in the previous paragraph is actually a bit of a cheat. I have explained the pricing of a *path-dependent* option purely via the shape of the PDF, which describes the probabilities of where spot ends up at expiry, but not *how it got there*. Clearly, the shape of the PDF is part of the story, but it is not the whole story. What is perhaps amazing is how well we *can* explain the valuation behaviour of exotic products using this simplistic approach. One way to understand this is to appreciate that the term structures of interest rates and volatilities do not usually contain lots of twists and turns, with the result that the place where spot ends up is a decent first-order indicator of the path it took to get there, and a good starting point for analyzing the effect of the smile on pricing exotics. Varying the exact nature of the spot path leads to smaller but still-significant effects, and we shall discuss this topic at greater length in the section on smile dynamics, Section 4.9.1.

So, what skews to TV do we predict for the corresponding contracts on USDTRY and AUDJPY? The PDF skew for USDTRY is a flipped version of that for EURUSD: strikes lower than spot have positive values and strikes higher than spot have negative values. We would therefore expect the skew to TV profile to be a flipped version of the EURUSD profile and have predominantly negative values, with some slightly positive values for barrier levels that are just a little bit lower than spot. The AUDJPY PDF skew, meanwhile, has the same qualitative form as for EURUSD, so

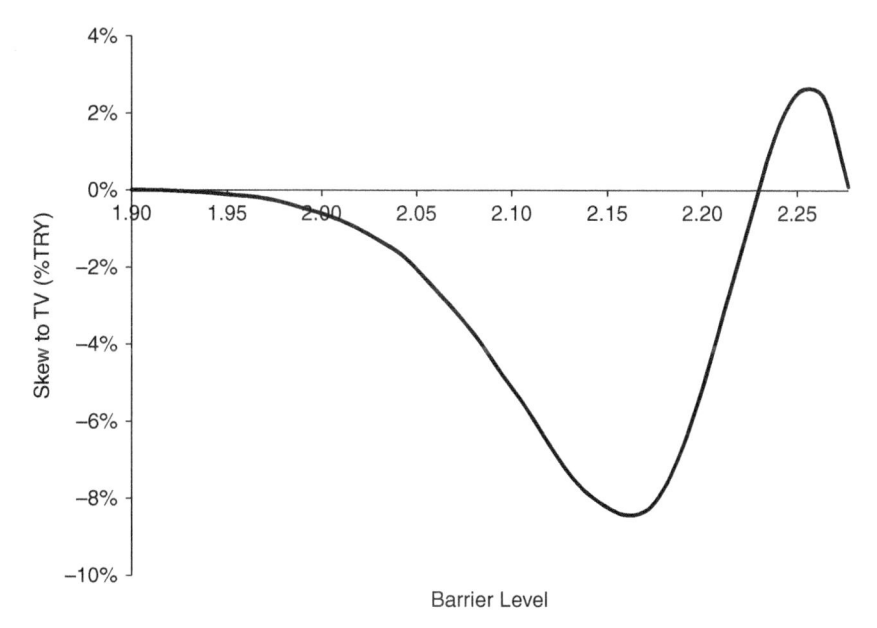

Figure 4.10 Variation with barrier level of the LV model skew-to-TV of a three-month USDTRY down-side one-touch paying in TRY

we would expect its skew to TV to have a similar profile to EURUSD. Lo and behold: the USDTRY and AUDJPY skews to TV, shown respectively in Figures 4.10 and 4.11, have exactly the qualitative behaviour we predicted.

We can furthermore assess the quantitative impact of the LV model on the three contracts by comparing the size of the skews to TV. For EURUSD, we already noted that the peak is over 4%. For USDTRY, the biggest magnitude of skew to TV is over 8%, whilst for AUDJPY it is about 7%.

Note that, for the purpose of better comparability, the three touch contracts we have just looked at are all paying in Domestic, but in practice these may not be the most common payment currencies. For instance, it is more common for USDTRY touches to pay in USD than in TRY.

Valuable as it is to compare three touch contracts using three separate graphs, it would be more revealing to be able to visually compare their behaviour by plotting their respective skews-to-TV on the *same* graph. The values are already in %Domestic, and can therefore be sensibly plotted on the same *y*-axis, but what should we plot on the *x*-axis of our graph? We cannot use the barrier level, as the different currency pairs have completely different spot levels. We could plot against barrier moneyness (barrier divided by spot or barrier divided by forward), but this is also unsatisfactory, as different currency pairs have substantially different drift rates and volatility bases, and therefore a given barrier moneyness corresponds

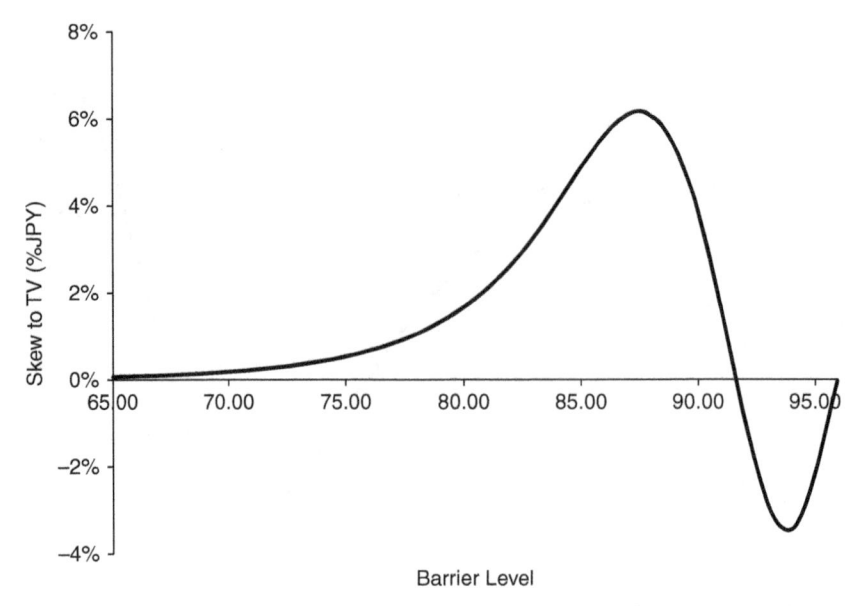

Figure 4.11 Variation with barrier level of the LV model skew-to-TV of a three-month AUDJPY down-side one-touch paying in JPY

to substantially different trigger probabilities for different currency pairs. A much better way to compare results for multiple currency pairs is to plot the skews-to-TV against the *TV itself*. The result is shown in Figure 4.12.

We can do exactly the same thing for the other touch contract types too. Figure 4.13 shows the results for up-side one-touches, which again can be interpreted in terms of the PDF skews. Take, for example, the AUDJPY skew to TV profile. It shows a prominent negative peak in the region below 50% TV, which corresponds to the region of negative PDF skew at higher future spot levels (around 105), as seen in Figure 4.7. The prominent positive peak in the region above 50% TV corresponds to the region of positive PDF skew at future spot levels just above current spot.

The results for down-side and up-side touch contracts essentially depend on the nature of the (expiry-time-dependent) distribution below and above spot respectively. In order to construct a single picture which reflects both sides of the distribution, a commonly applied trick exists whereby the two sets of results are plotted on the same graph, but with the data manipulated so that the two sets of results are contiguous, rather than lying on top of each other. The results of this trick for EURUSD are shown in Figure 4.14.

When we move to the case of the double touches, the contract has an extra degree of freedom, due to the second barrier, and we do not in general have a one-to-one correspondence between TV and barrier levels. In practice, double-touches are very

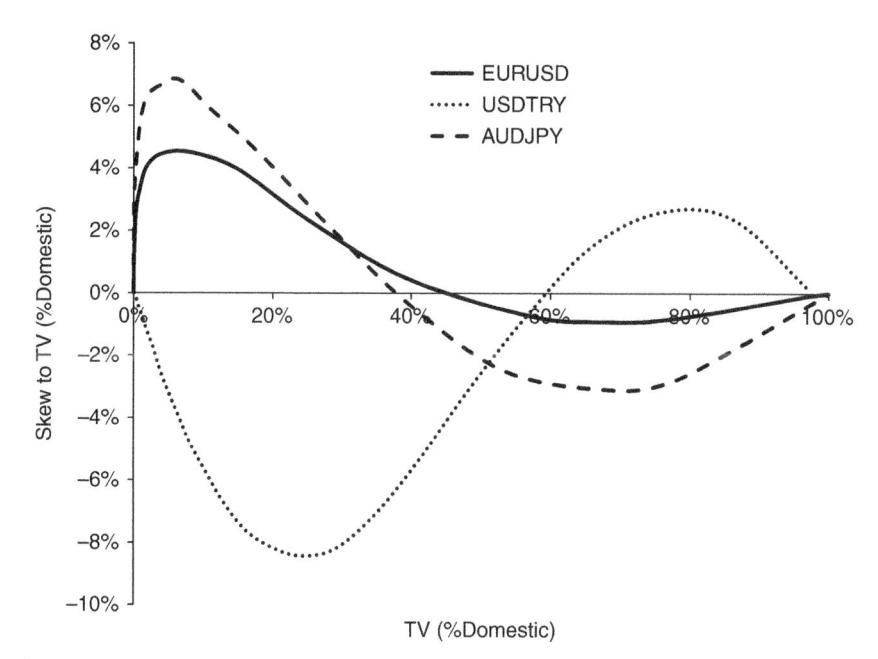

Figure 4.12 Variation with TV of the LV model skews to TV of three-month down-side one-touches on EURUSD, USDTRY and AUDJPY, all paying in Domestic

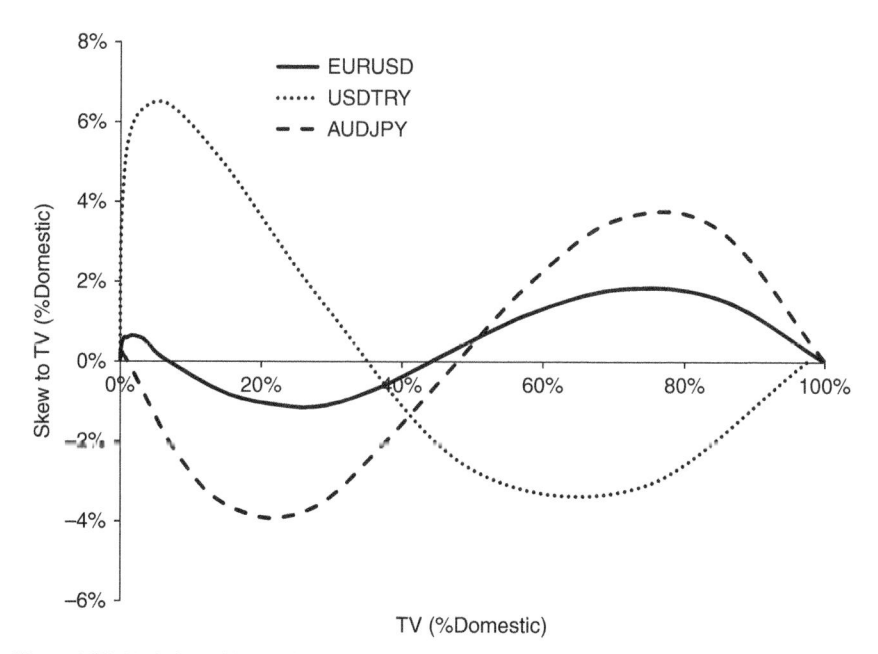

Figure 4.13 Variation with TV of the LV model skews to TV of three-month up-side one-touches on EURUSD, USDTRY and AUDJPY, all paying in Domestic

150 | FX Barrier Options

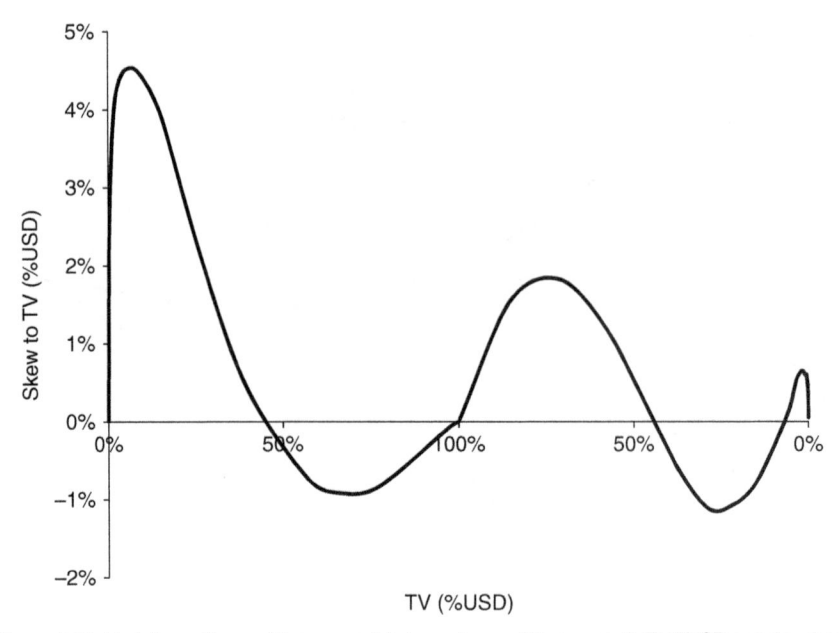

Figure 4.14 Variation with TV of the LV model skews to TV of three-month EURUSD one-touches, paying in USD. The down-side touches are plotted in the left-hand half, the up-side touches in the right-hand half

often set up to have barrier levels that are symmetric around the spot level prevailing at the time of trading. Although the set-up naturally departs from this symmetry as spot moves around after the option has been traded, we can conveniently use this initial symmetry as a constraint to simplify the examination of double-touch options. This symmetric set-up is also the most interesting double-touch set-up to examine, since if spot moves much closer to one of the two barriers than the other, it is intuitively clear that the option will behave something like a single-touch option based on the closer barrier.

Having constrained our double-touch options to have symmetric barriers, we further find that our policy of plotting results against TV nicely obviates the question of whether to plot the results against the lower barrier or the upper barrier. Figure 4.15 shows the variation of double no-touch skews to TV for our three benchmark currency pairs. There being two barriers, there are two effects in play related to PDF skew: the skew at the up-side barrier and the skew at the down-side barrier. The balance between these effects is different for the three different currency pairs.

Next, let us explore the behaviour of some barrier-contingent vanilla options. Here, we really are forced to deal with the extra degree of freedom arising from the strike, and we need a practical way of examining the two-dimensional variation of value with strike and barrier level(s). For our present purpose,

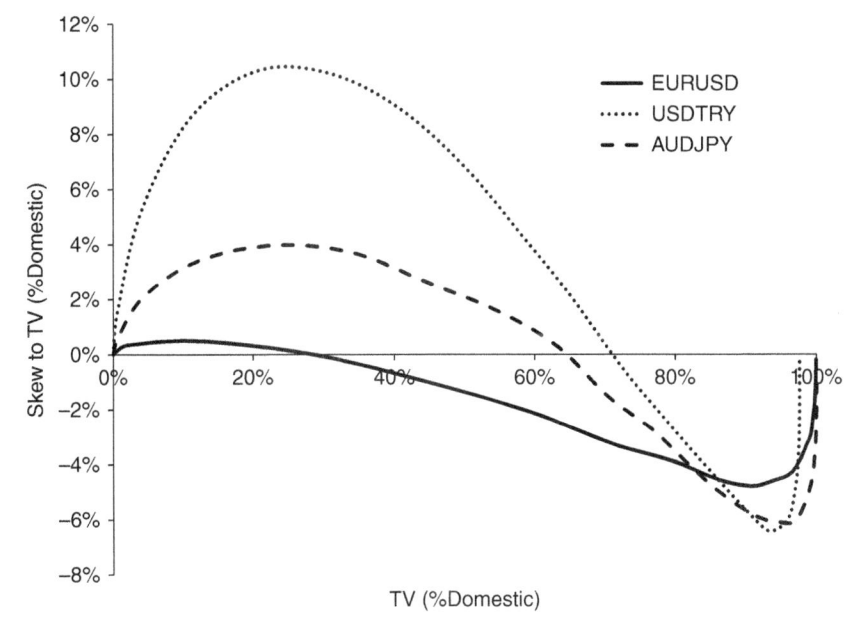

Figure 4.15 Variation with TV of the LV model skews to TV of three-month double no-touches on EURUSD, USDTRY and AUDJPY, all paying in Domestic

we will do this as follows: we will choose three strike levels – at-the-money, 25-delta out-of-the-money and 25-delta in-the-money – and for each of these strike levels we will vary the barrier level(s) (again with barriers symmetrically placed around spot in the case of double-barrier options). Results for three-month EURUSD up-and-out call (CNO) options with at-the-money, in-the-money and out-of-the-money strikes are shown, respectively, in Figures 4.16–4.18.

A subtle but significant feature of Figures 4.17 and 4.18 is that the skew to TV is non-zero at the non-zero-TV extreme. This is in contrast to the touch options, where the skew to TV was always zero at both extremes of TV. Why is this? Well, the non-zero-TV extreme represents the case where the barrier is very far away from spot and the barrier option then behaves essentially as a vanilla. It may at first seem surprising that vanilla options have a non-zero skew to TV, but that is indeed the case. The TV calculation values the vanilla under the TV vol, whereas the LV calculation, by virtue of calibration, values the vanilla to market. That is to say, the LV calculation values the vanilla consistently with the value that would be calculated from Black–Scholes using the volatility at its strike. When the strike is significantly away from the money, the volatility is significantly different from the TV volatility (the volatility is higher in the case of a smiley smile such as EURUSD) and so there is a significant skew to TV. Figure 4.19 shows the variation of the skew to TV of a EURUSD vanilla call option against strike.

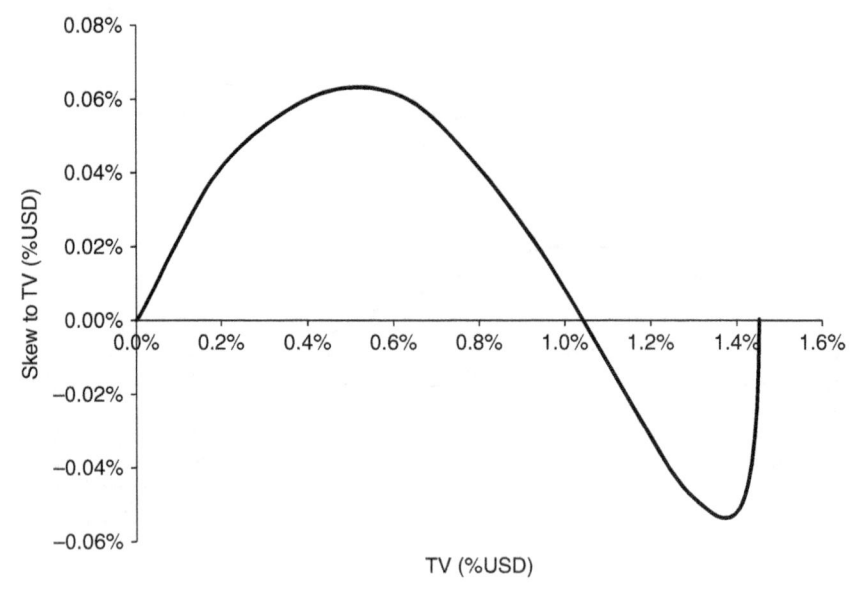

Figure 4.16 Variation with TV of the skew to TV of three-month 1.26-strike (at-the-money) EURUSD up-and-out call options under the LV model

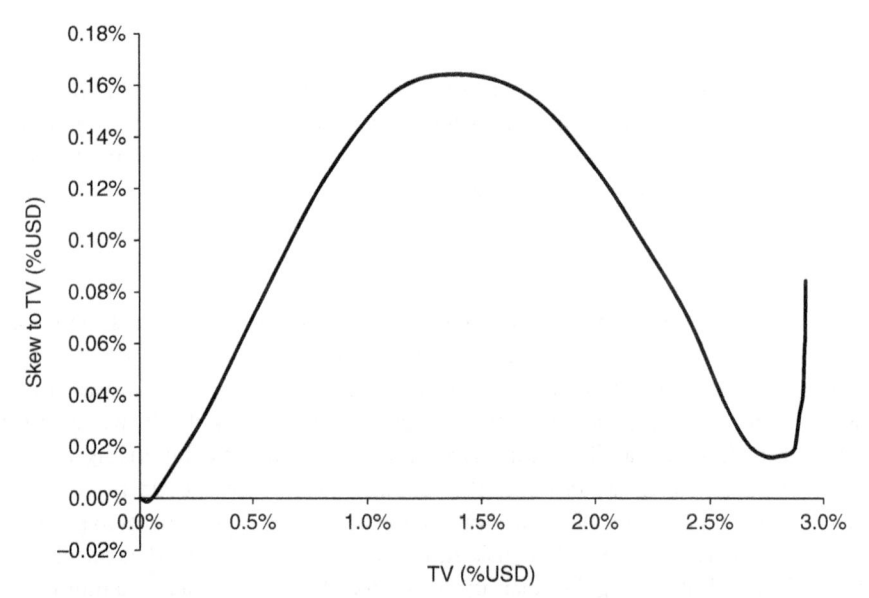

Figure 4.17 Variation with TV of the skew to TV of three-month 1.23-strike (in-the-money) EURUSD up-and-out call options under the LV model

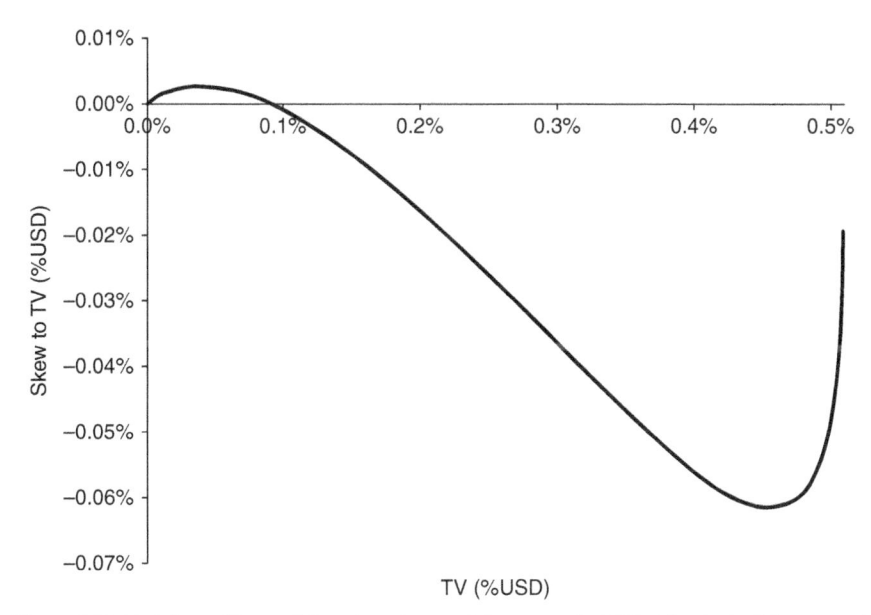

Figure 4.18 Variation with TV of the skew to TV of three-month 1.30-strike (out-of-the-money) EURUSD up-and-out call options under the LV model

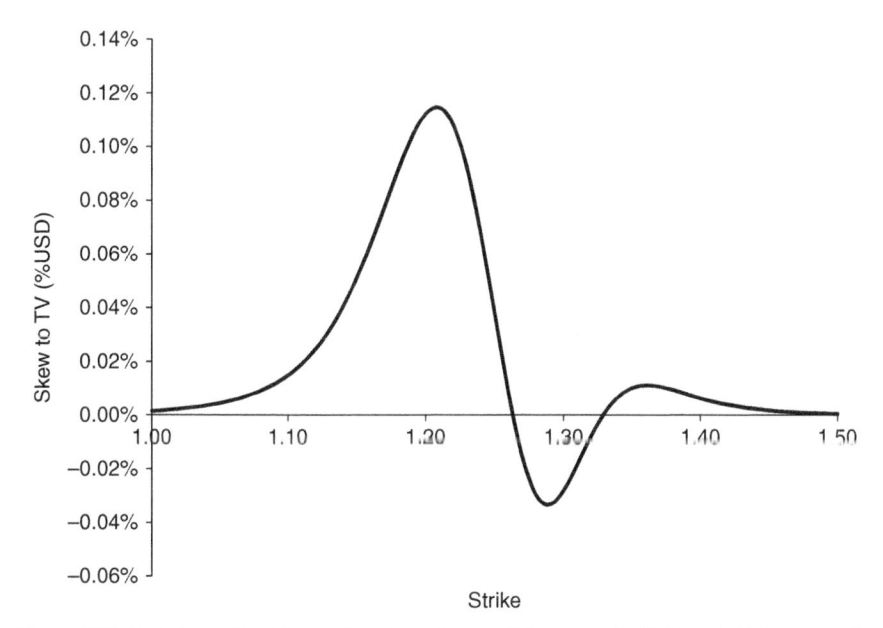

Figure 4.19 Variation with strike of the skew to TV of three-month EUR call/USD put vanilla options

At the zero-TV extreme of the barrier option graphs, the barrier is very close and the option is almost certain to knock out, so the price goes to zero under both TV and LV, and the skew to TV is correspondingly also zero.

Now, away from the TV extremes, the skew-to-TV behaviour of the barrier-contingent vanilla options exhibits two effects that we must consider and combine. The first effect is the likelihood of barrier trigger, which we discussed to a large extent for the touch options. Let's call this the "barrier skew effect". The second effect is the skew to TV of the vanilla aspect of the option, as described above and illustrated in Figure 4.19. Let's call this the "vanilla skew effect". We would expect that when the barrier is distant, the vanilla skew effect is very close to the vanilla skew to TV, but as the barrier comes nearer, the vanilla skew effect reduces in size. We are now ready to interpret the barrier-contingent results by combining these two effects, the vanilla skew and the barrier skew.

Let us start by looking at the at-the-money case shown in Figure 4.16. Its strike being at the money, the option is not affected by vanilla skew, so we would expect the skew to TV to be explained by barrier skew alone. The higher TVs correspond to more distant barriers, lying in the fat-tails area and therefore more likely to knock the option out, thus explaining the negative skew to TV. Lower TV values correspond to closer barriers, where PDF skew is negative, meaning the option is less likely to knock out and explaining the positive skew to TV.

Next let's look at the in-the-money case shown in Figure 4.17. The barrier skew effect should be similar to the at-the-money case, but there is now additionally a vanilla skew effect. Looking at Figure 4.19, we see that the vanilla skew for an in-the-money call (where strike is around 1.23) is positive, and a few basis points in size, so we would expect the skew-to-TV of the in-the-money barrier option to be a few basis points at the far-barrier extreme, with the effect decreasing as the barrier comes closer. That all ties up exactly with the plotted results.

Lastly, looking at the out-of-the-money case shown in Figure 4.18, we would again expect a similar barrier skew effect, but a different vanilla skew effect. The vanilla skew for an out-of-the-money call (where strike is around 1.30) is negative, and a few basis points in size (again reading off Figure 4.19), so we would expect the skew-to-TV of the out-of-the-money barrier option to be minus a few basis points at the far-barrier extreme, with the effect decreasing as the barrier comes closer. Again, that is indeed the case.

Lastly, we examine double-barrier-contingent vanilla options. Figure 4.20 shows the variation with TV of the skew to TV of three-month at-the-money EUR call/USD put options with symmetric double barriers. Its behaviour is very similar to that of the at-the-money reverse knock-out call discussed above, whose results are displayed in Figure 4.16. In both cases, the strike is at the money, so the options are unaffected by the vanilla skew effect and dependent only on the barrier skew effect.

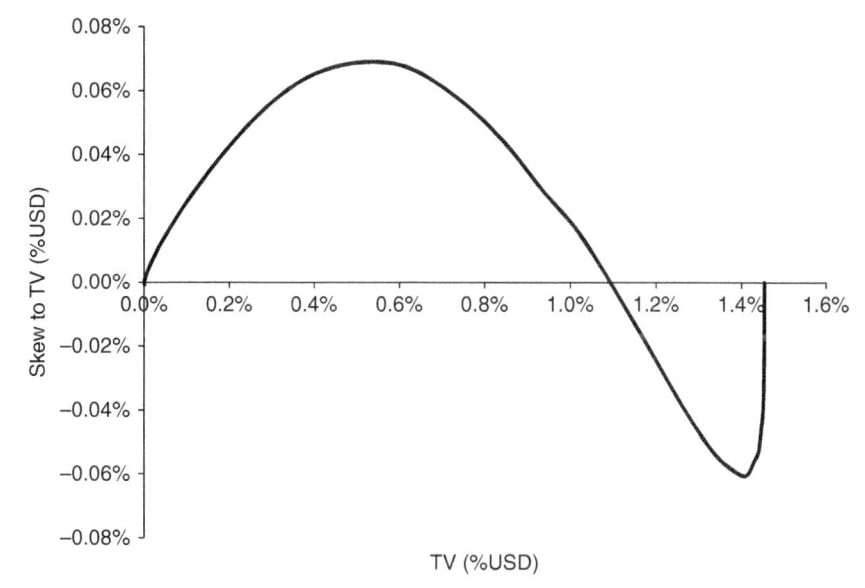

Figure 4.20 Variation with TV of the skew to TV of three-month 1.26-strike (at-the-money) EURUSD double knock-out call options under the LV model

4.9.1 It's the smile dynamics, stupid

So what's wrong with the local volatility model? We can calibrate it exactly to vanilla options at all strikes and maturities, and we can use it to price all our barrier options. The calibration process even automatically checks that our implied volatility surface is arbitrage-free. Surely it's the perfect model? Well not quite. As we discussed in Section 4.9, an important aspect of valuing exotic options is the question of how spot got where it did. In broad terms, we call this aspect of behaviour the **spot dynamics**. There are numerous angles from which we may examine spot dynamics, but one angle that stands out for its importance in the context of FX derivatives is the so-called **smile dynamics** of a model. There are two separate aspects of smile dynamics.

The first aspect is the way in which the model predicts the implied volatility smile will look as time moves forward. There are various assumptions under which one may calculate the implied volatility smile for future trading times, but in general terms, such a future smile is referred to as the **forward smile**. The forward smile dynamics are extremely important for forward-starting contracts, such as a forward-volatility agreement (FVA)[2], but less important for the barrier options that we have been considering.

---

[2] FVAs are especially sensitive to the forward smile when they are based on out-of-the-money options, but these are in practice uncommon, and the more common FVAs, which are based on at-the-money options, are very much less sensitive to the forward smile.

The second aspect of smile dynamics is the way in which the model predicts the implied volatility smile will look as spot moves around, and this aspect is crucial for modelling barrier options. I will call this **smile relocation**. Taking the example of our benchmark EURUSD surface, at the current (benchmark) spot and time, we have a smile which is very roughly symmetrical about the current forward curve. If spot were now to re-locate to a lower level, we would expect, in the absence of fundamental economic changes, that the whole forward curve would have moved lower with spot, and that the new market smile would be placed in the same way about the *new* forward curve. A common way of formalizing this is to assert that the implied volatility for a given strike changes, but that the volatility for a given *moneyness* stays constant. Smile dynamics based on this assertion are correspondingly known as **sticky-moneyness** dynamics. Conversely, if the implied volatility for a given strike did *not* change as spot moved, we would have **sticky-strike** dynamics. Market dynamics are generally much closer to sticky moneyness than to sticky strike. Unfortunately, that is not how the LV model behaves. The calibrated local volatility surface is "baked in" at the current time and spot price, with the result that the implied volatility for a given strike does not change much as spot moves, and the dynamics are closer to sticky strike.

If, after calibration, spot re-locates to some lower level, the model "sees" a smile which has a more negative skew. Conversely, if spot re-locates to a higher level, the model "sees" a smile with a more positive skew. Now, the skew (steepness) of an implied volatility smile is sensitively measured by the value of a risk reversal structure of the same expiry, as discussed in Section 4.4. Any steepening of the smile therefore changes the value of risk reversal positions, and in the industry parlance, when we are dealing with a model whose re-located smile steepens starkly as spot re-locates, we say that the model "realizes a large **risk reversal gamma**".

There is no standard industry convention for quantifying risk reversal gamma. Typically, we are interested in specific options, and it is their prices that we examine quantitatively, whilst using the term "risk reversal gamma" qualitatively. This may partly explain the slight oddity of our using the word 'gamma' even though the effect we are discussing involves the *first-order* change in risk reversal value as spot moves.

The local volatility model, then, is an example of a model that realizes a large amount of risk reversal gamma. Too large, as it happens. Because of its large risk reversal gamma, the LV model does not realistically represent the dynamics of typical FX markets, and despite its many benefits, we are therefore compelled to continue searching for a more suitable model.

4.10 Five things we want from a model

So it seems we need to update our wish list with another couple of items:

- The model can be calibrated to exactly price vanilla options at all strikes and maturities in any FX market.

- Calibration is straightforward and fast.
- The model may be used to calculate prices for all barrier options consistently with each other.
- The model involves a physical process for spot which is a reasonable representation of observed spot-market behaviour.
- The risk reversal gamma of the model realistically represents the dynamics of FX markets.

Our next step is to examine a different class of models.

4.11 Stochastic volatility (SV) models

The LV model local volatility at any future time t, $\sigma_{LV}(S(t), t)$, is a stochastic quantity, depending as it does on a stochastic variable, $S(t)$. However, the function itself is a deterministic function, and the overall model contains only one source of randomness. An obvious next step, then, is to introduce a second source of randomness, on which the instantaneous volatility depends. Such a model is called a **stochastic volatility model**. The class of these models is very wide, and we shall examine arguably the two most important examples.

4.11.1 SABR model

Developed by Pat Hagan et al., the SABR model [26] was originally applied to interest rate options and formulated in terms of forward rates. In the context of Foreign Exchange, the model is most usefully written in the following form:

$$dS = (r_d - r_f) S \, dt + \sigma_S S^\beta \, dW_t^S \qquad (4.32)$$

$$d\sigma_S = \alpha_\nu \sigma_S \, dW_t^\sigma \qquad (4.33)$$

In FX, the parameter β is almost invariably set equal to 1, and then the stochastic differential equation for spot, Equation 4.32, is of the form of a standard geometric Brownian motion, but with the instantaneous volatility σ_S itself a stochastic variable. The instantaneous volatility is governed by its own stochastic differential equation, Equation 4.33. The Wiener processes for spot and vol, W^S and W^σ, may in general be correlated:

$$\mathbb{E}\left[dW^S \, dW^\sigma\right] = \rho \, dt \qquad (4.34)$$

where ρ is called the **spot-vol correlation**. The parameter α_ν in Equation 4.33 is called the **volatility of volatility**.

The SABR ("Stochastic Alpha Beta Rho") model has both significant benefits and drawbacks. Its major benefit is that there exists a closed-form formula which gives a good approximation to the implied volatility for short-dated expiries. Vanilla options can therefore be priced extremely fast, and this fact, together with the model's small number of parameters (3), allows fast calibration of the model. The small number of parameters is also a drawback, however: we cannot hope to match a great deal of the implied volatility surface with so few degrees of freedom.

A further drawback of the model is that the volatility has rather unrealistic dynamics. Specifically, the volatility process is unconstrained, so there is nothing to stop the volatility becoming extremely large or small over time. As we shall see in the section on the Heston stochastic volatility, Section 4.11.2, it is possible to introduce "mean-reversion" in the volatility process, which helps to keep the volatility at sensible levels. The absence of mean-reversion in the SABR model becomes a larger problem as we consider longer maturities, and as a stochastic volatility process model, SABR is not often used, and then only for short maturities, say three months or less.

I wrote "as a stochastic volatility process model" in the previous paragraph, because SABR is extremely widely used in a different context: as an implied volatility smile model. Recall from Section 4.6 that we must calibrate a separate implied volatility smile model for each expiry. The ability to calibrate the SABR model fast is what makes it very suitable for use as a smile model.

4.11.2 Heston model

The stochastic volatility model developed and analyzed by Steven Heston [27] is a landmark in mathematical finance, and arguably the most popular stochastic volatility model used in the world of FX options. It can be written down as follows:

$$dS = (r_d - r_f) S \, dt + \sigma_H S \, dW_t^S \quad (4.35)$$

$$d(\sigma_H^2) = \kappa (\bar{\sigma}^2 - \sigma_H^2) \, dt + \alpha_v \sigma_H \, dW_t^\sigma \quad (4.36)$$

with the value of the parameter κ (Greek letter kappa) constrained to be positive:

$$\kappa > 0 \quad (4.37)$$

The stochastic differential equation for spot, Equation 4.35, is again in the familiar form of a geometric Brownian motion, but this time the instantaneous volatility σ_H is itself a stochastic variable. The volatility is governed by its own stochastic differential equation, Equation 4.36, which is constructed in terms of the *square* of the instantaneous volatility.

The square of the instantaneous volatility is often called the **instantaneous variance**, but as with the term "local variance", I prefer to avoid the term as the quantity is not really variance-like.

The first term of Equation 4.36 introduces no randomness to the process, but it has a stabilizing effect on it. If the volatility goes above $\bar{\sigma}$, the first term becomes negative, and the volatility falls. If the volatility goes below $\bar{\sigma}$, the first term becomes positive, and the volatility rises. Thus the effect of the first term is to draw the volatility back towards the fixed level $\bar{\sigma}$. This effect is known as **mean reversion**, the positive quantity κ is called the **mean-reversion speed**, and the quantity $\bar{\sigma}$ is called the **mean-reversion level**.

The randomness in σ_H is introduced by the second term of Equation 4.36, and is based on a Wiener process W^σ which is different from the one that appears in the spot SDE.

The Wiener processes W^S and W^σ may in general be correlated:

$$\mathbb{E}\left[dW^S dW^\sigma\right] = \rho\, dt \tag{4.38}$$

where ρ is called the **spot–vol correlation**. The parameter α_v in Equation 4.36 is called the **volatility of volatility** (almost always spoken "vol of vol").

Inspection of the dimensions present in Equation 4.36 reveals that the dimension of α_v is T^{-1} (one over time). Conventionally, quantities referred to as volatility usually have dimensions of $T^{-\frac{1}{2}}$, so we might think it more appropriate to say that the volatility of volatility is the *square root* of α_v. However, industry convention has it that we call α_v itself the volatility of volatility, so that is the terminology we shall use here. Whilst it is good to be aware of this pedantic distinction, it is probably more important to understand why it scarcely matters: we choose the model parameters not by measuring the properties of any actual process, but rather by calibration, as described later in this section.

4.11.2.1 *Mean-reversion vs volatility*

The balance between the stabilizing effect of the mean-reversion term and the volatilizing effect of the stochastic term is an important aspect of the Heston model. If the mean-reversion is very strong relative to the volatility of volatility, the instantaneous volatility is very unlikely to move far from its initial value. In the extreme case, when there is no volatility of volatility, the equation for the instantaneous volatility becomes:

$$d(\sigma_H^2) = \kappa(\bar{\sigma}^2 - \sigma_H^2)\, dt \tag{4.39}$$

which can be solved to give the following deterministic result:

$$\sigma_H^2(t) = \sigma_H^2(t_0) e^{-\kappa(t-t_0)} + \bar{\sigma}^2 \left(1 - e^{\kappa(t-t_0)}\right) \tag{4.40}$$

This "deterministic path" describes an exponential decay of volatility-squared from initial level $\sigma_H^2(t_0)$ at time t_0 to mean-reversion level $\bar{\sigma}^2$ at infinite time. The half-life τ of this decay is given by the time after which we are half-way from $\sigma_H^2(t_0)$ to $\bar{\sigma}^2$, hence:

$$e^{-\kappa\tau} = \frac{1}{2}$$
$$\Rightarrow \tau = \frac{\ln 2}{\kappa} \qquad (4.41)$$

This result gives us a useful way to judge what constitutes a weak or strong mean-reversion speed. For example, if we think a half-life of two months is realistic for a given market, we will calculate a mean-reversion speed of 4.2.

If the mean-reversion is instead very weak relative to the volatility of volatility, the volatility is very likely to move far away from its deterministic path. In this case, the volatility may become, and remain, very large, which is unrealistic and undesirable. Worse, the volatility-squared may become negative, after which the process cannot continue (with real values) without being modified in some way. A very useful result that helps us avoid negative process values is the **Feller condition** [28], which states that the process for σ_H^2 remains positive as long as the following (surprisingly simple) condition is satisfied:

$$2\kappa\bar{\sigma}^2 > \alpha^2 \qquad (4.42)$$

Note that this condition automatically enforces our earlier assertion that the mean-reversion speed κ must be positive.

4.11.2.2 Calibrating the Heston model

Combining as it does the effects of volatility of volatility and mean-reversion of volatility, the Heston model gives a qualitatively sensible physical representation of the real-world dynamics of FX spot prices. Other stochastic volatility models may give better representations of real-world dynamics, but the Heston model has a crucial benefit that makes it stand out from the rest: closed-form solutions exist for the prices of vanilla options under the model. This is crucial because when we come to calibrate the model to market implied volatilities, the calibration process involves repeatedly pricing options with different parameter sets. In the case of most stochastic volatility models, there is no closed-form solution for vanilla prices, and the only way forward is to price vanilla options numerically, which makes the calibration process prohibitively expensive. The availability of fast vanilla option pricing for the Heston model means that its calibration can be computationally tractable.

There are two catches, however. The first is that, whilst the Heston model contains more parameters than the SABR model, it's still only five parameters we're talking about, as follows:

1. mean-reversion speed κ;
2. mean-reversion level $\bar{\sigma}$;
3. volatility of volatility parameter σ_v;
4. spot-vol correlation ρ;
5. initial process volatility $\sigma_H(0)$.

Now is a good point at which to consider the effects of these parameters on the shape of the implied volatility surface. The initial process volatility $\sigma_H(0)$ and the mean-reversion level $\bar{\sigma}$ strongly influence the overall level of implied volatility, but have little effect on the smile's skew or convexity. When $\sigma_H(0)$ is much lower than $\bar{\sigma}$, the stochastic volatility process is likely to be upward sloping, and hence we would expect an upward-sloping term structure of at-the-money implied volatility. The spot-vol correlation ρ determines whether volatility tends to move up or down with spot, and as such it strongly influences the skew of the smile. The volatility of volatility parameter σ_v determines the convexity of the smile, but as discussed earlier in the context of the Feller condition, the mean-reversion speed κ serves as a kind of check on its effect.

By adjusting the parameters of the Heston model, we can attempt to match selected points in the implied volatility surface. What points should we select? Having discussed the effects of the parameters above, we know first that $\sigma_H(0)$ and $\bar{\sigma}$ do not much influence the shape of the smile but can help us modify the term structure, and second that σ_v and κ need to exist in some kind of balance. For this reason it is often impossible to fit five strike points at a single expiry time, and a better idea is to attempt to match three points at one expiry and two points at another. A common choice of calibration method is some kind of algorithm based on fitting of the smiles at the barrier option expiry time and at one earlier time.

Irrespective of our specific choice of points to match, the fact remains that we are forced to choose a small handful of points on the volatility surface to which to fit or maybe perform a best fit. We certainly cannot in general calibrate the Heston model to the entire vanilla implied volatility surface, as we could with the LV model. And the prices that we calculate for barrier options will then to some extent be dependent on our choice of calibration points, which is a rather unsatisfactory outcome.

The second catch is that we cannot even adjust the parameters with complete freedom. We have the Feller condition to think about. Ideally, we would like to calibrate the model to our chosen points subject to the constraint imposed by the Feller condition, but unfortunately it very often turns out that we cannot simultaneously calibrate the way we wish to and satisfy the Feller condition.

If the Feller condition is violated, and negative values arise in the volatility-squared process, it is not usually difficult to handle them. For example, if we are valuing exotic options using Monte Carlo simulation, we can simply adjust the the negative value of volatility-squared by replacing it with a non-negative one. There are two typical choices for the replacement value. We may replace the negative value by zero – this is often referred to as "absorption", even though the value does not actually remain at zero, thanks to the mean-reversion. Alternatively, we may replace the negative value by its modulus, to re-set the process to a positive value. However, the more often and more severely we have to adjust the process in this way, the further our adjusted process gets from the true Heston stochastic process.

Even when the Feller condition is satisfied, negative process values may arise in a discretized numerical method (such as Monte Carlo simulation). Finer time-stepping and improved choices of discretization method can significantly reduce the frequency with which negative process values are encountered. For example, Gatheral [29] describes how implementation of the Milstein discretization scheme in place of the usual Euler discretization scheme can substantially alleviate the problem of negative variances.

When I am working with Heston models, I find it useful to calculate and monitor a "**Feller Score**" $f = 2\frac{\kappa \bar{\sigma}^2}{\alpha^2}$. A Feller Score above (/below) 1 tells me that problems with negative process values are unlikely (/likely) to be encountered.

Despite all the above limitations, the Heston model remains popular, largely due to the existence of closed-form vanilla option pricing formulae.

We will see very shortly, in Section 4.12, that we can develop models containing stochastic volatility that we *can* calibrate to the entire implied volatility surface, so we will not now devote further time exploring the effects of the calibration choice on valuation under the Heston model. What we do need to consider now, however, is the nature of the *smile dynamics* of the Heston model.

When spot re-locates, the entire spot-process part of the Heston model (as governed by Equation 4.35) re-locates with it, whilst the volatility-process part of the model (as governed by Equation 4.36) is unaffected. The net result is that the implied volatility smile moves with spot, and there is very little or no steepening of the implied volatility. In other words, the Heston model realizes very little or no risk reversal gamma. This same property is possessed by the SABR model as well, and indeed by stochastic volatility models in general. The class of stochastic volatility models thus stands at the opposite extreme from the local volatility model, which realizes a large amount of risk reversal gamma. Whilst the Heston stochastic volatility model is closer to realistic market dynamics than the local volatility model, we would ideally like a model whose dynamics are somewhere in between.

4.12 Mixed local/stochastic volatility (LSV) models

The story so far: the local volatility model (see Section 4.9) can be calibrated to vanilla options, but has unrealistic spot dynamics and realizes far too much risk reversal gamma. Meanwhile, the Heston stochastic volatility model (see Section 4.11.2) has more realistic spot dynamics, but realizes too little risk reversal gamma, and it cannot be calibrated to vanilla options.

The denouement: we can *combine* elements of the local volatility and stochastic volatility models to construct a class of models with the following three crucial properties:

1. The spot dynamics are realistic.
2. The parameterization gives us control over how much risk reversal gamma is realized.
3. The model can be calibrated to vanilla options.

Such models are collectively referred to as **mixed local/stochastic volatility** (LSV) **models**. (Alternatively they are sometimes called SLV models.) They were introduced in 1999 by Mark Jex et al. [30], since when they have been studied, developed and described a great deal [31, 32, 33, 34, 5, 36, 37, 38]. They are now akin to an industry standard for model-driven valuation of FX barrier options.

I find it useful to start by considering a generic LSV model and writing the stochastic process for spot in the following form:

$$dS(t) = (r_d(t) - r_f(t)) S(t) \, dt + \sigma_0 \Lambda(S,t) \, \Xi(t) \, S(t) \, dW(t) \qquad (4.43)$$

The form of Equation 4.43 is familiar from previously described models, but now its volatility-like part is a product of three factors: σ_0, $\Lambda(S,t)$ and $\Xi(t)$.

The function $\Lambda(S,t)$ (Greek capital letter lambda) is a deterministic function, just like the $\sigma_{LV}(S,t)$ in the local volatility model. As we emphasized when discussing the LV model, in Section 4.9, the function is deterministic, but its values are random due to their dependence on spot. Λ provides the **local volatility component** of the model.

The variable $\Xi(t)$ (Greek capital letter xi) is stochastic, and contributes stochastic volatility to the LSV model in the same form as is obtained in a pure stochastic volatility model such as the Heston model. (We can think of $\Xi(t)$ as the equivalent of the Heston model's σ_H.) Hence $\Xi(t)$ provides the **stochastic volatility component** of the model.

The factor σ_0 is a constant volatility, called the **base volatility**, and is a representative volatility level for the market of interest, such as a short-term at-the-money volatility. It is clearly technically redundant, since its value can trivially be absorbed into one or both of the other two factors, but its presence effectively normalizes the quantities $\Lambda(S,t)$ and $\Xi(t)$, which makes their analysis and comparison much more intuitive. It also means we don't have to worry about "distributing the dimensionality" between $\Lambda(S,t)$ and $\Xi(t)$: σ_0 simply takes up the dimensionality of volatility, and $\Lambda(S,t)$ and $\Xi(t)$ are dimensionless.

The function Λ, whilst being *conceptually* equivalent to the function σ_{LV} in the local volatility model, is of course not the same function. To avoid confusion in discussions involving both functions, I shall refer to Λ as the **local volatility factor** of the LSV model, and to σ_{LV} as the **Dupire local volatility**.

Similarly, I shall refer to Ξ as the **stochastic volatility factor** of the LSV model.

There are various ways in which the stochastic volatility factor of our generic LSV model can be modelled. For example, we could use the Heston model form:

$$d(\Xi(t)^2) = \kappa(\bar{\Xi}^2 - \Xi(t)^2)\,dt + \alpha_v\,\Xi(t)\,dW_\Xi(t) \qquad (4.44)$$

where as before, $dW_\Xi(t)$ is in general correlated with the spot Wiener process $dW(t)$ with correlation ρ. This bestows the virtues of volatility mean-reversion on the LSV model. Moreover, we can meaningfully compare option valuation behaviour under the Heston-based LSV model to that under the pure Heston SV model, which is a significant advantage if we are already familiar with the Heston SV model and have used it for option valuation.

Other popular models for the stochastic-volatility component are the Ornstein–Uhlenbeck process [39]:

$$d\Xi(t) = \kappa(\bar{\Xi} - \Xi(t))\,dt + \alpha_v\,dW_\Xi(t) \qquad (4.45)$$

and the exponential Ornstein–Uhlenbeck process:

$$\Xi(t) = e^{Y(t)} \qquad (4.46)$$

$$dY(t) = \kappa(\bar{Y} - Y(t))\,dt + \alpha_v\,dW_\Xi(t) \qquad (4.47)$$

In line with the Heston nomenclature, the parameters κ, $\bar{\Xi}/\bar{Y}$ and α_v are called the mean-reversion speed, mean-reversion level and volatility of volatility, and again the Wiener process in the volatility process is in general correlated with the Wiener process in the spot process, with the spot–vol correlation denoted by ρ.

One further parameter to be chosen, whatever stochastic volatility model is used, is the initial value of the stochastic volatility factor Ξ.

Calibration of LSV models is achieved in two steps, at least conceptually, and very often also computationally. As a first step, we choose the parameters of the volatility process: the mean-reversion parameters, the volatility of volatility and the spot–vol correlation. The next step is to calibrate Λ, the local volatility factor, to our[3] implied volatility surface.

---

[3] I write "our", rather than "the" implied volatility surface, because as we discussed in Section 4.6, the implied volatility surface depends on our choice of volatility model.

The calibrated model can then be used for valuing barrier options (we discuss valuation methods later in this section), and of course we can (and do) tweak the parameters of the volatility process and iterate the calibration process. Very often, we are seeking to obtain a model which calibrates not only to vanilla options but also to selected highly liquid exotic contracts, such as a three-month 10%-TV symmetric double no-touch.

The calibration of the local volatility factor is achieved using numerical finite-difference methods, and is described in Appendix D. It is a crucial aspect of LSV models, is an extremely interesting numerical problem, and practically speaking tends to account for a large proportion of the total development effort expended on an LSV model. The relegation of its description to an appendix should in no way be seen as a belittling of its importance. It simply fits the structure of this book to encapsulate mathematical details of the calibration in an appendix and leave our path now clear to discuss the dynamics and behaviour of LSV models.

The fact that the calibration of the local volatility factor is performed using numerical finite-difference methods means that it is generally relatively straightforward to extend the volatility process parameters κ, $\bar{\Xi}/\bar{Y}$, α_v and ρ, to be *time-dependent*.

Whilst the particular choice of volatility process naturally makes a difference to the specifics of the spot dynamics, all LSV models share the fundamental property that the spot dynamics are a *mixture* of those of a pure (Dupire) local volatility model and those of a stochastic volatility model. We need to understand exactly what it means to mix two models, so let us start by considering each of the two extremes of this mixture.

Suppose we set the stochastic volatility factor to be a constant. This is easily achieved by setting the volatility of volatility equal to zero and the mean-reversion level equal to the initial level, for example: $\bar{\Xi} = \Xi(0)$. In this limit, any LSV model behaves exactly like the Dupire local volatility model, and the volatility in the spot process, $\sigma_0 \Lambda(S,t) \Xi(t)$, is equal to the Dupire local volatility σ_{LV}. We can say that "all the smile comes from the local volatility".

The opposite limit occurs when the stochastic volatility process is exactly calibrated to our implied volatility surface, whereupon the local volatility factor becomes a constant, and we can say that "all the smile comes from the stochastic volatility". Or at least, this limit would occur if such an exact calibration were possible, but as we saw when discussing the calibration of the Heston model, in Section 4.11.2, the limited number of stochastic volatility parameters means that an exact calibration is in general impossible. When the stochastic volatility parameters are made time-dependent, we can achieve a much better fit, but still cannot realistically calibrate to the entire implied volatility surface. Instead we can conceive of some "good" fit of the stochastic volatility process to our implied volatility surface, and the better this fit is, the closer the local volatility factor is to a constant.

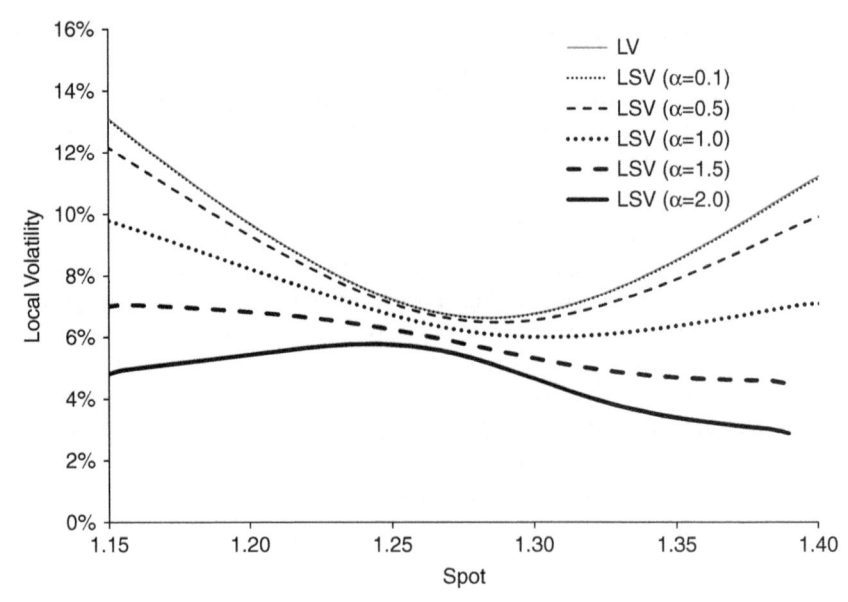

Figure 4.21 Variation with spot of the three-month EURUSD local volatility factor Λ for various different volatilities of volatility. The Dupire local volatility σ_{LV} is plotted alongside

In between these two extremes, we may set the stochastic volatility parameters in such a way that the stochastic volatility component of the model only *partially* reproduces the implied volatility surface. For example, we could set the volatility of volatility equal to half of its best-fit value. We can now say that some of the smile comes from the local volatility component and some from the stochastic volatility component.

We can visualize the balance of the mixture by examining the calibrated local volatility factor Λ and comparing it to the Dupire local volatility σ_{LV}. For this heuristic purpose, it is sufficient to examine Λ at a single time point, but it is important to keep in mind that calibration does not proceed time-point by time-point: it is the entire local volatility factor surface that must be calibrated to the entire implied volatility surface. Figure 4.21 shows, for EURUSD, how the three-month Λ (multiplied by σ_0, so that we have meaningful numbers) varies as the volatility of volatility parameter α is changed. (For simplicity, we leave all other stochastic volatility parameters unchanged.) When α takes the low value of 0.1, the local volatility factor behaves exactly like σ_{LV} and the two curves are barely distinguishable. As α increases, the local volatility factor curve flattens; less of the smile is coming from the local volatility component, and more from the stochastic volatility component. Eventually, α becomes so large that the local volatility factor turns into a **frown** (an upside-down smile). The smile being generated by the stochastic volatility component is now larger than the market smile and the local volatility component must compensate. It is common to establish a level $\alpha_{\max}$ which is the "maximum sensible" value of α: the one that gives rise to the flattest local volatility factor.

Computation of barrier option values under LSV models can be achieved numerically, using the same kinds of techniques that we discussed for the BSTS and LV models, to wit, finite-difference and Monte Carlo methods. Finite-difference methods solve the option pricing PDE, whilst Monte Carlo methods involve simulation of the LSV risk-neutral process given by Equation 4.43 together with whichever SDE is used for the stochastic volatility component. Finite-difference and Monte Carlo methods are discussed further in Chapter 6

The form of the option pricing PDE depends of course on the form of the stochastic volatility model chosen. Derivation of the option pricing PDE proceeds along lines similar to those described for the Black–Scholes model, but this time we need to hedge the volatility in addition to spot. The key to hedging volatility is to assume that we are able to hedge the vega of the option with an instrument whose value and Greeks are known (independently of the option pricing PDE that we are deriving). Yu Tian et al. [37] and Iain Clark [5] give some discussions and derivations of LSV option pricing PDEs. For our discussions here, let us take the example of the exponential Ornstein–Uhlenbeck process model, which gives rise to the following option pricing PDE (dropping the functional dependencies for the sake of clarity):

$$\frac{\partial V}{\partial t} + (r_d - r_f) S \frac{\partial V}{\partial S} + \frac{1}{2}\sigma_0^2 \Lambda^2 e^{2Y} S^2 \frac{\partial^2 V}{\partial S^2}$$
$$+ \kappa(\bar{Y} - Y)\frac{\partial V}{\partial Y} + \frac{1}{2}\alpha^2 \frac{\partial^2 V}{\partial Y^2} + \rho\sigma_0 \Lambda e^Y \alpha S \frac{\partial^2 V}{\partial S \partial Y} = r_d V \qquad (4.48)$$

Having laboriously examined and interpreted the individual terms of the Black–Scholes option pricing PDE back in Section 2.3.4, we are now well equipped to examine and interpret the LSV option pricing PDE. Even though Equation 4.48 relates to one specific stochastic volatility model (namely the exponential Ornstein–Uhlenbeck process), its terms are representative of LSV option pricing PDEs generally.

As we might have expected, the introduction of a stochastic volatility factor in addition to the spot factor results in extra terms in three partial derivatives: $\frac{\partial V}{\partial Y}$ (a vega-like quantity), $\frac{\partial^2 V}{\partial Y^2}$ (a volgamma-like quantity) and $\frac{\partial^2 V}{\partial S \partial Y}$ (a vanna-like quantity). I will refer to the corresponding terms of Equation 4.48 as the **vega term**, the **volgamma term** and the **vanna term**. They give us – at last – a formal representation of the value of volatility moves. The vega and volgamma terms are the volatility analogues of the delta and gamma terms. In the cases of both spot and volatility, the first-order terms (delta and vega) represent the value arising from *expected* moves, and their coefficients are the drift terms of the corresponding SDEs. If the spot process has a zero drift rate (due to the interest rate differential ($r_d - r_f$) being zero), there is no delta term; likewise if the volatility process has a zero drift rate (due to the mean-reversion speed κ being zero), there is no vega term.

The volgamma term is in many ways the term of greatest interest. When interpreting the terms of the Black–Scholes equation, in Section 2.3.4, we arrived at several important conclusions regarding the gamma term: first, that option gamma is worth something; second, that the gamma term of the Black–Scholes PDE measures this value; and third, that this term increases quadratically with the volatility of spot, σ. By analogy, we could have then guessed that option *volgamma* ought to be worth something under a model in which volatility is stochastic, and that this value must increase with volatility of *volatility*. And sure enough, the LSV option pricing PDE corroborates this, and shows that the volgamma term increases quadratically with α.

The vanna term is the cross-term between spot and volatility, and measures the value arising from correlation between the two stochastic quantities. This value is directly proportional to several quantities: the spot–vol correlation ρ, the local volatility factor Λ, the stochastic volatility factor (e^Y) and the volatility of volatility α. Note that if the correlation is zero, the vanna term is zero even if the vanna of the option is itself non-zero.

If we wished to obtain the most simplified LSV model, we could set to zero the spot–vol correlation and both of the drift terms, so that the delta, vega and vanna terms vanished. However, the gamma and volgamma terms will still be present:

$$\frac{\partial V}{\partial t} + \frac{1}{2}\sigma_0^2 \Lambda^2 e^{2Y} S^2 \frac{\partial^2 V}{\partial S^2} + \frac{1}{2}\alpha^2 \frac{\partial^2 V}{\partial Y^2} = r_d V \qquad (4.49)$$

This explains why the gamma and volgamma terms are of such interest.

The valuation behaviour of barrier options under LSV models reflects the interplay between the numerous different effects. We have already examined the effects of local volatility under the LV model, and these effects are essentially the same as those of the local volatility component of the LSV model. To get an idea of the effects of the stochastic volatility component of the LSV model, we can compare LSV values with LV values. Figures 4.22 and 4.23 show how the skew-to-TV profiles of down-side one-touches and double no-touches vary with α.

It is clear that the values can vary widely depending on the choice of α, and we can interpret these effects intuitively. For example, we saw in Section 3.2.1 that a three-month EURUSD 10%-TV double no-touch has a large positive volgamma. We would therefore expect that the value of this double no-touch increases with α (all other parameters remaining the same) – and sure enough, that expectation is borne out by Figure 4.24.

Smile Pricing | 169

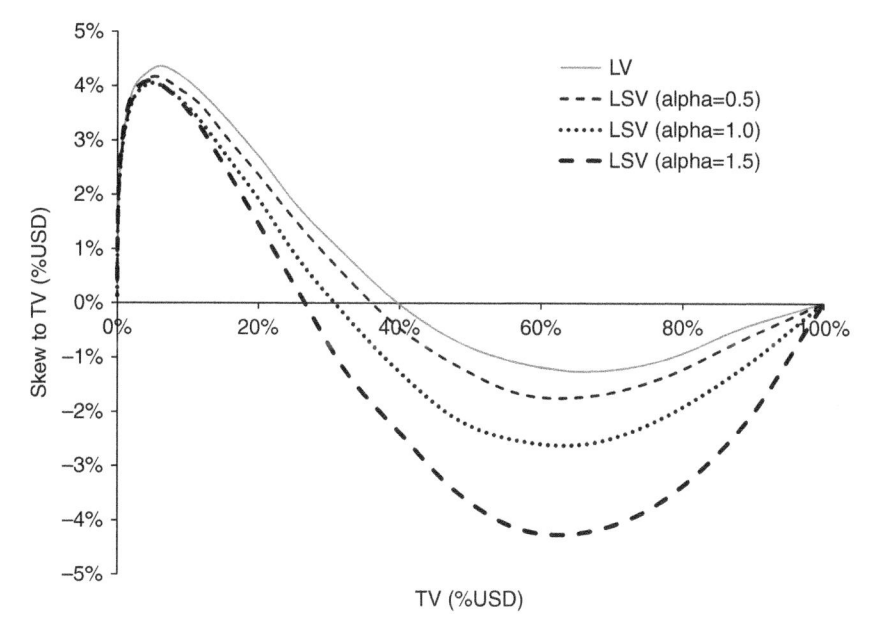

Figure 4.22 Variation with TV of the LSV model skews to TV of three-month EURUSD down-side one-touches paying in USD. Results are shown for two different values of LSV model parameter α, and the LV result is plotted alongside

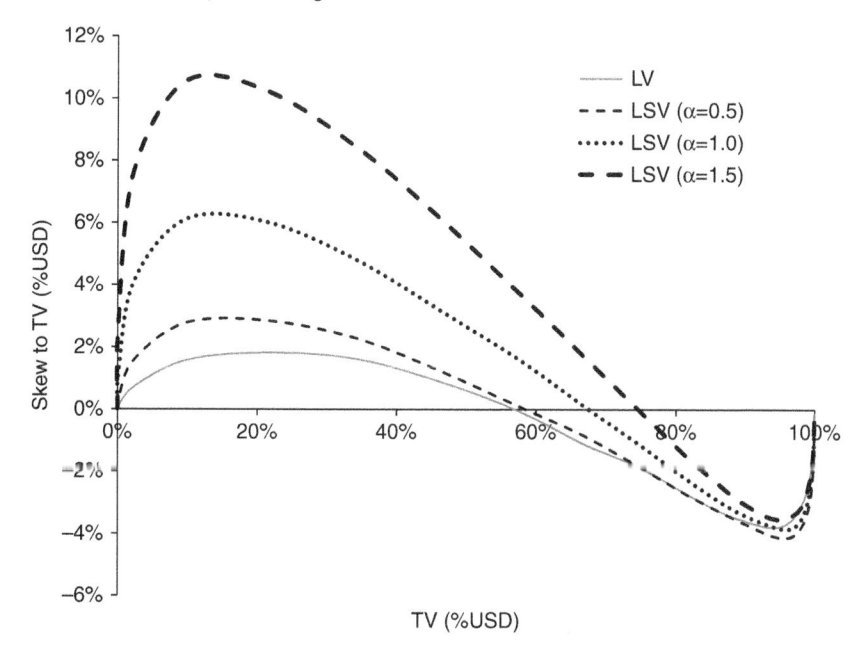

Figure 4.23 Variation with TV of the LSV model skews to TV of three-month EURUSD double-no-touches paying in USD. Results are shown for two different values of LSV model parameter α, and the LV result is plotted alongside

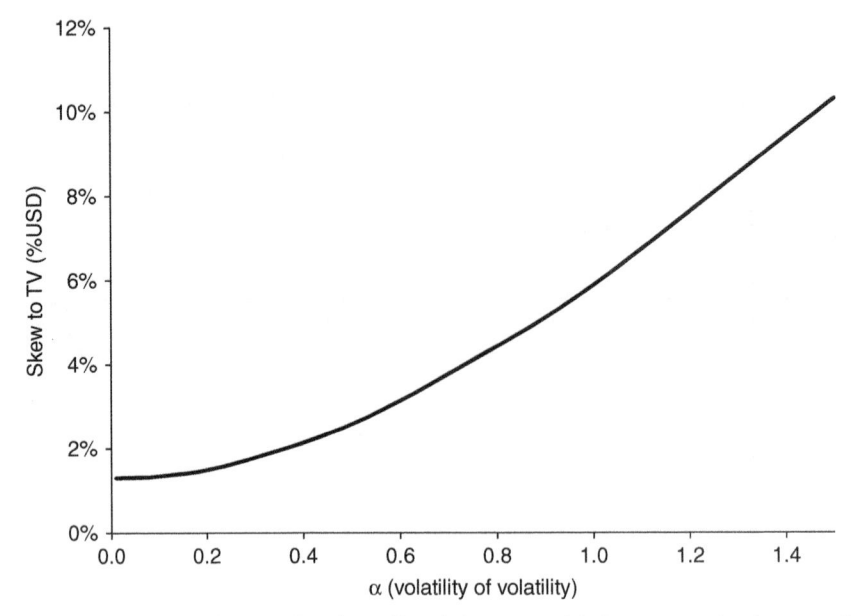

Figure 4.24 Variation with volatility-of-volatility of the LSV model skew to TV of a three-month EURUSD 10%-TV double-no-touch paying in USD

The question of what value of α we should use is obviously a crucial one. Clearly it needs to be somewhere between zero and α_{max} (the "maximum sensible" α). The markets of different currency pairs will have very different values of α_{max}, and to help us orientate ourselves in the domain of α, it is very common to calculate a normalized quantity, $\hat{\alpha}$, that runs from zero to one as α runs from zero to α_{max}:

$$\hat{\alpha} \doteq \frac{\alpha}{\alpha_{max}} \qquad (4.50)$$

This normalized quantity $\hat{\alpha}$ is called the **mixing factor**. For example, if we established for EURUSD that α_{max} was equal to 1.3 (see Figure 4.21), then an α value of 1 would correspond to a mixing factor of $\frac{1}{1.3} = 77\%$[4]. It may well be possible to calibrate the LSV model for values of mixing factor greater than 1, but these will result in local volatility factor curves that are frown-shaped.

4.12.1 Term structure of volatility of volatility

In practice it is found that short-term implied volatilities are consistently more volatile than long-term implied volatilities. A common form of historical analysis

---

[4] It is inevitable in the finance industry that any number that looks like it will take values between 0 and 1 will be quoted as a percentage.

examines the frequency distribution of ATM implied volatilities for a range of maturities (for a given currency pair), and then plots low- and high-percentile values against maturity. The distance between the resulting two lines decreases with maturity, and the plot is consequently referred to as a **volatility cone**. For this reason, it is desirable for an LSV model to admit a term structure of α. The calibration process for such an extended model must correspondingly be enhanced.

4.13 Other models and methods

So far, I have told a story of FX barrier option valuation that began with the Black–Scholes (BS) model, proceeded via Black–Scholes with term structure, Dupire local volatility and stochastic volatility models, and effectively culminated in the LSV models, a class of models which is today regarded as something akin to an industry standard. But exotic option pricing has a long and distinguished history, and a great many other valuation models and methods have been developed over the decades. Whether or not we wish to use these other models for barrier option valuation, it is important to be aware that they exist and to understand their properties, benefits and drawbacks. This section briefly describes a number of important models and methods.

4.13.1 Uncertain volatility (UV) models

Imagine if the only barrier option valuation tool available to us were a black box which implemented the Black–Scholes model for supplied inputs of trade and market data. Since we know that there is no single "correct" volatility, we could calculate the value of an option twice, using two different volatilities, and then combine the two values, perhaps by taking a weighted average. The option value thereby calculated would crudely reflect the stochastic nature of volatility. This is an example of an **uncertain volatility model**.

As a simple demonstration of the effect of mixing models in this way, let us value six-month EURUSD vanilla options over a range of strikes and back out the implied volatility. When the two volatilities used are respectively 2.5% higher and lower than the at-the-money volatility, the resulting UV-model implied volatility smile is as shown in Figure 4.25. Hey presto! We have created an implied volatility smile out of a smile-less model.

The same principle can be applied to the local volatility model. Here, instead of choosing two volatility numbers, we must choose two implied volatility surfaces, calibrate two LV models, and thus calculate two values. Such a model goes by various names, such as **uncertain local volatility** or **mixed Dupire**. The problem of choosing the two implied volatility surfaces presents a large number of degrees

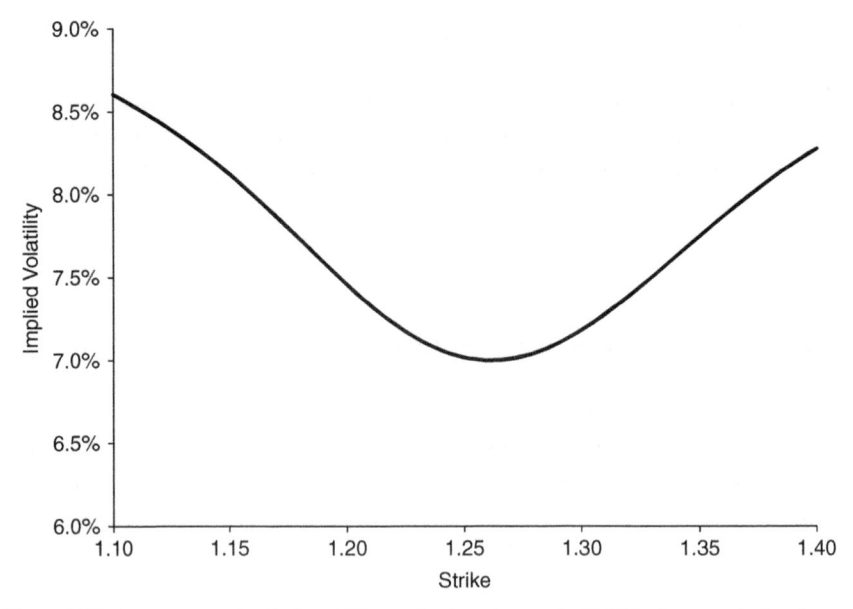

Figure 4.25 An example implied volatility smile for six-month EURUSD generated using an uncertain volatility model based on purely Black–Scholes calculations

of freedom, and the methods used in the industry to determine the surfaces can be very sophisticated.

The benefit of uncertain volatility models is that valuation is straightforward to implement, being based on simpler models. The principal drawbacks are twofold. First, there is no underlying physical process model, whose dynamics we can study and understand. Second, calibration is usually an unsatisfactory process: we cannot usually calibrate to the entire implied volatility surface, let alone to exotic prices, and there is invariably a degree of arbitrariness in the nature of the calibration.

4.13.2 Jump–diffusion models

All of the spot process models presented so far are *diffusive* models: their fundamental drivers of uncertainty are diffusion-based. Under such models, the probability of spot moving by a fixed amount upwards or downwards in a time interval $(t, t + \delta t)$ vanishes as δt tends to zero. As a result, diffusive models are incapable of making large sudden moves. Whilst such moves are uncommon events in Foreign Exchange spot, they do occur, a striking example being the EURCHF rate (Swiss francs per euro), which on 15th January 2015 fell nearly 30% in less than 15 minutes, after the Swiss National Bank unexpectedly removed its policy of keeping the exchange rate floored at 1.20 (a cap on the strength of the Swiss franc).

Jump–diffusion models add jump-based drivers of uncertainty to the process model. A common approach is to use a Poisson stochastic process to determine when jumps occur, and to draw the size of the jump (usually formalized as a proportion of prevailing spot) from a random distribution. The parameters of the jump-size distribution may be calibrated to historic data or marked to market prices of selected instruments.

The barrier options that we have been examining are typically not very sensitive to jumps, however, and the use of jump–diffusion models is rare. In practical terms, the limited gain from the use of jump–diffusion models does not easily justify the extra burden of calibration, calculation, parameter-marking and risk management that they require.

4.13.3 Vanna–volga methods

If we lived in a Black–Scholes world, there would be a single perpetual volatility for each market and we wouldn't have to worry about the consequences of volatility changing. But of course we don't, and we measure the sensitivity of option values to changes in volatility through the volatility Greeks: vega, volgamma and vanna. We have already understood the significance of these Greeks under an LSV model, where each of them contributes a term to the option pricing PDE. But without such a calibrated process model at our disposal, we could still seek to develop a heuristic method of calculating barrier option values which takes account of the volatility Greeks.

At first sight, it might look as if we have to take account of all three volatility Greeks, but that is not the case. Vanilla options, on whose market values we wish to base barrier option values, have non-zero vega, volgamma and vanna, and as a result can be used to hedge away some or all of the volatility risk. A useful way to do this is to seek a portfolio of vanilla options which hedges away all of one of the volatility Greeks. Invariably, it is the vega that is hedged away, leaving us with a portfolio Π which has zero vega but non-zero volgamma and vanna.

There are numerous ways in which the hedging portfolio of vanilla options can be sought. Amongst the many choices that must be made is that of the expiry times of the vanilla options. Simpler approaches use exclusively vanillas having the same expiry time as the exotic contract being valued. More sophisticated approaches recognize that the exotic contract may terminate sooner than its expiry due to barrier trigger, and use a range of vanilla expiries to reflect this fact.

The vega-hedged portfolio Π contains exotic and vanilla options, for both of which we can calculate a TV. The next step is to determine the skew to TV as the sum of the values of the portfolio's volgamma and vanna, which are generally assumed to be proportional to volgamma and vanna respectively:

$$\text{value of volgamma} = \alpha_{\text{volgamma}} \frac{\partial^2 \Pi}{\partial \sigma^2} \qquad (4.51)$$

$$\text{value of vanna} = \alpha_{\text{vanna}} \frac{\partial^2 \Pi}{\partial S \partial \sigma} \qquad (4.52)$$

There are two broad approaches to determining the multipliers α_{volgamma} and α_{vanna}. The first approach assumes our knowledge of market prices is confined to vanilla options, and uses the implied volatility smile to calibrate the multipliers from selected vanilla structures. For example, the skews to TV of a risk reversal structure and a strangle structure can be calculated using knowledge of the smile, and these values can then be used to solve Equations 4.51 and 4.52 simultaneously for α_{volgamma} and α_{vanna}. The second approach calibrates the multipliers to selected exotic contracts, such as one-touches and double no-touches. Given that highly liquid markets exist for these contracts, there is nowadays little reason to use the first approach. The second approach can be extended in various ways.

It is worth noting that the vanna–volga approach is usually called a "method" rather than a "model" – we are not modelling anything fundamental, and certainly not the market dynamics.

Vanna–volga methods for the valuation of exotic contracts were introduced (informally and without a name) by Lipton and McGhee [40], and have been studied further by Wystup [41, 42]. Castagna and Mercurio have shown how vanna–volga methods can also be used to construct implied volatility models [43].

5 | Smile Risk Management

The unexamined risk is not worth running.

In Chapter 3, we discussed how we can manage market risk when our valuation model is Black–Scholes. In this chapter we will go through some of the models that we described in the chapter on smile pricing, Chapter 4, and discuss the new or modified risk management issues that arise in each case. Specifically, we will discuss risk management under the following models:

- Black–Scholes with term structure (BSTS): see Section 4.2
- Local volatility (LV): see Section 4.9
- Mixed local/stochastic volatility (LSV): see Section 4.12

In each case, we will take care to clarify the nature of the risk factors.

5.1 Black–Scholes with term structure

The BSTS model is of course not actually a smile model, but it is a first important step beyond Black–Scholes, and it immediately raises an important question that also applies to smile models, namely: how should our risk management techniques change when the risk factors become *time-dependent*? In the BSTS case, the time-dependent risk factors are volatility and the Domestic and Foreign interest rates. Let us first consider volatility.

Our option value, irrespective of how we calculate it (analytically or numerically) now depends on a risk factor which is an entire term structure of volatilities rather than a single volatility number, so we can no longer simply calculate a single vega to represent first-order volatility (local) risk. Instead, we must define new ways of measuring the sensitivity of the option value to the volatility curve. We will refer to this category of risk broadly as **volatility term structure risk**.

So which volatility are we talking about anyway? The instantaneous volatility in the BSTS process, $\sigma_{\text{BSTS}}(t)$? Or the implied volatility $\Sigma(T)$? (Recall that t is the process time, and T is the expiry time of the vanilla option through which we define implied volatility.) Well we can easily convert between $\sigma_{BSTS}(t)$ and $\Sigma(T)$ using Equations 4.3 and 4.5, so we are at liberty to formalize our option value as a function of either $\sigma_{BSTS}(t)$ or $\Sigma(T)$. Since we are currently concerned with *market* risk management, we need to think of the option value as a function of *market* implied volatilities. At first sight, we might think that $\Sigma(T)$ is therefore the dependency we need, but that is not quite correct. Market quotes for implied volatility are only liquidly available at selected tenors, for example, one day, one week, two weeks, 1 month. As we discussed in Section 4.6, we require an *implied volatility model* to construct the entire implied volatility curve $\Sigma(T)$ out of individual quotes Σ_{1D}, Σ_{1W}, Σ_{2W} and so on. It is these individual implied volatility quotes that are the true market risk factors, and we can compute the sensitivity of our barrier option value to each of these factors.

Let us denote the individual quotes by Σ_i, the set of quotes by $\{\Sigma_i\}$, and the volatility-dependence of the option value function by $V(\{\Sigma_i\})$. Then the sensitivity to implied volatility quote j can be denoted by vega$_j$. Given that BSTS option values must in general be computed numerically, we define vega$_j$ on a finite-difference basis, as follows:

$$\text{vega}_j \doteq \frac{V(\{\Sigma_i'(j)\}) - V(\{\Sigma_i\})}{100\,\delta\Sigma} \tag{5.1}$$

$$\text{where } \Sigma_i'(j) \doteq \begin{cases} \Sigma_i + \delta\Sigma & i = j \\ \Sigma_i & i \neq j \end{cases} \tag{5.2}$$

Note that, in line with BS vega, the sensitivities are scaled for a 1% volatility move.

The set of sensitivities $\{\text{vega}_j\}$ generated by Equations 5.1 and 5.2 is collectively known as the **bucketed vega** or as a **vega ladder**. The individual vega$_j$ are referred to as the **vega buckets**. The bucketed vega for an option portfolio gives us a clear picture of the sign and size of volatility risk across all maturities, and as such provides a central and crucial risk report in any FX options business.

Now, if we run a bucketed vega report for, say, a four-month EURUSD barrier option, which buckets will have non-zero vega? (Recall that the set of straight dates for EURUSD includes 3M and 6M but not 4M, as shown in Table 4.1.) Certainly all the buckets for expiries up to and including three months will be non-zero (bar pathological cases), but what about the buckets for *later* expiries? The answer lies with the implied volatility model. An implied volatility model is essentially an interpolation algorithm, and if the algorithm is non-local, such that all the interpolated volatilities are affected by all the quotes (as is the case for some forms of spline interpolation), then all the buckets will show some non-zero risk. Even the one-year vega bucket would be non-zero (though probably very small) for our four-month barrier option. This phenomenon, whereby sensitivity to distant inputs is caused by non-local interpolation rather than by the direct dependence that one is trying to measure, is known as **ringing**. From a risk management point of view, ringing artefacts, such as the non-zero one-year vega, are unhelpful and distracting. For this reason, it is commonly the case that the implied volatility model – at least the one that is used for option valuation – employs an interpolation algorithm which depends on only the two quotes either side of the interpolation point. In this way, ringing is avoided, and the latest non-zero vega bucket will be the earliest one whose expiry is on or after the option's expiry. For our four-month barrier option example, the latest non-zero vega bucket will be the six-month one.

I wrote "at least the one that is used for option valuation" in the last paragraph because implied volatility models are also run by the tools that option market-makers use for *marking* volatilities. These may incorporate non-local interpolation algorithms without incurring the same problems.

Calculating bucketed vega reports is all well and good, but once we have measured our risk in this way, how can we *hedge* the risk? Let us assume that the market quotes used to construct the implied volatility curve are those for at-the-money (ATM) options, which is certainly the usual case. We can then hedge our portfolio vega using ATM options, and naturally, we will use ATM options with exactly the same expiries as the vega buckets. To hedge away all the vega risk, we will need exactly as many ATM options as there are non-zero vega buckets, and the question is then: *how much* (what principals) of each of the ATM options do we need to buy/sell to hedge our vega position? Each option hedge has vega exclusively in those buckets up to and including the hedging option's expiry. Hedging can therefore be achieved by an iterative process that starts with the hedge of the longest maturity and continues through hedges with successively shorter maturities. For our four-month barrier option example, we start by finding the amount of the six-month ATM vanilla option required to hedge the six-month vega of our portfolio. With this hedge added to the portfolio, we recalculate the portfolio bucketed vega, and then find the amount of the three-month ATM vanilla option required to hedge the three-month vega of our portfolio. This procedure continues until the earliest bucket is hedged.

Note that in the above hedging discussion, we didn't specify whether the ATM options used for hedging would be calls or puts. For *vega* hedging, it doesn't matter, and indeed can't matter, since a call and a put have the same vega. However, the *deltas* generated by the hedging options would of course be different.

It doesn't always make sense to employ the mechanical hedging approach described above. In particular, for small books, or where liquidity is thin, or for inactive books where the risk remains static for long periods of time, it is better to take a more subjective and tailored approach. (The same is true for books containing more complex and highly path-dependent exotic options.) But for large, liquid, simple and actively traded books, the mechanical approach is suitable.

A much simpler volatility risk measure, known as **parallel vega** and denoted by vega$_\|$, can be obtained by looking at the change in option value when *all* of the Σ_i change in parallel:

$$\text{vega}_\| \doteq \frac{V(\{\Sigma_i^\|\}) - V(\{\Sigma_i\})}{100\delta\Sigma} \tag{5.3}$$

$$\text{where} \quad \Sigma_i^\| \doteq \Sigma_i + \delta\Sigma \quad \forall i \tag{5.4}$$

An FX barrier option portfolio may well have large positive bucketed vega at some maturities and large negative bucketed vega at other maturities. Whilst the bucketed vega report will show this clearly, the parallel vega will mask all this detail and net the positive and negative vegas to a single number of smaller magnitude. Parallel vega on its own is thus not a reliable risk report for a portfolio. However, it can often be a simple and practical risk measure for a single barrier option, where it is uncommon to have both large positive and large negative vega buckets.[1]

A very useful companion to parallel vega is **weighted vega**, which again looks at the change in option value when all of the Σ_i change, but this time the changes are not equal. Instead, the volatilities at shorter maturities are shifted more than those at longer maturities. This reflects the fact that implied volatilities for short maturities tend to be much more volatile than implied volatilities for long maturities, as discussed in Section 4.12.1. The aim is to distil more information about the portfolio risk without the full-blown analysis of a bucketed vega report.

Very commonly, the desired bias towards shorter maturities is achieved by weighting the shifts *inversely to the square root of the maturity*, and choosing a **pivot maturity** (usually one month or three months) at which the volatility shift is $\delta\Sigma$. For example, the three-month weighted vega is calculated as follows:

$$\text{vega}_{3M} \doteq \frac{V(\{\Sigma_i^{3M}\}) - V(\{\Sigma_i\})}{100\delta\Sigma} \tag{5.5}$$

$$\text{where} \quad \Sigma_i^{3M} \doteq \Sigma_i + \sqrt{\frac{T_{3M} - t}{T_i - t}}\,\delta\Sigma \quad \forall i \tag{5.6}$$

In combination, the parallel vega and weighted vega provide, in two easy-to-digest numbers, a very good snapshot of the volatility risk of a portfolio position. For example, a position which is short parallel vega but long weighted vega will increase in value in response to an increase in short-term (spot-driven) implied volatilities, such as might follow a sharp move in spot.

---

[1] This is not the case for all types of exotic contract. A single forward volatility agreement (FVA) contract, for example, gives rise to a substantial negative vega at one maturity and a substantial positive vega at another.

Domestic and Foreign interest rate term structure risks are treated in exactly the same way as for volatility, leading to a **bucketed rho** report, a **parallel rho** and a **weighted rho** for each currency.

5.2 Local volatility model

Just as the spot-independent BSTS process volatility $\sigma_{\mathrm{BSTS}}(t)$ is calibrated to a strike-independent implied volatility curve $\Sigma(T)$, so the spot-dependent LV process volatility $\sigma_{\mathrm{LV}}(S,t)$ is calibrated to the strike-dependent implied volatility surface $\Sigma(K,T)$. There are several LV market risk factors, comprising not only ATM volatilities, but also delta-parameterized risk reversals and butterflies, as described in Section 4.4. Risk reports measuring the sensitivity of the portfolio value to the ATM volatilities are constructed in exactly the same way as for BSTS as described in Section 5.1. Risk reports for the risk reversals and butterflies, known as bucketed **rega** and **sega** reports respectively, are also constructed straightforwardly in a similar way. Each of the risk reports measures just one sensitivity; for example, one rega report might measure the sensitivity of the portfolio value to a change in 10-delta risk reversals, assuming that ATM volatilities, butterflies and 25-delta risk reversals remain *constant*. This is not necessarily realistic in terms of scenario analysis. For example, risk reversals and butterflies often show some correlation with ATM volatility, and risk reversals at different deltas move together, ditto butterflies. However, such separated risk reports do allow clear and consistent analysis of all option portfolios.

Whilst the generation of the risk reports is relatively straightforward, hedging the risk is another matter. This is because the market risk factors are not orthogonal, in the sense that the corresponding instruments will in general have sensitivity to all the market factors. For example, a 25-delta risk reversal structure will in general have some vega. We must therefore *solve* for the amounts of the hedging instruments required to cancel out all the market-factor risks for any given maturity bucket. The iterative technique described in Section 5.1, whereby we hedge the longest maturity first and work backwards, still applies.

The set of instruments types used for hedging does not have to consist of ATM options, risk reversals and butterflies. Often, individual vanilla options are used, such as an at-the-money call, an out-of-the-money call and an out-of-the-money put.

There can often be merit in additionally studying the sensitivity of portfolio values to the parameters of the implied volatility smile model. This is particularly true if the smile model is based on a process and has "physically meaningful" parameters, as is the case with the SABR model, for example. In this way one can obtain sensitivities to the volatility of volatility and to the spot–vol correlation. These parameters may also be a lot closer to orthogonal.

5.3 Spot risk under smile models

When spot moves, what happens to the other market risk factors in our models? In the cases of the BS and BSTS models, nothing. But under any model involving an implied volatility surface (such as SV or LSV), we must consider the *smile relocation dynamics*. We previously discussed smile re-location dynamics in the context of option valuation under the local volatility model (Section 4.9) and under stochastic volatility models (Section 4.11). As we saw, the natures of the respective models impose certain dynamics. Now, in the context of risk management, we are free, nay forced, to decide what dynamics we wish to impose on the model. Specifically, whenever we calculate a delta, we must decide whether the implied volatility surface changes as spot changes, and if so, how.

We have already met two forms of smile re-location dynamics. Under sticky-strike dynamics, the implied volatility remains constant for a given strike when spot moves. Under sticky-moneyness dynamics, the implied volatility remains constant for a given moneyness.

Let us formalize these statements mathematically. Suppose spot moves from S_{old} to S_{new}. Then under sticky-strike dynamics, we have:

$$\Sigma(S_{new}, K) = \Sigma(S_{old}, \tilde{K}) \tag{5.7}$$

$$\text{where} \quad K = \tilde{K} \tag{5.8}$$

so that the formula for the relocated volatility is simply:

$$\Sigma(S_{new}, K) = \Sigma(S_{old}, K) \tag{5.9}$$

Under sticky-moneyness dynamics, we have:

$$\Sigma(S_{new}, K) = \Sigma(S_{old}, \tilde{K}) \tag{5.10}$$

$$\text{where} \quad \frac{K}{S_{new}} = \frac{\tilde{K}}{S_{old}} \tag{5.11}$$

which we can solve trivially to get the following formula for the re-located volatility:

$$\Sigma(S_{new}, K) = \Sigma(S_{old}, \frac{S_{old}}{S_{new}} K) \tag{5.12}$$

Other forms of dynamics can be defined in a similar way. A very common form is **sticky-delta** dynamics, under which the implied volatility remains constant for a

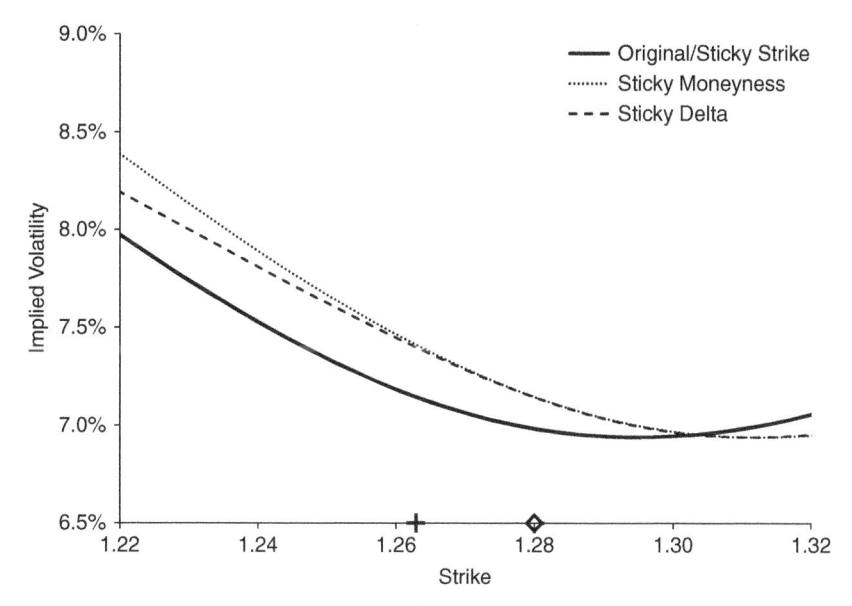

Figure 5.1 Smile re-location of three-month EURUSD under various dynamics. The original spot level is marked with a plus sign, the re-located spot level with a diamond

given delta:

$$\Sigma(S_{\text{new}}, K) = \Sigma(S_{\text{old}}, \tilde{K}) \qquad (5.13)$$
$$\text{where} \quad \Delta(S_{\text{new}}, K) = \Delta(S_{\text{old}}, \tilde{K}) \qquad (5.14)$$

In this case, the re-located volatility is computed numerically. Whilst the flavour of delta used *can* vary, Spot-Delta-in-Foreign is by far the most common flavour used in the context of imposing sticky-delta dynamics.

Figure 5.1 shows how the three-month EURUSD smile would behave if spot moved upwards, under various smile re-location dynamics. Under sticky-strike dynamics, the smile remains exactly as the original, by definition. With sticky moneyness or sticky delta, the smile moves with spot.

To understand how an option's delta might vary with the choice of smile dynamics, let us consider a vanilla option. Suppose we compute the Spot-Delta-in-Foreign of a three-month 1.28-strike EUR call/USD put option. Under sticky-strike dynamics, the volatility in play will be constant, whereas under sticky-moneyness or sticky-delta dynamics, it will *increase* with spot, because at 1.28, the sticky-moneyness volatility is greater than the sticky-strike volatility (seen by inspection of Figure 5.1). This will *add* value to the option, resulting in a larger positive delta for the sticky-moneyness case. If we change the option strike to 1.32, where the sticky-moneyness volatility is less than the sticky-strike volatility, the converse will be true, resulting in a smaller positive delta for the sticky-moneyness case.

Crunching the numbers, we calculate that the 1.28-strike option has a sticky-strike delta of 39% and a sticky-moneyness delta of 41%. Meanwhile the 1.32-strike option has a sticky-strike delta of 13% and a sticky-moneyness delta of 12%. QED.

5.4 Theta risk under smile models

Recall that there are two aspects to smile dynamics: what happens when spot moves; and what happens when time moves. Just as different assumptions about the former aspect lead to different deltas (sticky-strike, sticky-moneyness and so on), so different assumptions about the latter aspect lead to different *thetas*. Broadly speaking, assumptions need to be made about what happens to spot, to interest rates, to ATM volatilities, to risk reversals and to butterflies. That's a lot of assumptions that can vary, and can lead to a *lot* of different measures of theta!

Let us very briefly run through some of the variety of assumptions that can be made. Regarding spot, we may assume either that it stays constant or that it "follows the forward", that is, it moves to where today's forward curve (risk-neutrally) expects it to be. Interest rates may remain constant for a fixed tenor (time to maturity) or for a fixed maturity date. Likewise, ATM volatilities may remain constant for a fixed time to expiry ($T_e - t$) or for a fixed expiry time T_e. What happens to risk reversals and butterflies is a particularly complicated business: they may stay fixed, they may move together with ATM volatilities, or their moves may be modelled in some other way entirely.

Different institutions, and indeed different departments in the same institution, tend to take different approaches to theta calculation, and very often calculate several types of theta to compare.

5.5 Mixed local/stochastic volatility models

All of the risk management issues described already in this chapter apply to LSV models: volatility and interest rate term structure, bucketed vega reports, implied volatility smile risk reports, smile re-location dynamics, theta risks. In addition to all of these, LSV models introduce risk arising from the parameters of the stochastic volatility component. Of these parameters, it is more than anything else the volatility of volatility α (or equivalently the mixing factor $\hat{\alpha}$) to which barrier option values are sensitive. This parameter determines the mixture between local and stochastic volatility components, and it is of paramount importance that this **mixture risk** be managed.

If the LSV model used for valuation has a single α parameter, there will be a single mixture risk measure, which we may call **mixxa**, defined on the basis of the sensitivity of option values to α:

$$\text{mixxa} \doteq \frac{\partial V}{\partial \alpha} \qquad (5.15)$$

If, however, the LSV model admits a term structure of α, a bucketed mixxa report will be required, along the same lines as for bucketed vega.

5.6 Static hedging

All the hedging techniques described hitherto in this chapter have involved **dynamic hedging**. The hedging is repeated continually during the lifetime of the contract, and involves model-based re-calculation of the hedge ratios and rehedging of the portfolio. Whilst theoretically wonderful, model-based dynamic hedging presents many practical difficulties, not least because the models are based on hedging assumptions that are not valid in the real world. We discussed the hedging assumptions of the Black–Scholes model in Section 2.3.3, and all of them apply equally to the smile models we have examined.

Static hedging, in contrast, involves the design and construction of a one-time hedge, generally put in place at the time the contract is traded, which will remain relevant and effective throughout its life. To see how such a hedge can exist, it is useful to recall the method of images, which we discussed in Section 2.8 and illustrated in Figure 2.7. There, we showed how a barrier option could – almost – be replicated out of vanilla options. Static replication and static hedging of options are two sides of the same coin: if one set of vanilla option positions *replicates* an exotic option, then the set of opposite positions is a *hedge* for the exotic. For example, a long position in the normal knock-out put option illustrated in Figure 2.7 would be statically hedged using a short position in the 1.28-strike vanilla put and a long position in the 1.3107-strike vanilla call. Such a technique is a decent method of statically hedging a barrier option, but there are three caveats to bear in mind.

The first is the fact that the image option has to be valued using a "reflected market", whose Domestic and Foreign interest rates are transposed relative to the true market. (Hence the "almost" that I wrote above.) This caveat is often relatively minor, especially when the interest rates are low.

The second caveat: as Equation 2.90 shows, the principal of the image option depends on the value of spot! The further away spot moves from its original position, the poorer will be the quality of the static hedge. However, inspection of Equation 2.90 shows that the dependence on spot is fairly weak (and disappears entirely when the interest rate differential is zero). In our example case, the image principal changes by less than 1% for a big figure move in spot. To a good approximation, the principal of the image option equals that of the hedged option multiplied by the factor $\frac{K}{H}$, which does *not* vary with spot.

The third, and most significant, caveat relates – of course – to the *smile dynamics*. Specifically, it is the smile re-location dynamics (as opposed to the forward smile) that we are concerned with: when spot moves, the volatility surface responds in some way, but a static hedge set up according to the method of images knows nothing about the nature of that response.

Let us think more carefully about what specific aspects of smile re-location dynamics are important, and what effects they would have. When we discussed the effects of a change in spot under different smile dynamics in Section 5.3, we looked at a single strike, considering for example the delta of a 1.28-strike EUR call/USD put vanilla option under sticky strike, sticky moneyness and sticky delta dynamics. Here, however, we are concerned with two vanilla options, at different strikes, and by the nature of the method of images, we are always long the volatility at one strike and short the volatility at another strike. That is to say, these two options always form a *risk reversal*. We can thereby understand what aspect of smile re-location dynamics is important: it is the way in which *risk reversals* move when spot moves.

Now, what happens if spot reaches the barrier level during the option's lifetime? Well, the barrier option becomes worthless, and then we must close out the vanilla hedges, which involves buying the 1.28-strike vanilla put and selling the 1.3107-strike vanilla call. Under an ideal static hedge, this close-out would cost nothing (to match the value of the triggered barrier option), but we cannot assume that will be the case. Whether the close-out costs us money or makes us money, and how much, all depends on the level of risk reversal prevailing at the time we close out the hedge. A key requirement of better static hedging, then, is to be able to *hedge the close-out cost of the option hedge*. One route towards this aim is to somehow model the joint dynamics of spot and risk reversal.

The topics of static replication and hedging have been discussed from early on in the history of barrier options, for example by Derman, Ergener and Kani [44] and by Bowie and Carr [45]. More recently, Wilmott [3] and Joshi [46] both devote a chapter of their books to a systematic study and assessment of static hedging/replication.

5.7 Managing risk across businesses

The risk management techniques described in this chapter and in Chapter 3 are the primary techniques used by traders and risk-control functions to manage the market risk of option portfolios ("books") within a specific business. For example, FX options businesses with multiple trading desks, for FX vanilla options, FX barrier options, FX structured products and so on, will use these techniques to monitor and aggregate the risk across all its desks and books.

At a higher level, management of risk looks a bit different. For example, the head of an investment bank needs to monitor risk across multiple business areas and asset classes: not just foreign exchange, but also interest rates (often referred to as "fixed income"), inflation products, equities, commodities and credit derivatives. There may also be trading desks for "hybrid" products, which combine multiple asset classes. What needs to be monitored here is each business area's net portfolio value, referred to as its **P&L** (profit and loss), and also the total P&L of all business areas. The classic risk measure used to monitor risk across businesses in this way is called **Value at Risk (VaR)**. I will not go into this substantial topic in any detail, as for the most part, there is nothing about VaR that is specific to FX barrier options, and there are some excellent treatments of VaR in the literature, including books by Alexander [47] and Hull [48]. However, there are some situations in which a barrier option can have an unexpectedly large adverse impact on VaR, and it is worth understanding how such situations can arise.

A VaR figure tells us how much P&L could be lost due to adverse market moves. A typical calculation of VaR uses historic market data to estimate this loss. For example, the last 500 daily market moves might be used to estimate a probability distribution of the next daily market move and hence of tomorrow's P&L. The properties of the lower tail of this distribution would then be used to calculate a VaR. Now, if the historic data set contains a very large market move, any barrier options sensitive to such a move could lose a lot of value, contributing to an extended lower tail and a bigger VaR. For example, if the data set includes the EURCHF de-cap event of 15 January 2015, a large valuable position in a EURCHF down-side no-touch might be knocked out, resulting in an increased VaR.

To a large extent, the above adverse scenario also applies to vanilla options, but where barrier options present particular problems is if, as is often the case, the VaR calculation methodology approximates revaluations by extrapolation from the local option Greeks (that is, those at current market levels), instead of performing a full revaluation. As we saw in Chapter 3, the profiles of the Greeks for barrier options often contain a lot of turning points, with the result that the local Greeks may be so unrepresentative of the non-local risk as to render the VaR meaningless.

6 | Numerical Methods

Measure what is measurable, and make measurable what is not so.
Galileo Galilei

My intention in this chapter is to highlight a variety of specific numerical techniques that are of great value in the types of calculations and analysis required for FX barrier options. Of high importance are the two broad classes of numerical methods that are used for calculation of option values: **finite-difference methods** and **Monte Carlo simulation**. There is a lot of very good literature available on these two extensive subjects, so rather than re-introducing the subjects here, I will give references to published material and then point out some specific aspects of these subjects that are of particular importance.

6.1 Finite-difference (FD) methods

Daniel Duffy's book [49] is a very thorough introduction to finite-difference methods specifically for financial engineering. Each section is supported by a description of the underlying mathematics. Domingo Tavella and Curt Randall [50] have written a very accessible book which seeks to aid the understanding of how numerical schemes work, and of how the accuracy of the solution depends on the approximations made. Both books cover a variety of partial differential equations, boundary conditions and solution techniques. Morton and Mayers [51] take an approach to the subject which is not specific to financial engineering and is more mathematical – indeed their book was originally based on the content of a mathematics lecture course.

The field of finite-difference problems and techniques described in the literature is extremely wide, and it can be difficult to glean the practical priorities. Our purpose here is to highlight a number of the most important aspects of finite-difference methods.

6.1.1 Grid geometry

At the heart of finite-difference methods is a **grid**, which discretizes our continuous variables. For one-factor models, such as BS, BSTS and LV, the grid extends in time and spot, whilst for two-factor models, such as Heston and LSV models, the grid extends in time, spot and volatility. In describing the dimensionality of a grid, the time dimension is usually ignored; thus a BS grid is referred to as "1-dimensional" and an LSV grid as "2-dimensional".

The position of the grid nodes is referred to as the **grid geometry**. The process of choosing the grid nodes ("geometrizing the grid") is a subject of its own, and akin to an art form. There are two aspects: choosing the grid boundaries, and choosing the grid nodes within the boundaries.

Sometimes the boundary conditions of the physical problem impose the grid boundaries. Let us take a simple concrete example: suppose we need to set up a one-dimensional grid to find the value of a double knock-out call option. Denoting the strike by K and the lower and upper barrier levels by L and U respectively, the boundary conditions are:

$$V(S, T_e) = \max[0, S(T_e) - K] \tag{6.1}$$

$$V(L, t) = 0 \quad \forall t \tag{6.2}$$

$$V(U, t) = 0 \quad \forall t \tag{6.3}$$

In this problem, there is an entirely natural way for the boundaries of the grid to be defined: the time boundaries are $t = 0$ and $t = T_e$, whilst the spot boundaries are $S = L$ and $S = U$. This yields a rectangular grid.

In the absence of one or both barriers, we must decide how far the grid should extend in spot space. Ideally, we should run our FD calculation repeatedly to ensure that it is converged with respect to all its parameters, including the grid boundaries. Whilst this might be possible when we are poring over a single trade, and when we first enter a trade into a book, it is completely impractical when we are re-valuing a book containing hundreds or thousands of trades. A better way to choose the spot is on the basis of the risk-neutral distribution of spot at the time point in question: we choose a probability tolerance ϵ and calculate the inverse PDF of ϵ and of $(1 - \epsilon)$ to obtain the grid boundaries. Computation of the inverse PDF (twice at every time point in the grid) is computationally expensive though, and if we are valuing the same option repeatedly, as is often the case, re-computation of the inverse PDFs every time is superfluous. A very common practice adopted instead is to base the boundaries on a normal distribution and parameterized via a nominal volatility and two semi-widths (for lower and upper spot boundaries) specified in terms of numbers of standard deviations. For example, a EURUSD grid might be geometrized on the basis of the ATM volatility at the grid time point, seven standard deviations down, and five standard deviations up. (The asymmetry reflects the skew of the risk-neutral PDF, as shown in Figure 4.5.) The lower and upper spot boundaries at time point T, $S_L(T)$ and $S_U(T)$ can then be calculated as follows from the nominal volatility $\bar{\sigma}$ and the lower and upper widths w_L and w_U:

$$S_L(T) = F(T)e^{-w_L \bar{\sigma} \sqrt{T-t}} \tag{6.4}$$

$$S_U(T) = F(T)e^{+w_U \bar{\sigma} \sqrt{T-t}} \tag{6.5}$$

Note that these boundaries are time-dependent, and the grid is not rectangular.

Having determined the grid boundaries, we need to distribute the grid nodes. Since most process models for spot are based in some way on geometric Brownian motions (and the Black–Scholes model is exactly a geometric Brownian motion), it is almost always advisable to set up grids in the space of *log-spot* X instead of spot S. Let us consider a 1-D grid with N_T time points and N_X X-points, and denote the (zero-based) time index by l and the (zero-based) X index by i. Then we denote the time points by $T_{i,l}$, the log-spot points by $X_{i,l}$ and the option values by $V_{i,l}$. Since the time boundaries do not usually depend on spot (being specified by current time t and expiry time T_e), the time nodes do not usually depend on i.

A simple way of distributing the nodes is to space them *uniformly*. In the time dimension, this gives

$$T_l = t + l \Delta T \tag{6.6}$$

$$\text{where} \quad \Delta T = \frac{T_e - t}{N_T - 1} \tag{6.7}$$

whilst in the log-spot dimension we have:

$$X_{i,l} = X_L(T_l) + i \Delta X \tag{6.8}$$

$$\text{where} \quad \Delta X = \frac{X_U(T_l) - X_L(T_l)}{N_X - 1} \tag{6.9}$$

$$X_L(T) = \ln(S_L(T)) \tag{6.10}$$

$$X_U(T) = \ln(S_U(T)) \tag{6.11}$$

Uniform spacing is often the starting point for more sophisticated geometrization algorithms. For example, it is sometimes beneficial to ensure that special times and/or special spot levels lie on nodes, in which they can be added first and then the resulting partitions can be geometrized uniformly. Conversely, special points can be *avoided* by setting up an "exclusion zone" around them and then filling in the area outside the exclusion zone uniformly. The reason for avoiding certain points is that it is sometimes the easiest way of dealing with a singularity in a boundary condition. The classic, and extremely common, case is the strike in a vanilla option payoff. Tavella and Randall [50] give a nice explanation of how the quantization error due to the discontinuity in the gradient of the payoff at the strike level is minimized when the strike lies halfway between two nodes. If certain regions of spot or time require special attention, then the density of nodes can be increased in that region. This can be achieved by using uniform spacing of different densities in different regions. Alternatively, algorithms can be developed to place nodes in a special way according to the problem at hand.

6.1.2 Finite-difference schemes

A **finite-difference scheme** is a specific way of approximating a PDE by a finite-difference equation, or sometimes by multiple finite-difference equations. The finite-difference equations must then themselves be solved, using a numerical **finite-difference algorithm**, the nature of which can vary according to the scheme.

Many FD schemes are extremely well studied and documented, but it is always worth rehearsing for yourself the derivation of any scheme you need to implement, since this process helps to keep in mind the nature of the approximations being made. Let us take a concrete example: the LV model. The LV option pricing PDE is given by Equation 4.29:

$$\frac{\partial V}{\partial t} + (r_d(t) - r_f(t))S\frac{\partial V}{\partial S} + \frac{1}{2}(\sigma_{LV}(S,t))^2 S^2 \frac{\partial^2 V}{\partial S^2} = r_d(t)V$$

As explained in Section 6.1.1, we prefer to work in the space of log-spot ($X = \ln S$). Transforming Equation 4.29 to log-spot gives the following PDE in $v(X,t)$:

$$\frac{\partial v}{\partial t} + \left(r_d(t) - r_f(t) - \frac{1}{2}(\sigma_{LV}(S,t))^2\right)\frac{\partial v}{\partial X} + \frac{1}{2}(\sigma_{LV}(S,t))^2 \frac{\partial^2 v}{\partial X^2}$$
$$= r_d(t)v \qquad (6.12)$$

Let us suppose we have already geometrized the grid. Next, we must discretize Equation 6.12 in terms of the grid nodes, to obtain a finite-difference scheme. The most important part of this process is to approximate the partial derivatives in the PDE by finite differences. However, the design of a finite-difference scheme should not be seen as simply a matter of approximating the partial derivatives individually and plugging them back into the PDE. Rather, it is the *equation as a whole* that we are seeking to discretize.

The form of the option pricing problem means that we are always seeking to solve the PDE for an *earlier* time given the option value at a *later* time. (We know the option value at expiry – it is the option payoff – and are seeking to find its value today.) In discretized terms, this means that in each finite-difference step, we are seeking to calculate $V_{i,l}$ for all i given $V_{i,l+1}$ for all i. Now, the time partial derivative will need to involve both of these time points, l and $(l+1)$. But the spot partial derivatives may be written in terms of time point l, time point $(l+1)$, or some combination of the two. The analytically simplest (though, as we shall see, not numerically best) procedure is to write the spot derivatives purely in terms of time point $(l+1)$, so that there is only one term in l (from the time derivative), making the equation trivial to solve:

$$\frac{V_{i,l+1} - V_{i,l}}{T_{l+1} - T_l} + \left(r_{dl} - r_{fl} - \frac{1}{2}\sigma_{LV\,i,l}^2\right) \frac{V_{i+1,l+1} - V_{i-1,l+1}}{X_{i+1,l+1} - X_{i-1,l+1}}$$
$$+ \frac{1}{2}\sigma_{LV\,i,l}^2 \frac{V_{i+1,l+1} + V_{i-1,l+1} - 2V_{i,l+1}}{(X_{i+1,l+1} - X_{i,l+1})(X_{i,l+1} - X_{i-1,l+1})} = r_{dl}V_{i,l+1} \quad (6.13)$$

Before we discuss the pros and cons of this scheme, there are two subtle points to note. The first is that in Equation 6.13 I have used an equality sign $=$, not an approximation sign $\simeq$. Whilst the solution $V_{i,l}$ of the FD equation is an approximation to the solution $V(S,t)$ of the PDE, it is an *exact* solution to the FD equation. We clearly require our FD scheme to have the property that its solution converges to the PDE solution in the limit as the time and spot spacings tend to zero (a limit which we will refer to as the **infinitesimal-difference limit**). This fundamentally important property is called **consistency**, and is discussed in Duffy [49] and in Tavella and Randall [50].

With the consistency property in mind, we can understand the second subtle point, which is that the FD option value at a given grid node does not actually have to be equal to the true option value at the spot and time of that node! In other words, $V_{i,l}$ does not have to be equal to $V(X_{i,l}, T_l)$ – it must only tend to the correct value in the infinitesimal-difference limit. This fact can come in very useful when faced with singularities, such as the gradient discontinuity at the strike in a vanilla option payoff that we discussed in Section 6.1.1. If a grid node lies exactly on a singularity, the tactic of setting its value equal to the average of values in the neighbourhood of the singularity reduces the error without violating consistency. Again, this is discussed in Tavella and Randall [50].

This second point applies equally to the known quantities, r_d, r_f and σ_{LV}. Since their values at all time and spot points are known up front, they can be discretized using any combination of time and log-spot indices. For example, a popular technique is to use time-averaged expressions for the interest rates, and a time- and spot-averaged expression for the local volatility:

$$r_{dl} = \frac{1}{2}\big(r_d(T_l) + r_d(T_{l+1})\big) \quad (6.14)$$

$$r_{fl} = \frac{1}{2}\left(r_f(T_l) + r_f(T_{l+1})\right) \tag{6.15}$$

$$\sigma_{LV\,i,l} = \frac{1}{4}\big(\sigma_{LV}(X_i, T_l) + \sigma_{LV}(X_i, T_{l+1}) \\ + \sigma_{LV}(X_{i+1}, T_l) + \sigma_{LV}(X_{i+1}, T_{l+1})\big) \tag{6.16}$$

The finite-difference scheme described by Equation 6.13 is called an **explicit scheme** (specifically, it is the "explicit Euler scheme"), since it allows us to calculate option values at time point l explicitly in terms of the option values at time point $l+1$. The benefit of this scheme is that it is simple to implement and computationally undemanding. Its immense drawback is that it is only stable under certain conditions, namely when the time step size ΔT is sufficiently small in comparison to the log-spot spacing size ΔX. Tavella and Randall [50] show that, for constant volatility σ, the stability condition is given by:

$$\Delta T \leq \frac{(\Delta X)^2}{\sigma^2} \tag{6.17}$$

As an example of what this result implies: if we wished to obtain EURUSD spot resolution of one small figure, with a volatility of 7%, we would need a time step of 40 seconds! This means we would need about 200,000 time steps to price a three-month option! Conversely, if we wished to take daily time steps, we could achieve a spot resolution of no better than about half a big figure. Whilst it is possible to obtain useful results from the explicit scheme, its conditional stability is highly restrictive.

Rewriting Equation 6.13 with the spot derivatives purely in terms of time point l, we get the following finite-difference scheme:

$$\frac{v_{i,l+1} - v_{i,l}}{T_{l+1} - T_l} + \left(r_{dl} - r_{fl} - \frac{1}{2}\sigma_{LV\,i,l}^2\right)\frac{v_{i+1,l} - v_{i-1,l}}{X_{i+1,l} - X_{i-1,l}} \\ + \frac{1}{2}\sigma_{LV\,i,l}^2 \frac{v_{i+1,l} + v_{i-1,l} - 2v_{i,l}}{(X_{i+1,l} - X_{i,l})(X_{i,l} - X_{i-1,l})} = r_{dl}v_{i,l} \tag{6.18}$$

This equation can be solved using linear algebra: we first note that it can be written in the following form:

$$Av_{i-1,l} + Bv_{i,l} + Cv_{i+1,l} = Dv_{i,l+1} \tag{6.19}$$

where the A, B and C are known quantities which depend on grid geometry and market data. Equation 6.19 has the form of the following matrix equation:

$$\mathbf{M}_{ij}v_{j,l} = Dv_{i,l+1} \tag{6.20}$$

where **M** is a **tridiagonal matrix** – only the diagonal and off-diagonal elements are non-zero. Tridiagonal matrix equations can be solved simply and efficiently, as described by Press et al. [52].

The finite-difference scheme described by Equation 6.18 is called an **implicit scheme**. The great benefit of this scheme is that it is unconditionally stable. For a given grid geometry, it is computationally more expensive to compute, due to the tridiagonal matrix solution, but its stability properties mean we can generally use a grid geometry that is temporally much less dense. Its accuracy is the same as that of the explicit scheme, namely it is first-order in the time step size. The properties of the implicit scheme are discussed and demonstrated in Tavella and Randall [50] and in Morton and Mayers [51].

As I wrote above, the spot partial derivatives may be written in terms of time point l (yielding the implicit scheme), time point $(l+1)$ (yielding the explicit scheme), or some combination of the two. It turns out that "some combination of the two" yields a scheme which is both unconditionally stable and which has far better accuracy than the implicit scheme. Introducing an **implicitness** parameter θ, we can construct a weighted average of the explicit and implicit schemes:

$$\frac{v_{i,l+1} - v_{i,l}}{T_{l+1} - T_l} + \left(r_{\mathrm{d}l} - r_{\mathrm{f}l} - \frac{1}{2}\sigma_{\mathrm{LV}\,i,l}^2\right)\left[\theta\frac{v_{i+1,l} - v_{i-1,l}}{X_{i+1,l} - X_{i-1,l}} + (1-\theta)\frac{v_{i+1,l+1} - v_{i-1,l+1}}{X_{i+1,l+1} - X_{i-1,l+1}}\right]$$

$$+ \frac{1}{2}\sigma_{\mathrm{LV}\,i,l}^2\left[\theta\frac{v_{i+1,l} + v_{i-1,l} - 2v_{i,l}}{(X_{i+1,l} - X_{i,l})(X_{i,l} - X_{i-1,l})}\right.$$

$$\left. + (1-\theta)\frac{v_{i+1,l+1} + v_{i-1,l+1} - 2v_{i,l+1}}{(X_{i+1,l+1} - X_{i,l+1})(X_{i,l+1} - X_{i-1,l+1})}\right] = r_{\mathrm{d}l}v_{i,l} \qquad (6.21)$$

Solution of this mixed scheme (sometimes called the **theta scheme**) again requires use of the tridiagonal matrix equation method.

The choice of $\theta = \frac{1}{2}$ yields the famous **Crank–Nicolson** scheme [53], which is accurate to *second order* in the time step size, and is also unconditionally stable. As a consequence of these beneficial properties, the Crank–Nicolson scheme is a very commonly used finite-difference scheme for option valuation under one-factor models.

Two-factor models present us with additional challenges. Consider for example the LSV model option pricing PDE given by Equation 4.48 and the LSV calibration PDE equation given by Equation D.10. Explicit schemes for such PDEs can be designed without difficulty, but like their 1-factor counterparts, they are of limited use due to their conditional stability. Meanwhile, implicit schemes can be derived, but, due to the extra dimensionality, they cannot be solved using the tridiagonal matrix method or any other straightforward method. Instead, a technique very often used is to approximate the complex two-dimensional dynamics of a single time step as a sequence of two time steps with simpler dynamics. To implement this, each time step is split into two sub-steps, where one sub-step is solved implicitly in one dimension and the other sub-step implicitly in the other dimension. Such techniques are known as **operator splitting** techniques. The schemes that result are referred to either as **Alternating-Direction Implicit (ADI)** schemes or as **Implicit/Explicit (IMEX)** schemes. Examples are described and discussed in Duffy, [49], Morton and Mayers [51] and Clark [5]. Of particular interest is the Craig–Sneyd scheme [54], which is suitable for the LSV calibration and option pricing PDEs.

6.2 Monte Carlo (MC) methods

Like finite-difference methods, the subject of Monte Carlo simulation is a wide one, and it is well covered in the literature. Of particular interest are books by Peter Jäckel [55] and Paul Glasserman [56]. My purpose here is to highlight some important aspects of Monte Carlo methods.

First of all, in an effort to conceptually link up the methods of finite-difference and Monte Carlo, let us briefly remind ourselves how we derive option pricing PDEs. We start with a stochastic process model for the market, we devise a dynamic hedging strategy that allows us to construct a riskless portfolio, we equate the rate of growth of that riskless portfolio to a conceptual risk-free interest rate, and we thereby derive a relationship that the option value must satisfy, namely the option pricing PDE. Now the risk-neutral approach taken in this derivation also yields a *risk-neutral process*, as discussed in Section 2.7.2. For example, the risk-neutral process for the Black–Scholes model is given by Equation 2.71. Monte Carlo option valuation methods are based on the **simulation** of such risk-neutral processes.

As usual, we prefer to work in log-spot space, and continuing with the BS example, the risk-neutral process for log-spot X is given by:

$$dX = \left(r_d - r_f - \frac{1}{2}\sigma^2\right)dt + \sigma\,dW \qquad (6.22)$$

The time-discretized risk-neutral process is:

$$\delta X = \left(r_d - r_f - \frac{1}{2}\sigma^2\right)\delta t + \sigma\,\delta W \qquad (6.23)$$

We can now use random numbers to simulate the change in the Wiener process δW. Knowing that δW is normally distributed with a mean of zero and a variance of δt, we can simulate it as follows:

$$\delta W = \phi \sqrt{\delta t} \tag{6.24}$$

where ϕ is a random number drawn from a standard normal distribution.

Inserting Equation 6.24 into Equation 6.23, we get:

$$\delta X = \left(r_d - r_f - \frac{1}{2}\sigma^2\right)\delta t + \sigma \phi \sqrt{\delta t} \tag{6.25}$$

$$\Rightarrow X(t+\delta t) = X(t) + \left(r_d - r_f - \frac{1}{2}\sigma^2\right)\delta t + \sigma \phi \sqrt{\delta t} \tag{6.26}$$

Converting back to spot space, we get:

$$S(t+\delta t) = S(t)\exp\left((r_d - r_f - \frac{1}{2}\sigma^2)\delta t + \sigma \phi \sqrt{\delta t}\right) \tag{6.27}$$

Equations 6.26 and 6.27 allow us to simulate log-spot and spot from today's known values to any future time point. In practice, in order to avoid having to perform the computationally expensive exponential function any more often than necessary, it is advisable to simulate in X space as far as possible (using Equation 6.26), and only convert to spot space when strictly necessary. To determine whether a barrier level H has triggered, rather than converting from X to spot at every time point of every simulation, it is preferable to calculate the logarithm of the barrier once up front and store it with the contract data so that it can be compared against the simulated X values. With this practical proviso in mind, I will henceforth use the term "simulate spot" to mean simulating either S or X, for the sake of simplicity.

6.2.1 Monte Carlo schedules

How large should δt be? At this point we need to differentiate between the sequence of time points required for contract evaluation (the **contract schedule**) and the sequence of time points over which the simulation is to be performed (the **simulation schedule**). The contract schedule is dictated by the terms of the contract, for example, the nature of barrier monitoring and the expiry payoff calculation. For example, for a vanilla option, there is only one time point in the contract schedule, namely the expiry time. For a discrete barrier option, the contract schedule must contain all of the barrier monitoring times. For a continuous barrier option, we must approximate the continuous monitoring with some choice of monitoring frequency. As we discussed in Section 2.10,

Broadie et al. [21] show how discrete barrier options can be valued in terms of continuous barrier options. This "continuity correction" to the barrier level can be applied in reverse, to yield a technique that allows us to value continuous barrier options in terms of discrete barrier options. This is here a very useful technique, because discrete monitoring is the only kind, strictly speaking, that we can handle with Monte Carlo. Another useful technique in Monte Carlo for handling continuously monitored barriers is the **Brownian Bridge**; this is described in Section 6.2.4.

The simulation schedule must satisfy two requirements: it must include all of the time points in the contract schedule, and it must be sufficiently fine to accurately approximate the continuous stochastic process. As we highlighted in Section 2.2, the Black–Scholes SDE for log-spot can be integrated over large time steps, which in the context of Monte Carlo means that we can accurately simulate the SDE using arbitrarily large time steps in Equation 6.26. The Black–Scholes SDE is an exception in this respect, albeit an important one. In general, the SDE cannot be integrated, and we must take care to ensure that our calculation is converged with respect to the fineness of simulation time steps. The convergence behaviour will depend to some extent on market data: higher volatilities and steeper term structures will in general require finer time stepping.

For continuous barrier options, it makes sense for the contract and simulation schedules to be the same, since we wish to monitor the barrier as often as possible.

6.2.2 Monte Carlo algorithms

Using *independent* random numbers, we successively simulate over all N_T time steps from now until the option's expiry time, thereby generating a set of simulated spot rates, which we will refer to as a **spot path** and denote $\mathbb{S}$. For barrier options, a spot path $\mathbb{S}$ is all we need to calculate the option payoff $P(\mathbb{S})$. (This does not hold for all options; notably American options require information regarding optimal exercise.)

Given N spot paths $\mathbb{S}_i$ (each containing N_T simulated spot levels), and N corresponding payoffs P_i, we now calculate the value of the option using a **Monte Carlo standard estimator** $\hat{V}$:

$$\hat{V} \doteq \frac{1}{N} \sum_{i=1}^{N} e^{-\bar{r}_d (T_{\text{pay}_i} - t)} P_i \qquad (6.28)$$

where T_{pay_i} is the payment time: the time at which the option payoff i occurs. For barrier-contingent vanilla options and pay-at-maturity barrier-contingent payments, the payment time is fixed (it is the settlement date), but for pay-at-hit contracts the payment time will vary with the spot path.

For conciseness we will denote the discounted payoff by $\tilde{P}$:

$$\tilde{P}_i \doteq e^{-r_\text{d}(T_{\text{pay}\,i}-t)} P_i \qquad (6.29)$$

so that Equation 6.28 becomes:

$$\hat{V} = \frac{1}{N} \sum_{i=1}^{N} \tilde{P}_i \qquad (6.30)$$

We can check that $\hat{V}$ is an unbiased estimator by calculating its expectation:

$$\mathbb{E}\!\left[\hat{V}\right] = \mathbb{E}\!\left[\frac{1}{N} \sum_{i=1}^{N} \tilde{P}_i\right]$$

$$= \frac{1}{N} \sum_{i=1}^{N} \mathbb{E}\!\left[\tilde{P}_i\right]$$

$$= \mathbb{E}\!\left[\tilde{P}\right] \qquad (6.31)$$

$$\Rightarrow \mathbb{E}\!\left[\hat{V}\right] = V \qquad (6.32)$$

More interestingly, we can calculate the *variance* of $\hat{V}$:

$$\text{Var}\!\left[\hat{V}\right] = \text{Var}\!\left[\frac{1}{N} \sum_{i=1}^{N} \tilde{P}_i\right]$$

$$= \frac{1}{N^2} N \text{Var}\!\left[\tilde{P}\right]$$

$$= \frac{1}{N} \text{Var}\!\left[\tilde{P}\right] \qquad (6.33)$$

where we have used the fact that all the spot paths and therefore all the payoffs are independent of each other, having been generated using independent random numbers.

Equation 6.33 is a very important and useful result. That the variance of the estimator is proportional to the variance of the payoff is unsurprising and reassuring. But the fact that the variance decreases as $\frac{1}{N}$ is critical, because this means that the *error* of a Monte Carlo calculation (represented by the standard deviation of the estimator) will decrease as $\frac{1}{\sqrt{N}}$. In other words, to *halve* the error, we must run four times as many spot paths. This rate of convergence is the reason Monte Carlo is sometimes spoken of as a "slow" or "inefficient" numerical method.

6.2.3 Variance reduction

There are many ways to improve on the standard estimator $\hat{V}$ defined by Equation 6.28. Techniques that reduce the variance of the estimator are collectively known as **variance reduction** techniques. We will discuss and compare two very popular and common variance reduction techniques: **antithetic variables** and **control variates**.

6.2.3.1 Antithetic variables

The symmetry of the standard normal distribution of the random numbers means that ϕ and $-\phi$ have the same probability distribution. This motivates us to simulate *two* log-spot levels X^+ and X^- from each random number drawn, one using ϕ and the other using $-\phi$. We call X^+ and X^- **antithetic variables**, and we use them to compute two payoffs $\tilde{P}^+$ and $\tilde{P}^-$. We can then construct a new estimator, $\hat{V}_{av}$:

$$\hat{V}_{av} \doteq \frac{1}{N} \sum_{i=1}^{N} \frac{1}{2} \left(\tilde{P}_i^+ + \tilde{P}_i^- \right) \tag{6.34}$$

and compute its variance:

$$\text{Var}\left[\hat{V}_{av}\right] = \frac{1}{4N^2} \left(N \text{Var}\left[\tilde{P}^+\right] + N \text{Var}\left[\tilde{P}^-\right] + 2N\rho_{\pm} \sqrt{\text{Var}\left[\tilde{P}^+\right] \text{Var}\left[\tilde{P}^-\right]} \right)$$

$$= \text{Var}\left[\hat{V}\right] \times \frac{(1+\rho_{\pm})}{2} \tag{6.35}$$

So, the variance of the antithetic-variable estimator equals that of the standard estimator multiplied by a factor that depends on $\rho_{\pm}$, the correlation between $\tilde{P}^+$ and $\tilde{P}^-$. If this correlation is zero, the variance will be $\frac{1}{2}\hat{V}$. If this correlation is positive, as is the case for, say, a straddle or a strangle structure, the variance of $\hat{V}_{av}$ will be somewhere between $\frac{1}{2}\hat{V}$ and $\hat{V}$. In the limiting case where $\tilde{P}^+$ and $\tilde{P}^-$ are identical, the variances of the two estimators are equal. However, if the correlation is negative, as is the case for, say, a risk reversal structure, the variance of $\hat{V}_{av}$ will be somewhere between zero and $\frac{1}{2}\hat{V}$. And in the limiting case where $\tilde{P}^+$ and $\tilde{P}^-$ are equal and opposite, the variance of $\hat{V}_{av}$ goes to zero. In practice, we do not get anywhere near the limiting cases for real options, and so we can conclude that the variance of the antithetic-variable estimator is always significantly better (smaller) than that of the standard estimator $\hat{V}$. Thus, from the point of view of variance reduction, it is always advisable to use antithetic variables.

The variance-reduction point of view is not the only one to consider, however. The estimator $\hat{V}_{av}$ computes the payoff twice as often as $\hat{V}$, and if the payoff computation is a relatively expensive part of the overall calculation, the use of antithetic variables may slow the calculation down. This is rarely the case, and it is common for industrial Monte Carlo valuation tools to use antithetic variables as a matter of course.

6.2.3.2 Control variates

This technique involves the use of a **control variate payoff** $\tilde{P}^0$ whose value V^0 is known accurately via some non-Monte Carlo route, perhaps from a closed-form formula derived by analytical methods. We now use Monte Carlo to calculate the *difference* between the payoff of the contract we wish to value and the control variate contract, and we add this difference to the known value V^0. We can write our estimator as follows:

$$\hat{V}_{cv} \doteq V^0 + \frac{1}{N}\sum_{i=1}^{N}\left(\tilde{P}_i - \tilde{P}_i^0\right) \tag{6.36}$$

As before we calculate the variance of the estimator:

$$\mathrm{Var}\left[\hat{V}_{cv}\right] = \frac{1}{N^2}N\left(\mathrm{Var}\left[\tilde{P}\right] + \mathrm{Var}\left[\tilde{P}^0\right] - 2\rho_{cv}\sqrt{\mathrm{Var}\left[\tilde{P}\right]\mathrm{Var}\left[\tilde{P}^0\right]}\right)$$

$$= \mathrm{Var}\left[\hat{V}\right] \times \left(1 + \frac{\mathrm{Var}\left[\tilde{P}^0\right]}{\mathrm{Var}\left[\tilde{P}\right]} - 2\rho_{cv}\sqrt{\frac{\mathrm{Var}\left[\tilde{P}^0\right]}{\mathrm{Var}\left[\tilde{P}\right]}}\right) \tag{6.37}$$

where ρ_{cv} is the correlation between $\tilde{P}$ and $\tilde{P}^0$. As before, the variance of the control variate estimator equals that of the standard estimator multiplied by a factor, but this time the factor depends on both ρ_{cv}, the correlation between $\tilde{P}$ and $\tilde{P}^0$, and also on the ratio of the variances of the two payoffs. These two quantities will determine how good the control variate is at reducing the variance of the calculation. In practice, this is often tested simply by running Monte Carlo calculations with and without a given control variate, and comparing their convergence properties. Just to get a feel for the effect, we can simplify the situation by assuming that the two variances are similar in size, in which case the factor is approximately equal to $2(1-\rho_{cv})$. Any correlation greater than $\frac{1}{2}$ will reduce the variance, with the variance tending to zero as the correlation tends to 1. However, correlations less than half will *increase* the variance.

In conclusion, not all control variates will reduce variance, even if they are positively correlated with the payoff being valued. This is in contrast to the technique of antithetic variables, which can only reduce variance. Care must be taken to choose a good control variate – it is better to use no control variate than a poor one.

6.2.4 The Brownian Bridge

As we discussed in Section 6.2.1, we must approximate the continuous monitoring of a barrier with some choice of discrete monitoring frequency. Ideally, we would increase the barrier monitoring frequency until the option value has converged, but in practice this can turn out to require such a high monitoring frequency that the calculation becomes prohibitively slow. For example, convergence of the value of a three-month normal knock-out might require the barrier to be monitored every few hours. One technique that helps enormously is the *barrier continuity correction* mentioned in Section 6.2.1. Another very helpful technique is to use the properties of the **Brownian Bridge**, a stochastic process whose value is known ("pinned") at each of two points in time, and behaves similarly to a Brownian motion in between. (Actually Brownian Bridges can also be of the "cantilever" variety, pinned at only one point in time.) We exploit the fact that we can analytically calculate an expression for the probability p_{trigger} that a Brownian Bridge process triggers a barrier level H in a time interval (T_1, T_2), conditional on its values at time points T_1 and T_2. Under a model where spot S follows a geometric Brownian motion with volatility σ, the expression for the conditional trigger probability is as follows:

$$p_{\text{trigger}} = \exp\left(-2\frac{\ln\left(\frac{S(T_1)}{H}\right)\ln\left(\frac{S(T_2)}{H}\right)}{\sigma^2(T_2 - T_1)}\right) \quad (6.38)$$

We can easily see by inspection that this expression satisfies various limiting cases. For example, for very distant barriers, the argument of the exponential becomes large and negative, so that the probability of trigger tends to zero. Conversely, for very near barriers, the argument tends to zero, so that the probability of trigger tends to unity.

To employ the Brownian Bridge technique in practice, we work in terms of *barrier survival probabilities*. The survival probability over a given time step is given by $(1 - p_{\text{trigger}})$, and the running barrier survival probability is then simply the product of the survival probabilities over individual time steps. As we simulate a spot path, we keep track of the running survival probability, and then at expiry, if the barrier has not been triggered, we *weight* the payoff calculation according to the survival probability. For example, a no-touch would not pay out the principal, but the principal *multiplied* by the survival probability. For double-barrier contracts, we keep track of two barrier survival probabilities, one for each barrier, and make the simple assumption that the overall survival probability is their product.

Equation 6.38 is not computationally insignificant, requiring as it does two logarithms and one exponential per barrier and *per time step*. It is well worth optimizing its calculation, by checking the sizes of the arguments to the transcendental functions to determine whether it is really worth calling them. (An analytic approximation for the logarithm function helps here.) If both spot levels $S(T_1)$ and $S(T_2)$ are far from the barrier level, and the argument of the exponential function is, say -10, the time-step survival probability can simply be set to unity.

Equation 6.38 is exact for the Black–Scholes model, with its inherent geometric Brownian motion, but we can also use the technique for other models, substituting the fixed volatility in the expression for the instantaneous or local volatility for the time and spot level of interest. The technique works extremely well for all models, which is perhaps unsurprising given that the region in which we are applying the analytic formula is highly localized in both spot (the barrier level) and time (a single MC time step), and is therefore effectively "locally geometric Brownian Motion".

Steve Shreve [10] gives a thorough coverage of Brownian Bridges, devoting to them an entire section of the chapter on stochastic calculus.

6.2.5 Early termination

The value of many barrier-based contracts can become known before the expiry time. For example, the value of any no-touch (single or double) becomes zero as soon as a barrier is triggered, whilst the value of a one-touch becomes known upon trigger if (and only if) it pays in Domestic currency. For such contracts, it is highly advisable to set up the Monte Carlo framework so that it stops simulating once the payoff is known. This technique is known as **early termination**. It is simple but highly effective, especially for contracts where barrier trigger is highly likely, such as the popular 10%-TV double no-touches.

6.3 Calculating Greeks

6.3.1 Bumped Greeks

When discussing the spot Greeks in Section 3.1.4, I mentioned that there were sometimes good and legitimate reasons for preferring bumped Greeks even when analytically calculated Greeks are available. High amongst these is the fact that the changes in P&L predicted by bumped Greeks can be reproduced exactly by bumping the market data and re-calculating option values. This is something that is easily and typically done when using an industrial-strength FX risk management system. For example, suppose we are risk-managing an option book and know its current value and delta. If we bump spot up by 1% and re-calculate the book's value, we would very much like to see the book's value move by exactly the delta. That will happen if the delta we compute is a bumped delta, but if we are using an analytic delta, the move in P&L will not quite match.

Another motivation for calculating Greeks by bumping is consistency. Analytically calculated Greeks are typically available only for some option types and some models, and it may be operationally preferable to calculate all Greeks in the same way (by bumping) than to have to administer a mixture of analytically and numerically calculated Greeks across products and models.

Irrespective of our reasons for calculating Greeks by bumping, there are a number of challenges that we have to negotiate, and we discuss them now.

6.3.1.1 Bumping spot near a barrier

Recall from Section 3.1.4 that the value of a barrier option can exhibit a discontinuity in its gradient at the barrier level, and that the delta correspondingly has a discontinuity in its value (the "delta gap"). Consider the example shown in Figure 3.8. Now, if spot is just below the barrier level, and if in our attempt to compute the bumped delta we bump spot *over* the barrier level, we will not calculate the gradient of the value profile at all, but some other (much less steep) gradient, and we will end up with completely the wrong delta. It is therefore of paramount importance that spot lies the same side of the barrier for both the unbumped and bumped calculations. This is not an issue when spot is far from the barrier, but numerical methods must be written in such a way that they recognize that a barrier is nearby, and take alternative action accordingly. One possible alternative action is to bump spot by a smaller amount, so that it does not cross the barrier. Whilst this works in many cases, it leads to increasingly poor accuracy in the derivative as spot approaches the barrier and we are dividing one very small numerical difference by another. A far better alternative action is to bump spot *away* from the barrier. The spot bump size can then remain the same, and the calculations of the Greeks are much more stable.

For gamma, two spot bumps are required, and we would like to allow *both* of them to be away from the barrier when the barrier is nearby. This can be achieved by bumping spot away from it by δS and $2\delta S$ and using quadratic polynomial fitting to calculate the gamma at the unbumped spot.

6.3.1.2 Arbitrage in bucketed vega reports

Naively, we might calculate a given vega bucket for a bucketed vega report (see Section 5.1) by bumping the volatility at that tenor up and recalculating the option value. For example, we might calculate the one-month vega as:

$$\text{vega}_{1M} = \frac{1}{100\delta\Sigma}[V(\Sigma_{1D}, \Sigma_{1W}, \Sigma_{2W}, \Sigma_{1M}+\delta\Sigma, \Sigma_{2M}, \Sigma_{3M}, \cdots)$$
$$- V(\Sigma_{1D}, \Sigma_{1W}, \Sigma_{2W}, \Sigma_{1M}, \Sigma_{2M}, \Sigma_{3M}, \cdots)] \qquad (6.39)$$

This is inadvisable, however. Such a point-wise bump increases the slope of the volatility curve before the bumped point and decreases its slope after the point. The former effect causes no problem, but the latter effect can introduce *falling variance arbitrage* after the bumped tenor. We discussed this form of arbitrage, also known as calendar arbitrage, in Section 4.2 (in the context of the BSTS model) and in Section 4.9 (in the context of the LV model). Bumping the volatility down is not a solution, as arbitrage can potentially then be introduced *before* the bumped tenor.

A robust solution to this problem is to bump up *all later tenors* together with the desired tenor. Our example one-month vega would then be calculated as follows:

$$\text{vega}_{1M} = \frac{1}{100\delta\Sigma}[V(\Sigma_{1D}, \Sigma_{1W}, \Sigma_{2W}, \Sigma_{1M} + \delta\Sigma, \Sigma_{2M} + \delta\Sigma, \Sigma_{3M} + \delta\Sigma, \cdots) \\ - V(\Sigma_{1D}, \Sigma_{1W}, \Sigma_{2W}, \Sigma_{1M}, \Sigma_{2M} + \delta\Sigma, \Sigma_{3M} + \delta\Sigma, \cdots)] \qquad (6.40)$$

The calculation of a bucketed vega report then proceeds as follows: first we have all the volatilities unbumped; then we have the volatility at the last tenor bumped up; then we have the volatilities at the last two tenors bumped up, and so on. This **incremental bumping** technique specified by Equation 6.40 requires no more valuation calculations than the naive technique of Equation 6.39.

A similar alternative solution involves bumping volatilities *down*, at the desired tenor and all *earlier* tenors.

Note that we are always talking about avoiding the *introduction* of arbitrage: if the volatility curve or surface already contains arbitrage, the incremental bumping technique will not remove it.

6.3.2 Greeks from finite-difference calculations

Finite-difference calculations naturally yield option values at multiple spot levels, since the FD problem is solved on a grid. A delta and a gamma can therefore easily be calculated using these values. Whilst this is very useful, it is important to understand that the spot Greeks calculated in this way represent the risks under a specific form of smile dynamics. The local volatility surface (whether for the LV model or an LSV model) is the same for all the spot values, so we may call these dynamics **sticky local volatility**.

To obtain the spot risks under other dynamics, such as sticky strike or sticky delta, and to obtain other risks, such as vega and volgamma, we must recalibrate the local volatility surface for the bumped spot or volatility, and re-run the finite-difference calculation. Crucially, though, we do not have to *regeometrize* the FD grid, and in fact we should not do so: using different geometries for the unbumped and bumped calculations can introduce a significant amount of noise. If we use the same grid geometry for the unbumped and bumped calculations, the numerical noise in the calculated Greek is vastly reduced. When designing FD calculation tools, it is advisable to distinguish two markets: the one used for geometrization and the one used for valuation. As long as the valuation market is only a small bump away from the geometrization market, the same grid geometry will be appropriate. However, this technique should not be used for large-scale market shifts, such as those required for spot ladders and vega ladders.

6.3.3 Greeks from Monte Carlo

Traditional methods for computing Monte Carlo Greeks are fraught with numerical error. Recall that option values are computed using *estimators*, whose errors are computationally expensive to reduce, as discussed in Section 6.2.2. Computation of Greeks then involves taking *differences* between such error-containing values, or even (for second-order risks) differences of differences – a numerical recipe for noisy results.

Parallel processing of Monte Carlo calculations vastly improves the situation, and is done routinely in the industry. Monte Carlo simulations can be easily parallelized, since the simulations do not depend on each other. For example, a calculation involving a million paths could be distributed over 100 processors (or processor cores), and would then take roughly as long as a 10,000-path calculation on a single processing unit. This approach comes at some cost, however: dedicated collections of processors for Monte Carlo (known as **Monte Carlo farms** or **compute grids**) must be continually maintained, in terms of both hardware and software. In particular, all the software installed on the farms must be compatible with that installed on the client machines from which the distributed calculations are launched.

Some steps can be taken to reduce the noise for a given number of simulations. For example, the simulations used for the bumped and unbumped calculations can be orchestrated so that they use exactly the same random numbers, which substantially reduces the noise compared with the use of different random numbers. (Such orchestration must be sophisticated enough to take into account any early-termination techniques used.)

The combination of highly parallelized calculations and other noise-reducing techniques allow us to reach the point where deltas can be calculated with adequate precision in an acceptable calculation time. Gammas improve greatly too, but usually remain unsatisfactorily noisy. And ladder reports and bucketed risk reports, with their large numbers of inputs to be bumped, remain extremely slow.

Many other powerful techniques have been developed for improving Monte Carlo Greeks, but often there are reasons that they are not well suited to FX barrier options. One example is the **pathwise method**, discussed in Glasserman [56] and Jäckel [55]. This works by simulating not the contract's payoff but its sensitivity to a market parameter, effectively interchanging the order of differentiation and expectation. This method cannot be used for discontinuous payoffs, however, thereby ruling out many barrier option types. Even when the payoff is continuous, the method does not lend itself to variation of the smile dynamics, since the simulated process is held constant. Another example is the technique of **adjoint algorithmic differentiation (AAD)**, developed by Mike Giles and Paul Glasserman [57]. The technique improves matters dramatically where the number of inputs to be bumped is large compared to the number of contracts to be risk-managed, but this is far from the standard FX options case, where the top priority is to calculate a handful of Greeks for portfolios containing thousands of contracts.

7 | Further Topics

> If you ask ten different traders what they want from your model, you will get twelve different answers.
>
> *A trader quant*

7.1 Managed currencies

All of the currencies in the benchmark currency pairs that we have used for illustrating results – EUR, USD, TRY, AUD and JPY – are (at the time of writing) examples of **free-floating currencies**: their exchange rates with respect to other currencies are determined by market forces, rather than being set by monetary authorities, such as the central bank of the country which issues the currency. A currency which is not free-floating is described as **managed**. Subtle distinctions between different types of managed currencies can additionally be made [58].

Note that a currency that is not managed may still be subject to **intervention**, whereby a monetary authority intervenes in the FX markets occasionally in an attempt to strengthen or weaken its currency. For example, the Japanese yen has been subject to several interventions by the Bank of Japan over the years in attempts to curb its strength.

The Danish krone (DKK) is an example of a managed currency: the Danish central bank ensures that the EURDKK rate is held in a narrow range around 7.46. We say that the krone is **pegged** to the euro. Similarly, the Hong Kong dollar (HKD) is pegged to the US dollar; the Hong Kong Monetary Authority ensures that the USDHKD rate is held in a range 7.75–7.85. Other examples of pegged currencies abound.

Standard diffusion models represent floating currencies well, but what do we need to do differently to model pegged exchange rates? As a minimum, we must ensure that the implied volatility model that we use is able to match the market prices of any liquid options for the pegged currency pair, and it may well be that we need a specialized pegged implied volatility model for that purpose. To see why that is the case, it is useful to picture the shape of the PDF that we might expect for a currency pair whose values cannot go outside a given range: it will have very little or no weight outside the range – a bell curve that is truncated on one or both sides. For the risk-neutral PDF to take such a peculiar shape, the implied volatility smile will also need to take on a peculiar shape, which may not be easily calibrated by smile models that were primarily designed for unmanaged currencies.

We may go further and create a specialized spot process model which reflects the idiosyncratic economics of the pegged currency pair. The advantages of this approach are clear: such a process will far better represent the dynamics that we are trying to model, and will probably be a lot easier to calibrate as a result. The drawback is that we must then re-develop our valuation models for all contract types to additionally handle the new pegged-currency model.

Perhaps the most interesting and instructive case of currency management in recent years is the Swiss franc. As described in Section 4.13.2, the Swiss franc (CHF) was **pegged** to the euro for a period, which came to an abrupt end on 15 January 2015. The pegged period began in September 2011, when the Swiss National Bank announced [59] that it would "no longer tolerate a EUR/CHF exchange rate below the minimum rate of CHF 1.20. The SNB will enforce this minimum rate with the utmost determination and is prepared to buy foreign currency in unlimited quantities."

This case highlights the fact that our valuation and risk management models must not only take account of pegs that are currently active, but they must also handle **de-peg risk**: the possibility that the peg is *removed*. Such a **de-peg event** would likely cause spot to jump substantially and could therefore have a catastrophic effect on the P&L of a pegged-currency barrier options book, and so it is vital that any serious pegged-currency model is able to measure the size of the de-peg risk.

7.2 Stochastic interest rates (SIR)

The aim of this section is to explain the issues that arise when interest rates are no longer assumed to be deterministic. Seminal work in this area was performed by Amin and Jarrow [60], and their results are still used today. We will start our analysis by re-visiting the Black–Scholes PDE of Equation 2.21 and reminding ourselves exactly where the dependencies on interest rates occur. The interest rates are to be seen in two places: the carry term is proportional to the interest rate differential $(r_d - r_f)$, and the cash account term is proportional to the Domestic interest rate r_d. (See Section 2.3.4 for descriptions of the terms.) Notably, the Foreign interest rate does not appear on its own. We can immediately deduce that any FX model which includes stochastic interest rates must be able to model these two quantities in a realistic way. In particular, the volatility of the interest rate differential will be strongly dependent on the *correlation* between the two interest rates.

An excellent introduction to interest rates is to be found in Hull [2]. He describes and discusses the nature of interest rate instruments (such as futures, swaps, caplets and swaptions), the interest rate market, and a variety of models.

Interest rate models fall very broadly into two categories: models of market instruments, such as the LIBOR market model of Brace, Gatarek and Musiela (BGM) [61], and models of the instantaneous short interest rate, such as the famous and popular Hull–White model [62].

The interest rates we have used in our FX models have been short rates, so let us treat them using the Hull–White model, writing it in the following form:

$$dr = \kappa(\bar{r}(t) - r(t))dt + \sigma_r dW_t^r \quad (7.1)$$

The first term on the right-hand side represents mean-reversion of the interest rate, and in that respect is similar to the corresponding term in the Heston model, which we discussed in Section 4.11.2. The second term is a Brownian motion with volatility σ_r. Note that the volatility in the Hull–White model has the dimensions of time$^{-\frac{3}{2}}$, not time$^{-\frac{1}{2}}$ as for FX spot models. Very broadly speaking, typical values of the volatility would lie in the range 0.5%–1.5%.

Using the Hull–White model of Equation 7.1 for each of the interest rates, and using the risk-neutral Black–Scholes SDE of Equation 2.71 for the FX spot rate, we can construct the following three-factor model (dropping the t-dependencies of the interest rates for the sake of clarity):

$$dS = (r_d - r_f)S dt + \sigma_S S dW^S \quad (7.2)$$
$$dr_d = \kappa_d(\bar{r}_d - r_d)dt + \sigma_d dW^d \quad (7.3)$$
$$dr_f = \kappa_f(\bar{r}_f - r_f)dt + \sigma_f dW^f \quad (7.4)$$

where the three Wiener processes are correlated:

$$dW^S dW^d = \rho_d dt \quad (7.5)$$
$$dW^S dW^f = \rho_f dt \quad (7.6)$$
$$dW^d dW^f = \rho_{d,f} dt \quad (7.7)$$

The individual Hull–White models can be calibrated to the market prices of liquid interest rate instruments, typically caplets and swaptions. This process entails numerous choices, as described for example by Gurrieri et al. [63]. The calibration of the spot volatility must take into account both the calibrated interest rate models and also the FX market. Specifically, we need to calibrate to FX market instruments that depend on FX spot and on interest rates. The simplest such instruments are *FX forward contracts*.

As a reminder, the fair forward rate is the strike at which a forward contract has zero value. In Section 1.2.2, we derived an expression for the forward rate, and the replication argument we used there extends to the case of stochastic interest rates. For current time t and settlement date T_s, the forward rate $F(t, T_s)$ is given by Equation 1.10, which we reproduce here:

$$F(t, T_s) = S(t) \exp\left(-\int_{t'}^{T_s} (r_d(u) - r_f(u)) \, du\right)$$

We can use Itô's lemma to express the change in the forward rate in terms of the changes in spot and the interest rates. This exercise generates a lot of drift terms (in dt), but we do not need to evaluate them all in order to obtain the result we are after. Instead, I will write the result as follows:

$$dF = \text{(drift coefficients)} \, dt$$
$$+ \sigma_S F \, dW^S + (T_s - t') F \sigma_d \, dW^d - (T_s - t') F \sigma_f \, dW^f \quad (7.8)$$

If we now assume that the forward process, like spot, follows a geometric Brownian motion:

$$dF = \mu_F F \, dt + \sigma_F F \, dW^F \quad (7.9)$$

we obtain the following relationship between the four Wiener processes:

$$\sigma_F \, dW^F = \sigma_S \, dW^S + \sigma_d \tau \, dW^d - \sigma_f \tau \, dW^f \quad (7.10)$$

where I have written $\tau = T_s - t'$ for brevity. Squaring both sides and taking expectations, we derive the following important and interesting relationship:

$$\sigma_F^2 = \sigma_S^2 + \sigma_d^2 \tau^2 + \sigma_f^2 \tau^2 + 2\rho_d \sigma_S \sigma_d \tau - 2\rho_f \sigma_S \sigma_f \tau - 2\rho_{d,f} \sigma_d \sigma_f \tau^2 \quad (7.11)$$

This relates the volatility of the forward to the volatility of spot, the volatilities of the interest rates and the three correlations between spot and interest rates.

As already described, the interest rate volatilities come from the calibration of the interest rate models to market prices of interest rate instruments. The volatility of the forward is closely related to at-the-money implied volatilities, and so can be estimated from market prices of vanilla options. It is the volatility of spot that affects barrier options: all other things being equal, *the greater the volatility of spot, the more likely the barrier is to be triggered.* We therefore need to solve Equation 7.11 for the spot volatility, which is easily done as it is in the form of a quadratic equation:

$$\sigma_S^2 + 2\tau(\rho_d\sigma_d - \rho_f\sigma_f)\sigma_S + \left(\sigma_d^2 + \sigma_f^2 - 2\rho_{d,f}\sigma_d\sigma_f\right)\tau^2 - \sigma_F^2 = 0 \qquad (7.12)$$

This is the **calibration equation for the volatility of spot** under our chosen three-factor model.

Equation 7.12 shows that, in the absence of any correlations, the volatility of spot is less than the volatility of the forward, and hence barriers are less likely to be triggered. However, the effect is proportional to the square of the maturity τ, and therefore only becomes significant for longer maturities. For example, with interest rate volatilities of 1%, the reduction in spot volatility is about two basis points for a six-month maturity, and even when the maturity is three years the reduction only reaches 85 basis points (0.85%).

The introduction of non-zero correlations changes everything. For a start, the stochastic interest rate effect can be either positive or negative: the correlation terms contain a mixture of signs and the correlations themselves may take either sign. Furthermore, some of the effects are proportional to τ rather than τ^2 and so are greater for short maturities.

Let us take the specific example of USDTRY. Suppose that market economics suggest that an increase in TRY interest rates is likely to be accompanied by a loss in the value of the Turkish lira, and hence an increase in USDTRY spot. Thus spot would be strongly positively correlated with the Domestic interest rate. Assuming for simplicity that the other correlations are zero and that the interest rate volatilities are still 1%, Figure 7.1 illustrates this effect for various levels of correlation. Two things are very clear: first, this effect results in a significant reduction in the volatility of spot, and second, the effect is strongly sensitive to the correlation.

How should we choose the correlations in our model? Unfortunately, there is no clear answer, and the reason is that there is no clear choice of market instruments to which we can calibrate these correlations. This is a desperate situation for anyone wishing to make prices and risk-manage positions in the competitive market of FX barrier options. And in such desperate situations, it is not uncommon to turn to historic data, and compute historic correlations as a guide to the values to be used in the model.

Needless to say, there exist models for FX and stochastic interest rates which are far more sophisticated than the treatment above, for example models having the ability to calibrate to the entire FX implied volatility surface. (Many such models are proprietary.) However, the same difficulty of calibrating the correlation parameters remains, and in fact if the model admits a term structure of correlations, calibration is an even greater challenge. In summary, perhaps the greatest difficulty associated

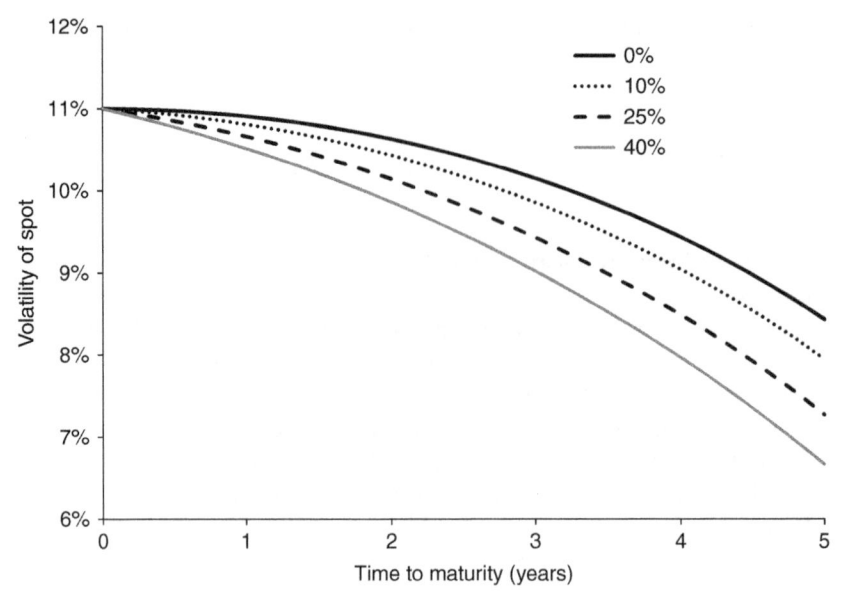

Figure 7.1 Variation of the calibrated volatility of USDTRY spot with maturity of calibration forward contract, for various levels of correlation between spot and TRY interest rate. The FX forward volatility is 11%

with the use of stochastic interest rate models for FX is the question of how to calibrate the correlation parameters.

7.3 Real-world pricing

What, you may rightfully ask, was not "real-world" in everything we have discussed hitherto? Not too much, thankfully, but there nevertheless remain a small handful of crucial practical issues which we need to understand.

7.3.1 Bid–offer spreads

When a market-maker (such as an FX options trader at a bank) quotes a price to a counterparty, the price that is quoted for the counterparty to buy at is called an **offer price**, whilst the price that is quoted for the counterparty to sell at is called the **bid price**. In order for the market-maker to be able to earn a margin, the offer price must be higher than the bid price. The **mid price** is defined as the price exactly halfway between bid and offer prices.

In the FX barrier options market, market-makers usually quote both the bid and offer prices, called a **two-way price**. Usually, market-makers don't know whether the counterparty is interested in buying or selling, or even has a preference – but they may well try and guess! The difference between the prices in a two-way quote is called the **bid–offer spread**.

In a highly competitive market such as the FX barrier options market, it is vital to calculate bid–offer spreads to accurately reflect the costs of trading. If the quoted bid–offer spread is too narrow, counterparties will trade heavily, but the margin earned will not cover the costs of managing the trade and running the market-making business generally. If the spread is too wide, few counterparties will trade, and again the business cannot turn a profit.

Part of the bid–offer spread for a barrier option comes from the spreads on the underlying market variables: FX spot, Domestic interest rate, Foreign interest rate, at-the-money vanilla option prices and delta-parameterized risk reversals and butterflies. Whilst it is in principle possible to set up a mathematical model which inherently includes these underlying spreads, this is very rarely done in practice. There are a number of reasons for this. For a start, the simultaneous modelling of the spreads on several different market variables would quickly make even the simplest option valuation model hugely cumbersome. Furthermore, we would have to completely re-think the nature of many aspects of our models. For example, the continuous delta-hedging strategy that underlies many of our models would be useless, because it would lead to infinite hedging costs – we would be crossing the spread infinitely often in finite size. Similarly, the concept of a local volatility function would need to be extended to depend on a two-way spot and would need to be derived on the basis of a two-way implied volatility surface. And all our numerical methods would also need to be extended to handle the effects of two-way prices. And at the end of the day, this enormous extra complexity would bring us little benefit, as there would still be extra issues that had to be handled on top, such as anticipated lack of liquidity or depth in the spot market around certain times. Thus it is far preferable to set up our mathematical models to calculate fair values with no spreads and then add spreads on top.

So the challenge then becomes this: even once we are given a fair option value based on our valuation model of choice, how should we generate a two-way price? A clue to help us meet this challenge is to recall that the meaning of "fair value" for an option is the cost of *hedging* that option. Now, the costs of a dynamic hedging strategy are not known up front, because by its very nature they vary through the contract's lifetime. But, if we can find a good *static hedge* for our barrier contract (of the kind discussed in Section 5.6), we can examine *its* market bid–offer spreads in order to come up with a bid–offer spread for the barrier contract price.

Note that the bid and offer prices may be spread from the fair value by asymmetric amounts, with the result that the mid-price is not necessarily the same as the fair value.

The static hedging example we discussed in Section 5.6 involved a single barrier option, but very often a market-maker must quote a two-way price on an *option structure*. The way in which the bid–offer spread of the structure should be computed from the bid–offer spreads of the underlying options is called **netting**, and depends intimately on the nature of the structure. For example, a **ratchet option** is a structure consisting of a ladder of KIKOs, whereby one KIKO knocks out at exactly the barrier level that another one knocks in. Despite the fact that numerous barrier options are involved in the structure, only one of them will be delivered, and the bid–offer spread need only be wide enough to account for one option. Computing and netting bid–offer spreads accurately for options and structures is crucial to the success of an FX options business, and industrial algorithms for doing so are highly developed and can be extremely sophisticated.

7.3.2 Rules-based pricing methods

For some kinds of products, such as complex and long-dated structures, it is worthwhile for a trader and/or structurer to take time to analyze a trade before coming up with a price quote. For others, such as flow barrier options, which are traded in high volumes, the focus is on making prices quickly, so that option price quotes can be distributed electronically to customers in real time. This need for speed means that fair value calculations based on a model, such as an LSV model, may simply be too slow. Given that such calculations only produce a fair value anyway, and that an additional infrastructure of algorithms is needed to calculate bid–offer spreads (as discussed in Section 7.3.1), it makes sense to try and set up algorithms that actually calculate the price itself. Such **rules-based pricing methods** examine and combine a variety of different effects. The pricing rules are usually based to some extent on static hedging, but static hedges are not always available that are sufficiently good for price-making, and in practice, a mixed approach is usually taken, involving a static hedge plus an estimation of *re-hedging* costs. The smile-based volatility Greeks are therefore amongst the key ingredients required by the pricing rules. Other ingredients include barrier over-hedging adjustments (as described in Section 3.5) and estimates of capital costs.

For many contracts, the prices that come out of rules-based methods are sufficiently reliable that they can be used not only for *quoting* to customers, but also to *deal*, electronically and in real time. The consequent potential for high trading volumes have made such **eCommerce** systems a focus for many market-making FX options businesses.

Whether a given contract is sufficiently benign to allow it to be safely traded without the intervention of a human dealer depends both on the contract type and also on the contract parameters. Examples of factors that make a contract less safe to be dealt automatically are: a highly in-the-money or out-of-the-money strike or barrier; a very large principal; or a very short or very long maturity. Electronic price distribution platforms are designed to detect such factors and distinguish the status of the corresponding price quotation accordingly. For example, it might be that a price which is safe to deal is designated "Live", one which requires checking by a trader is designated "Indicative", and one which cannot reliably be calculated using the pricing rules is designated "Refer to dealer".

7.4 Regulation and market abuse

There are a handful of regulatory aspects of barrier options that are worth being aware of. Perhaps the thorniest is the occurrence of scenarios where spot is near a barrier level and a dealer places a large FX spot order which appears to have the effect of pushing spot through the barrier level – to the dealer's benefit. A clear case of market abuse? Far from it. Consider an FX options trader who has sold a reverse knock-out call and is managing its risk. As we discussed in Chapter 3.1.4, the contract has a large negative delta gap at the barrier, meaning that a short position has a large positive delta, which must be hedged with a large short spot position. If spot crosses the barrier, this position will need to be closed out, by placing a large buy order for spot. Now, if spot rallies towards the barrier, a trader may judge it very likely that the large buy order will be needed imminently, and in such a situation it makes sense to *start* executing the order slightly ahead of the barrier level, with the aim of getting the overall order filled at a reasonable rate. This is known as **pre-hedging**, and is accepted practice. Thus, a legitimate risk management tactic may look like market manipulation and invite the scrutiny of the regulators.

Of course the reverse situation is equally problematic: a dealer who actually manipulates the market will attempt to explain it away in terms of hedging. The nub of the matter, therefore, is that it can sometimes be extremely difficult to distinguish market abuse from genuine risk management – a frustrating situation for regulators and regulated alike.

The question of how to detect and prove market abuse is one that is being addressed by regulators globally. For example, in the UK, a debate on this topic (amongst others) has been initiated by a "Fair and Effective Markets Review" consultation document written jointly by the Bank of England, the UK Treasury and the UK Financial Conduct Authority [64]. A specific question in this document is:

> Do trading practices involving barrier or digital options pose risks to the fairness and effectiveness of one or more FICC[1] markets? How hard is it to distinguish between hedging and 'defending' such options in practice? Should further measures be taken to deal with the risks posed by barrier options, whether through market-wide disclosure of significant barrier positions, an extension of regulation or some other route?

---

[1] The acronym FICC is commonly used to denote the set of asset classes: Fixed Income, Currencies (meaning Foreign Exchange) and Commodities.

At the time of writing, numerous responses to the review have been submitted, and the industry awaits its recommendations.

A more fundamental problem is that there is no clear consensus as to precisely what market event constitutes a barrier trigger. And the reason for this, perhaps alarmingly, is that there is no clear consensus as to exactly where the FX spot market is trading at any given time. Regulatory changes since the credit crisis have caused liquidity to become fractured. Multiple trading venues now operate and it is even possible for multiple spot rates to be seen on the same venue by different market participants. The legal contracts for barrier options generally specify a **calculation agent**, who is responsible for determining whether the barrier levels in the contract have been triggered. Before the fracture of the FX spot market, disputes were relatively easy to resolve, as multiple banks were able to testify to the same market observations, but these days that is not reliably the case.

That a book describing cutting-edge models for FX barrier options should end by noting that FX spot is not always well defined is, aside from slightly comical, a salutary reminder that in this complex financial world in which we live, we should take nothing for granted.

A | Derivation of the Black–Scholes Pricing Equations for Vanilla Options

> Junior quant: 'Should I be surprised that μ drops out?'
> Senior quant: 'Not if you want to keep your job.'

This appendix describes the procedure for deriving closed-form expressions for the prices of vanilla call and put options, by analytically performing integrals derived in Chapter 2. In that chapter, we derive two integral expressions, either of which may be used to calculate the Black–Scholes value of a European option. One of the integral expressions yields the value in terms of the transformed variable X (Equation 2.64):

$$v(X,\tau) = \int_{-\infty}^{\infty} \frac{1}{\sqrt{2\pi\sigma^2\tau}} e^{-\frac{(X-X')^2}{2\sigma^2\tau}} \bar{P}(X')\,dX'$$

The other integral expression yields the value in terms of the original financial variable S (spot price) (Equation 2.65):

$$V(S,t) = e^{-r_d(T_s-t)} \int_0^{\infty} \frac{1}{\sqrt{2\pi\sigma^2(T_e-t)}} \frac{1}{S} \exp\left(-\frac{(\ln F - \ln S')^2}{2\sigma^2(T_e-t)}\right) P(S')\,dS'$$

We will here perform the integral in Equation 2.64 in order to obtain the pricing formulae. The transformed payoff function $\bar{P}(X)$ takes the following form for a vanilla option:

$$\bar{P}(X) = \max\left(0, \phi\left(F_0 e^X - K\right)\right) \qquad (A.1)$$

where ϕ is the option trait (+1 for a call; −1 for a put) and F_0 is the arbitrary quantity that was introduced in the transformation process for the purpose of dimensional etiquette.

The zero floor in the payoff function has the result that the integrand vanishes for a semi-infinite range of X' values. For $\phi = +1$, the integrand vanishes for $X' < \ln(K/F_0)$, whereas for $\phi = -1$, the integrand vanishes for $X' > \ln(K/F_0)$. In general, we may write the integral in terms of lower limit a and upper limit b:

$$v(X,\tau) = \int_a^b \frac{1}{\sqrt{2\pi\sigma^2\tau}} e^{-\frac{(X-X')^2}{2\sigma^2\tau}} \max\left(0, \phi\left(F_0 e^{X'} - K\right)\right) dX' \quad (A.2)$$

where the limits a and b depend on the option trait ϕ in the following way:

$$a = \begin{cases} \ln\left(\frac{K}{F_0}\right) & \phi = +1 \\ -\infty & \phi = -1 \end{cases} \quad (A.3)$$

$$b = \begin{cases} \infty & \phi = +1 \\ \ln\left(\frac{K}{F_0}\right) & \phi = -1 \end{cases} \quad (A.4)$$

Let us write the two terms in Equation A.2 explicitly as such:

$$v(X,\tau) = I_1 - I_2 \quad (A.5)$$

where

$$I_1 \doteq \phi F_0 \int_a^b \frac{1}{\sqrt{2\pi\sigma^2\tau}} e^{-\frac{(X-X')^2}{2\sigma^2\tau}} e^{X'} dX' \quad (A.6)$$

and

$$I_2 \doteq \phi K \int_a^b \frac{1}{\sqrt{2\pi\sigma^2\tau}} e^{-\frac{(X-X')^2}{2\sigma^2\tau}} dX' \quad (A.7)$$

The integrand of Expression I_2 is the probability density function (PDF) of a normal distribution with mean X and variance $\sigma^2\tau$. This can be written in terms of the special function $N(\cdot)$, which is the cumulative distribution function (CDF) of a standard normal distribution:

$$I_2 = \phi K \left(N\left(\frac{b-X}{\sigma\sqrt{\tau}}\right) - N\left(\frac{a-X}{\sigma\sqrt{\tau}}\right) \right) \quad (A.8)$$

In Expression I_1, completion of the square in the exponent gives:

$$I_1 = \phi F_0 e^{X + \frac{1}{2}\sigma^2\tau} \int_a^b \frac{1}{\sqrt{2\pi\sigma^2\tau}} e^{-\frac{(X'-(X+\sigma^2\tau))^2}{2\sigma^2\tau}} dX' \quad (A.9)$$

As with I_2, the integrand is again the probability density function (PDF) of a normal distribution, and the variance is again $\sigma^2\tau$, but this time the mean is $(X + \sigma^2\tau)$. Again, this can be written in terms of $N(\cdot)$:

$$I_1 = \phi F_0 e^{X + \frac{1}{2}\sigma^2\tau} \left(N\left(\frac{b-X-\sigma^2\tau}{\sigma\sqrt{\tau}}\right) - N\left(\frac{a-X-\sigma^2\tau}{\sigma\sqrt{\tau}}\right) \right) \quad (A.10)$$

Derivation of the Black–Scholes Pricing Equations for Vanilla Options | 217

The closed-form expressions for I_1 and I_2 given by Equations A.10 and A.8 respectively can now be inserted into Equation A.5 to give a closed-form expression for v. Since the quantities a and b depend on the option trait ϕ (see Equations A.3 and A.4), we will separate the call and put cases.

For calls ($\phi = +1$), I_1, I_2 and v are given as follows:

$$I_1 \text{ (call)} = F_0 e^{X + \frac{1}{2}\sigma^2 \tau} \left(N(\infty) - N\left(\frac{\ln\left(\frac{K}{F_0}\right) - X - \sigma^2 \tau}{\sigma \sqrt{\tau}} \right) \right)$$

$$= F_0 e^{X + \frac{1}{2}\sigma^2 \tau} \left(1 - N\left(\frac{\ln\left(\frac{K}{F_0}\right) - X - \sigma^2 \tau}{\sigma \sqrt{\tau}} \right) \right)$$

$$= F_0 e^{X + \frac{1}{2}\sigma^2 \tau} N\left(\frac{-\ln\left(\frac{K}{F_0}\right) + X + \sigma^2 \tau}{\sigma \sqrt{\tau}} \right) \tag{A.11}$$

$$I_2 \text{ (call)} = K \left(N(\infty) - N\left(\frac{\ln\left(\frac{K}{F_0}\right) - X}{\sigma \sqrt{\tau}} \right) \right)$$

$$= K \left(1 - N\left(\frac{\ln\left(\frac{K}{F_0}\right) - X}{\sigma \sqrt{\tau}} \right) \right)$$

$$= K N\left(\frac{-\ln\left(\frac{K}{F_0}\right) + X}{\sigma \sqrt{\tau}} \right) \tag{A.12}$$

$$\Rightarrow v_{\text{call}} = F_0 e^{X + \frac{1}{2}\sigma^2 \tau} N\left(\frac{-\ln\left(\frac{K}{F_0}\right) + X + \sigma^2 \tau}{\sigma \sqrt{\tau}} \right) - K N\left(\frac{-\ln\left(\frac{K}{F_0}\right) + X}{\sigma \sqrt{\tau}} \right) \tag{A.13}$$

For puts ($\phi = -1$), I_1, I_2 and v are given as follows:

$$I_1 \text{ (put)} = -F_0 e^{X + \frac{1}{2}\sigma^2 \tau} \left(N\left(\frac{\ln\left(\frac{K}{F_0}\right) - X - \sigma^2 \tau}{\sigma \sqrt{\tau}} \right) - N(-\infty) \right)$$

$$= -F_0 e^{X + \frac{1}{2}\sigma^2 \tau} N\left(\frac{\ln\left(\frac{K}{F_0}\right) - X - \sigma^2 \tau}{\sigma \sqrt{\tau}} \right) \tag{A.14}$$

FX Barrier Options

$$I_2 \text{ (put)} = -K\left(N\left(\frac{\ln\left(\frac{K}{F_0}\right) - X}{\sigma\sqrt{\tau}}\right) - N(-\infty)\right)$$

$$= -KN\left(\frac{\ln\left(\frac{K}{F_0}\right) - X}{\sigma\sqrt{\tau}}\right) \quad \text{(A.15)}$$

$$\Rightarrow v_{\text{put}} = -F_0 e^{X + \frac{1}{2}\sigma^2\tau} N\left(\frac{\ln\left(\frac{K}{F_0}\right) - X - \sigma^2\tau}{\sigma\sqrt{\tau}}\right) + KN\left(\frac{\ln\left(\frac{K}{F_0}\right) - X}{\sigma\sqrt{\tau}}\right) \quad \text{(A.16)}$$

The similarities between Equations A.13 and A.16 allow us to recombine the call and put results into a single vanilla result, like so:

$$v_{\text{vanilla}} = \phi\left[F_0 e^{X + \frac{1}{2}\sigma^2\tau} N\left(\phi \frac{X - \ln\left(\frac{K}{F_0}\right) + \sigma^2\tau}{\sigma\sqrt{\tau}}\right) - KN\left(\phi \frac{X - \ln\left(\frac{K}{F_0}\right)}{\sigma\sqrt{\tau}}\right)\right] \quad \text{(A.17)}$$

We now have a closed-form expression for the transformed value variable $v(X, \tau)$. To obtain an expression for the original value variable $V(S, t)$, it only remains for us to undo the four transformations of Section 2.7.1 one by one.

Undoing Transformation 4 gives us an expression for undiscounted vanilla prices in terms of the forward:

$$\tilde{U}(F, \tau) = \phi\left[FN\left(\phi \frac{\ln\left(\frac{F}{K}\right) + \frac{1}{2}\sigma^2\tau}{\sigma\sqrt{\tau}}\right) - KN\left(\phi \frac{\ln\left(\frac{F}{K}\right) - \frac{1}{2}\sigma^2\tau}{\sigma\sqrt{\tau}}\right)\right] \quad \text{(A.18)}$$

Undoing Transformation 3 gives us an expression for undiscounted prices in terms of spot:

$$U(S, \tau) = \phi\left[Se^{(r_d - r_f)\tau} N\left(\phi \frac{\ln\left(\frac{S}{K}\right) + (r_d - r_f + \frac{1}{2}\sigma^2)\tau}{\sigma\sqrt{\tau}}\right) - KN\left(\phi \frac{\ln\left(\frac{S}{K}\right) + (r_d - r_f - \frac{1}{2}\sigma^2)\tau}{\sigma\sqrt{\tau}}\right)\right] \quad \text{(A.19)}$$

Derivation of the Black–Scholes Pricing Equations for Vanilla Options | 219

Undoing Transformation 2 gives us an expression for discounted prices in terms of spot:

$$\tilde{V}(S,\tau) = \phi\left[Se^{-r_f\tau}N\left(\phi\frac{\ln\left(\frac{S}{K}\right) + (r_d - r_f + \frac{1}{2}\sigma^2)\tau}{\sigma\sqrt{\tau}}\right) - Ke^{-r_d\tau}N\left(\phi\frac{\ln\left(\frac{S}{K}\right) + (r_d - r_f - \frac{1}{2}\sigma^2)\tau}{\sigma\sqrt{\tau}}\right)\right] \quad (A.20)$$

Lastly, undoing Transformation 1 gives us an expression for discounted prices in terms of spot, with explicit reference to the time variable t:

$$V(S,t) = \phi\left[Se^{-r_f(T-t)}N\left(\phi\frac{\ln\left(\frac{S}{K}\right) + (r_d - r_f + \frac{1}{2}\sigma^2)(T-t)}{\sigma\sqrt{T-t}}\right) - Ke^{-r_d(T-t)}N\left(\phi\frac{\ln\left(\frac{S}{K}\right) + (r_d - r_f - \frac{1}{2}\sigma^2)(T-t)}{\sigma\sqrt{T-t}}\right)\right] \quad (A.21)$$

If it seems that we have laboured the working, it is for a reason: each of the forms of expression we have presented can be useful in its own right. All of the forms of expression shown above may be found in the literature. The long expressions that form the arguments of the normal CDF are commonly given their own symbols. For example, following the conventions in Hull [2], we define:

$$d_1 = \frac{\ln\left(\frac{S}{K}\right) + (r_d - r_f + \frac{1}{2}\sigma^2)(T-t)}{\sigma\sqrt{T-t}} \quad (A.22)$$

$$d_2 = \frac{\ln\left(\frac{S}{K}\right) + (r_d - r_f - \frac{1}{2}\sigma^2)(T-t)}{\sigma\sqrt{T-t}} \quad (A.23)$$

whereupon our formula for the discounted prices in terms of spot becomes:

$$V(S,t) = \phi\left[Se^{-r_f(T-t)}N(\phi d_1) - Ke^{-r_d(T-t)}N(\phi d_2)\right] \quad (A.24)$$

The value V here is for an option with unit Foreign principal ($A_f = 1$); to get the value for non-unit-principal options, we simply need to multiply V by A_f.

B | Normal and Lognormal Probability Distributions

B.1 Normal distribution

In the case where Z follows a **normal** distribution, its density function $f_Z^{\mathcal{N}}$ has the form:

$$f_Z^{\mathcal{N}}(z) = \frac{1}{\sqrt{2\pi \sigma_Z^2}} \exp\left(-\frac{(z - \mu_Z)^2}{2\sigma_Z^2}\right) \tag{B.1}$$

where z may take any real value.

The mean of the distribution equals μ_Z, and its variance equals σ_Z^2. The **standard normal distribution** is a normal distribution which has mean equal to zero and variance equal to one. We denote the PDF and CDF of the standard normal distribution by special functions $n(\cdot)$ and $N(\cdot)$ respectively:

$$n(z) = \frac{1}{\sqrt{2\pi}} \exp\left(-\frac{z^2}{2}\right) \tag{B.2}$$

$$N(z) = \int_{-\infty}^{z} \frac{1}{\sqrt{2\pi}} \exp\left(-\frac{x^2}{2}\right) dx \tag{B.3}$$

B.2 Lognormal distribution

In the case where Z follows a **lognormal** distribution, its density function $f_Z^{\mathcal{LN}}$ has the form:

$$f_Z^{\mathcal{LN}}(z) = \frac{1}{\sqrt{2\pi \sigma_Z^2}} \frac{1}{z} \exp\left(-\frac{(\ln z - \ln \mu_Z)^2}{2\sigma_Z^2}\right) \tag{B.4}$$

where $z > 0$.

C | Derivation of the Local Volatility Function

C.1 Derivation in terms of call prices

Our aim here is to derive an expression for the local volatility (LV) function $\sigma(S,t)$ that appears in the local volatility model of Equation 4.21:

$$dS = (r_d - r_f)\,S\,dt + \sigma(S,t)\,S\,dW_t$$

Central to the derivation is the probability density function (PDF) of spot. This quantity provides the crucial link between the dynamics of spot and the values of options. We introduced the PDF in the special case of the Black–Scholes model, in Section 2.7.2. With volatility equal to a constant, as we had there, we were able to write down an explicit expression for the PDF (Equation 2.69) in the form of a lognormal distribution for spot. In the context of a general implied volatility surface, the PDF is not lognormal and is no longer given by Equation 2.69.

The core of our derivation involves two relationships: first, the relationship between the PDF and call option values, and secondly, the relationship between the PDF and spot dynamics. Since the derivation involves both the time- and spot-dependence of the PDF, we will introduce the notation of a function p which depends explicitly on both variables:

$$p(s,t) \doteq f_{S(t)}(s) \tag{C.1}$$

Relationship 1 – between PDF and call option values – is the more straightforward one. To derive it, we use the fact that the value c of a call option equals the discounted risk-neutral expectation of its payoff, which can be written in terms of the risk-neutral PDF of spot at expiry:

$$c(K,T) = B(t,T')\,\mathbb{E}[\max(0, S(T) - K)] \tag{C.2}$$

$$= B(t,T')\int_K^\infty p(s,T)(s-K)\,ds \tag{C.3}$$

where K is the strike of the call option, T is its expiry time (dropping the subscript e for brevity), and B is the discount factor to option settlement time. The lower bound of the integral is set to K because the payoff is zero when $S(T)$ is below this level.

Now the discounting is not of relevance to the current derivation, so we can simplify things a little by working in terms of the *undiscounted* call value C (the value at settlement date), defined as:

$$C(K,T) \doteq B^{-1}(t,T')\, c(K,T) \tag{C.4}$$

Relationship 1 then becomes:

$$C(K,T) = \int_K^\infty p(s,T)(s-K)\,ds \tag{C.5}$$

Relationship 2 – between the PDF and spot dynamics – is given by the following equation:

$$\frac{\partial p}{\partial t} + (r_d - r_f)\frac{\partial}{\partial s}(sp) - \frac{1}{2}\frac{\partial^2}{\partial s^2}\left(\sigma^2 s^2 p\right) = 0 \tag{C.6}$$

This equation is known as the Fokker–Planck equation or the Forward Kolmogorov equation, and its derivation is given in Appendix E.

We now need to combine Relationships 1 and 2 (Equations C.5 and C.6). We can easily differentiate Equation C.5 with respect to T, to get:

$$\frac{\partial C}{\partial T} = \int_K^\infty \frac{\partial p}{\partial T}(s-K)\,ds \tag{C.7}$$

Equation C.6 gives us an expression for $\frac{\partial p}{\partial T}$, which we can substitute into Equation C.7, to produce:

$$\frac{\partial C}{\partial T} = \int_K^\infty \left\{ -(r_d - r_f)\frac{\partial}{\partial s}(sp) + \frac{1}{2}\frac{\partial^2}{\partial s^2}\left(\sigma^2 s^2 p\right) \right\}(s-K)\,ds$$

We break this expression down into two integrals:

$$\frac{\partial C}{\partial T} = -(r_d - r_f) I_1 + \frac{1}{2} I_2 \tag{C.8}$$

where

$$I_1 = \int_K^\infty (s-K)\frac{\partial}{\partial s}(sp)\,ds \tag{C.9}$$

$$I_2 = \int_K^\infty (s-K)\frac{\partial^2}{\partial s^2}\left(\sigma^2 s^2 p\right)\,ds \tag{C.10}$$

To help us tackle the integrals, we revisit Relationship 1 (Equation C.5) and calculate its first and second strike-derivatives to obtain the following relationships:

$$\frac{\partial C}{\partial K} = -\int_{K}^{\infty} p(s, T) \, ds \qquad \text{(C.11)}$$

$$\frac{\partial^2 C}{\partial K^2} = p(K, T) \qquad \text{(C.12)}$$

These two relationships are not only useful for evaluating the integrals; they also have very practical interpretations. A European digital call with strike K can be structured out of two vanilla call positions with strikes closely spaced around K: a long position at the lower strike and a short position at the upper strike. In the limit of infinitesimal strike spacing, and with principals inversely proportional to the strike spacing, the undiscounted value of this structure equals $-\frac{\partial C}{\partial K}$. Hence, using Equation C.11, we can see that the undiscounted European digital call price equals the integral of the PDF from K to infinity, which equals one minus the CDF at K. Meanwhile, the undiscounted European digital *put* price is precisely the CDF at K.

Along similar lines, the limiting case of a butterfly with very closely spaced strikes has undiscounted value equal to $\frac{\partial^2 C}{\partial K^2}$. Equation C.12 then tells us that this butterfly value is precisely the PDF.

In addition to Equations C.11 and C.12, we also note the following useful result:

$$C - K\frac{\partial C}{\partial K} = \int_{K}^{\infty} s\, p(s, T) \, ds \qquad \text{(C.13)}$$

Integrating I_1 and I_2 by parts gives:

$$I_1 = -C + K\frac{\partial C}{\partial K} \qquad \text{(C.14)}$$

$$I_2 = \sigma^2 K^2 \frac{\partial^2 C}{\partial K^2} \qquad \text{(C.15)}$$

where we have made certain assumptions regarding the asymptotic behaviour of the PDF, for example that it tends to zero faster than quadratically as spot tends to infinity:

$$\lim_{s \to \infty} s^2 p = 0 \qquad \text{(C.16)}$$

Inserting Equations C.14 and C.15 into Equation C.8 gives:

$$\frac{\partial C}{\partial T} = (r_d - r_f)(C - K\frac{\partial C}{\partial K}) + \frac{1}{2}\sigma^2 K^2 \frac{\partial^2 C}{\partial K^2} \qquad \text{(C.17)}$$

Rearranging this equation gives us the result we need:

$$\sigma(K, T) = \sqrt{\frac{\frac{\partial C}{\partial T} - (r_d - r_f)(C - K\frac{\partial C}{\partial K})}{\frac{1}{2}K^2 \frac{\partial^2 C}{\partial K^2}}} \tag{C.18}$$

This equation is the **formula for calculating the LV model local volatility in terms of undiscounted call prices**.

To obtain the corresponding equation in terms of *discounted* call prices c, we use Equation C.4, together with its derivatives with respect to strike and maturity:

$$\frac{\partial C}{\partial T} = B^{-1}(t, T')\left(r_d(T')c(K, T) + \frac{\partial c}{\partial T}\right)$$

$$\frac{\partial C}{\partial K} = B^{-1}(t, T')\frac{\partial c}{\partial K}$$

$$\frac{\partial^2 C}{\partial K^2} = B^{-1}(t, T')\frac{\partial^2 c}{\partial K^2}$$

The result is:

$$\sigma(K, T) = \sqrt{\frac{\frac{\partial c}{\partial T} + r_f c + (r_d - r_f)K\frac{\partial c}{\partial K}}{\frac{1}{2}K^2 \frac{\partial^2 c}{\partial K^2}}} \tag{C.19}$$

This equation is the **formula for calculating the LV model local volatility in terms of discounted call prices**.

The partial derivatives with respect to strike and maturity in Equations C.18 and C.19 are the "co-Greeks" which we introduced in Section 3.6.

Whilst perfectly correct, Equations C.18 and C.19 are not actually the equations best used in practice to calculate local volatilities. The reason is their numerical stability. At very high and very low strikes, the numerator and denominator of the fraction inside the square root both become very small, and the error in their quotient becomes large. It is easy to see why the numerator and denominator become small for very high strikes: the value of the call option tends to zero, and correspondingly all its co-Greeks do too. To see why it is also the case for very low strikes, we note that a call option tends to a forward as its strike tends to zero. The co-gamma in the denominator measures convexity, which is zero for a forward. A little analysis of the numerator (left as an exercise for the reader) shows that it is zero for a forward, in fact at any strike. We should not be surprised by this asymptotic behaviour; it would after all be odd if we could somehow deduce a volatility (even an infinite one) from the price of a forward, which has no sensitivity to volatility.

C.2 Local volatility from implied volatility

The challenge of deducing volatilities from options which have vanishing volatility-dependence, as described at the end of Section C.1, arose long before the LV model was developed: the same challenge needs to be addressed in order to make vanilla option prices in the first place. A vanilla option market-maker may be asked to make prices at any strikes, and therefore requires an implied volatility model which is able to produce sensible vols for very low and very high strikes. With such an implied volatility model at our disposal, if we were able to compute local volatilities from implied vols instead of from call prices, then we would expect much better numerical stability. Partly for this reason, and partly because we anyway generally prefer to work in volatility space than in price space, it is common practice to calculate local volatilities from implied volatilities. We now show how to transform Equations C.18 and C.19 to a form involving implied volatilities.

Formally, the implied volatility $\Sigma(K, T)$ at strike K and expiry time T is related to call prices by the Black–Scholes pricing formula. From the results in Appendix A, we can write:

$$C(K, T) = FN(d_1) - KN(d_2) \tag{C.20}$$

where

$$d_1 = \frac{\ln\left(\frac{F}{K}\right)}{\Sigma\sqrt{T-t}} + \frac{1}{2}\Sigma\sqrt{T-t} \tag{C.21}$$

$$d_2 = \frac{\ln\left(\frac{F}{K}\right)}{\Sigma\sqrt{T-t}} - \frac{1}{2}\Sigma\sqrt{T-t} \tag{C.22}$$

These relationships allow us to compute the co-Greeks $\frac{\partial C}{\partial T}$, $\frac{\partial C}{\partial K}$ and $\frac{\partial^2 C}{\partial K^2}$ in terms of derivatives of the implied volatility Σ.

Since the implied volatility always appears multiplied by the square root of the time to expiry, we can simplify the notation a little by defining a new quantity Ω by:

$$\Omega(K, T) \doteq \Sigma(K, T)\sqrt{T-t} \tag{C.23}$$

We will call the quantity Ω the implied standard deviation. The expressions for d_1 and d_2 now simplify to:

$$d_1 = \frac{\ln\left(\frac{F}{K}\right)}{\Omega} + \frac{1}{2}\Omega \tag{C.24}$$

$$d_2 = \frac{\ln\left(\frac{F}{K}\right)}{\Omega} - \frac{1}{2}\Omega \tag{C.25}$$

and the results for the co-Greeks are as follows:

$$\frac{\partial C}{\partial T} = (r_d - r_f)FN(d_1) + Fn(d_1)\dot{\Omega} \tag{C.26}$$

$$\frac{\partial C}{\partial K} = Fn(d_1)\Omega' - N(d_2) \tag{C.27}$$

$$\frac{\partial^2 C}{\partial K^2} = n(d_2)\left[K\Omega'' + \Omega' + \frac{(1 + d_1 K\Omega')(1 + d_2 K\Omega')}{K\Omega}\right] \tag{C.28}$$

where we have used the following shorthand forms for the derivatives of Ω:

$$\dot{\Omega} \doteq \frac{\partial \Omega}{\partial T} = \dot{\Sigma}\sqrt{T-t} + \frac{\Sigma}{2\sqrt{T-t}} \tag{C.29}$$

$$\Omega' \doteq \frac{\partial \Omega}{\partial K} = \Sigma'\sqrt{T-t} \tag{C.30}$$

$$\Omega'' \doteq \frac{\partial^2 \Omega}{\partial K^2} = \Sigma''\sqrt{T-t} \tag{C.31}$$

Collecting everything together, we obtain the result:

$$\sigma(K,T) = \sqrt{2\frac{\dot{\Omega} + (r_d - r_f)K\Omega'}{K^2\Omega'' + K\Omega' + \Omega^{-1}(1 + d_1 K\Omega')(1 + d_2 K\Omega')}} \tag{C.32}$$

This equation is the **formula for calculating the LV model local volatility in terms of implied standard deviations**.

If we need an expression with explicit dependence on the implied volatility Σ, we evaluate Equations C.29–C.31 in terms of Σ:

$$\dot{\Omega} \doteq \frac{\partial \Omega}{\partial T} = \dot{\Sigma}\sqrt{T-t} + \frac{\Sigma}{2\sqrt{T-t}} \tag{C.33}$$

$$\Omega' \doteq \frac{\partial \Omega}{\partial K} = \Sigma'\sqrt{T-t} \tag{C.34}$$

$$\Omega'' \doteq \frac{\partial^2 \Omega}{\partial K^2} = \Sigma''\sqrt{T-t} \tag{C.35}$$

and insert the results into Equation C.32, to get:

$$\sigma(K,T) = $$

$$\sqrt{2\frac{\dot{\Sigma}(T-t) + \frac{1}{2}\Sigma + (r_d - r_f)(T-t)K\Sigma'}{K^2\Sigma''(T-t) + K\Sigma'(T-t) + \Sigma^{-1}(1 + d_1 K\Sigma'\sqrt{T-t})(1 + d_2 K\Sigma'\sqrt{T-t})}} \tag{C.36}$$

Derivation of the Local Volatility Function | 227

This equation is the **formula for calculating the LV model local volatility in terms of implied volatilities**.

C.3 Working in moneyness space

As described in Section 2.7.3.4, it is often beneficial to work in terms of moneyness instead of strike. For that reason, we will now transform our local volatility formulae into moneyness terms. Let us take the example of the formula for local volatility in terms of discounted call prices (Equation C.19). We first define a new function in terms of moneyness:

$$\tilde{c}(k, T) \doteq c(K, T) \tag{C.37}$$

Then we evaluate the partial derivatives needed for the local volatility formula:

$$\frac{\partial c}{\partial K} = \frac{1}{F} \frac{\partial \tilde{c}}{\partial k} \tag{C.38}$$

$$\frac{\partial^2 c}{\partial K^2} = \frac{1}{F^2} \frac{\partial^2 \tilde{c}}{\partial k^2} \tag{C.39}$$

$$\frac{\partial c}{\partial T} = \frac{\partial \tilde{c}}{\partial T} - k(r_d - r_f) \frac{\partial \tilde{c}}{\partial k} \tag{C.40}$$

Inserting these transformed partial derivatives into Equation C.19, we get the result:

$$\sigma(K, T) = \sqrt{\frac{\frac{\partial \tilde{c}}{\partial T} + r_f \tilde{c}}{\frac{1}{2} k^2 \frac{\partial^2 \tilde{c}}{\partial k^2}}} \tag{C.41}$$

This equation is the **formula for calculating the LV model local volatility in terms of discounted call prices in moneyness space**.

A similar transformation on Equation C.18 (setting $\tilde{C}(k, T) \doteq C(K, T)$) gives:

$$\sigma(K, T) = \sqrt{\frac{\frac{\partial \tilde{C}}{\partial T} - (r_d - r_f) \tilde{C}}{\frac{1}{2} k^2 \frac{\partial^2 \tilde{C}}{\partial k^2}}} \tag{C.42}$$

This equation is the **formula for calculating the LV model local volatility in terms of undiscounted call prices in moneyness space**.

Likewise, defining $\tilde{\Omega}(k, T) \doteq \Omega(K, T)$, Equation C.32 can be transformed to:

$$\sigma(K, T) = \sqrt{2 \frac{\dot{\tilde{\Omega}}}{k^2 \tilde{\Omega}'' + k \tilde{\Omega}' + \tilde{\Omega}^{-1} \left(1 + d_1 k \tilde{\Omega}'\right) \left(1 + d_2 k \tilde{\Omega}'\right)}} \tag{C.43}$$

This equation is the **formula for calculating the LV model local volatility in terms of implied standard deviations in moneyness space**.

Note that the transformation to moneyness space *simplifies* the expressions.

C.4 Working in log space

Another beneficial transformation is to work in terms of the logarithm of strike or moneyness. For example, we define the *log-moneyness* κ by:

$$\kappa \doteq \ln(k) \tag{C.44}$$

Taking the case of implied standard deviations, we define a new function as follows:

$$\bar{\Omega}(\kappa, T) \doteq \tilde{\Omega}(k, T) \tag{C.45}$$

and we then express the derivatives of $\tilde{\Omega}$ in terms of the derivatives of $\bar{\Omega}$:

$$\frac{\partial \tilde{\Omega}}{\partial k} = e^{-\kappa} \frac{\partial \bar{\Omega}}{\partial \kappa} \tag{C.46}$$

$$\frac{\partial^2 \tilde{\Omega}}{\partial k^2} = e^{-2\kappa} \left(\frac{\partial^2 \bar{\Omega}}{\partial \kappa^2} - \frac{\partial \bar{\Omega}}{\partial \kappa} \right) \tag{C.47}$$

$$\left.\frac{\partial \tilde{\Omega}}{\partial T}\right|_k = \left.\frac{\partial \bar{\Omega}}{\partial T}\right|_\kappa \tag{C.48}$$

The expression for local volatility then becomes:

$$\sigma(K, T) = \sqrt{2 \frac{\dot{\bar{\Omega}}}{\bar{\Omega}'' + \bar{\Omega}^{-1}(1 + d_1 \bar{\Omega}')(1 + d_2 \bar{\Omega}')}} \tag{C.49}$$

This equation is the **formula for calculating the LV model local volatility in terms of implied standard deviations in log-moneyness space**.

Similarly, the *log-strike* X is given by:

$$X \doteq \ln K \tag{C.50}$$

and we can introduce a function $\hat{\Omega}$ that gives the implied standard deviation as a function of log-strike:

$$\hat{\Omega}(X, T) \doteq \Omega(K, T) \tag{C.51}$$

Derivation of the Local Volatility Function | 229

The expression for local volatility then becomes:

$$\sigma(K,T) = \sqrt{2\frac{\dot{\hat{\Omega}} + (r_d - r_f)\hat{\Omega}'}{\hat{\Omega}'' + \hat{\Omega}^{-1}\left(1 + d_1\hat{\Omega}'\right)\left(1 + d_2\hat{\Omega}'\right)}} \qquad (C.52)$$

This equation is the **formula for calculating the LV model local volatility in terms of implied standard deviations in log-strike space.**

All the expressions in terms of implied volatility and implied standard deviations (Equations C.32, C.36, C.43, C.49 and C.52) are numerically better behaved than the expressions in terms of call prices (Equations C.18, C.19, C.41 and C.42).

C.5 Specialization to BSTS

It may come as a surprise to note that the formulae for the local volatility in terms of call prices (for example, Equations C.18 and C.19) are not merely *applicable* to the BSTS model, but they are exactly the same: the formulae cannot be simplified even though the BSTS model itself is much simpler than the LV model. It is only when we come to re-write the formulae in terms of implied volatility that the BSTS version becomes different – and much simpler! Setting to zero the strike derivatives of the implied standard deviation Ω in Equation C.32, and converting back to implied volatility Σ, we obtain:

$$\begin{aligned}\sigma_{\text{BSTS}}(K,T) &= \sqrt{2\Omega\dot{\Omega}} \\ &= \sqrt{\Sigma^2 + 2\Sigma\dot{\Sigma}(T-t)} \\ &= \sqrt{\frac{\partial}{\partial T}\left(\Sigma^2(T-t)\right)} \end{aligned} \qquad (C.53)$$

This is the **formula for calculating the BSTS model instantaneous volatility in terms of implied volatilities.**

Equation C.53 can be inverted straightforwardly:

$$\Sigma(t,T) = \sqrt{\frac{1}{T-t}\int_t^T \sigma_{\text{BSTS}}^2(u)\,du} \qquad (C.54)$$

This is the **formula for calculating the BSTS model implied volatility in terms of its instantaneous volatility.**

D | Calibration of Mixed Local/Stochastic Volatility (LSV) Models

This appendix describes the calibration of the local volatility factor Λ in the LSV model introduced in Section 4.12. At this stage, we assume that the stochastic volatility process parameters (mean-reversion parameters, volatility of volatility and spot–vol correlation) have already been determined.

The key equation that provides the basis for calibration is a relationship derived in 1996 by Bruno Dupire [65] and independently in 1998 by Emanuel Derman and Iraj Kani [66]. This relationship states that the expectation of the square of the instantaneous volatility at a given time, conditional on the spot price at that time being at a particular level, equals the square of the local volatility at that time and that spot level:

$$\mathbb{E}\left[\sigma^2 | S(T) = K\right] = \sigma_{\mathrm{LV}}^2(K, T) \tag{D.1}$$

It is straightforward to see how this relationship holds for the LV model: the instantaneous volatility in this model is the deterministic local volatility function $\sigma_{\mathrm{LV}}(S, T)$, whose expectation conditional on $S(T) = K$ is trivially $\sigma_{\mathrm{LV}}(K, T)$.

Inserting instead the instantaneous volatility for the LSV model gives:

$$\mathbb{E}\left[\sigma_0^2 \, \Lambda^2(S(T), T) \, \Xi^2(T) | S(T) = K\right] = \sigma_{\mathrm{LV}}^2(K, T) \tag{D.2}$$

Again the conditional expectation of the deterministic local volatility function (the local volatility factor Λ) is straightforwardly taken out of the expectation, as is the constant base volatility level, yielding:

$$\sigma_0^2 \, \Lambda^2(K, T) \, \mathbb{E}\left[\Xi^2(T) | S(T) = K\right] = \sigma_{\mathrm{LV}}^2(K, T) \tag{D.3}$$

Λ is then given by the following expression:

$$\Lambda^2(K, T) = \frac{\sigma_{\mathrm{LV}}^2(K, T)}{\sigma_0^2 \, \mathbb{E}\left[\Xi^2(T) | S(T) = K\right]} \tag{D.4}$$

Computation of Λ relies on evaluation of the conditional expectation of Ξ. The latter can be written in terms of the joint probability density function of $S(T)$ and Ξ, which we will denote $p_{S,\Xi}$:

$$\mathbb{E}\left[\Xi^2(T)|S(T)=K\right] = \frac{\int \xi^2 p_{S,\Xi}(K,\xi,T)\,d\xi}{\int p_{S,\Xi}(K,\xi,T)\,d\xi} \tag{D.5}$$

The expression for Λ is then given by:

$$\Lambda^2(K,T) = \frac{\sigma_{LV}^2(K,T)}{\sigma_0^2} \frac{\int p_{S,\Xi}(K,\xi,T)\,d\xi}{\int \xi^2 p_{S,\Xi}(K,\xi,T)\,d\xi} \tag{D.6}$$

If Ξ is modelled as the exponential of a process, as for example in the exponential Ornstein–Uhlenbeck LSV model described in Section 4.12, it is useful to write the conditional expectation in terms of the joint density function of S and $Y(=\ln \Xi)$, denoted $p_{S,Y}$:

$$\Xi = e^Y \tag{D.7}$$

$$\mathbb{E}\left[e^{2Y(T)}|S(T)=K\right] = \frac{\int e^{2y} p_{S,Y}(K,y,T)\,dy}{\int p_{S,Y}(K,y,T)\,dy} \tag{D.8}$$

The expression for Λ is in that case given by:

$$\Lambda^2(K,T) = \frac{\sigma_{LV}^2(K,T)}{\sigma_0^2} \frac{\int p_{S,Y}(K,y,T)\,dy}{\int e^{2y} p_{S,Y}(K,y,T)\,dy} \tag{D.9}$$

We demonstrated the derivation of the Fokker–Planck equation in the case of the LV model in Appendix E. Exactly the same approach based on our chosen form of LSV model yields the joint density function p required to evaluate either of Equations D.6 and D.9. For example, for the exponential Ornstein–Uhlenbeck model, the Fokker–Planck equation is:

$$\frac{\partial p}{\partial t} + (r_d - r_f)\frac{\partial}{\partial s}(sp) - \frac{1}{2}\sigma_0^2 e^{2y}\frac{\partial^2}{\partial s^2}(\Lambda^2 s^2 p) + \kappa \frac{\partial}{\partial y}((\bar{Y}-y)p)$$
$$- \frac{1}{2}\alpha^2 \frac{\partial^2}{\partial y^2}(p) - \rho \sigma_0 \alpha \frac{\partial^2}{\partial s \partial y}(\Lambda e^y sp) = 0 \tag{D.10}$$

We can use finite-difference methods to compute the solution of Equation D.10 numerically, as described in Chapter 6.

E | Derivation of Fokker–Planck Equation for the Local Volatility Model

We derive here the Fokker–Planck equation for the local volatility model. We will not be focusing on all of the mathematical conditions which the various quantities and functions need to satisfy. For a more mathematically thorough derivation, including all the conditions of behaviour we need to satisfy, see Shreve [10].

Our aim is to derive an equation of motion for the probability density function (PDF) of the spot price $S(t)$ whose dynamics are given by the LV stochastic differential equation (SDE) of Equation 4.21:

$$dS = (r_d - r_f) S\, dt + \sigma(S,t)\, S\, dW_t$$

Let $g(\cdot)$ be an arbitrary function, and define a stochastic variable G_t by:

$$G_t \doteq g(S(t)) \tag{E.1}$$

Then, using Itō's Lemma, the SDE for G_t is given by:

$$dG = \left[(r_d - r_f) S \frac{\partial g}{\partial S} + \frac{1}{2}\sigma^2 S^2 \frac{\partial^2 g}{\partial S^2}\right] dt + \sigma(S,t) S \frac{\partial g}{\partial S} dW_t \tag{E.2}$$

We can then write down the following equation of expectations:

$$\underbrace{\frac{\partial \mathbb{E}[G_t]}{\partial t}}_{\text{lhs}} = \underbrace{\mathbb{E}\left[(r_d - r_f) S \frac{\partial g}{\partial S} + \frac{1}{2}\sigma^2 S^2 \frac{\partial^2 g}{\partial S^2}\right]}_{\text{rhs}} \tag{E.3}$$

The expectations on the left-hand side and right-hand sides can each be written in terms of an integral involving the PDF $p(S,t)$, and the time partial derivative on the left-hand side can be taken inside the integral:

$$\text{lhs} = \frac{\partial}{\partial t} \int_0^\infty g(s) p(s,t)\, ds$$

$$= \int_0^\infty g(s) \frac{\partial p}{\partial t}\, ds \tag{E.4}$$

Derivation of Fokker–Planck Equation for the Local Volatility Model

$$\text{rhs} = \int_0^\infty \left[(r_d - r_f) s \frac{\partial g(s)}{\partial s} + \frac{1}{2} \sigma^2 s^2 \frac{\partial^2 g(s)}{\partial s^2} \right] p(s,t) \, ds \tag{E.5}$$

The right-hand side can furthermore be integrated by parts, to give:

$$\text{rhs} = -(r_d - r_f) \int_0^\infty \frac{\partial}{\partial s}(sp) g \, ds + \frac{1}{2} \int_0^\infty \frac{\partial^2}{\partial s^2} \left(\sigma^2 s^2 p \right) g \, ds \tag{E.6}$$

In the above step, we have assumed various quantities vanish for infinite spot. For example, we have assumed:

$$\lim_{s \to \infty} \frac{\partial}{\partial s} \left(\sigma^2 s^2 p \right) g = 0$$

which assumes certain asymptotic properties of g. Equating LHS and RHS, we can now write that, for any function g with suitable asymptotic behaviour, the following equation holds:

$$\int_0^\infty \left\{ \frac{\partial p}{\partial t} + (r_d - r_f) \frac{\partial}{\partial s}(sp) - \frac{1}{2} \frac{\partial^2}{\partial s^2} \left(\sigma^2 s^2 p \right) \right\} g(s) \, ds = 0 \tag{E.7}$$

We deduce that the quantity in curly braces must equal zero:

$$\frac{\partial p}{\partial t} + (r_d - r_f) \frac{\partial}{\partial s}(sp) - \frac{1}{2} \frac{\partial^2}{\partial s^2} \left(\sigma^2 s^2 p \right) = 0 \tag{E.8}$$

This is **the Fokker–Planck equation for the local volatility (LV) model.**

Bibliography

[1] A. Lipton. *Mathematical Methods for Foreign Exchange.* World Scientific, 2001.
[2] J. Hull. *Options, Futures and other Derivatives (9th Ed.).* Prentice Hall, 2014.
[3] P. Wilmott. *Paul Wilmott on Quantitative Finance.* Wiley, 2006.
[4] K. Pilbeam. *International Finance.* Palgrave Macmillan, 2013.
[5] I. J. Clark. *Foreign Exchange option pricing.* Wiley, 2011.
[6] U. Wystup. *FX options and structured products.* Wiley, 2006.
[7] R. Brown. A brief account of microscopical observations made in the months of june, july, and august, 1827, on the particles contained in the pollen of plants; and on the general existence of active molecules in organic and inorganic bodies. *Edinburgh new Philosophical Journal*, 358–371, 1828.
[8] F. Black and M. Scholes. The pricing of options and corporate liabilities. *Journal of Political Economy*, 81(3):637–654, 1973.
[9] K. Itô. On stochastic differential equations. *Memoirs of the American Mathematical Society*, (4):1–51, 1951.
[10] S. Shreve. *Stochastic Calculus for Finance II.* Springer, 2004.
[11] W. Doeblin. Sur l'équation de kolmogoroff. *C. R. Ser. I*, 331:1059–1102, 1940.
[12] P. Austing. *Smile Pricing Explained.* Palgrave Macmillan, 2014.
[13] M. Fourier. *Théorie analytique de la chaleur.* 1822.
[14] R. C. Merton. Theory of rational option pricing. *The Bell Journal of Economics and Management Science*, 4(1):141–183, 1973.
[15] Espen Gaarder Haug. *The Complete Guide to Option Pricing Formulas (2nd Ed.).* McGraw-Hill, 2007.
[16] E. Reiner and M. Rubinstein. Breaking down the barriers. *Risk Magazine*, 4(8):28–35, 1991.
[17] S. Shreve. *Stochastic Calculus for Finance I.* Springer, 2004.
[18] U. Wystup. Ensuring efficient hedging of barrier options. *http://www.mathfinance.de*, 2002.
[19] E. Reiner and M. Rubinstein. Unscrambling the binary code. *Risk Magazine*, 1991.
[20] C. H. Hui. One-touch barrier binary option values. *Applied Financial Economics*, 6:343–346, 1996.
[21] M. Broadie, P. Glasserman, and S. Kou. A continuity correction for discrete barrier options. *Mathematical Finance*, 7(4):325–348, 1997.
[22] R. C. Heynen and H. M. Kat. Partial barrier options. *Journal of Financial Engineering*, 3:253–274, 1994.
[23] F. Mercurio. A vega-gamma relationship for european-style or barrier options in the black-scholes model. *Banca IMI*.
[24] O. Reiss and U. Wystup. Computing option price sensitivities using homogeneity and other tricks. *The Journal of Derivatives*, 9(2):41–53, 2001.
[25] B. Dupire. Pricing with a smile. *Risk Magazine*, 7(1):18–20, 1994.

[26] P. S. Hagan, D. Kumar, A. S. Lesniewski, and D. E. Woodward. Managing smile risk. *Wilmott Magazine*, July:84–108, 2002.
[27] S. Heston. A closed-form solution for options with stochastic volatility with applications to bond and currency options. *The Review of Financial Studies*, 6(2):327–343, 1993.
[28] W. Feller. Two singular diffusion problems. *Annals of Mathematics*, 54(1):173–182, 1951.
[29] J. Gatheral. *The Volatility Surface*. Wiley, 2006.
[30] M. Jex, R. Henderson, and D. Wang. Pricing exotics under the smile. *J.P.Morgan Securities Inc. Derivatives Research*, 1999.
[31] A. Lipton. The vol smile problem. *Risk Magazine*, February:61–65, 2002.
[32] K. Said. Pricing exotics under the smile. *Risk Magazine*, November:72–75, 2003.
[33] P. Henry-Labordère. Calibration of local stochastic volatility models to market smiles: A monte-carlo approach. *SSRN*, http://ssrn.com/abstract=1493306, 2009.
[34] P. Henry-Labordère. Calibration of local stochastic volatility models to market smiles. *Risk Magazine*, September:112–117, 2009.
[35] G. Vong. Turbo-charged local stochastic volatility models. *SSRN*, 2010.
[36] P. Karasinski and A. Sepp. The beta stochastic volatility model. *Risk Magazine*, October:66–71, 2012.
[37] Y. Tian, Z. Zhu, F. Klebaner, and K. Hamza. A hybrid stochastic volatility model incorporating local volatility. *2012 Fourth International Conference on Computational and Information Sciences (ICCIS). Available at SSRN: http://ssrn.com/abstract=2074675*, 2012.
[38] C. Homescu. Local stochastic volatility models: calibration and pricing. *SSRN*, 2014.
[39] G. E. Uhlenbeck and L. S. Ornstein. On the theory of the brownian motion. *Physical Review*, 36(5):823–841, 1930.
[40] A. Lipton and W. McGhee. Universal barriers. *Risk Magazine*, May:81–85, 2002.
[41] U. Wystup. The market price of one-touch options in foreign exchange markets. *Derivatives Week*, XII(13), 2003.
[42] U. Wystup. Vanna-volga pricing. *Frankfurt School of Finance and Management*, (11):1–23, 2008.
[43] A. Castagna and F. Mercurio. The vanna-volga method for implied volatilities. *Risk Magazine*, January:106–111, 2007.
[44] E. Derman, D. Ergener, and I. Kani. Static options replication. *Goldman Sachs Quantitative Strategy Research Notes*, 1994.
[45] J. Bowie and P. Carr. Static simplicity. *Risk*, 7(8):44–49, 1994.
[46] M. Joshi. *The Concepts and Practice of Mathematical Finance*. Cambridge University Press, 2008.
[47] Carol Alexander. *Market Risk Analysis*. Wiley, 2009.
[48] John C. Hull. *Risk Management and Financial Institutions*. Wiley, 2012.
[49] D. Duffy. *Finite Difference Methods in Financial Engineering*. Wiley Finance, 2006.
[50] D. Tavella and C. Randall. *Pricing Financial Instruments*. Wiley, 2000.
[51] K. W. Morton and D. F. Mayers. *Numerical Solution of Partial Differential Equations*. Cambridge University Press, 2005.
[52] W. H. Press, S. A. Teukolsky, W. T. Vetterling, and B. P. Flannery. *Numerical Recipes*. Cambridge University Press, 2007.

[53] J. Crank and P. Nicolson. A practical method for numerical evaluation of solutions of partial differential equations of the heat-conduction type. *Advances in Computational Mathematics*, 6(1):207–226, 1996.

[54] I. J. D. Craig and A. D. Sneyd. An alternating-direction implicit scheme for parabolic equations with mixed derivatives. *Computers and Mathematics with Applications*, 16(4):341–350, 1988.

[55] P. Jäckel. *Monte Carlo Methods in Finance*. Wiley, 2002.

[56] P. Glasserman. *Monte Carlo Methods in Financial Engineering*. Springer, 2003.

[57] M. Giles and P. Glasserman. Smoking adjoints: fast monte carlo greeks. *Risk Magazine*, January:88–92, 2006.

[58] Credit Suisse. Emerging markets currency guide. *Credit Suisse*, www.credit-suisse.com, 2013.

[59] Swiss National Bank. Swiss National Bank sets minimum exchange rate at CHF 1.20 per euro. *Swiss National Bank Press Release*, 2011.

[60] K. Amin and R. Jarrow. Pricing foreign currency options under stochastic interest rates. *Journal of International Money and Finance*, 10:310–329, 1991.

[61] A. Brace, D. Gatarek, and M. Musiela. The market model of interest rate dynamics. *Mathematical Finance*, 7(2):127–155, 1997.

[62] J. Hull and A. White. Pricing interest rate derivative securities. *Review of Financial Studies*, 3(4):573–592, 1990.

[63] S. Gurrieri, M. Nakabayashi, and T. Wong. Calibration methods of hull–white model. *SSRN*, http://ssrn.com/abstract=1514192, 2009.

[64] Bank of England, HM Treasury, and Financial Conduct Authority. How fair and effective are the fixed income, foreign exchange and commodities markets? *Fair and Effective Markets Review*, 2014.

[65] B. Dupire. A unified theory of volatility. *Paribas Capital Markets discussion paper*, 1996.

[66] E. Derman and I. Kani. Stochastic implied trees: Arbitrage pricing with stochastic term and strike structure of volatility. *International Journal of Theoretical and Applied Finance*, 1(01):61–110, 1998.

Index

10%-TV double no-touch, 108, 110, 134, 165, 168, 200
2-way price, 210
25-delta, *see* delta, strike quotation method
3-factor models, 207–210

AAD, *see* adjoint algorithmic differentiation
accumulators, 1, 27
adjoint algorithmic differentiation, 204
adjusted barriers, 119
adjusted drift rate, 37
American bets, 23, 94
American binaries, 23, 94
American options, 23
analytic Greeks, 86
analytical methods, 80–81
antithetic variables
    Monte Carlo, 197–199
arbitrage
    calendar, 124, 143
    distributional, 143
    falling variance, 124
    no-arbitrage conditions, 143
    no-arbitrage principle, 15, 41
Asian options, 19
at-the-money conventions, 129–131,
    see also moneynesses
    at-the-money forward, 129
    delta-neutral straddle, 129–130
at-the-money strikes, 58–59, 134
at-the-money volatility, 128–131, 137
    relationship to smile level, 131

barrier bending, 119
barrier continuity correction, 80, 195
barrier over-hedging, 91
barrier radar reports, 119

barrier survival probability, *see* survival probability
barrier trigger probability, *see* trigger probability
barrier types, 26–27
    continuously monitored, 26
    discretely monitored, 26–27
    Parisian, 27
    partial, 26
    re-setting, 26
    time-dependent, 26
    window, 26
barrier-contingent payments, 23–25
    Black–Scholes pricing, 73–80
    local volatility model pricing, 144–150
    local/stochastic volatility model pricing, 168
barrier-contingent vanilla options, 16–23
    Black–Scholes pricing, 64–73
    local volatility model pricing, 150–154
    local/stochastic volatility model pricing, 168
base volatility, 163
basis points, 119, 154, 209
    definition, 4
benchmark market data
    spot, 3, 4
    volatility surfaces, 126
bid–offer spreads, 42, 210–212
big figures, 4, 30
bips, 4
Black–Scholes model, 33–81
    barrier-contingent payments, 73–80
    barrier-contingent vanilla options, 64–73
    conceptual inputs and outputs, 38
    discrete barrier options, 80
    equation for spot price, 33
    numerical pricing methods, 81

Index

Black–Scholes model – *continued*
  option pricing PDE, 37–42
    boundary conditions, 45
    derivation, 39
    payoff solution, 66
    supplementary solution, 66
    transformation, 48
  role in options markets, 133
  vanilla options, 47–59
    derivation of formulae, 215–219
    formulae, 57–59
  window barrier options, 80
Black–Scholes with term structure, 123
boundary conditions
  barrier-contingent vanilla, 65
  vanilla options, 53
broker markets, 135–136
Brownian Bridge, 195, 199–200
BS, *see* Black–Scholes model
BSTS, *see* Black–Scholes with term structure
bumped Greeks, 86
butterflies, 128–137
    relationship to smile convexity, 133
    relationship with risk-neutral PDF, 223
    smile vs market, 137

calculation agents, 214
call options, *see* vanilla options
call spreads, 16
carry trade, 44
CDF
  normal distribution, 220
co-Delta, 120
co-Gamma, 120
co-Greeks, 119–120, 138, 224
co-Theta, 120
common misconceptions, 90, 92–94, 99, 126, 136
continuously monitored barriers, 19, 26, 194
contract type codes
  CNN, 86
  complete list, xxviii
  DII, 75
  DII_H, 76
  DIN, 75
  DIN_H, 76
  DNI, 75
  DNI_H, 76
  DNN, 45, 115
  DNO, 75
  DON, 75
  DOO, 75
  FNI, 77
  FNN, 46
  FNO, 76
  FOO, 78
  WNN, 47
control variates
  Monte Carlo, 197–199
Crank–Nicolson scheme, 192
currency pair inversion, 29, 31, 76
currency pair symbols, 2–4
currency pairs
  AUDJPY, 3, 4, 29, 33, 59, 60, 86, 126, 131, 138, 146, 150
  BRLJPY, 130
  Domestic vs Foreign, 3–4
  EURCHF, 172, 185, 206
  EURGBP, 3
  EURUSD, 1–4, 6–14, 16–25, 29, 33, 60, 66, 70, 76, 86, 87, 91–94, 97, 98, 104–110, 126, 128, 131, 132, 136, 138, 145, 150, 166, 168
  quote order, 2–5
  USDTRY, 3, 29, 60, 77–80, 95, 126, 131, 138, 146, 150, 209

d-Vega-d-Vol, *see* volgamma
Danish krone, 205
datetime, 5
de-peg event, 206
de-peg risk, 206
delta, 39–41, 44–45, 83–95
  Forward-Delta-in-Domestic, 84
  Forward-Delta-in-Foreign, 84
  hedge, 40–41
  premium adjustment, 84–85
  Spot-Delta-in-Domestic, 84
  Spot-Delta-in-Foreign, 39–41, 84
  strike quotation method, 88–90
delta exchange, 136
delta gap, 91, 201
delta hedging, 83

delta-neutral straddle, 129
derivatives, 11
diffusion equation, 52
discount factors, 4–5
   definition, 5
discretely monitored barriers, 26–27, 194
DNS, *see* delta-neutral straddle
Domestic currency, 3–4, *see also* Foreign currency
double knock-ins, 22
double knock-outs, 21
double no-touches, 134
   vega, 108–110
   volgamma, 108–110
downward-sloping volatility curve
   BSTS, 124
drift rate, 34
dual Greeks, *see* co-Greeks
Dupire local volatility, 164, *see also* local volatility model
dVega, *see* volgamma
dynamic hedging, 39, 183

eCommerce, 212–213
electronic price distribution, 212–213
euro, *see* EUR
European derivatives, 14
European digitals, 15–16, 19, 31, 213
   relationship with risk-neutral CDF, 223
European options, 14, 53
exchange houses, 135
exchange rate, *see* spot rate, forward rate
exotic contracts, 19
exotic options, 19
expected rate of return, 34
expiry cuts, 14
expiry times
   standardized, 129
explicit scheme
   finite-difference methods, 189–191

F, *see* fair forward rate
fair forward rate, *see also* forward points, *see* forward rate
   formula, 8–12
fair value
   as risk-neutral expectation, 55

definition, 42
Feller Score, 162
finite-difference methods, 30, 81, 186–193
   algorithms, 189
   explicit scheme, 189–191
   implicit scheme, 191–192
   implicit-explicit schemes, 193
   local/stochastic volatility models, 167
   operator splitting, 193
first exit time, *see* first passage time
first passage time, xxvii, 73
first-generation exotic options, 26
flat volatility curve
   BSTS, 124
flies, *see* butterflies
flow products, 26
Fokker–Planck equation, 222
   local volatility model, 232–233
   local/stochastic volatility models, 231
Foreign currency, 3–4, *see also* Domestic currency
forward contracts, 6–12, 208
   payoff, 10
   replication, 9, 31
forward curve, 7
forward Kolmogorov equation, 222
forward market, 6–12
forward points, 7–8
   quotation convention, 8
   scaling factor, 8
forward rate, 7
forward smile, 155
forward volatility agreements, 155
free-floating currencies, 205–206
frown, *see* implied volatility frown
funding valuation adjustment, 5
FVA, *see* forward volatility agreements, *see* funding valuation adjustment

gamma, 44–45, 83–95
   mathematical, 85
   practitioner, 86
gamma of vega, *see* volgamma
gamma of vol, *see* volgamma
geometric Brownian Motion, 34
geometry
   finite-difference grid, 186–189

Greeks, 40, 83, 99, *see also* individual Greeks
   analytic, 86
   bumped, 86

heat equation, 52
hedge ratios, 83, *see also* Greeks
Heston model, 158
   risk reversal gamma, 162
Hong Kong dollar, 205
Hull–White model, 207–210

IMEX, *see* implicit/explicit
implicit scheme
   finite-difference methods, 191–192
implicit/explicit schemes
   finite-difference methods, 193
implicitness parameter
   finite-difference, 192
implied standard deviation, 225
implied variance, 142–143
implied volatility, 121
   at-the-money volatility, 129–131
   butterfly, 132–133
   curve, 123
   definition, 125–126
   fly, 132
   frown, 133, 166, 170
   market, 122
   models, 136–137
   smile risk reversal, 131–132
   smiles, 126
   surface
      spot dynamics, 179–182
   surfaces, 126
   term structure, 123
      interpolation model, 137
in-the-money strikes, 58–59
incremental bumping, 202
industry parlance, 1, 3, 7, 131, 156
infinitesimal-difference limit
   finite-difference grid, 190
initial-value problem, 53
instantaneous variance, 158
instantaneous volatility
   BSTS, 123
   Heston, 158, 159

LV, 141
SABR, 157
inter-bank markets, 135
interest rates
   assumed deterministic, 5
interventions, 205
intrinsic value, 57–58
inversion method, *see* currency pair inversion
Itô's lemma, xxi, 36–37
Itô process, 36

KIKOs, 25–26
   sequential vs non-sequential, 26
   structurable vs non-structurable, 26

lagless approach, 38–39
leptokurtic distributions, 138
local variance, 142–143, 230
local volatility component
   of LSV model, 163
local volatility factor
   of LSV model, 164
local volatility model, 141–154
   barrier-contingent payments, 144–150
   barrier-contingent vanilla options, 150–154
   calibration, 221–229
   Fokker–Planck equation, 232–233
   Monte Carlo methods, 144
   option pricing PDE, 144
   risk-neutral process, 144
local/stochastic volatility models, 162–171
   barrier-contingent payments, 168
   barrier-contingent vanilla options, 168
   calibration, 164–165, 230–231
      EURUSD, 166
   finite-difference methods, 167
   Fokker–Planck equation, 231
   generic form, 163
   Monte Carlo methods, 167
   option pricing PDE, 167–168
log-moneyness, 228
log-spot, 35
lognormal distribution, 220

Index | 241

LSV, *see* local/stochastic volatility models
LV, *see* local volatility model

managed currencies, 205–206
market abuse, 213–214
market roll, 122
maturity, 31
  of forward, 6
  of option, 39
mean reversion, 159
mean-reversion level
  Heston, 159
  Ornstein–Uhlenbeck, 164
mean-reversion speed
  Heston, 159
  Ornstein–Uhlenbeck, 164
method of images, 67
mid prices, 210
mio (million), 29
mixed Dupire model, 171
mixed local/stochastic volatility, *see* local/stochastic volatility model
mixing factor, 170, 182
mixture risk
  local/stochastic volatility models, 182–183
mixxa, 183
moneyness, 58–59, 227–228
  lines of constant moneyness, 143
Monte Carlo methods, 81, 125, 186, 193–200
  adjoint algorithmic differentiation, 204
  antithetic variables, 197–199
  Brownian Bridge, 199–200
  compute grids, 203
  contract schedule, 194–195
  control variates, 197–199
  early termination, 200
  estimators, 195
  farms, 203
  Greeks, 203
  local volatility model, 144
  local/stochastic volatility models, 167
  pathwise method, 203
  simulation schedule, 194–195
  variance reduction, 197–199

Monte Carlo simulation, *see* Monte Carlo methods

netting
  of bid–offer spreads, 212
New York expiry cut, 14
no-arbitrage principle, 15, 41
non-deliverable currencies, 130
non-sequential KIKOs, 26
normal distribution, 220
  standard, xxvii, 194, 220
normal knock-outs, 19–21, 31, 71, *see also* reverse knock-outs
notional amounts, 1
numerical methods, 80–81

offer prices, 210
operator splitting
  finite-difference methods, 193
option inversion, 29
option pricing PDEs
  local volatility model, 144
  local/stochastic volatility models, 167–168
options
  holder, 31
  premium, 13
  vanilla, 12–15
  writer, 31
Ornstein–Uhlenbeck process, 164
  exponential, 164
orthogonality of risk factors, 179
OTC, *see* over-the-counter
out-of-the-money strikes, 58–59
outright forward rate, 8, 31, *see also* fair forward rate
over-hedging, 117–119
over-the-counter markets, 135

P&L, 185
Parisian barriers, 27, 31
Parisian options, 27, 32
partial barriers, *see* window barriers
pay-at-hit, 24, *see also* pay-at-maturity
pay-at-maturity, 24, *see also* pay-at-hit

payoff profiles
  definition, 11
payoff spike, 19
payoffs
  accumulators, 27–28
  barrier-contingent payments, 23–25
  barrier-contingent vanilla options, 16–23
  forward contract, 10
  KIKOs, 25–26
  vanilla options, 12–14
PDEs
  option pricing, *see* option pricing PDEs
PDF
  lognormal distribution, 220
  normal distribution, 220
  risk-neutral, *see* risk-neutral
  skew, 138
pegged currencies, 205–206
pips, 4, 32
pivot maturity, 178
pre-hedging, 213
premium
  of option, 13
premium currency, 130
premium-adjusted delta, 84–85
price quotation styles, 59–60
pricing rules, *see* rules-based pricing methods
principal amounts, 1, 32
probability distributions
  lognormal, 220
  normal, 220
pseudo term sheet, 28–29
put options, *see* vanilla options
put spreads, 16
put–call parity, 14–15, 32

quantitative analysts, xx
quote order convention, 3

ranges, 23, 32, 78
ratchet option structure, 212
re-setting barriers, 26
rebates, 25
reflection principle, 69
regulation, 213–214
return, 34

reverse knock-outs, 19–21, 32, *see also* normal knock-outs
  similarity to barrier-contingent payments, 94
rho, 113–115
  bucketed, 179
  discounting effect, 115
  forward effect, 115
  parallel, 179
  weighted, 179
ringing, 177
risk analysis
  spot, 83–97
    local, 83–95
    non-local, 83, 96–97
risk ratios, 83, *see also* Greeks
risk reports
  spot, 97
risk reversal gamma, 156
  Heston model, 162
  local volatility model, 156
  local/stochastic volatility models, 162–163
risk reversals, 128–137, 156, 184
  option structure, 131–132
  relationship to smile skew, 132
risk-neutral CDF
  relationship with European digitals, 223
risk-neutral distributions, 55, 76, 100, 137, 138, 143, 221
risk-neutral drift rate, 55
risk-neutral expectation, 47, 55, 56, 115, 221
risk-neutral measure, 55
risk-neutral PDEs, 42, 55
  BS, 42
risk-neutral PDF
  relationship with butterflies, 223
risk-neutral processes
  BS, 55
  BSTS, 125
  local volatility model, 144
  LV, 141
risk-neutral valuation, 4, 42, 55, 83
  definition, 42
rules-based pricing methods, 212–213
rungs, 97

SABR model, 157
schedules, 27, 194–195
schemes
    finite-difference, 189
sequential KIKOs, 26
settlement date
    of spot trade, 1
settlement lags, 2, *see also* settlement rules
settlement rules, 2–32
short rates, 5
short-dated forwards, 7
short-term interest rate trading, 10
sibling options, 22, 24, 71
simulation
    Monte Carlo, *see* Monte Carlo methods
SIR, *see* stochastic interest rates
skew to TV, 134, 144–154
    vanilla options, 151
SLV, *see* local/stochastic volatility models
small figures, 4, 32
    spot move, 191
smile convexity
    relationship to butterfly, 133
smile dynamics, 154–156, 184, 202
    re-location, 179–182
smile level
    relationship to at-the-money volatility, 131
smile re-location, 156
smile skew
    relationship to risk reversal, 132
spikes in payoff, 19
spot dates, 2, 32
spot dynamics, 155
spot exchange rate, *see* spot rate
spot ladders, 97
spot lags, 2, 32, *see also* settlement rules
    lagless approach, 38–39
spot market, 1–5
spot price, *see* spot rate
spot rate, 2, 32
spot trades, 1–5, 32
spot–vol correlation
    Heston, 159
    Ornstein–Uhlenbeck, 164
spot-vol matrix, 113

standard normal distribution, *see* normal distribution
static hedging, 183–184
static replication, 183–184
sticky local volatility, 202
sticky moneyness, 156
sticky strike, 156
stochastic interest rates, 206–210
stochastic processes, 35
stochastic volatility component
    of LSV model, 163
stochastic volatility factor
    of LSV model, 164
stochastic volatility models, 157
    Heston, 158
    SABR, 157
stochastic/local volatility model, *see* local/stochastic volatility models
straddle, 129
    delta-neutral, *see* delta-neutral straddle
straight dates, 129, 137
strangle
    smile vs market, 137
strike, 32
    of forward, 7
strike rate, *see* strike
structured products, 27–28, 212
survival probability, *see also* trigger probability, 73–76
SV, *see* stochastic volatility models
swap points, *see* forward points

tenors, 129
term sheet, 28–29
terminal spot rate, 14, 32
theoretical value, 133–136
theta, 115–117, *see also* implicitness parameter
    mathematical, 115
    scaled mathematical, 116
theta scheme
    finite-difference, 192
time value, 61–64
time-dependent barriers, 26, 32
trade date, 2
trade time, 2
trading book, 82

trait, xxvii, 53
trigger probability, *see also* survival probability, 73–76
TV, *see* theoretical value

uncertain volatility models, 171–172
underlying, 11
units
   drift rate, 34
   interest rate, 5
   time, 5
   volatility, 35
upward-sloping volatility curve
   BSTS, 124

Value at Risk (VaR), 185
vanilla options, 12–15
   boundary condition, 53
   definition, 13
   market, 126–137
      standardized quotes, 128
   structures, 128
   trait, 53
vanna, 110–112, 173–174
   gap, 112
   term of local/stochastic volatility model PDE, 167–168
vanna–volga methods, 173–174
VaR, *see* Value at Risk
variance reduction
   Monte Carlo, 197–199
vega, 97–110, 129, 173–174
   bucketed, 176–178
   ladders, 112

mathematical, 99
parallel, 177–178
practitioner, 99
term of local/stochastic volatility model PDE, 167–168
weighted, 178
vol convexity, *see* volgamma
volatility
   Black–Scholes, 35
   cone, 171
   ladders, 112
   risk reports, 112–113
volatility Greeks, 173–174
volatility of volatility, 182
   Heston, 159
   Ornstein–Uhlenbeck, 164
   term structure, 170–171
volatility swaps, 1
volatility term structure risk, 175
volga, *see* volgamma
volgamma, 99–110, 173–174
   heuristic, 102
   other names, 99
   term of local/stochastic volatility model PDE, 167–168
vomma, *see* volgamma

weighted vega, *see* vega, weighted
Wiener processes, 34–35
window barriers, 26

zero-coupon bond, 135
zero-delta straddle, *see* delta-neutral straddle

Printed and bound by CPI Group (UK) Ltd, Croydon, CR0 4YY